W9-BYG-429

THE NEW GUIDE TO
SKIING

Martin Heckelman

W. W. NORTON & COMPANY

NEW YORK · LONDON

REVISED · EDITION ·

THE NEW GUIDE TO
SKIING

Martin Heckelman

For information about permission to reproduce selections
from this book, write to Permissions,
W. W. Norton & Company, Inc.,
500 Fifth Avenue, New York, NY 10110

The text of this book is composed
in Simoncini Garamond
with the display set
in Trade Gothic
Composition by Sylvie Vidrine
Book design by Bill Harvey
Cover photograph: Scott Spiker

Library of Congress Cataloging-in-Publication Data

Heckelman, Martin
The new guide to skiing / Marty Heckelman.-- Rev. ed.
    p. cm.

    ISBN 0-393-31966-0 (pbk.)

    1. Skis and skiing. I. Title

    GV854 .H378 2000
    796.93--dc21

                                         00-055004

W. W. Norton & Company, Inc.
500 Fifth Avenue, New York, NY 10110
www.wwnorton.com

W. W. Norton & Company Ltd.
10 Coptic Street, London WC1A 1PU

1 2 3 4 5 6 7 8 9 0

ACKNOWLEDGEMENTS

To thank all the people who have helped me during my long career in the USA, Europe and South America would require too much space. All the students I have had the pleasure of being with on the mountains, as well as other ski instructors, racers and ski school directors, have taught me something. I therefore would like to extend my gratitude collectively to all of them.

Thanks too, to all my many friends and family who have been there when needed and who have helped to make life a wonderful experience.

I would like to give a special thanks to Ian Beveridge, a good friend and BASI ski instructor. Ian's scientific nature has led him to assiduously study the mechanics, dynamics and physics of skiing and modern ski racing techniques. Our many technical discussions, on and off the slopes, have helped me refine my understanding of how to properly make use of the new ski equipment. I'm also very grateful for Ian's photographic skills, which account for the majority of the splendid photos that accompany the text.

Additional thanks are extended to Gordon Maclean who generously gave of his time and talent to provide the remainder of the photos.

I'm also indebted to, and would like to thank, Tyrolia bindings, Head skis and boots, Nevica clothing, Pouilloux-Vuarnet France sunglasses, Reusch gloves, Fuji Film France, Dann photo, and La Poudreuse ski shop for providing their excellent equipment and service.

A final special acknowledgement is due to the vast ski areas of Tignes and Val d'Isere (L'espace Killy), where all the photographs were taken.

CONTENTS

benefit greatly from this book as you will learn to initiate turns the modern way, by rolling your feet and ankles and leaning your hips, rather than by flexing and extending your legs. While this new method of skiing is very easy to perform on shaped skis, it also works fine with traditional skis. In fact, all traditional skis of the past ten years or so are somewhat shaped: the shovel and tail are wider than the waist of the ski, though less so than in the shaped ski.

INTRODUCTION

More than a decade has passed since I wrote the first edition of this book. Since then, I have continued to teach skiing. I've also studied and analyzed modern teaching methods and changes to ski design to see how they work and how they can make both the process of learning skiing and the skiing itself easier, more efficient, and more enjoyable.

This new edition of the book reflects the results of my studies and experimentation.

Over the past 30 years or so, the major changes to skis have been in the ski construction. They've gone from wood, to metal, to plastics, to high-tech fibers like carbon and titanium — all in an effort to make the skis lighter, livelier, and more responsive. Each development has made it easier to turn and steer the skis.

Up until recently, skis remained pretty much the same shape. Now this has changed. Ski manufacturers are making skis in a multitude of shapes and sizes that have revolutionized the way we ski and learn to ski.

These shaped skis (also called carving skis) make it much easier to initiate a turn, hold an edge, and ski faster in control. They are also less tiring to ski than traditional skis. With these skis, beginners and intermediates can make much faster progress to advanced skiing levels.

This new edition shows how to ski the modern way on these skis. You will learn how to use the shaped skis correctly to get the optimum performance from them, as well as how to ski with more ease, precision, and control.

If you are skiing on traditional skis, you too will

Skiing is one of the easiest sports to learn when taught correctly. Unlike tennis or golf, skiing does not require years or even months of practice and training to become reasonably proficient, and most ski schools can have first-time skiers skiing down easy slopes in a week.

The ski schools that incorporate shaped skis are achieving even better results. The students learn from the beginning how to properly use the ski edges and the curved shape of the skis to steer their turns. This enables them to ski with good control and quickly builds their confidence.

The teaching exercises presented in this book have been designed for shaped skis, though they can be performed on any skis. By following and practicing the exercises presented in Section One, and Two, complete novices should be able to confidently make controlled parallel turns on intermediate slopes, making the same type of turns as those made by advanced skiers. Furthermore, they will develop the correct basic skills that will equip them to progress quickly to the more advanced skiing maneuvers described in Sections Three, Four, and Five.

Intermediate and advanced skiers would benefit from reviewing the exercises presented in Sections One and Two. Especially important are the exercises that teach how to roll the feet and ankles and how to apply pressure to the skis to initiate and control the turns. These exercises form the foundation for turning on shaped skis. Another useful exercise is skating, which unfortunately is often omitted in many current teaching methods for adults.

I especially recommend that intermediate skiers,

and even many of you who consider yourselves to be advanced skiers, practice the "staircase sidesliding" exercises at slow speed in order to improve your feet sensitivity and edge control. This exercise will help you become a more precise skier.

Section Three explains how to ski all types of bumps. You will learn how to turn both over and around them and ski in control on even the big, steep ones. It also explains how to safely ski icy bumps, slush bumps and those nasty, chopped off bumps with cliff-like faces.

Section Four is intended for intermediate skiers ready to become advanced skiers, and for experienced skiers wishing to improve their technique and skills. This Section explains and demonstrates how to perform the advanced skiing techniques and maneuvers which enable you to ski the steeper slopes in good control. You will learn how to start your turns easily and finish them safely. In addition, it teaches how to ski on ice and hardpacked snow, gullies, and steep mountain faces.

Section Five is devoted to learning how to ski in powder snow. Intermediate and advanced skiers are shown how to adjust their basic technique to ski the many types of powder snow. This section demonstrates and explains a number of different ways of initiating turns in varied snow conditions.

Skiers planning on taking lessons in a ski school — whatever the country — should find the photographs and descriptions of the many exercises very useful as a supplement to their ski school lessons. In fact, regardless of which country they are in, they will recognize many of the same exercises that they are being taught. I am a keen advocate of ski lessons and recommend that you take lessons and use this book in conjunction with them.

For the benefit of those of you who intend to use this book to help you improve your technique and further your skiing ability, the book has been organized as a self-teaching manual that takes you step-by-step from beginner to advanced skier. Naturally, learning from a book is not as easy as having a competent instructor in front of you, demonstrating the maneuvers and correcting any errors you may be making on the spot. I have therefore tried to make the explanations of the various steps clear and precise, and have made extensive use of detailed stop-action photographs to complement the text. Furthermore, I have attempted, through the numerous Special Tips and Notes, to supplement the basic explanations to help you understand the key or secrets of each maneuver.

I hope that all of you who read this book will find the details on ski techniques valuable, and that by practicing and incorporating these you will be able to ski more safely and easily and will gain greater enjoyment of one of the world's finest sporting activities. My ultimate aim is that you should continue to use this book to help develop the skills that will allow you to ski every type of terrain, in every possible snow condition, with complete confidence.

Alpine skiing

Skiing is a wonderful individual and family sport and is a very healthy, fun-filled way to enjoy winter. It is one of the very few sports where grandparents, parents and children of all ages can participate together. In fact, much to the consternation of many parents, children pick up the sport so quickly that they very soon become better skiers than their parents.

There are two primary types of skiing — Alpine and Nordic — and they require very different equipment and locales. Most Nordic skiing, which is also referred to as cross-country skiing, is performed primarily on flat or gently rolling terrain. The skis used are quite narrow and very light, the shoes are similar to running shoes, and the bindings allow the heels of the shoes to lift, enabling the skier to glide, walk, or run on the skis.

Alpine skiing is performed on snow-covered hills and mountains that vary in gradient from very gentle inclines to extremely steep mountain faces. A novice skier naturally starts on the gentle terrain and progresses to the more demanding terrain after developing the necessary technique and capability to control his or her skis on the steeper slopes and at higher speeds.

Alpine skiis have slippery plastic soles and sharp metal edges that are used for controlling and steering the skis. The ski boots are made of plastic and are heavier and much stiffer than ordinary street shoes. They are designed to fit comfortably on the foot and hold the foot and ankle firmly in place so that they do not feel any strain during the skiing movements. The boots allow the ankle to bend forward, but not sideways. The bindings, which secure the skis to the boots, contain springs designed to release the boot and skier during a fall.

A form of skiing combining Alpine and Nordic skiing is growing in popularity in many parts of the world. It is known as three-pin, skinny-skis, Norpine, or Telemark skiing, and is performed on a lightweight ski similar to a Nordic ski, though slightly wider, with metal edges. The binding is called a three-pin and lifts at the heel. The boots used are lighter and more flexible than Alpine ski boots.

Another Alpine event that has become very popular is snowboarding. Snowboarding is performed on a wide board with both feet attached to the board. The stance and the technique for turning are similar to water surfing. One can snowboard using either hard ski boots or soft boots similar to after-ski boots. This book teaches how to Alpine ski, which is the most popular form of skiing.

Choosing your equipment and physical fitness

While most modern ski equipment can be quite expensive, especially at the top end of the range, beginners do not need to purchase the most expensive equipment. Manufacturers make many different skis, each designed for a specific skiing level, with the beginners' skis being the least expensive. Similarly, boot manufacturers offer models for all standards of skiers, with prices corresponding with the standard of the boot.

It is advisable for beginners to rent their equipment from a reliable ski shop or rental company rather than purchasing it. By renting, you have the opportunity to try a variety of products before deciding what is best for you. Furthermore, a beginner will probably prefer relatively short skis to start with and then progress to longer skis as improvement is made. Renting lets you easily upgrade your equipment to correspond to your current level and type of skiing. Most ski areas have good rental shops with a wide variety of the latest equipment to choose from.

Whether you plan to buy or rent your ski equipment, you should always deal with a reputable ski shop which employs knowledgeable staff. It is worth speaking with the salesperson and allowing him or her to help you choose the right gear.

Skis

Shaped skis have changed the way one chooses the correct length of ski to use. We used to employ charts that correlated a skier's weight, height, and skiing ability to determine a recommended ski length. Now skis can have so many different shapes that even tall, advanced skiers may decide to ski on very short skis with an extreme sidecut in order to have fun on the groomed runs. A number of ski schools start complete beginners (whatever their size) on 110- or 113-cm (centimeter) skis and then move them progressively up to 120-cm and then to 135-cm skis. When the beginner can get around the easy slopes making controlled turns, the next step is to choose skis in the 150 cm-180 cm range.

The shorter the skis, the easier it is to maneuver them. A longer ski will provide better stability at high speeds. Therefore I recommend that you start on short skis, and as you progress and start to ski faster, move on to longer skis. Intermediate and advanced skiers shifting to shaped skis should use skis that are 10-20 cm shorter than their traditional skis. It's best to try out various brands and models in different sizes to determine which feel the best for you.

The brand of ski that you choose can be based on appearance or cost; provided you buy skis from a well-known manufacturer, they will conform to the specifications laid down. A good ski shop should have literature from ski manufacturers describing the intended uses for their different models.

Ski boots

This is probably the most important piece of ski equipment that you will use, and therefore you should take the most care in choosing it since skiing with aching, uncomfortable feet can be very painful and tiring and can cause you to develop poor skiing habits.

To ski properly and remain in control, you need to have a pair of boots that will give you good overall support and proper fit. When buckled, the boot should fit snugly at the heel and fit firmly around your instep without squeezing your foot. It's okay if your heel lifts a tiny amount — approximately 6 mm (1/4 in). When you stand up straight, your toes should just touch the front of the boot, and when you bend your knees you should no longer feel that contact — your toes should be able to wiggle up and down. For modern skiing, ski boots need to have good lateral support or you can easily develop ankle pains. If the boots fit too tightly, in addition to discomfort and/or foot cramping you may experience a decrease in the blood circulation to your feet, causing them to become very cold. So take your time selecting a pair of boots that is right for you.

In the early days of modern skiing the boots were made of leather. If a pair of boots felt good in the shop they would probably be unsatisfactory on the slopes, since they would usually stretch with use and would no longer give the firm support required. Consequently, the rule of thumb was that a pair of boots needed to feel too tight when worn in the shop. With the advent of plastic boots, this philosophy no longer applied; a plastic boot that feels comfortable in the shop will probably feel comfortable on the slopes. A boot that hurts your foot in the shop will definitely hurt your foot on the slopes.

Most of the ski shops at ski areas carry one or two brands of rental boots. Try several pairs of boots, both in the shop and on the slopes, until you find a pair that feels comfortable. If none of the boots in your selected ski shop feels right, try some different brands of boots in other ski shops until you find the right pair. The shop personnel can help you.

When you find the right boot you may decide to purchase a pair of the same model. If the new boots

A properly equipped skier should have warm and waterproof outer garments, Gore-Tex or leather insulated gloves, high-quality sunglasses, well tuned skis, properly set bindings, and firm and comfortable ski boots.

have an anatomic flow inner system (which takes the form of your foot and ankle) you may have to wear them for some hours until the flow adjusts to your feet. In this case it is best to have the boots buckled loosely at first and tighten them as the inner boots mold themselves to your feet.

One system which provides very good comfort and control is a foam- or silicon-injected inner boot that is pressure-molded to the shape of your foot. Some boot manufacturers offer foam or silicon injection in their higher performance models. You can also purchase a separate inner boot that can be injected into any make of outer shell to ensure a very comfortable, snug fit. Footbeds, or better still, orthotics that are molded to the shape of the bottom of your foot and can then be inserted into the boots, are very welcome additions. Resting your feet on soles specially designed for them provides great comfort and aids in controlling ski edging.

Ski bindings

While ski boots are the most important equipment for comfort, ski bindings are the most important for safety. Regardless of your skiing ability you must have a safe, reliable binding that will open and release you from your skis during awkward falls.

Each manufacturer makes a number of very good bindings designed for different skiers. Racers and heavy, fast skiers need a binding with a very strong spring, while lighter skiers, children, and beginners require a spring that will release with less stress. A good ski shop can help you choose the binding that is designed for you and, using DIN calculations, adjust it to the proper setting.

When buying new skis, it is advisable to purchase

new bindings rather than transfer old bindings from an old pair of skis, since bindings need to be clean and in good working order to function properly.

Ski poles

Ski poles are quite inexpensive. A good pole should be light and strong, and should have a comfortable hand grip with some form of safety strap or grip that allows your hand to release easily from the pole in a fall or if the pole gets snagged. An easy way to determine the proper length for your ski poles is to invert the pole, rest the end of the grip on the floor, flex your knees, and grasp the pole just under the basket. The length is correct when your forearm is parallel to the ground.

Ski clothing

It is much more comfortable, and much warmer, to wear a number of thin layers than to wear one or two very heavy, bulky garments. New fabrics have made a huge change in the level of skiers' comfort. Fleece is warm, light and very insulating. On very cold days I wear two or three thin fleece layers, which don't bulk me up yet keep me very warm. Closest to the skin it is best to wear a pair of thin tights or longjohns made of polypropylene or chlorofiber (which transfers body moisture away to the outer garments). On top of this you can wear a turtleneck shirt and a fleece or woolen sweater. For the outer garment, a down, "Thinsulate," or fibre-filled jacket or parka should keep out most chills. On especially cold days, you may want to add an additional layer, such as a woolen shirt or another fleece. On warm days you can, of course, remove as many layers as you wish. A useful feature of modern ski clothing is that it can be fashionably worn at home as well as on the slopes, so that you are not limiting your investment in top-quality clothing to skiing holidays.

Trousers

The best outfit to wear is one designed especially for skiing, as it will keep you dry as well as warm. One-piece insulated ski outfits provide excellent protection. Two-piece outfits, consisting of a jacket and bib ski pants with 'over the shoulder' straps, are also very good.

An inexpensive way to keep dry is to wear a pair of outer pants made of nylon or Gore-Tex over a pair of jeans or cotton trousers.

Socks

The rule of thumb used to be to wear two pairs of socks; generally a silk or cotton pair under a thicker woolen pair. Modern ski boots usually are made with insulating materials for warmth, and for the best fit it is now generally recommended that you wear one pair of medium-thick socks only. The best socks for skiing are socks that 'wick away' moisture, which you can find in most ski shops. My experience is that except on the very coldest days one pair of ski socks is sufficient to keep your feet comfortable. On extremely cold days you can keep your feet warm by adding battery-operated heaters to your boots or wrap your ski boots in special insulating boot covers.

Gloves

A good pair of leather, nylon, or Gore-Tex insulated gloves or mittens is essential to keep your hands warm. A pair of mittens with woolen liners also works well. On very cold days, if your gloves or mittens are not warm enough, you can wear thin silk gloves closest to the skin to add a layer of warmth. I have found down- or 'Thinsulate'-filled leather mittens to be the warmest.

Hats

A warm hat that covers your ears is very important when trying to keep warm, since a great deal of body heat is lost via an uncovered head.

Sunglasses and goggles

Sunglasses are extremely important. The sun's rays are very strong at high altitudes and their effect is multiplied by the reflection from the snow. This can cause serious problems to unprotected eyes. It is therefore worth investing in good-quality sunglasses that filter out the sun's damaging ultra-violet rays. These same sunglasses will be very useful for boating or beach activities in the summer months. Every skier should also own a good pair of "fog-free" goggles for safe skiing on those days when the sun is hiding behind the clouds, making the terrain difficult to see (a condition known as "flat light"), or it's snowing.

Accessories

Weather in the mountains can change very rapidly, and a skier should always be prepared for these sudden climatic changes. A knapsack or fanny pack is very useful for carrying the extra gear to cope with changes in the weather. It's a good idea to carry a nylon windbreaker which takes up very little space when folded, but adds considerable warmth when worn either under or over your jacket. A face mask made of neoprene, silk, fleece, or wool can come in handy when caught in a blizzard or riding up chairlifts. A wool or fleece neck warmer will help prevent loss of body heat. An extra pair of mittens or an inner glove liner can be carried in case the weather becomes particularly cold. A good pair of fog-free goggles should also be stowed in the bag, as well as a warm hat and an extra pair of dry ski socks. It's good to have a high-energy snack, such as a bar of chocolate, an energy bar, or a bag of nuts and raisins, available when needed. It is also worth carrying a bar or tube of ski wax that can be rubbed on the bottoms of your skis if the snow conditions cause them to stick to the snow, and a screwdriver, Swiss army knife, or binding adjustment key for coping with binding problems.

Because the snow reflects the heat and rays of the sun, it can often get very warm during the afternoons when the sun rises overhead, so a ski sack is a handy place to stow unneeded layers of clothing. Suntan cream with a high sunscreen factor should be applied often to your face, ears, and lips for protection from the sun and wind. In the springtime it is a good idea to apply the cream several times a day.

Getting into shape

Skiing can be exhausting, because you use muscles that you don't often use in daily living. Consequently a beginner, or even an experienced skier starting a new season, may ache or feel tired after a few ski sessions. It is advisable, therefore, to get yourself into good physical condition before heading out to the ski slopes. There are different approaches to fitness, but whichever one you use, make sure you work on aerobic, anaerobic, and physical conditioning. It's also equally important to be very loose and flexible, so you should do a lot of preseason stretching and flexibility training.

Some good activities include jogging, running, fast walking, bicycling, rollerblading, competitive rowing, speed or distance ice skating, swimming, cross-country skiing, skipping with a rope, modern dance routines, and participation in a daily aerobic exercise program.

Physical conditioning can be done in your home or at a gymnasium or fitness center, and should consist of a program of muscle stretching and exercises designed to increase your strength. Important areas to concentrate on are your thighs, calves, stomach, and lower back. Dead weights, springs, proprietary exercise equipment, or simple exercises such as sit-ups and leg lifts can be used to build up and, more importantly, tone your muscles. The better shape you are in when you start to ski the easier you will find it, and the quicker your progress will be.

BEGINNERS' BASICS

section one

The goal of this section is for you to learn the fundamental skiing skills which will enable you to feel comfortable while standing, walking, gliding and turning on skis. These skills are the basis for all the more advanced skiing techniques taught throughout the book.

A series of interlocking steps are presented in an organized order, starting with simple maneuvers and going on to more complex maneuvers. Each step is designed to build upon the fundamentals that you will have learned in the previous steps, in the same way that a building is constructed - layer upon previous layers.

It starts with the basic skiing position and basic exercises to help you become more familiar and comfortable on your skis. You will learn how to use the edges of the skis to grip the snow and the smooth bases to glide. The "wedge stop" will enable you to ski to a stop on easy runs at slow speeds. The "traverse position" is the position that a skier is in almost all the time and the exercises are designed to teach you how to comfortably ski in this position. Most of the exercises presented in this section are actual ski maneuvers used in advanced skiing. Thus, while you are practicing these exercises in order to develop your basic skills, you will be at the same time perfecting advanced skiing capabilities.

Experience from teaching novices has convinced me that those who practice the exercises and acquire the fundamentals make the best and fastest progress afterwards, so I recommend that you take the time to practice and perfect as many of the exercises presented in this section as possible, in the order shown.

BEGINNER EXERCISES

The purposes of these exercises are:

- To learn to feel the skis as an extension of your body;

- To learn to develop your body awareness and stability on the skis while gliding and schussing;

- To learn to shift your weight from ski to ski;

- To learn to change direction;

- To learn to climb a hill;

- To learn to get up after a fall;

- To learn to do a kick turn (conversion); and

- To learn to stop at slow speeds on gentle terrain.

When learning any new sport there is an initial period of difficulty as your body adapts to the new demands placed upon it. In skiing, first boots are attached to your feet, then skis are attached to your boots, and suddenly you have a foot or two extension in front of your toes and behind your heel. When you try to turn in the normal manner you find that you step on your skis. Your boots seem heavy and the skis clumsy, and when you stand on a slight gradient, your skis want to slide away from you. All beginners go through this frustrating period so there is no need for undue concern. The Beginner Exercises teach your body to adjust to the fact that your feet have now "grown" fore and aft, and that they now have slippery plastic bottoms and sharp metal edges.

By the end of the beginner exercises you will realize that the plastic bottoms allow the skis to slide, and that the metal edges digging into the snow

enable the skis to turn or stop. You will also feel more comfortable on the skis and will be ready to learn more advanced maneuvers. It is advisable to follow the exercises in the order presented.

The basic position on skis

These exercises are to be performed on flat terrain

1) The basic position on skis PHOTOS 1+4B

The basic position is the position you will be in when skiing straight down a slope and when you are walking or gliding on a flat area. Photo 1 shows the position from the side. Photo 4B shows it from the front.

To assume the basic position stand over your skis with your weight equally distributed over both skis and have the skis a little less than hip distance apart. Relax and bend your knees slightly so that your shins are lightly touching against the fronts of your ski boots. Try to keep your back in a normal, relaxed position and bent slightly forward so that when you slide you do not tilt backwards. Keep your head centered, your shoulders relaxed and your arms held in front of your body with your elbows bent, as though you were carrying a tray or holding the handlebars of a bike. The ski poles should be pointing backwards as shown.

SPECIAL TIP

◎ The ski poles should be worn around the wrist so that you grasp the strap and the grip simultaneously. An easy way to learn to do this is to hold one pole in front of you and let the strap dangle. Place your hand

Walking and gliding on skis

Turning in position using tails as pivots

up from the bottom through the strap, and then grasp the strap and the grip.

2) Walking and gliding on skis — with and without ski poles PHOTOS 2A-B

Keeping the body in the basic position, begin to "walk" forward by pushing one foot in front of the other. This is accomplished by shuffling one ski forward and then shuffling the other ski forward, shifting your weight alternately from the front foot to the back foot. It is best to try this with the aid of the ski poles for a few strides and then, as in pictures 2A and 2B, by holding the ski poles in the middle and gliding forward without their aid.

3) Turning in place using tails and tips as pivots PHOTOS 3A-H

Now that you have taken a few paces forward, it is

time to turn around to walk back. This is easily accomplished by taking little steps so that you turn in place, using either the tails (backs of the skis) or tips (fronts of the skis) to pivot about. Let's start with the tail pivot and turn to the left (counter-clockwise), as shown in pictures 3A-3D.

Keeping your body in the basic position, lean on the right foot so as to reduce the weight on the left foot and, leaving both ski tails in the same place, step the front of the left ski to the left. (3A) Now lean on this ski and lift the front of the right ski and bring it alongside the left ski, leaving the tails in the same place. Repeat this motion of stepping the front of the left ski to the side, followed by the front of the right ski, leaving the tails of both skis in place, until you are turned around. This procedure should then be repeated to the right (clockwise), again using the tails as a pivot.

SPECIAL TIP

◎ If you find that you are placing one ski on the other it is because you are not leaving the tails in place in the snow.

Turning in place with tips as pivots

The same exercise should be performed using the tips of the skis as a pivot. In doing this maneuver, the tips of the skis are kept in place and the tails are stepped around. Turn first by stepping your tails to the left (clockwise) and then to the right (counter-clockwise).

These exercises are to be performed on a gentle slope with an uphill runout

4) Straight schussing down the fall-line PHOTOS 4A-B

First, it is necessary to understand the term "fall-line." This is the steepest path down the section you are on, and thus the direction in which you would slide if you fell, or the path down which a snowball would roll. The significance of the fall-line is that when your skis are pointing down it, they will automatically slide; only when your skis are perpendicular or at right angles to the fall-line will you be able to stand still without relying on your ski poles. This exercise is the first time that you will experience the feeling of skiing, in other words, the skis sliding over

Straight schussing down the fall-line.

the snow — hopefully with you standing on them!

Assume the basic position again, pointing down the fall-line, with your ski poles in the snow preventing you from sliding forwards. So that you do not fall backwards, it is very important to keep your knees bent and to lightly lean your shins against the front of the ski boots as the skis slide and not to lean backwards. Maintain the weight on both feet, relax, release the ski poles with a little push (pictures 4A and 4B), and try to keep your balance as you glide down the hill. If you are on a hill with an uphill runout, as suggested, you will stop automatically as you lose momentum on the uphill slope.

At this point, having successfully made it down the hill, most of my students break out into their first big happy smile, and the ones that get a particular gleam in their eyes are the ones that I know are hooked on skiing for life.

Sidestepping up the hill.

5) Sidestepping up the hill PHOTOS 5A-C

Having made it down, it would be fun to do it again. To get back up, we sidestep.

This is a simple maneuver achieved by keeping the skis perpendicular to the fall-line and walking the skis up the hill using the metal edges to bite into the snow to prevent the skis slipping sideways.

Assuming the basic position, you should stand with your skis perpendicular to the fall-line, as shown in picture 5A. It is absolutely essential to incline your feet and ankles towards the uphill slope the entire time in order that the ski edges bite into the snow so that they don't slip. Lean on the lower ski and move the upper ski up the hill in a small step, as shown in picture 5B. Place the ski in the snow perpendicular to the fall-line and place your weight on this ski, pressing so that the edge bites into the snow. Now lift the lower ski and place it alongside the uphill ski. Then transfer your weight back on to this lower ski. You should now be standing the same way that you started, only one step further up the hill. Now repeat these steps until you are up the hill.

SPECIAL TIPS

◎ If you are slipping backwards, it is because your ski tails are lower than your ski tips; vice-versa, when you are sliding forwards, your ski tips are lower than your tails.

◎ This maneuver should be practiced on both sides, so that you feel equally comfortable climbing to the left and right. It should also be performed both with and without using ski poles.

◎ I have found that closing the eyes for a few steps while climbing helps enormously, enabling the feet to "feel" the position of being perpendicular to the fall-line.

6) Diagonal sidestepping PHOTOS 6A-D

This maneuver is similar to the previous one, only this time the ski is stepped slightly forward at the same time as you step it up the hill (as shown in pictures 6A-6D) so that you are climbing on a diagonal path, rather than straight up the hill. The skis, of course, remain perpendicular to fall-line even as you climb diagonally.

SPECIAL TIP

◎ This maneuver is especially useful when climbing a relatively steep slope, as it is less tiring than straight climbing.

Diagonal sidestepping

Schussing down the fall-line lifting tails alternately

7) Schussing down the fall-line lifting tails alternately PHOTOS 7A-B

Here is a good exercise to help develop body awareness as you shift your weight from ski to ski. This maneuver is similar to straight schussing down the fall-line. The variation is that you alternately lift the tails of your skis as you schuss down the slope.

Start off in the basic position with your skis facing down the fall-line. Start gliding and, as you pick up speed, lift the tail of one ski (by leaning your weight over the other ski) for a count of two. Place the tail back on the snow, lean on this ski and lift the tail of the other ski for a count of two. Repeat until you automatically stop on the uphill runout.

SPECIAL TIP

◎ Try to maintain your balance as you lean over the ski that is on the snow, as in pictures 7A and 7B.

Schussing down the fall-line picking up gloves

8) Schussing down the fall-line picking up gloves PHOTOS 8A-C

This maneuver forces you to bend down and relax. Place a few gloves in the snow, just to the sides of the fall-line. Start in the basic position with your skis pointing down the hill. Hold your ski poles without putting your hands through the straps. Now push off and leave your poles behind. As you slide down the hill, bend down and lift each glove as you pass alongside it, as shown in pictures 8A-8C. Stand up between gloves.

SPECIAL TIPS

◎ If the practice slope is long enough, try to place at least four gloves in the snow.

◎ Drop each glove as you stand up.

9) Bending under ski pole arches PHOTOS 9A-C

This is another fine maneuver, and is as good for adults to practice as it is for children-although children tend to beat adults at it! Arrange ski poles in a series of arches by placing one pole horizontally through the straps of two vertical poles planted in the snow as in pictures 9A-9C. Stand in the basic position above the ski pole arches and start to slide. As you approach the first arch, bend your knees, lower your hips and crouch low to the ground so that you pass under the horizontal pole, as in picture 9A. As you pass the arch, rise up (picture 9B), and then bend again as you pass under the next horizontal pole (picture 9C).

SPECIAL TIPS

◎ If there is enough room and you can borrow

Bending under ski pole arches

Getting up after a fall

But it is still preferable to fall sideways if you can.

Having said that, after you fall and are splayed across the snow with legs and arms pointing in all directions, what should you do next? Generally, at the slow speeds you will be traveling during basic exercises, the skis will remain on when you fall. So the first step is to arrange yourself so that you are sitting with your skis together, perpendicular to the fall-line, and with your body uphill of your skis. Your legs should be bent and your knees tucked up towards your chest. Now, remove your hands from the ski pole grips and place the ski poles in front of your chest with their tips in the snow next to your uphill thigh. Place one hand on top of the grip and the other either just above the basket or on the snow at your side and you will be in the "ready" position, as shown in picture 10A. The trick to getting up effortlessly is to lean your chest forward the entire time. Now push yourself upward with your lower hand and simultaneously press down on the top of the grip with your upper hand. If you accompany this action by leaning your torso forward so that your knees are bent towards your chest, you should come up very simply, as in pictures 10B, 10C and 10D.

SPECIAL TIPS

◎ Due to gravity it is much easier to get up while on a hill than it is while on the flat. The point to remember when on a hill is that the skis must be below you, perpendicular to the fall-line, and when you start to roll up, be certain that the edges of the skis bite into the snow so that they do not start to slide away as you lean on them.

◎ Should your skis come off during the fall, collect them, open the bindings, place the skis perpendicular to the fall-line and stand alongside them. Using your ski poles for support, step into the binding of your lower (downhill) ski and then, standing with your weight on this lower ski, step into the binding of your upper (uphill) ski. If you are on an incline, you should roll your lower ski on to its uphill edge before stepping on to the uphill ski so that you don't slide down the incline.

◎ If you find it too difficult trying to get up with your skis attached, it may prove better to remove your skis and follow the above procedure.

enough ski poles place four or five arches down the slope.

◎ Be sure to rise up between the arches.

10) Getting up after a fall   PHOTOS 10A-D

Everyone falls, and so everyone must get up. But trying to get up incorrectly can be very exhausting and frustrating. Getting up correctly, while not easy in the beginning, soon becomes a habit and is not tiring or difficult once mastered.

When you fall, it is best to try and fall sideways with the skis parallel, as this is the least likely way to get injured. Naturally it is not always possible for you to fall as you would like, but modern release bindings are designed to kick the boot out of the ski in a fall, so it is pretty difficult to injure yourself these days.

The kick turn

11) The kick turn PHOTOS 11A-E

There are some ski schools that don't teach this until you are an advanced skier. They believe that it is potentially too dangerous for beginners. My experi-

ence is that when taught correctly a kick turn is the easiest and safest way of turning your skis through 180° when standing still on a hill. In all of my years of teaching I have never seen a beginner get hurt performing a properly executed kick turn.

The key to success in the kick turn is to prepare yourself correctly and then to perform the move in three fluid parts. The preparation consists of standing perpendicular to the fall-line, facing downhill. Both the ski poles should be placed in the snow uphill of you, one on either side of your body, and you should lean on these poles, as in picture 11A. It is very important that you face downhill with your hands visible in front of you. It is equally important that your top ski is very secure in the snow so that when you put your weight on it, it does not slide forwards or backwards. Once the preparation is completed, the turn can be performed.

Step one (picture 11B): swing (do not lift) the lower

The herringbone climb

ski forward and up, place the ski tail in the snow as far forward as you can and as close to the uphill ski as possible with your knee as straight as possible. If performed correctly you should be well balanced, leaning slightly uphill on the edge of your uphill ski, being supported by the ski poles.

Steps two and three are to be done in tandem, though not hurriedly. Step two (picture 11C): lower the tip of the vertical ski and place it perpendicularly across the fall-line next to the upper ski and in the opposite direction. The tail of the lower ski should not have moved. (I call this the "ballet step," though you don't have to be a Nureyev to do it.) The trick to make the step easy, is to bend your downhill knee and to lean your torso downhill over the bottom or downhill ski, as you place the ski on the snow. People who experience difficulty at this point do so because they lean backwards up the hill rather than downhill. If you lean downhill as suggested, bending the lower knee, it is extremely easy to perform step two and then step three.

Step three (pictures 11D and 11E): lean on the lower ski and bring the uphill ski around and place it parallel and next to the lower ski, completing the kick-turn maneuver. Be sure to keep the skis edged, i.e., rolled to the uphill side.

SPECIAL TIP
◎ To help you make this turn easily, keep the ski poles behind you until the last part of the maneuver. Many people try to bring the ski pole around before

the ski, and end up stepping on the pole. The pole and uphill ski should be swung around together, with the ski being planted first, followed by the pole.

◎ It is safest to practice this maneuver the first few times with a ski instructor or a friend who's a good skier standing in front of you and who can assist you.

To summarize, the kick turn is performed as follows: preparation; step 1-swing lower leg up and plant ski tail forward and close to uphill ski; step 2-leave tail in place, lower the tip of vertical ski, bend the knee, place the ski alongside uphill ski in the opposite direction, and lean out from the waist over the downhill ski; step 3-bring uphill ski around, followed closely by the ski pole.

12) The herringbone climb   PHOTOS 12A-B
The herringbone climb is a means of climbing straight up a fairly gentle hill by walking the skis up the slope in a "wishbone" fashion. This is performed by leaning against the fronts of the boots, keeping the tails of the skis close together and spreading the ski tips apart. As you step up the hill, you plant the ski on its inner edge in order to get a good grip in the snow so as to not slide backwards, as shown in picture 12A. When you have all your weight on this ski, you step the other ski farther up the hill, again with the tip pointing away from the fall-line and step on to this inner edge to get a grip in the snow (picture 12B). This is then repeated as you progress up the hill. This maneuver can be performed with and without the use of ski poles.

NOTE
◎◎◎ Apart from learning to climb up a hill, the herringbone climb is a useful exercise because it teaches you how to set your ski edges, push off these edges and shift your weight from ski to ski as you walk up the hill. These body movements are essentially the same as the movements used for "skating."

13) Beginners' "Tuck" position   PHOTO 13
This position, which is also known as a schuss or egg position, is similar to one that we often see ski racers in as it enables a skier to ski faster. Little kids usually love going down slopes like this. The "tuck" position is mainly used by beginners when they want

Beginners' "tuck" position

The wedge (snowplow)

to get up enough speed to make it up an uphill grade.

To ski in a "tuck" position, (picture 13), lower your hips and bend forward from the waist until you are crouching just about as far as you can. Have your skis quite wide apart (just less than hip distance). Hold your arms out in front of you, resting your forearms or elbows on your knees or thighs and point your ski poles backwards. Lightly lean your shins forward against your boots and keep your head up to see where you are going.

NOTE

◎◎◎ Because of the wide tips on "shaped skis," one has to be careful to keep the skis very flat on the snow when "schussing" straight down the fall-line. If you roll the skis at all inwards (on to their inner edges), the tips may catch the snow and the skis could cross, which could cause a nasty fall.

14) The wedge (snowplow)
PHOTO 14A-C

The wedge (or snowplow) is a means of slowing down or stopping on a gentle gradient at slow speeds. Though some ski schools don't teach this movement to beginners, many ski schools do. I personally feel that the wedge stop is a very useful ski maneuver for intermediate and advanced skiers, but is potentially dangerous for beginners to perform. It gives them a false sense of confidence, making them believe that they can stop when they lose control and are going too fast. As the knees are in a twisted position in the wedge, using this maneuver at high speeds may put too much stress on the legs and knees, and a fall could possibly result in spiral leg fractures or ligament tears. Furthermore, when beginners lose control they tend to lean backwards, which further aggravates the situation.

Consequently, I make sure that skiers skiing with me only use the "wedge stop" to stop on gentle slopes at slow speeds and I check that the bindings are set on a light setting so that the skis will come off easily should the skier fall.

Since this book is designed to help you if you are teaching yourself, and as you may find yourself in situations when it would be useful to have such a means of slowing up or stopping, I am including the wedge stop in the basic exercises. It is very important to remember that this movement should only be performed by beginners on gentle slopes at slow speeds. (Should you begin to lose control and start skiing too fast, it is preferable to fall sideways, swing your skis below you, and use the ski edges to bite into the snow to slow you to a stop.)

To perform the "wedge stop" (snowplow), choose a smooth, gentle slope with an uphill runout at the end. Face down the fall-line in the basic body position as described on page 10 and allow your skis to slide (picture 14A). Be sure to lean your shins against the front of your ski boots throughout the entire maneuver. As you gain momentum, roll your knees and ankles towards each other and, keeping the ski tips fairly close together, begin to lower your hips and push your feet outwards (picture 14B). Try to keep your weight equally distributed over both feet as you press down, with your upper body balanced midway between the skis. Continue pushing outwards until your skis form a "V" and you stop (picture 14C).

It is advisable to practice the "wedge stop" first on the flat, and "walk" the skis to the side until you are in the full wedge position, as shown (picture 14C). Keep practicing on the flat until you feel completely comfortable with the final stopping position before trying it on the gentle slopes.

SPECIAL TIPS

◎ Your weight should be over the middle of both ski boots as your skis are on their inner edges (not on the heels).

◎ Continually lean your shins against the fronts of the ski boots.

◎ As you push the skis apart, keep your knees and ankles rolled towards each other so that you cause the edges of the skis to dig into the snow.

◎ Try not to let the tips of the skis cross nor separate too far apart. Your skis should be angled in a "V," rather than parallel to each other.

◎ Try to keep your upper body naturally upright and relaxed the entire time, with your head centered and your arms held in the "tray holding" position with your ski poles pointed backwards.

TRAVERSE
The purposes of these exercises are:

▪ **To learn to feel the skis as an extension of your body;**

▪ **To learn to maintain the correct body position while skiing across a slope;**

▪ **To learn to control and steer the downhill ski;**

▪ **To learn to use the edges of the skis;**

▪ **To learn to shift your weight from ski to ski; and**

▪ **To learn to change direction and stop.**

A skier is almost always in the traverse position. It is the position you are in when skiing across a slope, and the position you are in before and after a turn. The only time you are not in a traverse position is when skiing the fall-line in a straight schuss position — and this is normally only done at the bottom or runout of a slope.

Since many runs are cut across the fall-line, even when skiing straight down the run without turning, the skier is generally not on the fall-line and therefore must assume the traverse position. My experience is that if you learn the correct traverse position as early as possible you will make the fastest progress. The biggest difficulty I have with students who come to me as intermediate skiers wanting to improve, is correcting their basic traverse position. Often these skiers have poor traverse positions and lack control when initiating and finishing turns. I find that I have to spend a great deal of time correcting these problems before I can make progress. When performed correctly, traversing is very easy and requires remarkably little movement of the parts of the body.

These exercises are to be performed on a gentle hill (beginners' slope)

1) The basic traverse position   PHOTO 15

As can be seen in picture 15, rather than facing the skis straight down the fall-line as in the straight schuss position, the skis are pointed across the fall-line. The speed of descent is determined by whether the skis are pointing closest to the perpendicular to the fall-line or to the fall-line itself. Naturally the position closest to the perpendicular - called a "shallow" traverse - will cause the slowest descent, and that closest to the fall-line - called a "steep" traverse - will be the fastest descent in traverse. Whenever the skis are across the fall-line (shallow, steep or any stage in between), your body should be in the traverse position.

NOTE

◎◎◎ On traditional skis I recommend that you have the skis 2-5 in. apart (5-12cm). On shaped skis I find it better to have the skis wider apart, approximately 4-7 in. (10-18cm). As you ski, you can vary the spacing to find the ski distance that feels the best for you.

To assume the traverse position, as shown in picture 15, all the uphill parts of your body should be slightly in front of their downhill counterparts. Start with the skis spaced apart (as noted above) and extend the uphill ski forward about a quarter to a half of a boot length. (The uphill foot is now automatically in front of the downhill foot, and the uphill knee is automatically in front of the downhill knee.) Now twist your body slightly so that the uphill side of your hip is in front of the downhill side, and turn your shoulders so that the uphill shoulder is slightly in front of the downhill shoulder. Your body should therefore be facing slightly downhill. Your head should be relaxed and centered, and facing the direction of the traverse, so that when you start to ski you can see where you are going. Your arms should be held still, as though you are carrying a tray. Your ski poles should be held at your sides pointing slightly backwards. The next requirements are very important in order to control the skis.

Relax and lower your hips a little bit and lightly lean your shins against the fronts of the ski boots so that you have a space between the calf muscles and the backs of the ski boots. Your top buckle should

The basic traverse position

not be so tight as to prevent you from leaning comfortably against the front of your boot, nor so loose that you have no support. Modern boots, made of strong plastic, support the body well and help prevent muscle pains. Skiers who suffer from painful shins are those who do not continually lean against the fronts of their boots but rather bang against them as they try to lean forward to regain control.

Next, incline your feet and ankles towards the uphill slope so that your skis are no longer flat on the snow but are making contact on their uphill edges. Lastly, lean your upper body down the hill so that most of your weight is over your downhill ski. Your torso should remain natural and relaxed and your knees relaxed and slightly bent.

NOTE

◎◎◎ On shaped skis I generally like to keep some weight on both skis in order to carve using both ski edges, so I do not lean my upper body as far down the hill as I do on traditional skis. The key point to remember is that most of your weight should be over your downhill ski.

SPECIAL TIPS

◎ This is the normal traverse position for skiing on packed snow. When skiing on icy snow the weight needs to be more over the downhill ski. This is accomplished by bending your upper body farther over the downhill ski. When skiing in powder snow, the weight should be over the heels and more evenly distributed over both skis. Skiing on ice and in powder snow are

16A

16B

16C

16D

Finding the "sweet spot" of the ski

advanced skiing maneuvers, and are explained in greater detail in Sections Four and Five. When learning the traverse position, it is best to be on packed snow.

◎ When skiing on steeper slopes modify the basic traverse position by rolling your feet and ankles slightly more uphill (thereby "edging" the skis more) and leaning your upper body more downhill, over your downhill ski.

2) Finding the "sweet spot" of the ski
PHOTOS 16A-D

The "sweet spot" of a tennis racket is the area on the face of the racket where you want to hit the ball as that is where the ball comes off the racket with the most force. The reason for this is that area is where the racket transmits the most energy to the ball. It also feels the best.

Likewise, skis also have a "sweet spot." That is the place where the skis transmit the most energy to a turn when pressed on and released. Standing on the "sweet spot" of the skis also feels the best and provides the most control.

To find the "sweet spot" of your skis, ski on a shallow traverse track across a slope and lean your body about, pressing on different places under your feet (pictures 16A, 16B and 16C). Vary your upper body lean both in a forward/backward direction and down the hill over your downhill ski. Also tilt your lower body forward and backward and try to find the position that feels the best. That position should place you over the "sweet spot" of your skis (picture 16D).

3) Shallow traverse — lifting tail of uphill ski PHOTO 17

Start in a traverse position close to the perpendicular to the fall-line and push off with your ski poles. While traversing across the slope, lift the tail of your uphill ski, as in picture 17. This is accomplished by leaning over the downhill ski in order to take your weight off the uphill ski. (If you are leaning on the uphill ski you cannot lift the tail.) Hold the ski tail in the air for a count of three and then place it back alongside the downhill ski. As you are in a shallow traverse, you will stop as you lose momentum.

Repeat this maneuver in the opposite direction and practice lifting the other ski. Most people find this easier on one side than on the other, so be certain to also work on the less favorable side since skiing requires equal control in both directions.

4) Shallow traverse — touching bottom of downhill ski boot PHOTO 18

Start as in the previous exercise and, while moving, lean over and touch the bottom of the downhill ski boot just where the arch of the boot comes in contact with the ski (picture 18). Hold this position for a count of three and then stand up again, assuming a good traverse position. Repeat in the opposite direction.

SPECIAL TIPS

◎ The trick here is to incline the downhill knee and ankle more towards the hill, making it easier to lean over sideways.

◎ This is an excellent exercise to "feel" how to ride on the uphill edge of the downhill ski.

5) Shallow traverse — holding ski poles across chest PHOTO 19

Hold your ski poles horizontally in front of your chest with the palms downwards and with one hand just below the grips and the other just above the baskets, as in picture 19. Since your chest is facing downhill, the ski poles are across the fall-line. Traverse across the slope in this position.

This exercise can also be performed lifting the tail of the uphill ski as a means of combining this and exercise 2. Repeat in the opposite direction.

NOTE

◎◎◎ I have found that this is a very good corrective exercise for intermediate and advanced skiers with incorrect traverse positions. I therefore recommend that all intermediate and advanced skiers execute this maneuver in both directions to ascertain whether or not you have a flawless traverse position.

6) Shallow traverse — alternately lifting tail and touching boot

As you traverse across the slope, hold the tail of the uphill ski in the air for a count of three, and then traverse with both skis in the snow for a count of three. Now bend down and touch the downhill ski boot for a count of three and then stand up and finish by traversing to a stop. Repeat to the opposite side.

Shallow traverse — lifting tail of uphill ski

Shallow traverse — touching bottom of downhill ski boot

Shallow traverse — holding ski poles across chest

Stepping uphill to stop

7) Stepping uphill to stop PHOTOS 20A-D

While you are skiing on a shallow traverse you will not have to worry about stopping, as you will run out of momentum naturally. But when you start performing these maneuvers on steeper traverses it will be necessary to have a means of stopping in order to prevent yourself from going off the side of the run. This stepping uphill maneuver not only teaches the proper use of the edges as well as how to shift the weight from one ski to the other, but also allows you to slow up or stop by stepping your skis up the hill into a shallower traverse until you stop naturally.

This maneuver should be practiced first on the flat, then on a gentle slope while standing still, then on a shallow traverse using a small push of the ski poles to get you into a very slow glide, then with a

longer glide and finally, after a complete traverse across the slope.

NOTE

◎◉◎ When performing this on the flat your body should "realize" that this maneuver is essentially the same as the Beginner Exercise, "turning in position using the tails as a pivot." The difference is that while gliding you have to maintain your stability on one ski at a time while you are moving.

To perform the stopping maneuver from a slow glide, start in a traverse position on a shallow traverse with your weight on your downhill ski (picture 20A). Push off with your ski poles so that you start to glide slowly. During the glide, lift the tip of your uphill ski and turn the ski so that it points more up the hill. Then step this ski slightly up the hill, leading with the ski tip, as in picture 20B. Place the ski on the snow and lean on the uphill edge (to prevent the ski from sliding sideways) — picture 20C.

Maintain your traverse position with your uphill shoulder and hip in front of the downhill counterparts so that your body is still facing downhill. (You must resist the tendency to twist your body in the direction you are stepping.)

The weight is now on the uphill ski. Now bring the downhill ski parallel to the uphill ski (picture 20D) and once more put your weight on the downhill ski. You will now be in a traverse position on a shallower traverse. If you are still going too fast the procedure should be repeated until you are on a traverse that will permit your skis to stop naturally. Repeat in the opposite direction.

SPECIAL TIPS

◎ Remember to practice this maneuver first on the flat, and then on a slope while standing still. After practicing with a short glide, increase your speed and length of glide.

◎ Your shins should be touching the fronts of the boots throughout this exercise, your knees should be relaxed, the uphill knee, hip, shoulder and arm should be leading, and your weight should be over the middle of your downhill foot.

◎ The trick to this maneuver is to leave the tails of the skis in place when stepping the skis up the hill. If you lift the whole ski and place it a full step up the

Traverse, touch boot and step uphill to stop

ver. My experience is that people want to slow down too quickly and consequently try to take a large, abrupt step up the hill, which inevitably leads to a fall while doing "the splits."

◎ Try to be graceful and allow the skis to glide as you are making small steps.

8) Traverse, touch boot and step uphill to stop PHOTOS 21A-E

You are now ready to apply what you have learned so far. Start in a medium traverse and push off with the ski poles (picture sequence 21). While gliding, bend down and touch your downhill boot and then stand up and continue gliding in the same traverse. Then, step the skis up the hill and glide to a stop. Repeat in the opposite direction.

hill in a parallel traverse direction to the one you are in, you will not slow down.

◎ If you take small steps and don't hurry the movements you should find it easy to perform this maneu-

9) Steeper traverse exercises

Now that you can safely and confidently step to a stop to both sides, all the traverse exercises can be performed on a steeper traverse path, in other words, closer to the fall-line. As your confidence grows you should increase the steepness of the traverse until you are starting just off the fall-line. Referring to Figure 1 you should begin each exercise in traverse A, a shallow traverse, close to the perpendicular to the fall-line; then repeat in traverse B, a slightly steeper traverse, closer to the fall-line; then in traverse C, D and E, each traverse becoming steeper and closer to the fall-line.

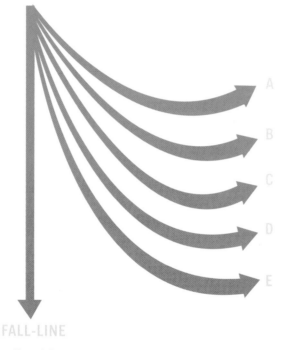

Figure 1: Start excercises in shallow traverse (A) and increase the steepness until you are starting just off the fall-line.

Hopefully you have become aware that all the maneuvers described so far have been done with your lower body. Your upper body has done little except to remain relaxed, and has been used only to maintain your balance over the instep of either your downhill or uphill ski. As you progress to more advanced maneuvers you will find this still to be the case.

Skiers who use their upper body too much tend to throw themselves off balance and are constantly seeking to regain their balance. I prefer a relatively "quiet" or "still" upper body for most ski maneuvers.

At this point you should be feeling much more confident on your skis. Your skis and boots should be feeling less alien, and you should be starting to enjoy the new sensations of gliding movement on the snow.

NOTE

◎◎◎ One of the nice things about skiing as a recreational sport is that it is non-competitive and you can go at your own pace. So take your time and practice each exercise until you feel ready to move on to the next one. I have never seen a determined person fail to learn to ski!

SIDESLIDING
The purposes of these exercises are:

- To learn how to correctly use the ski edges for sidesliding and control;

- To learn to use the feet and ankles to control the amount of edging required to cause the skis to either grip in the snow or to make them slide sideways;

- To reinforce the traverse position while sidesliding; and

- To teach your body the subtlety of lower body movements required for the transition from traversing to sidesliding.

All the sidesliding exercises should be performed on a short, steep slope

1) Sidesliding — pushing with ski poles PHOTOS 22A-D

Start in a traverse position with your skis perpendicular to the fall-line and with both ski poles planted in the snow uphill (similar to the start of the kick turn). Your upper body should be facing straight down the fall-line. Place the ski poles close to the skis (picture 22A) and start pushing the poles backwards. Release your ski edges slightly by rolling your feet and ankles in the downhill direction. Maintain

Sidesliding — pushing with ski poles

your skis perpendicular to the fall-line as you are pushing on your poles, and allow the skis to slip gently sideways down the fall-line as in picture 22B. When your hands are fully extended behind you, as in picture 22C, bring the ski poles back to the original position close to the skis and again push them away from you. Repeat this maneuver facing in the opposite direction.

SPECIAL TIPS

◎ The trick to this maneuver is to not roll your feet and ankles too far downhill or you will catch the downhill edge and fall over it.

◎ Try to maintain your proper traverse position with your weight over your downhill ski.

◎ As you sideslide, keep your knees relaxed and your shins leaning on the fronts of the ski boots.

2) Sidesliding — one foot at a time
PHOTOS 23A-C

Start in a traverse position with your weight on the instep of the downhill ski boot, the shins against the fronts of the ski boots and your arms and ski poles held comfortably in the "tray carrying" position, with the elbows bent. Push the downhill ski down the fall-line, keeping the ski perpendicular to the fall-line. (Your weight will shift to your uphill ski.) When your ski is extended to a point well before you do the splits, get a good grip with the edge biting into the snow, transfer your weight back on to this edge and slide the uphill ski alongside the lower ski. Again, push your downhill ski down the fall-line and bring the uphill ski alongside. Continue these movements until you feel comfortable and in control of your skis, and then repeat in the opposite direction.

Sidesliding — one foot at a time

3) Straight sidesliding PHOTOS 24A-D & PHOTOS 25A-C

Assume a proper traverse position with your arms in the "tray carrying" position for balance. Keep your weight on the instep of your downhill ski boot and roll your feet and ankles downhill. Your skis, as they start to flatten, will begin to slide down the fall-line (picture 24B). Try to control the slide so that the skis remain perpendicular to the fall-line as they are sliding. When you are ready to stop, roll your feet and ankles uphill again and your edges will begin to dig into the snow (picture 24D).

SPECIAL TIP

◎ The tricks here are to constantly maintain shin contact with the fronts of the ski boots, to keep your weight on the downhill ski and not to over roll your feet and ankles. (You don't want the skis totally flat on the snow or you might fall over the downhill edge.)

NOTES

◎◎◎ On wet, sticky snow, it is necessary to wax the skis so that they slide easily. Almost every ski shop has a hot-waxing machine that can wax your skis for the prevailing snow conditions and it is a good idea to bring your skis in and have them properly prepared. Properly waxed skis are safer than skis that stick to the snow as they react quicker to your movements and will respond as directed. Skis that stick may cause you to fall at slow speeds, which can be potentially dangerous. Furthermore, sidesliding is difficult with sticky skis, as the snow gathers under them.

Straight sidesliding

Straight sidesliding (detail)

◎ This exercise teaches the nuance of movement required to start the skis sliding.

Picture sequence 25A-C shows a close-up of the lower body during the sidesliding movement. Notice how the skis flatten when the feet and ankles are rolled downhill (which starts the skis sliding) and how the skis are edged when the feet and ankles are rolled back uphill to stop the slide.

4) Diagonal sidesliding PHOTOS 26A-D

I find that many people have trouble with this maneuver when they try mentally to force themselves to slide down the hill sideways and go forward at the same time, so I use a little trick which almost never fails. Instead of thinking of diagonal sidesliding as a separate maneuver, think of it as traversing to a point on the other side of the slope with your skis flattened a little. (It is actually easier to sideslide than to traverse, since during sidesliding you do not have to put as much pressure on the edges as you do when traversing.)

To perform this maneuver, assume a proper traverse position. While standing still, roll your feet and knees downhill (just enough so the skis are still on their edges but almost flat on the snow). Now when you try to traverse, because your skis are less edged, they will slide downhill as you are moving forward. In picture sequence 26A-D, you see the diagonal track being engraved in the snow during a diagonal sideslide.

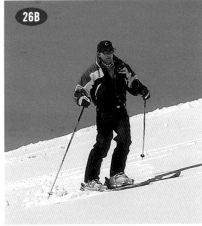

Diagonal sidesliding

SPECIAL TIPS
◎ Keep your eye on the point you've chosen across the slope (a run marker, a tree, or a lift tower) and try

Staircase sidesliding

to keep your ski tips pointed towards this object as you descend. This will help prevent your skis from running away down the hill.

◎ Be sure to maintain your shins in contact with the front of your ski boots with a gap between your calf muscles and the backs of the ski boots, otherwise your weight can tilt backwards and you will have trouble controlling your skis.

◎ Throughout the maneuver your weight should be over the instep of your downhill ski boot.

◎ Try to keep your upper body still.

5) Staircase sidesliding PHOTOS 27A-F

This is one of my favorite exercises, and one which has remained a constant feature in my teaching through all the years of experimentation and innovation. I especially like this maneuver because it teaches the subtlety of feet and ankle movement and gives beginners great confidence on their skis as a conse-

quence of the control that they learn to acquire. I also like this maneuver because it is extremely useful when skiing a narrow run that is on a bias to the fall-line, especially when the run is crowded.

It is best to practice this on a wide, intermediate grade slope on packed snow, remaining aware of other skiers who are descending on the run in order to avoid collision.

Staircase sidesliding is nothing more than a combination of straight sidesliding and traverse, both of which you have already performed. It is called staircase sidesliding, not surprisingly, because the track in the snow resembles a staircase, as can be seen in picture 27F.

To perform this maneuver, traverse across an intermediate grade slope, as shown in picture 27A. After going some 6 to 10 ft (2 to 3 meters), roll your feet and ankles downhill and, without stopping, begin to sideslide (picture 27B). Continue to sideslide for approximately 3 to 5 ft (1 to 1.5 meters) and then roll your feet and ankles towards the hill and press your downhill ski edges into the snow (picture 27C). Without stopping, and with your skis rolled towards the hill, traverse again for some 6 to 10 ft (2 to 3 meters) — picture 27D.

Continue to repeat these alternating movements until you have crossed the slope. Repeat the maneuver in the opposite direction.

SPECIAL TIP

◎ To test your capability, sideslide diagonally rather than straight every other traverse, and try to perform this maneuver very slowly.

NOTES

◎◎◎ Whenever I have intermediate and advanced skiers wanting to improve, but who tend to make too many movements with their upper bodies, I have them perform this exercise at very slow speeds. It always amazes them that they find it difficult to do.

◎◎◎ Many skiers get into the bad habit of throwing their hips to turn their skis, and often lose — or never establish — the sensitive contact between their feet and the snow. This exercise is designed to help establish that contact.

◎◎◎ You will find sidesliding to be a very useful maneuver when you start to ski the runs on mountains, for whenever you encounter a pitch on a slope that you feel is too steep to ski, too narrow to allow you to confidently make turns, or too icy or rocky, you can always sideslide safely. No matter how advanced a skier you become you will always encounter places where you must sideslide. Therefore, learn to sideslide confidently and you will always have a safety maneuver when needed.

You have now learned the two most important safety maneuvers; "sidesliding" for beginner and intermediate skiers, and the "kick turn" for advanced skiers. I have lost count of the number of times I have led advanced skiers off the packed slopes into the back-bowls and have come to a place where for one reason or other we have had to turn around to get down another way, only to be told that they cannot "kick turn." Thus they have had to walk backwards along treacherous cliffs in order to find room to turn around. I now make skiers demonstrate to me the "kick turn" before I lead them "off-piste." So, as beginners, I recommend that you go back and practice your kick turn now until it is as easy to do as signing your name. Similarly, practice sidesliding whenever you can, so that these techniques are ready to be used when needed.

SKATING
The purposes of these exercises are:

▥ To learn how to shift your weight from one ski to the other;

▥ To help achieve better balance and stability while gliding;

▥ To practice pushing off the ski edges and gaining a better understanding of the use of the ski edges;

▥ To learn to change direction while moving;

▥ To practice leg "flexion and extension;" and

▥ To practice independent action of the legs.

"Skating" is a ski maneuver that many ski schools do not teach to adults, but only include in their teaching curriculum for children. This, I feel, is a serious mistake, as skating is one of the most beneficial skiing maneuvers to help anyone's body feel comfortable and relaxed on skis. While skating, the legs are taught how to "flex" and "extend," which are the same movements used for more advanced skiing, the body is trained to shift its weight from ski to ski and one learns how to change direction easily while moving. Skating also helps to improve a skier's body awareness and balance. Skating is also fun to do.

I have always observed that at the end of the skating exercises students feel very familiar and at ease with their skis and consequently make excellent progress in the subsequent skiing maneuvers. I therefore recommend that all beginners and intermediate skiers who are not comfortable skating spend the time necessary to practice all the exercises in this section.

NOTE

◎◎◎ It is best to practice the basic skating movements on the flat and then, when they are learned, practice the gliding exercises on a gentle slope. Start

Skating on the flat — with exaggerated body movements

with very little exaggeration of body movement. When you begin to "feel" the skating movements, exaggerate the leg thrusts. As you become more advanced you will find that eventually you will be able to skate even on the more difficult slopes.

1) Skating on the flat PHOTOS 28A-D

This maneuver should be performed first with very little exaggeration of body movements and then with more exaggerated body movements, and can be thought of as roller skating, roller blading or ice skating with longer blades. Refer to pictures 28A-28D. Spread the tips of the skis slightly apart so that the ski tails are closer together than the ski tips. Now "set" the edge of one ski by rolling your foot and ankle inward. Push off with that ski and glide on the other ski. While gliding, roll your other foot and ankle inward, lower your hips, set the edge, and push off on

the other ski. Do at least four or five of these skating maneuvers.

SPECIAL TIPS

◎ You will find that if you do not roll your foot and ankle inwards, the ski will remain flat on the snow and when you push off the edge, the ski will slide away. Therefore, it is necessary to "set" that edge so that you have a firm grip when you push off.

◎ The other trick to this maneuver is, after you push off, lean out over the gliding ski (as in pictures 28C and 28D) so that you don't find yourself caught between the skis. (Your body should be moving from side to side as you push and glide.)

These exercises should be performed on a gentle slope.

Skating using poles as foils

2) Skating down the fall-line —
skating as a "fencing" maneuver
PHOTOS 29A-E

The motion required is the same as skating on the flat, only now you will have more gliding speed and the setting of the edges will require more precision.

At this point, I should like to point out that there is a great similarity of body movements in different sports. This is natural, since the body is only capable of just so many movements. It is as well to realize that although you are in a new medium using different equipment, the actual body movements required have already been learned via some other activity. Skating is a motion very similar to fencing. As you can see in picture sequence 29A-29C, if you hold your ski poles as you would a fencing foil and imagine your opponent up the hill from you, in order to thrust at him

you must bend your lower leg, point your upper leg (and ski), push off the lower leg (downhill ski) and lean over the thrusting leg (uphill ski). As on a flat surface, and even more so on a slope, it is necessary to set the edge of the downhill ski so that you have a firm grip from which to push off.

If you now hold your ski poles in the normal fashion, as in picture sequence 29D-29E, and perform exactly the same movement as the fencing thrust, you should find skating easy.

On a gentle beginners' slope with an uphill or flat runout, skate a path straight down the fall-line. Start with little exaggeration and then exaggerate the flexing and thrusting movements. Concentrate on setting your edges and shifting your weight from ski to ski.

Skating — holding poles normally

Skating uphill

SPECIAL TIPS

◎ As you are gliding, start to lower your hips as you roll your foot and ankle inwards, so that you can get a hard edge set when you are ready to thrust in the new direction.

◎ When you are moving quickly, it is best to lift the stepping ski so that the tail is slightly higher than the tip (as in picture 29D) and cross it over the pushing ski, keeping the boots fairly close together. Place the stepping ski in the snow with the tip first, followed smoothly by the rest of the ski as your body weight transfers to this ski during the glide (picture 29E).

3) Skating uphill PHOTOS 30A-C

I recommend that you briefly repeat "stepping uphill to a stop" which was practiced during the Traverse exercises (page 28). This maneuver is nothing more than half a skating step. In this movement one ski becomes the stepping and gliding ski while the other remains the pushing ski. (In sequence 30A-30C, the right ski is the pushing ski and the left ski the stepping and gliding ski). Take as many steps up the hill as you need to stop. Having already practiced skating from one ski to the other you should find this exercise easy to do. Try to exaggerate the flexing and thrusting movements as you "half-step" your skis to a stop.

4) Skating to a stop

This maneuver is simply a combination of skating down the fall-line and then skating uphill to a stop. Start by facing down the fall-line and begin skating down the fall-line. When you have done four or five skating steps start leaning in one direction and skate to a stop with a number of small half-steps up the slope away from the fall-line. Repeat this exercise and skate to a stop in the opposite direction.

5) Skating across the fall-line

This and the next exercise will determine how comfortably you are skating and whether you have mastered the use of your ski edges. Start by skating down the fall-line and after two or three skating steps start half-skating to one side. Instead of skating to a stop, however, start to half-skate down the hill to the opposite side so that you are having to turn across the fall-line. Your stepping/gliding ski now becomes your pushing ski, and vice-versa.

After crossing the fall-line, again change your stepping/gliding ski and pushing ski and half-skate downhill across the fall-line so that you are making a series of skating turns down the hill.

SPECIAL TIPS

◎ The trick to this maneuver is to be certain to lean your body in the direction you are heading so that it will be over the leading ski, especially as you change direction.

◎ A further trick is to lead with the knee that is in the direction you wish to head.

6) Skating a figure-of-eight
PHOTOS 31A-E

Perform this, the culmination of skating maneuvers,

31A

31B

31C

31D

31E

Skating a figure-of-eight

on a very gentle slope, as part of the maneuver will require you to ski uphill. Refer to picture sequence 31A-E. Start in a traverse position and half-skate across the fall-line to the right (pictures 31A and 31B). Then, after crossing the fall-line, half-skate to the left as you proceed down the hill (picture 31C). So far, this is the same as the previous maneuver. Now comes the demanding part as, instead of continuing to skate downhill across the fall-line, you must continue half-skating up the hill (picture 31D), completing a circle, crossing your track at midpoint and then, changing directions, continue half-skating uphill until you are at your starting point, completing the figure-of-eight (picture 31E.

SPECIAL TIP

◎ The uphill part of the figure-of-eight requires strong leg thrusts and speed when changing direction. As in the previous exercise, lead with the knee that is in the direction you want to head, and lean the upper body well forward and over the gliding ski (picture 31C). Naturally there will not be too much glide as you push uphill.

Skiing a figure-of-eight is a "fun" maneuver and not absolutely necessary for everyone to perform; but if you are strong and able and want to see how well you have mastered skating, give it a try.

Whether you've performed the figure-of-eight or not, you should be feeling much more at ease on your skis than before, and should be finding it easy to control and steer your skis. You are now ready to move on to the skiing lessons that will show you how to carve parallel turns.

CARVING TURNS

    This section will teach you how to properly ski smooth, graceful turns with very little effort. You will learn how to employ hip lean, edging, and pressure to make controlled parallel turns on easy and intermediate ski runs.

    The exercises are presented in a step-by-step format with each step building upon the previous steps. By practicing the exercises in the order shown, you will be preparing yourself for the following lessons while you do them.

    You will first learn how to turn the skis parallel using just your feet and ankles, and use hip lean to make large-radius turns on easy slopes. The next step in the progression will show you how to make medium- and short-radius turns so that you will be able to ski in control on steeper runs.

    The last series of exercises demonstrates high-energy carving and shows you how to get top performance from your shaped skis. These maneuvers, done properly, will enable you to ski at high speeds, as well as ski race.

CARVING TURNS

The purposes of these exercises are:

- To understand "why" skis turn;

- To learn how to correctly use the feet and ankles to place the skis on their edges;

- To learn how to employ hip lean to initiate turns;

- To learn how to employ edging and pressure to steer turns;

- To learn how to turn your skis uphill to a stop;

- To learn how to carve parallel turns;

- To learn how to perform leg flexion and extension;

- To learn "dynamic" skiing and fundamental racing skills; and

- To have fun.

Why skis turn

Although I emphasize learning to ski by "feeling" the various movements, I believe it can be useful for skiers to understand why their skis turn.

When I learned how to ski, we used an exaggerated upward movement which lifted the ski tails off the snow and we jumped the tails across the fall-line, landing with the skis pointing in the new traverse position. This was hard on the knees and quite tiring for all but the youngest and fittest. As the use of modern technologies became incorporated into ski manufacture, so an understanding of ski dynamics influenced ski design, and the skis that are used today are much more sophisticated than those with which I started.

We are also indebted to the racing circuit, since racers and manufacturers have always constantly sought ways of making skis turn more easily to give them the advantage over their competitors. These improvements have found their way into our recreational skis, resulting in skis that essentially turn by themselves with very little effort on the part of the skier. No longer do we have to thrust our skis into the air, winding and unwinding our bodies like coiled springs to turn the skis. All we have to do is press on the ski edges in a particular manner, and the shape of the ski and the energy transmitted to it automatically cause it to turn, making skiing as physically easy for older skiers as for youngsters.

To understand the technicalities of why skis turn, begin by learning the basic construction of modern skis. Figure 2 shows a ski on a flat surface.

Ski camber

Notice that the ski does not lie flat on the surface but rather is arched so that only the front and back parts of the ski contact the surface. This feature is called "ski camber." When you stand on the middle of your skis, your weight is distributed along their entire length. Naturally, since the front and back part of the skis are always in contact with the snow, the front and back parts are pressed even harder into the snow when you stand on them.

Ski sidecut

Notice also in Figure 2 that the skis are not evenly broad over their entire length. They are widest at the tip (shovel), narrowest at the waist, and wide at the tail. This narrowing is called "ski sidecut" and, combined with ski camber, is responsible for the way skis carve in the snow during a turn.

Because the shovel and tail of a ski are wider than its waist, when you roll your ski onto its edge and press down with your foot the contact resistance created along the length of the ski is greater at these wider points than at the middle. Since the resistance is greatest at the shovel, the ski will start to turn around that point.

NOTE

◎◦◦ To help visualize how this resistance works, imagine pushing a shopping cart sideways with the brake applied to the front wheels. Rather than move sideways, the cart will pivot around the front wheels because the resistance at the back wheels is less than at the front wheels.

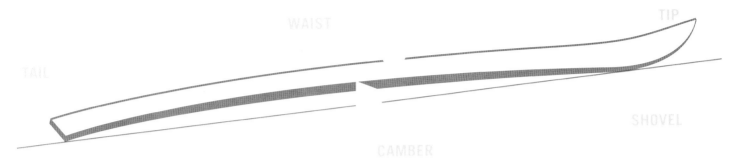

Figure 2: Parts of a ski

Reverse camber

When you press down on the middle of a ski on a compressible substance such as snow, the center of the ski bends more than the ends, causing the ski to bow in the reverse direction. This is referred to as "reverse camber." The amount of reverse camber and the dimensions of the sidecut determine the arc of a carved turn.

Reverse camber is also one of the factors that enables a skier to initiate turns without exaggerated and exhausting body movements. When a ski is bowed in reverse camber, it is stressed and stores energy. As the skier takes his weight off the middle of the ski, it starts to return to its original shape and the stored energy helps spring the skier into the turn much as a diving board springs a diver into the air or a bow releases an arrow.

Torsional resistance

Another feature built into skis is torsional resistance. This quality allows the ski to twist as it is turning and untwist after the turn, so the edges maintain constant biting contact with the snow. When you initiate a turn, the front of the ski starts to turn and the back follows. If you immediately initiate a turn in the opposite direction, torsional resistance permits the backs of the skis to complete the last turn while the fronts of the skis twist in the new direction.

Torsional resistance varies with ski design. A beginner usually finds it easier to use a ski with less torsional resistance, while a racer would prefer one with more.

Ski flexion

Another property of modern skis is ski flexion, or how the ski flexes, or bends, as it passes over undulations in the snow. A "soft" ski will flex more than a "stiff" one. The flex pattern of a ski determines the way the ski bends in reverse camber.

The amount of flexion required in a ski depends on the type of skiing that you intend to do. For skiing on hard or icy conditions and for fast skiing, it is preferable to have a reasonably stiff ski. For slower skiing and for powder snow many people prefer a soft ski.

While camber, sidecut, torsional resistance, and flexion are the main features that determine how a ski will turn, there are a number of additional qualities built into skis that improve their overall performance at various speeds but add to their cost. Some better quality skis have layers of rubber or torsional flex bars to help dampen ski vibrations — the shaking or chatter that occurs at high speeds. Generally, the more expensive skis are constructed with sophisticated materials, such as kevlar, graphite, or titanium, which add to their lightness, liveliness, and durability.

Now that you have a basic understanding of the way skis are designed to turn, you can appreciate how much easier skiing can be if you ski in such a way as to utilize these features. My experience is that those who have been skiing for many years have been taught, or learned on their own, to use exaggerated movements of the body to start the skis turning. Even though they are now using modern skis, they have not yet caught on to the joys and simplicity of their modern skiing equipment. If you are just beginning to ski, you can learn to ski the easy way: turning your skis with a minimum of effort. So continue on with

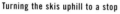
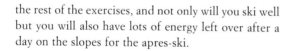

Turning the skis uphill to a stop

the rest of the exercises, and not only will you ski well but you will also have lots of energy left over after a day on the slopes for the apres-ski.

These exercises should be performed on a gentle slope

NOTES

◎◎◎ These exercises are designed to build your confidence by making use of the same fan pattern that was used for the traverse exercises (Figure 1). You'll start out skiing slowly, turning uphill from a shallow traverse, and then increase your speed gradually by starting the turns from steeper traverses until you are turning uphill from the fall-line. The next step will be to turn downhill across the fall-line to both sides and then link a series of parallel turns down the slope.

◎◎◎ Perform all the exercises of the series to one side and then repeat the series to the other side.

1) Turning the skis uphill to a stop

A) Starting on a shallow traverse, turning uphill using the feet and ankles **PHOTOS 32A-F**

The first exercise of the series is to show you how to turn your skis uphill by simply rolling your feet and ankles (pictures 32A and 32B). Start on a shallow traverse with your body in a good traverse position and your skis slightly edged, and gather some speed (picture 32C). When you are ready to turn, simply roll your feet and ankles up the hill and hold the ski edges gripping in the snow (pictures 32D and 32E). The skis will turn up the hill to a stop (picture 32F).

Repeat the exercise, and this time, when you roll your feet and ankles, hold them for a count of three and then roll them back to their original traverse position and glide again. Then roll them up the hill again. Try to notice how the skis turn when you roll your feet and ankles.

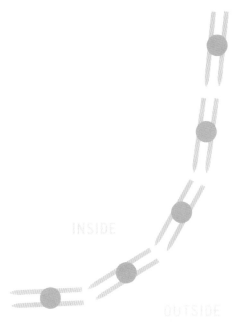

Figure 3 Outside/Inside ski

Lowering hips to apply pressure

SPECIAL TIPS

◎ As you are rolling your feet, try to focus on rolling your uphill little toe and your downhill heel.

◎ Don't try to turn the skis by turning your feet in the direction of the turn! This action will most likely cause the skis to skid. Be patient and try to feel yourself riding on the edges of the skis as they turn. (The skis turn when you put them on their edges because of their shape and design.)

Definition of outside/inside ski

If you look at the track that skis make in the snow (Figure 3), you will see that each turn inscribes an arc. The circle has an inside and an outside. Logically, we refer to the ski that is on the outside of the circle as the outside ski and the ski on the inside of the circle as the inside ski. I have found that students often find it easier to visualize which ski I am referring to when I refer to the skis as inside or outside rather than as uphill or downhill — terms which I also will employ for clarity for many ski maneuvers. In pictures 32C-32F, which show a turn to the left, the right ski is the outside ski and the left ski is the inside ski.

B) Lowering hips to apply pressure **PHOTOS 33A-C**
Repeat the first exercise. As you roll your feet and ankles up the hill, begin lowering your hips to apply pressure to the skis. This will cause your skis to turn more up the hill. You should find that the pressure applied to the ski edges makes your skis turn very easily.

Traverse, flatten skis, turn uphill

Traverse, flatten skis, turn more to the fall-line, turn uphill

◎ It is important to keep your upper body and hips facing to the outside of the turn (i.e., toward the outside ski), with most of your weight over your outside ski.

C) Traverse, flatten skis, turn uphill **PHOTOS 34A-D**
Begin on a shallow traverse (picture 34A). As you are gliding, roll your feet and ankles slightly down the hill to flatten your skis (picture 34B). Allow the skis to start to turn toward the fall-line and gather speed. As soon as they do, edge them by rolling your feet and ankles back up the hill and lower your hips to apply pressure to the skis (picture 34C) as in the previous exercise and turn the skis uphill to a stop.

D) Traverse, flatten skis, turn more to the fall-line, turn uphill **PHOTOS 35A-D**
Repeat the same exercise. This time after you flatten the skis, let the skis turn closer to the fall-line (picture 35B) and gather more speed before turning them uphill to a stop.

E) Traverse, flatten skis, turn to the fall-line, turn uphill **PHOTOS 36A-D**
Repeat the same exercise. This time, after you flatten the skis, let the skis turn to the fall-line (picture 36B) before turning them uphill to a stop.

NOTE

◎◎◎ Notice in picture sequence 36A-D how the upper body remains still during this maneuver. Beginners often try to pull themselves around by leaning their upper body in the direction they want to go. That doesn't work! In fact, that is like climbing up a steep hill with slippery shoes; the shoes keep slipping out from under you because there is no friction — in other words, no resistance. The reason you roll your feet and ankles up the hill is to put the skis on their edges. By pressing down on the edges you force them to bite into the snow, thereby creating friction along the edges (hence a resistance between the skis and the snow) which, because of the shape of the skis, causes them to turn. If you try to pull yourself around, you will be taking the weight off the instep of the downhill foot and therefore off the edge of the downhill ski, and the ski will either carry on in the same direction or skid.

Traverse, flatten skis, turn to the fall-line, turn uphill

F) Garlands (scallop-shell pattern) PHOTOS 37A-D

See if you can create a scallop-shell pattern, known as a garland, in the snow by linking a series of these uphill turns. (At this point in the learning sequence it's okay if your skis sideslip a little as they are turn-ing.) Start skiing on a shallow traverse and flatten your skis (picture 37A). When they turn toward the fall-line, edge, press down, turn uphill and ski to a stop, as you've done in the previous exercises (pic-tures 37B and 37C). Then lower the ski tips down the

Garlands (scallop-shell pattern)

One turn across the fall-line, flattening skis

hill and traverse again and repeat the same movements. Continue making these linked uphill turns until you have created a garland or scallop-shell pattern in the snow (picture 37D).

SPECIAL TIP
◎ This is best performed on a wide, uncrowded slope so that no one runs into you.

2) Parallel turns downhill across the fall-line PHOTOS 38A-E

A) One turn across the fall-line, flattening skis
This time you will make your first parallel turn downhill across the fall-line. The movements are essentially the same as those used for the uphill turn. The difference is that after you flatten your skis and they turn to the fall-line, continue to roll your feet and ankles across the fall-line so that your skis roll onto the other set of edges.

To make a downhill turn, start traversing as before with most of your weight on your downhill ski (picture 38A). When you pick up some speed, roll your feet and ankles toward the fall-line to flatten your skis so that they turn toward the fall-line

Linked parrallel turns, flattening skis between turns

(picture 38B). When the skis are running down the fall-line, begin to shift your weight to the other ski (this ski will be the outside ski of the turn, and after the turn will be your new downhill ski) and continue to roll your feet and ankles in the same direction until you've rolled them over to the other side (picture 38C). (Most of your weight should now be over this new downhill ski.) You will find that your skis will roll onto their other set of edges and turn across the fall-line. After the skis cross the fall-line, continue to roll your feet and ankles up the hill and begin to lower your hips to apply some pressure to the edges, and your skis will continue to turn up the hill to a stop (picture 38D). Repeat this exercise to the other side.

SPECIAL TIPS

◎ As you are turning, keep your chest and hips facing the outside ski of the turn. The key point is to not turn your chest and hips in the same direction as the skis are turning.

◎ Try to maintain a relaxed stance on your skis and note how the skis actually turn across the fall-line by themselves in a large, curved arc.

B) Linked parallel turns, flattening skis between turns
PHOTOS 39A-F

This time, rather than stopping after the turn, link together two turns. Start traversing and as you pick up speed, flatten the skis, roll your feet and ankles toward the fall-line, and when the skis are running down the fall-line, continue to roll your feet and ankles across the fall-line and place more weight over the outside ski. Then, as the skis cross the fall-line, lower your hips to apply some gentle pressure to the edges. The skis will continue to turn up the hill as before. But this time, rather than skiing to a stop, start to flatten the skis again by rolling your feet and

Turning in a tuck position

ankles down the hill and repeat the same movements to make a turn in the other direction. Stop after this turn.

When you feel confident making two turns, link a long series of parallel turns down the slope, rolling from one set of edges to the other.

C) Turning without flattening skis

Now that you are able to roll your feet and ankles to turn your skis across the fall-line, you should be capable of making turns without first intentionally flattening the skis as a separate movement. It's best to start in a tuck position and then perform the turns in an upright stance. Turning in a tuck position will limit unnecessary upper body and hip movements so that you can concentrate on just rolling your feet and ankles and feel the effect on the edges of your skis.

C1) Turning in a tuck position **PHOTOS 40A-D**

On a very gentle slope, assume a tuck position with your skis held wide apart (just less than hip width) and start traversing the slope. When you are ready to turn, slowly roll your feet and ankles in the direction of the turn

Turning in an upright stance

so that the skis gradually roll onto the other set of edges and make a turn across the hill. When the skis have turned, slowly roll your feet and ankles in the other direction and make another turn across the hill. Try to make very smooth, large-radius turns down the slope.

C2) Turning in an upright stance **PHOTOS 41A-G**
On the same easy slope, perform the same turns in an upright stance. As you ski, try to stand on your skis so that you are riding the edges and the skis are not slipping.

N O T E
◎◦◦ This may feel a bit stiff, but at this point you should just be interested in learning how to turn your skis by only rolling your feet and ankles. After you practice some of the following exercises, it will feel and look more relaxed and natural.

3) Hip lean
The next series of exercises will show you that you can also place your skis on their edges by leaning your hips in the direction of the turn. As you did in the previous series, you will start by leaning your hips up the hill to turn uphill and then lean them down the hill to carve downhill turns across the fall-line.

A) Turning uphill by leaning hips **PHOTOS 42A-F**
On a gentle slope, start traversing and then lean your hips up the hill. Your shaped skis should turn up the hill automatically. See if you can feel how your skis start to turn as soon as they are placed on their edges. Do it again with more hip lean and note how much more the skis turn the further you lean your hips. Repeat to the other side.

N O T E
◎◦◦ Try to imagine that you are leaning against a stool that is up the hill by the side of your uphill hip. Thus, to lean against the stool, you have to lean your hip to the side. Be careful to not lean backwards.

S P E C I A L T I P
◎ As you lean your hips, bend your upper body down the hill slightly so that you keep most of your weight on your downhill ski and don't topple over. The more you lean your hips, the more you have to lean your upper body.

Turning uphill by leaning hips (rear view)

Turning uphill by leaning hips
(front view)

Downhill turns with hip lean

B) Downhill turns with hip lean PHOTOS 43A-D
See if you can make some downhill turns by leaning your hips from one side to the other, in the direction of each turn. Start to traverse and when you are ready to turn, simply lean your hips in the direction of the turn to place your skis on their edges. The skis should carve a turn across the fall-line. As you lean your hips, try to keep more weight over the outside ski.

4) Edging and pressure
The two major variables that you can play around with to steer and control your skis are edging and pressure. Two very good exercises to help you learn how to control these variables are as follows:

**A) Constant pressure and changing edge angles
PHOTOS 44A-C**
For this exercise try to keep the pressure on the skis constant. Vary the edge angle (i.e., the amount of edging) by rolling your feet and ankles and leaning your hips more up the hill.

Start traversing with your skis slightly edged and apply a small amount of pressure to the skis. Then, keeping the pressure unchanged, tilt the skis uphill more and note how the skis turn further up the hill. Continue to roll your feet and ankles to the side and lean your hips, so as to tilt your skis as far over as you can. You should find that the more the skis are edged, the more they turn up the hill.

**B) Constant edge angle and changing pressure
PHOTOS 45A-B**
For this exercise try to keep the edge angle constant and vary the pressure by lowering your hips to press down on the skis.

Start traversing with your skis slightly edged and keep the skis on the same edge angle during this maneuver. Begin by standing quite tall and increase

Constant pressure and changing edge angles

the pressure on the skis by gradually lowering your hips. Start off by pressing very lightly and then increase the pressure until you are pressing as hard as you can. Note how much more the skis turn up the hill as you increase the pressure on the skis.

NOTE

⊚⊚⊚ These two variables, edging and pressing, are essentially what put you in control of your skis, so it would be useful to consciously play around with different combinations while practicing turns, noting what happens each time.

5) Weight transfer PHOTOS 46A-C

A useful exercise for learning when to transfer your weight from ski to ski is to practice this weight transfer exercise. In this maneuver you will lift the tail of the unweighted ski.

Start traversing an easy slope with your weight on your downhill ski (picture 46A) and make a downhill turn. As your skis start turning, lean your body over your outside ski and lift the tail of your inside ski (picture 46B). After the turn, place the tail of the ski back in the snow and repeat the same movements in the opposite direction for the next turn. Continue these movements, linking a series of turns down the slope.

NOTE

⊚⊚⊚ You should notice where in the turn you shift your weight. Expert skiers shift their weight to their outside ski very early in the turn so as to have the best control throughout the turn. So practice transferring

Constant edge angle and changing pressure

Weight transfer

Press and release practice — with skis

squeeze the sponge ball, it will compress. When you release the pressure it will expand back to its original shape. If you release the pressure gradually, the sponge ball will expand back gradually; if you release the pressure quickly it will expand back quickly. This is very similar to what happens to your skis when you press on them, putting them in reverse camber. If you release the pressure gradually as you transfer your weight from one ski to the other, the bent ski will gradually and smoothly return to its normal camber. If you release the pressure abruptly as you transfer your weight, the bent ski will quickly spring back to its normal camber.

By varying the way you release the pressure on the skis, you can make large-, medium- or short-radius turns. The more slowly you release the pressure the larger the turn will be. Conversely, to make short-radius turns you release the pressure quickly.

NOTE

◎◎◎ You may find it helpful to imagine that you have the sponge balls under your skis, beneath your arches, so that when you press down on your skis you are trying to squeeze the sponge balls. (I actually have my clients stand on real sponge balls which I place under their boots and have them practice pressing and releasing.)

A1) Press and release practice PHOTOS 47A-D
Traverse an intermediate slope and during the traverse, practice pressing on your downhill ski and varying the speed with which you release the pressure. Release the pressure gradually a few times, then press and release the pressure somewhat more quickly. Then press and release the pressure very quickly. Do this to both sides.

NOTE

◎◎◎ To release the pressure on the ski rapidly, pull your leg up. Do this by keeping your knees and hips relaxed and pull up with your thigh muscles.

A2) Linked medium-radius turns PHOTOS 48A-E
Ski on an intermediate-grade slope. Initiate a turn across the fall-line by rolling your feet and ankles in the direction of the turn, as you have done in the previous exercises. As the skis turn toward the fall-line,

your weight as soon in the turn as you feel able to lift the inside ski and control the outside ski.

6) Medium-radius turns and short-radius turns

At this point you should be able to comfortably carve large-radius turns on the easy slopes. However, if you try this same type of turn on steeper slopes, you will undoubtedly pick up a great deal of speed. To control your speed you need to make tighter turns, either medium-radius or short-radius. These turns will enable you to ski more slowly.

A) Medium-radius turns

For the purpose of analogy it is useful to compare the concept of ski camber to a sponge ball. When you

48A

48B

48D

48C

48E

Linked medium-radius turns

roll your feet and ankles in the new direction. At the same time that you are releasing the pressure on one ski, you should be starting to apply pressure to the other ski. Try to ski to a smooth rhythm so that as one leg is flexing the other is extending.

NOTES

◎◎◎ Describing this action makes it seem much more complicated then it actually is. In fact it is very easy to do! You can think of the action as a pedalling motion on a bicycle or step machine — one foot presses down as the other rises up. The only difference in skiing is that as the feet go up and down, they are also rolling from side to side.

◎◎◎ The pressing and releasing should be a very fluid and rhythmic motion. You may find it helpful to hum or sing a song and press and release to the rhythm of the song. An old song that I've always found appropriate for medium-radius turns is a slow

start to press down on the outside ski and continue to press while the skis turn across the fall-line. Almost immediately after the skis have crossed the fall-line, start to release the pressure on the ski and begin to

Short radius turns

version of "Tea for Two." (Another song I use with children is a very slow version of "Twinkle, Twinkle, Little Star.")

B) Short-radius turns PHOTOS 50A-C

To make short-radius turns, you have to press and release the skis more quickly than you do for medium- and large-radius turns. Again, it might help to imagine that you have sponge balls under your skis. When you are ready to turn, press down on the imaginary ball under your downhill ski. Then release the pressure quickly as you start to transfer your weight to the other ski and start to roll your feet and ankles in the other direction, so that the ball springs back to its original shape. As you release the pressure, immediately press down on the imaginary ball under your other ski.

Mixed-radius turns

To practice these movements, ski down an intermediate-grade slope and make a series of downhill turns. Try to press and release the pressure on the skis more quickly than you did for the medium-radius turns. As was the case for the previous exercise, it may help to sing or hum a song to establish a rhythm. (I sing a faster version of "Tea for Two" with adults and a normal version of "Twinkle, Twinkle, Little Star" with children. You may wish to choose a different song.)

With practice, you should start to feel the buildup of energy in your skis as you apply pressure, and should soon discover the perfect release point so that the skis will help to spring you from one turn to the next.

NOTE

⊚⊚⊚ As you are skiing, try to keep your upper body relaxed and centered over a straight path down the slope as you press and release the ski edges, so that your legs and skis swing back and forth beneath your upper body. In technical terms, this action is known as "cross-under," and is a fun maneuver to perform on high-energy shaped skis.

C) Mixed-radius turns PHOTO 50D

Try varying the pressure and release so that you make different radius turns. Release the skis slowly for some turns and more quickly for others, and note the differences.

◎ Whichever turns you are making, you want to ski from the feet upward. Your brain, of course, tells your feet where you want to go, but then you need to learn to feel what the skis are doing in the snow and respond accordingly. You can think of it as a chain reaction that works its way rapidly up the body once you roll your feet and ankles and press on the ski edges. Essentially you are building an intelligence in your feet, ankles, knees, hips, and upper body so that they become sensitive to, and work in harmony with, the feel of the skis as they turn.

NOTE

◎◎◎ At this point, you should be having lots of fun on your skis and should be able to confidently ski many of the trails on the mountain.

7) Ski separation PHOTOS 51A-B

How far apart you should keep your skis depends on what distance feels most comfortable to you. Some instructors recommend skiing with a wide stance. Others say a narrow one is better. I think the distance should vary according to your build, how fast you are skiing, the steepness of the slope, the type of snow, and what gives you the best security.

When I started skiing, the goal was to ski with the skis almost locked together. These days most people ski with their feet spaced somewhat apart.

Shaped skis that are held very close together (picture 51A) can bang at the tips and tails and create problems. Skis held farther apart than hip distance (picture 51B) will be difficult to control for most ski maneuvers.

I find that I generally have my shaped skis somewhat farther apart than I would my traditional skis when skiing on packed snow and ice. In powder I bring the skis closer together. You need to experiment and find what seems right for you.

8) Pole planting PHOTOS 52A-D

On traditional skis, pole planting is an important part of the turn, as it is used in conjunction with hip flexion and extension to time and initiate a turn. On shaped skis, many turns can be initiated without planting the ski poles. In fact, very often, people using short, shaped skis ski with no poles at all.

Skis too close

Skis too wide

Pole planting

There are times however, such as when you are skiing on bumps or very steep slopes, when it is useful and advisable to plant your ski poles to "trigger your turns," so it is worthwhile practicing correct

Dynamic leg extension — weight transfer to outside ski

pole planting.

Traverse across a slope on a shallow traverse and hold your downhill ski pole vertical, ready to be planted. Practice lightly touching the pole in the snow as you press and release the pressure on your downhill ski. Touch the pole in the snow when you flex your legs (picture 52B) and lift it out of the snow when you extend your legs (picture 52C). Do this to both sides.

Now start skiing turns with pole planting and practice getting the timing right, coordinating the pole planting movements with the release of the turn.

NOTES

◎◉◎ When skiing in a good traverse position your arms should be held in front of you with your elbows bent and your ski poles pointing backward. When you are ready to plant the downhill pole, merely cock your wrist to swing the ski pole vertical. After you plant the pole, immediately push your wrist forward so that you end up in a good traverse position after the turn.

◎◉◎ You don't need to jab the poles hard! All you need to do is touch your pole in the snow to trigger your turn.

◎◉◎ Exactly where you plant your ski pole depends on a number of factors. Normally you plant the pole where your hand is. On a very steep slope you will most likely have your upper body turned to the fall-line. Therefore you will be planting your downhill ski pole further back than you would when skiing on an easy slope. (In Section Four, you will learn how to anticipate the turns, planting the ski poles further back on steeper slopes.) When skiing bumps quickly, one normally plants the ski pole near the tips of the skis on the front flank of the bump. When skiing in powder, skiers hold their hands wider apart and tend to plant their ski poles more to the sides. If you are in a good traverse position, skiing at moderate speeds on easy or intermediate runs, it should feel most natural to plant your ski poles just where your hands are held.

9) Dynamic skiing

This series of exercises will teach you how to get the best performance from your shaped skis. You will

Dynamic leg extension — weight transfer to inside ski

learn how to ski at high speeds and remain in good control, while having fun and developing the fundamentals of good racing skills. These exercises will work with all types of skis so they are helpful for everyone, though they are especially effective on shaped skis.

There is so much energy built into the new shaped skis, and they are so dynamic, that they can be thought of as performing tools that can be easily used to achieve high-energy skiing and precise carving.

The following exercises will teach you how to obtain this type of performance from your shaped skis.

A) Dynamic leg extension PHOTOS 53A-G & 54A-C

Dynamic leg extension is the movement of pushing off the outside ski to accelerate a turn. The motion is similar to the way you push from ski to ski when you skate with exaggerated body movements.

Start skiing on an intermediate-grade slope and make a few medium-radius turns as you've done previously. On the third or fourth turn, after you press on the outside ski. rather than just releasing the pressure as you get ready to initiate the next turn, powerfully push off the ski and extend your leg as you thrust into the next turn. (You can start pushing from around the middle of the turn or closer to the end of the turn.) As you push off, roll your feet and ankles in the new direction and transfer your weight onto the new outside ski. This action should be very dynamic. Continue these same movements and make a series of high-energy turns down the slope. It can

Dynamic leg extension and leg retraction

also be useful, especially if you plan to ski race, to practice transferring your weight on to the new inside ski (pictures 54A-C). In this case, after you extend

56A

56B

56C

56D

Leg retraction only

your leg to initiate the turn and roll your ankles across the fall-line, you finish the turn with your weight on the same ski. For this turn, the weight transfers from edge to edge of the same ski, rather than from ski to ski.

B) Dynamic leg extension and leg retraction
PHOTOS 55A-D

This exercise combines dynamic leg extension with leg retraction to add power and quickness to the turn. During this action you retract your leg before you finish the extension movement, as follows:

Make a few turns using the dynamic leg extension movements of the previous exercise. After the third or fourth turn, start to press on the outside ski (picture 55A) and then, rather than pushing off the ski to thrust into the next turn, quickly release the pressure by pulling your leg up, that is, retract it (picture 55B). As you retract your leg, roll your feet and ankles in the new direction and transfer your weight onto the new outside ski (picture 55C).

If you get the timing right, you should find that you will make a very smooth, rapid, and controlled turn. When you extend your outside leg to press on the outside ski as the ski is turning, you are loading up the ski with energy by putting it in reverse camber and making it bite into the snow and direct the turn (picture 55A). When you retract your leg, you release this energy, causing a rapid and fluid movement of your body downhill across the skis (picture 55B). This enables you to very quickly press onto the new outside ski, which will allow you to carve the ski very early in the turn.

C) Leg retraction only **PHOTOS 56A-D**

This movement is useful when making large-radius turns at high speeds. The retraction is basically a flexion (compression) movement of the two legs, which absorbs the forces acting on the body at the end of a turn and allows you to get your body across the skis in the direction of the next turn very early in the turn. Aside from being good fun, retraction permits very dynamic, controlled skiing. It also enables you to carve your skis very smoothly into the next turn.

The way to ski with leg retraction is to start skiing some fast, large-radius turns, using just your feet

Hip angulation — in tuck position

and ankles to initiate the turns. After three or four turns, when you are ready to make the next one, quickly retract both your legs and roll your feet and ankles in the new direction. After the skis cross the fall-line, extend your legs back to a neutral position. Continue this as you go down the slope and make a long series of leg retraction turns.

You can either transfer your weight from ski to ski as you have done in the previous exercises, or ski with your weight on both feet (keeping a bit more weight over the downhill ski) as you retract and extend your legs. Skiing with your weight on both skis will allow you to carve the turns with both skis, an action known as double carving.

NOTE
◎◎◎ I like the feeling of double carving so much that I do it whenever the snow conditions and the slope allow me to ski in control with my weight on both feet.

D) Hip angulation PHOTOS 57A-D & 58A-C
I've noted the importance of keeping your upper body facing the outside of the turn. This helps create hip angulation. It's worthwhile practicing some large-radius turns, specifically concentrating on turning your upper body toward the outside of the turn.

Practice on an easy slope. Ski a run or two in a tuck position, turning the skis just by rolling your feet and ankles. Always try to turn your upper body to the outside of the turn. Then ski the same easy run in an upright stance and concentrate on keeping your upper body turned to the outside of the turn.

Hip angulation — in upright stance

Inclination

E) Inclination PHOTOS 59A-F

This is an interesting and useful whole body action that leads to very smooth transitions from turn to turn. (This should only be performed by good inter-mediate or advanced skiers. It can be confusing to beginners, who need to concentrate on keeping the upper body turned to the outside of the turn.) This action works along with angulation to make for very

Fault: Swinging the upper body and hips in the direction of the turn

Correction

Fault: During the turn, leaning up the hill with the back straight, putting the weight on the uphill ski

Correction

fluid skiing.

As in the previous exercise, practice first in a tuck position and then again in a normal upright position. Start skiing in a tuck and make large-radius turns as before, concentrating on keeping your body in an angulated stance. After two or three turns, start to introduce the inclination movement in the last third of the turn.

Inclination movement:

After you've begun a large-radius turn with hip angulation, and the skis are turning in an arc (picture 59A), as they start to turn into the fall-line, slowly turn your chest so that it squares up over your skis, facing the ski tips (pictures 59B and 59C). Reducing the angulation in the last third of the turn by squaring up with the skis allows you to incline your body more into the turn. Then make another turn across the fall-line, repeating the same upper body movement. Try to keep the body movements smooth and fluid. When you get the timing right you should find that one turn flows into the next very smoothly.

NOTE

◉◉◉ As you are turning your upper body, it is important that you don't overswing your hips. They should be kept slightly countered (facing the outside of the turn).

10) Common faults and corrections

There are many faults that skiers make. You may find yourself making some of them. Following are a few of the most common faults and their corrections.

1A) Fault: Swinging the upper body and hips in the direction of the turn. **PHOTO 60A**

1B) Correction **PHOTO 60B**
Two good exercises to correct this problem are:
a) Hold your ski poles horizontally across the hill at chest level and ski large-radius turns on an easy slope, keeping the poles still and perpendicular to the fall-line the entire time (picture 60B). (Don't allow the poles to swing in the direction of the turn.)
b) Ski a series of large-radius turns on an easy slope and place both your hands on your outside knee as you are turning.

2A) Fault: During the turn, leaning up the hill with the back straight, putting the weight on the uphill ski. **PHOTO 61A**

2B) Correction **PHOTO 61B**
As you turn, tilt your upper body slightly over the outside ski to keep most of your weight on this ski. (This ski becomes the downhill ski after the turn.) A good exercise is to lift the tail of your unweighted ski as you are turning (see page 57, picture 46B).

Fault: Leaning on back of boots

From left to right: extreme backward lean, extreme forward lean, correct-neutral position

Fault: Legs too straight and stiff

Correction

3A) Fault: Leaning on backs of boots **PHOTO 62A**

3B) Correction **PHOTO 62B-D**
Lean your shins forward so they are touching the tongues of your boots and try to mentally focus on continually feeling that contact. (You should have a space between your calf muscles and the backs of the boots.)

A useful exercise is to traverse across a slope and exaggerate leaning backward and forward (pictures 62B and 62C). First lean backward on the backs of the boots, then lean far forward (pressing hard against the fronts of the boots), and then try to lean correctly so that your shins are just lightly leaning against the tongues of the boots (picture 62D).

NOTE
◎◉◉ Another valuable exercise to help you establish

a good sense of body position is to ski a series of turns on an easy slope with your boots open.

4A) Fault: Skiing with tensed feet, with the toes curled up

4B) Correction
Ski a series of turns on an easy slope and intentionally wiggle your toes. Try to relax your feet and, as you are skiing, move your toes up and down.

5A) Fault: Legs too straight and stiff **PHOTO 63A**

5B) Correction **PHOTO 63B**
As you are skiing, try to relax your legs and knees. Try shaking them rapidly as though they were made of jelly. If you lean against the fronts of your ski boots and lower your hips slightly, your knees will bend automatically.

BUMP SKIING

section three

No ski area is free of bumps! You may find a slope from time to time without them, but that is the exception. Though some bumps are permanent, having been formed by snow piling onto a big boulder or over a natural mound, most are formed by skiers turning their skis in the same place, carving out the snow beneath the turn and spraying it to the side. This continuous carving of the snow results in a mound of snow. The steeper the slope, the more turns skiers make, producing numerous bumps that are usually quite large. On a gentle slope, most skiers make fewer turns and press less hard on the edges of the skis, so the bumps tend to be smaller.

In most ski areas, machines are used to flatten the bumps and redistribute the snow in order to maintain an even snow base throughout the slope; however, no sooner are the bumps flattened by the machines than new ones are being formed by skiers. It is therefore evident that sooner or later you will have to ski bumps in order to get down a slope. Thus it is wise to learn how to do it properly so that you won't fear them and try to avoid them (as I did when I first learned to ski). In fact, once you become proficient at skiing bumps, you will see that they can be great fun.

The goal of this section is to help you achieve that proficiency by explaining and demonstrating a number of different ways of skiing the varied types and shapes of bumps that you are likely to encounter.

NOTE: Bumps are also known as *moguls*.

A bump field

GETTING STARTED

1) Turning around bumps

Shaped skis are very good for skiing bumps. The fact that the skis are designed to turn makes skiing the bumps even easier on shaped skis than on traditional skis.

The easiest way to start skiing bumps is to turn around them, starting each turn before a bump and making the turn in the trough around it. This is essentially the same as turning on a smooth, bump-free slope, since you will be skiing on a reasonably smooth path between the bumps.

A) Turning around small bumps on easy intermediate runs
PHOTOS 64A-D

To learn to ski around bumps, start on an easy, intermediate-grade slope with small bumps. Stand in a good traverse position with your weight on your downhill ski and ski toward a bump. As you approach the bump, prepare to plant your downhill ski pole on its front flank (picture 64A). Then make the same type of turn around the bump that you have made on the smooth slopes (picture 64B). Be sure to transfer your weight onto your new outside ski and recover your inside arm by pushing your hand forward after you plant your ski pole (picture 64C). Try

to swing a large arc so that you turn your skis completely around the bump, making the turn in the trough between the bumps (picture 64D). Practice turning in both directions.

B) Linking turns while turning around bumps
PHOTOS 65A-D

Once you feel comfortable turning to the left and to the right around the bumps, you should practice linking your turns. Begin by linking two turns and stopping. When you have mastered this, link together three and then four turns and finally ski through the bump field turning around as many bumps as you can. Concentrate on trying to get the timing right and also concentrate on finishing your turns so that you remain in good control at all times.

C) Turning around medium bumps on steeper runs
PHOTOS 65A-D

When you feel comfortable turning around the small bumps on the easy intermediate runs, gradually progress to turning around larger bumps on steeper runs (pictures 65A-D).

NOTE

◉◉◉ You can turn around bumps making any of the turns that you've practiced in Section Two. It's a good idea to try using each method to see the differences and to determine which works best for you. At slow speeds on small bumps, you can turn by simply rolling your feet and ankles and applying some pressure to the outside ski. On larger bumps, on steeper trails, and at higher speeds, you should find that the leg extension turns work better.

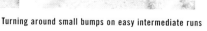
Turning around small bumps on easy intermediate runs

2) Turning over bumps

An easy way to ski bumps at slow speeds is to ski over their tops. The rise of the bump helps the timing of the turn, and the summit of the bump offers very little resistance, as only the portions of the skis that are under your feet are in contact with the snow when you make the turn. Turning on the tops of the bumps is a very good way to reinforce the parallel turn, since the two skis turn very easily as a result of this low resistance.

A) Turning over small bumps on easy intermediate trails
PHOTOS 66A-D

To learn to turn over bumps, start on an easy intermediate-grade slope with small bumps. Stand in a good traverse position, ski toward a bump with your weight on your downhill ski, and aim to pass over the top of the bump. As you approach, lower your hips to press down on your downhill ski (picture 66A). Then, as you are skiing up the bump, plant your ski pole to the side of the summit, extend your legs, and roll your feet and ankles in the new direction (across the fall-line), and turn over the top (picture 66B). Transfer your weight to your new outside ski and press down on this ski to finish the turn on the back side of the bump (pictures 66C and 66D). Repeat, turning in both directions.

NOTES

◎◎◎ Try to time the turning movements so that as you turn on top of the bump, only the portion of the skis that is under your feet is in contact with the snow.

◎◎◎ It's very important that you do not swing your upper body in the direction of the turn, as this will cause your skis to over-turn and you'll lose control. (Try to keep your upper body relaxed and still and facing the outside of the turn.)

B) Linking turns while turning over bumps

Follow the same progressive approach as you did when turning around the bumps: Once you feel comfortable turning to the left and to the right over the bumps, practice linking your turns. Begin by linking two turns and stopping. When you have mastered this, link together three and then four turns and finally ski through the bump field turning over as many bumps as you can. Between turns, assume a neutral, relaxed traverse position so that you can flex your

Turning around medium bumps on steeper runs

Turning over small bumps on easy intermediate trails

hips before the next turn.

When you feel confident linking turns over small bumps on easy intermediate slopes, start linking turns over larger bumps on progressively steeper runs. Try to ski slowly and in control.

SPECIAL TIPS

◎ Be sure to immediately push your hand forward after you plant your ski pole to recover your inside arm (picture 66C). I've noticed that many skiers have a tendency to leave this arm trailing behind as they cross the fall-line, causing the inside shoulder to be pulled backward and resulting in an incorrect traverse position and a loss of control.

◎ As you crest the bump, press your hips forward and lean your shins against the fronts of your boots, or else you may find your weight shifting backward and your skis shooting away.

NOTE **PHOTOS 67A-C**

◎◎◎ Turning over the bumps should be done only at slow speeds. If you try to turn over the top of a bump when you are skiing too fast on even a gentle or intermediate trail, you will find it difficult to keep your skis in contact with the snow — often you will fly off the top of the bump and have to turn your skis in the air and try to regain your balance on landing. (This, by the way, can be fun once you get the hang of it. During lessons with advanced skiers we sometimes play games by skiing down a bump run, jumping off the tops of the bumps and trying to pass over two or three of them before turning our skis and landing in the new direction. Obviously, this type of jump turn should not be attempted until you are ready for it.) If a bump is too large or steep, if it is a rock partially covered with snow, or if there is an obstacle such as a tree or lift tower sticking out of it, it is much easier and safer to ski around it.

Turning around obstacles

3) Bumps as friends

One of the biggest problems skiers have with bumps is that they see them as enemies — monsters waiting to grab them and knock them over — rather than as friends waiting patiently to make turning easier. This is a very important *attitude* problem which generates fear and causes the body to tense up. Once you come to understand and trust that you can use the bumps to both control your speed and help make the turn, I'm sure you will feel happier skiing bumps and hopefully, you'll eventually start to look for bumps to play with, as the good bump skiers do.

4) Using the front slopes of large bumps to slow down

Skiers very often get frightened when they have to ski down a long, steep slope full of big bumps. There's an interesting point that I think may help you overcome some of this fear: The front slope of every bump is a curved wall rising up!

It's common knowledge that you can't ski very far up a wall, so instead of seeing all the cliffs on the backs of the bumps when you look down a slope, see instead all the walls on the fronts of the bumps. All you need to do to ski slowly and safely is use these walls to slow down. You do this by swinging very large arcs so that you turn completely around the bumps, steering your skis so they ride up the steep front slopes of the neighboring bumps. This will cause you to lose speed as you complete each turn.

5) Foot swivelling PHOTOS 68A-D

A very good exercise to practice before you start skiing the big bumps at high speeds is to "foot swivel" on the tops of the bumps. This is an excellent way to build confidence on very big bumps or bumps on steep slopes, as you will be able to ski totally in control, turning slowly on the tops of the bumps and then slowly descending their backs.

Another advantage to foot swivelling is that it will help you develop a good feel for different snow textures, which will serve you well whenever you ski.

To learn to foot swivel, stand on a bump with your hips slightly lowered, with only the portion of the skis that is beneath your feet in contact with the snow (the tips and tails should be in the air) as in picture 68A. Press your shins forward against your

boots, turn your upper body in the direction of the turn (anticipation position) and plant your ski pole down the fall-line (picture 68B). Keep your weight over both feet. Now relax your legs and hips and swivel your feet so that your skis turn beneath you (picture 68C) and you end up on the same spot, but facing in the opposite direction (picture 68D). Practice this to both sides.

NOTES

◎◎◎ Be sure that the skis are not too far apart, so they are turning at essentially the same place on the bump.

◎◎◎ It is important to plant the ski pole down the fall-line so that you have to reach downhill.

◎◎◎ Try to keep the ski pole vertical as you make the turn.

To make an active foot-swivel turn, slowly ski toward a big bump. As you approach the summit of the bump lower your hips slightly, anticipate the turn as you did above, plant your ski pole down the fall-line, and swivel your feet (your momentum should

Foot swivelling

slowly propel you over the top of the bump as your skis are turning). As you crest the bump press down on your skis on the back of the bump and slowly steer your skis to the top of the next one.

SPECIAL TIP

◎ Imagine that you are standing on two jam jars, trying to open their lids by twisting your feet. You have to press down as you are swivelling!

◎ Foot swivelling is also very useful when skiing in whiteout conditions or during snowstorms when the bumps get covered with new snow. Each time you feel a bump under your feet, you can slowly foot swivel over the top and thus not get thrown by the bumps.

ABSORBING BUMPS
6)   Absorption (Avalement)

Absorption was developed by ski racers as a means of keeping their skis in constant contact with the snow on grooved and bumpy race courses. As it helps the racers from being thrust airborne by the bumps, so absorption can help all skiers keep their skis on the surface on any uneven trail. In fact, absorption may be the single most useful advanced skiing maneuver for all levels of skiers, and should become second nature when passing over bumps at high or medium speeds. Knowing how to stay in control on bumps will help you conquer your fear that the bumps will knock you over and you will go tumbling down the slope.

A) Basic absorption

If you were driving a new car on a bumpy road, you would probably be very upset if the entire chassis went up and down each time the car passed over a bump. Indeed, you would probably bring the car back to the dealer to have the suspension system overhauled. What you would expect is that the suspension springs would compress, absorbing the bump as the wheels passed over it, and then extend again after passing over the bump. The chassis would remain quiet and still, regardless of the road conditions.

Figure 4: Suspension springs compressing and extending as car passes over a bump in the road.

Figure 5: As the body passes over a bump, during absorption the knees are "pushed up" towards the chest, "absorbing" the bump.

To help understand absorption (also called, *avalement*) it is useful to look at a simplified car-suspension system (Figure 4) and understand how it works. The chassis of a car constantly exerts a downward force, causing the wheels to press against the road surface. As the wheels meets a bump, the bump pushes up against the wheels, which starts to compress the suspension springs. The chassis attitude remains constant. As the wheels approach the peak of the bump, the springs continue to compress and are most compressed at the summit of the bump. As the wheels start to descend the bump, the springs begin to extend back to the neutral position and are completely neutral when the wheels have fully descended the bump and are back on the flat surface.

Figure 5 shows how the body can be compared to a car. If you think of your head and torso as the chassis, your hips, knees, and legs as the suspension springs, and the skis as the wheels, then we can make a direct comparison with the previous example.

Your "chassis" is heavy and is constantly exerting a downward force. As your skis reach a bump, they should push up against your "suspension system" and the suspension system should compress — your knees should push up toward your chest with your hips as the pivot point. Obviously this will not occur if your knees and hips are rigid. Instead, your entire body will ride up over the bump and, if you are skiing fast, you will become airborne as you shoot off the top. So keep your knees and hips relaxed to allow the bumps to compress the knees.

As you start to pass over the back of the bump, you have to push your feet downward to keep your skis in constant contact with the snow. When you have descended the bump, your legs and knees should be back in a relaxed position.

Absorption Position PHOTOS 69A-B

So that you are not thrown backward when your knees are thrust upward by the bump, when skiing with absorption you should sit slightly lower and bend your chest slightly forward from the waist so that your center of gravity is always over the middle of the ski boots. (Picture 69A shows a normal traverse position; picture 69B shows the body modification required for absorption skiing.)

Absorbtion position

SPECIAL TIPS

◎ Always keep your shins touching against the fronts of the ski boots.

◎ Resist the temptation to lower your hips as you pass over the bump. It is not the hips that go down, but the knees that are pushed up!

◎ Some of my students have found it easier to visualize absorption if they think of it as a pumping motion of the knees. The knees pump up (flex) as you ski up the bump and pump down (extend) as you ski down the bump, in much the same way that a car's shock absorbers work.

◎ Absorption turns can be performed either with your weight equally spread over both skis, or with the weight shifting from ski to ski.

B) Absorption while traversing

Prior to learning the absorption turn, it is a good idea to practice traversing across a series of bumps, passing over the tops of each bump in your path and absorbing it as you ride up, over and down it, keeping your skis in total contact with the snow. Even if you decide not to learn absorption turns, knowing how to absorb bumps with your knees at high (or out-of-control) speeds can be very useful and should be learned by every skier.

The following exercises should be performed on an easy intermediate slope

Shallow traverse

7) Shallow traverse over small bumps

1) Shallow traverse PHOTOS 70A-D

The best learning sequence is to start with bumps that are quite small and then advance to larger bumps. Choose a shallow traverse track that will take you over a series of small bumps. Keep your weight mostly over your downhill ski. Press down constantly, but keep your knees and hips relaxed.

Start to traverse and, as you reach the first bump, assume an absorption —position and allow the bump to compress your knees so that they are fully compressed or flexed at the top of the bump (pictures 70A and 70C). As you start to descend the bump, press your feet downward and extend your legs to keep your skis in contact with the snow (pictures 70B and 70D). Throughout the maneuver, maintain a good traverse position with most of your weight on the instep of your downhill ski boot and with the skis well edged. Repeat to the opposite side.

2) Steeper traverse over small bumps

On the same slope, choose a steeper traverse track over a series of small bumps and repeat the absorption movements. Repeat again on a very steep traverse, being certain that you have sufficient space after the short bump field to regain control. Repeat to the opposite side.

3) Shallow traverse over large bumps

Repeat exercise 1, choosing a shallow traverse track that passes over a series of larger bumps. Repeat to the other side.

4) Steeper traverse over large bumps

Repeat exercise 2 over large bumps.

5) Traversing bumps on an advanced intermediate slope

When you feel confident absorbing the bumps while traversing on the easy, intermediate slopes, repeat the same series of exercises on a more difficult slope.

NOTE

◉◉◉ When you attempt to ski absorption on a steep traverse track over large bumps on steep trails, you will probably be hitting each bump very hard and your knees may be driven with considerable force toward your chest. I therefore recommend this exercise only for those of you who are very fit, very daring, and very confident using absorption. I also recommend that you choose a very short bump field with a large smooth runout.

8) Absorption turns

When you have mastered the sensation of absorbing the bumps with your legs, you will be ready to turn your skis using absorption. When making an absorption turn you turn over the summit of the bump and complete the turn as you descend the back of the bump. It is best to learn uphill turns before turning the skis downhill across the fall-line. It is also advisable to practice first on an easy intermediate slope and then, once the maneuver is mastered, to move on to an advanced intermediate slope.

1) Absorption turn uphill — starting on a traverse PHOTOS 71A-C

Start on a traverse on an easy intermediate slope, holding your uphill ski pole vertical, and aim for a medium-sized bump (picture 71A). As you ride up the bump, plant your ski pole on its summit and

Absorption turn uphill

absorb the bump as you did in the previous exercises. When you reach the summit of the bump and your knees are most compressed (picture 71B), turn your skis uphill. As you pass over the crest of the bump, start extending your legs while you descend the back (picture 71C). Push your uphill hand forward to recover your arm so that you are in a good traverse position and continue steering your skis up the hill to a stop. Repeat this to the opposite side.

SPECIAL TIPS

◎ Keep your upper body facing the outside of the turn throughout the turn.

◎ Initiating the turning of the skis at the summit of the bump is very easy and is similar to the foot swivel maneuver (exercise 5, page 73), since only the part of the ski beneath your feet is making contact with the snow.

◎ When making uphill turns, keep most of your weight on the instep of your downhill ski boot.

2) Absorption turn uphill — turning from the fall-line
PHOTOS 72A-C
This time, start by pointing your skis straight down the fall-line and repeat the same maneuver as above. As you start to ride up the bump, bring one ski pole forward and prepare to plant it at the summit of the bump (picture 72A). At the summit, absorb the bump and turn your skis uphill (picture 72B) as you did in the previous exercise, turning around the ski pole.

Complete the turn by extending your legs as you

Absorption turns uphill — turning from the fall-line

Absorption turn downhill

3) Absorption turn downhill PHOTOS 73A-D

On the same slope that you have used for the previous exercises, ski toward a large bump in a steep traverse (picture 73A). As you start to ride up the bump, bring your downhill ski pole forward, ready to plant on the top of the bump (picture 73B). As you arrive at the summit of the bump, plant your ski pole at the summit and transfer your weight to the outside ski. While your legs are absorbing the bump, simply turn your feet downhill across the fall-line and push your wrist forward (picture 73C). Continue turning your skis across the fall-line as you extend your legs on the back of the bump (picture 73D). End in a good traverse position ready for the next turn. Repeat, making a turn downhill to the opposite direction.

SPECIAL TIPS

◎ Be sure to keep your upper body bent slightly forward at the waist and constantly facing toward the fall-line during the turn over the bump.

◎ To prevent your skis from slipping and sliding, keep them on their edges as you make your turns.

4) Linked absorption turns

Once you can make absorption turns to both sides, it is very easy to link the turns. The key to linking turns is to ensure that you are in a good traverse position at the end of the turn so that you are in control to start the next turn.

Choose a field of small bumps on an easy intermediate slope to practice on, and link a series of absorption turns over them. When you can ski these small bumps with good control, choose a similar gradient slope with larger bumps and link a series of absorption turns. The next step is to practice on an advanced intermediate slope with small bumps and then, finally, ski through a field of large bumps on this slope, making controlled absorption turns.

SPECIAL TIPS

◎ To help keep your weight forward and your skis in contact with the snow, *press the balls of your feet down* as you pass over the tops of the bumps.

◎ Skiing with absorption is an excellent way to ski bumps that are lightly buried or hidden by freshly fallen snow and in whiteout conditions when you can't see the bumps.

descend the back of the bump (picture 72C), push your hand forward, and continue steering your skis up the hill to a smooth stop.

SPECIAL TIPS

◎ Since this is a very dynamic maneuver, you must be sure to be in the absorption position (picture 72B) with your upper body bent slightly forward at the waist, so that you are not thrown backward when the bump compresses your knees.

◎ Be sure to push your wrist forward as you pass your ski pole (picture 72C) so that the ski pole does not pull your arm back, resulting in an improper traverse position at the end of the turn.

◎ Practice this with your weight on the outside ski, then with your weight over both skis.

ADVANCED BUMPS

9) Wedeln turns (Wiggle turns)

If you intend to become a good bump skier making fast runs down the fall-line of a bumpy trail, you will need to learn how to wedeln your skis.

Wedelning is the technique of making very fast turns using just your feet to steer your skis. This can be referred to as "foot power." When done correctly, foot power provides you with instant and total control of your skis.

NOTES

◉◉◉ When wedelning, you steer with your feet rather than using the ski edges to turn the skis. This can be done using both traditional and shaped skis.

◉◉◉ The word wedeln comes from Austria and means the wagging of a dog's tail. So be true to the name — try to wedeln (or wiggle) with quick, fluid motions.

A) Learning foot power (wedelning) PHOTOS 74A-C

A good exercise to learn to wedeln is to ski down a very gentle, smooth slope (with no bumps) trying to rapidly turn both skis at the same time.

NOTE

◉◉◉ It's best to keep your weight evenly over both feet and turn both skis as though they were a single wide ski, rather than shifting your weight from ski to ski.

Start with your skis separated about 3-6 inches (8-15 cm). Hold your arms in the tray-holding position and lower your hips a little more than usual, so that you are sitting slightly with your knees relaxed and with your weight evenly spread over both feet, as shown in picture 74A. Keep your upper body pointing down the fall-line.

Start to glide and, *using only your feet*, turn your skis rapidly from side to side as you descend the fall-line (picture sequence 74A-C). It's fun to count your turns and try to make as many as possible. If you are on a short slope, ride back up the lift and repeat this maneuver a number of times. Try to feel the power in your feet! When you feel that you are controlling and steering the turns with your feet, begin to smooth out

Learning foot power

the turns by slowing down the tempo of the turning movements and, with each descent, start to bring your skis closer together. Eventually you should be able to place your skis together and, using only as much foot power as is necessary, smoothly and elegantly wedeln down the fall-line.

Planting ski poles

Planting ski poles with feet close together (detail)

B) Planting ski poles   **PHOTOS 75A-E**
When skiing on bumps you will need to plant your ski poles, so repeat the above exercises planting your ski poles before each turn.

◎ Be sure to not swing your hips or upper body to start the skis turning.
◎ Face your upper body down the fall-line the entire time.

When you feel confident wedelning on the gentle slopes, you can try it on smooth, intermediate slopes, skiing a very narrow path straight down the trail. When you feel confident on these slopes you should be ready to wedeln through the bumps.

NOTE
◎◎◎ On smooth slopes, wedelning is usually performed with the skis kept quite flat on the snow, with very little edging. Though some very good bump skiers can ski bumps with flat skis, to have control on bumps you should be skiing on the edges of your skis. Thus it is worthwhile practicing rolling your skis from edge to edge as you wedeln down the smooth slopes.

C) Wedelning bumps   **PHOTOS 76A-C**
Start off by skiing quick wedeln turns down a run of small bumps on an easy slope. Than gradually progress to larger bumps on steeper slopes.

CHOOSING SKI LINES
10) Choosing ski lines   PHOTO 77
When you are skiing bump trails it is a good idea to look down the slope and pick a route that you plan to ski. A hot bump skier will usually pick a route that runs straight down the fall-line and try to turn around each bump along the way. The end of one turn becomes the start of the next turn and the skis do not swing very far away from the fall-line. This is known as "skiing a fast line" (A in picture 77).

Another way to ski the bumps is to swing large turns around each one so that you approach each bump from a shallow rather than a steep angle. By making wide turns, you will also finish each turn on a shallow angle. Skiing these wide turns will allow you to ski more slowly. This is known as "skiing a slow line" (B in picture 77).

Obviously it is best to start off skiing bumps on a slow line and progressively build up your confidence to ski faster and faster lines.

Wedelning bumps

One can also ski a bump trail in very good control by turning around two or three bumps, rather than turning around every bump straight down the slope (C in picture 77).

Choosing ski lines

SPECIAL TIP

◎ When you are skiing on a fast ski line, try to visualize an imaginary line running straight down the slope and constantly lean your upper body toward this line. This will keep your body well balanced as you are turning your skis from side to side.

NOTE

◎◎◎ When you are skiing for fun and are not in a bump competition, feel completely free to change your ski line during the descent so as to get the most enjoyable run through the bumps.

11) Independent leg action

If you want to minimize the number of times that you fall when skiing on both smooth slopes and bumps, it is very useful to develop the independent action of your legs. With independent leg action, each leg will be able to operate on its own and not be locked in to the movements of the other leg.

Following are some exercises that I've found very useful for developing independent leg action.

Skiing on one ski with one ski lifted

A) Skiing on one ski with one ski lifted **PHOTOS 78A-C**
On a very easy, smooth slope, ski a series of turns with one ski lifted off the snow. Try to roll from edge to edge while turning (pictures 78A-C).

B) Skiing on one ski **PHOTOS 79A-C**
You can do the same exercise as above with just one ski attached. Do this on both feet.

C) One ski schussing and the other ski wedelning **PHOTOS 80A-C**
On a gentle, smooth slope, spread your skis apart and ski down the fall-line. Try to wedeln just one ski (fast turning using foot power as described on page 79)

while you keep the other ski running straight down the slope (pictures 80A–80C). Then switch and wedeln on the other ski.

NOTE
⊚⊚⊚ The exercises demonstrated on pages 102–105 for Skiing with the weight on the uphill ski will also help you refine and further develop the independent action of your legs.

BUMP CONDITIONS
12) Icy bumps **PHOTO 81**
Icy bumps seem to cause the greatest fear in skiers.

Skiing on one ski

One ski schussing and the other ski wedelning

This is made even worse when the bumps are big as well as icy. While icy bumps may not be as much fun as soft bumps, with sharp ski edges, care, and a positive attitude you can ski them in good control using the same basic techniques that you use for skiing soft ones. (Refer to pages 95-96 which explain how to ski smooth, icy ski runs.)

A) Partially icy bumps

Often you'll find that a bump is not completely icy. The icy part may be on the front flank, the top or the back of the bump. Usually you'll find the top and back to be icy since most people turn on the top and slide down the back, skidding off the snow. The trick is to observe where the softer snow is and ski in that rather than on the ice. If the snow on the back of a bump has been skied off, it will be lying in the hollow between the bumps or partially up the front flank of the next bump. So make large turns around the icy bumps by starting the turns in the soft snow in the trough and swinging a large arc as you turn so that you complete the turn in the soft snow in the next trough. Then continue skiing from trough to trough.

B) Solidly icy bumps

Sometimes the bumps will be solidly icy. In this case, assume the ice position (picture 81), with your feet wider apart, your body lower, essentially all your weight on your downhill ski, and your hands held lower. Allow your skis to sideslip toward the bump and as soon as your skis touch it, plant your ski pole

Ice position

on the bump and initiate a turn around it. Use gentle movements and try to control the slideslip as you aim for the next bump. It is very important that you keep your upper body facing down the fall-line.

On large, solidly icy bumps on steep slopes, you may find it safer to foot swivel on the tops of the bumps and sideslip down their backs as you complete your turns. As long as fear doesn't cause you to lean your body back up the hill, you should be able to get down these slopes safe and sound.

NOTE

◉◉◎ If you can confidently ski on ice on smooth slopes and have sharp ski edges, you can ski icy bumps the same way, using your sharp edges to carve turns around them.

13) Chopped-off bumps PHOTO 82

"Chopped Off" bumps

Very often skiers trying to get down a steep slope of bumps that they find beyond their ability traverse from side to side, thereby chopping off the backs of the bumps and creating a series of cliffs (picture 82). Skiing these bumps is not fun, as it is difficult to establish a rhythm; turning over the tops is out of the question because of the sheer drops on the backs.

The best way to ski these bumps is to take it slowly and carefully and make large turns around them, sidesliding wherever necessary so that you don't risk tumbling off the backs. Often on these slopes there are easier, smaller bumps on the edges of the trail on which you can either sideslide slowly, if you want to be very cautious and safe, or ski in the normal manner if you feel that you can ski with enough control to avoid going off the edge of the trail.

If you are a good bump skier and can handle steep runs confidently, you can link turns through these big, chopped-off bumps by choosing your route carefully and turning around the cliffs, in the troughs between the bumps.

14) Slush bumps

In the springtime, the lower trails on the mountain often become quite mushy and the bumps very soft and wet. One way to handle these bumps is to ski them as though you are skiing powder. That means you should be in the powder position (pages 119–120), with your weight slightly back over your heels and more evenly distributed over both feet (if your weight is all on your downhill ski, that ski can easily sink in the soft snow and you could topple over).

Since the bumps are very slushy, if you try to turn over the tops your skis will likely sink into the snow, so it is better to ski around them, turning in the troughs where the snow is more compressed.

If you are a good enough skier and can ski with your weight on the uphill ski as well as on the downhill ski (as explained on pages 136–138), you can use this technique to ski slushy bumps. Keep the skis well edged, with your weight over the uphill edge of the uphill ski, and turn from uphill edge to uphill edge, using the downhill ski as an outrigger to test the snow and help maintain your balance. By pressing down on the uphill edge of the uphill ski, you should be able

Fault: hands at the side

to steer and control your turns.

If you are able to ski quick, tight turns down the fall-line on bump runs, and like a bit of wild fun, another way to ski these slush bumps is to ski them

Fault: Back too straight/stiff legs and knees

very aggressively and use foot power to power your way through the slush.

NOTE

⊚⊚ When skiing fast and aggressively you have to have very quick feet and be very alert, as the soft snow often grabs the skis, throwing you out of balance. It helps to be able to make jet turns (pages 98–100) which can help you recover your correct position so that you remain in control.

Common faults and corrections

Skiers make many of the same faults when skiing bumps that they make on smooth slopes. The problem is compounded by the fact that bumps are harsh taskmasters — the faults that you can get away with on smooth slopes can throw you on the bumps, so if you make an error, you'll probably fall over!

Following are some of the more common faults that I've observed skiers committing on bumps, and their corrections.

1A) Fault: hands at the side   PHOTO 83A-C

Skiers who ski with their hands at their sides have to swing their arms forward to plant their ski poles. This action hinders making quick linked turns because of the time it takes to lift the arms. Often the hand comes up too late for the turn and by the time the pole is planted, the skier finds himself turning on the wrong part of the bump. Swinging the arms also upsets the skier's balance.

1B) Correction

Hold your arms well out in front of you at all times, as though you are carrying a tray, and plant the poles with a firm wrist action. Holding your arms out in front will help you maintain your balance on the bumps and help keep your weight forward.

2A) Fault: back too straight   PHOTOS 84A-C

Skiing with an upright stance is okay on the smooth slopes. However, when you are skiing quickly and absorbing the bumps with your lower body, you will find yourself thrown backward unless you bend slightly forward from your waist.

2B) Correction

Stand on your skis in an absorption (avalement) position when you set off to ski bumps at speed. Lower your hips and keep your upper body bent slightly forward.

3A) Fault: stiff legs and knees   PHOTOS 84A-C

If you're skiing with stiff legs and knees, keep away from bumps as you will be sure to get knocked about by them and lose control. If you hit a bump at speed with stiff knees and legs, you'll most probably get thrown airborne.

3B) Correction

If you find that you have stiff legs and knees, consciously try to relax them. Often the problem is caused by being frightened. You can automatically keep your knees bent by leaning on the fronts of your boots and crouching a bit by lowering your hips. Try

85A

85B

85C

Fault: looking down at the skis

to imagine your legs as springs and concentrate on feeling the springs compressing and expanding as you ski over the bumps.

4A) Fault: skis too flat

If you turn over or around bumps with your skis too flat, you won't be able to carve the completion of your turns and it's likely that you will slide harshly into the next bump.

4B) Correction

Try to roll from one set of edges to the other as you are turning and keep your skis on their edges at the ends of the turns.

NOTE

◉◉◉ Some advanced bump skiers like to keep their skis fairly flat so that they can ski as fast as possible down the bumps. I think it's best to leave flat-ski skiing to the bump competitors.

5A) Fault: looking down at the skis   PHOTOS 85A-C

I'm always amazed to see skiers looking down at their skis. I suppose they want to be sure that their skis are turning. The most obvious problem is that they don't see where they are going and can run into someone or some obstacle. Another problem is that they will find it difficult to choose and follow a ski line through the bumps.

5B) Correction

Keep your head up and look ahead three or four turns. Before setting off down a bump trail, look down the trail and roughly plan your route. Try to visualize yourself making the first three or four turns. Also look for escape places where you can safely turn off if you make a mistake and lose control. Be aware where the edges of the trail are and know what is on the other side, especially if there are cliffs and trees.

SPECIAL TIPS AND SAFETY CONSIDERATIONS

◉ When there are other skiers in your intended way it is always better to break your rhythm and change your route rather than risk a collision.

◉ Because other skiers may inadvertently cut across your route, be prepared to stop.

◉ The skier above always has the responsibility to avoid hitting skiers below, so whenever possible, pass behind slow or stopped skiers.

◉ Whichever way you decide to ski bumps, finish your turns so that your skis cross the fall-line and are well edged. The more you steer your skis across the fall-line, the slower you will ski. When you gain confidence you can ski faster by turning your skis closer to the fall-line.

◉ When you are skiing quick turns on large bumps in an absorption position, you will probably find that your normal length ski poles are too long, since your hands will often end up too high when you plant them on the bump — at times even higher than your head. You will be more comfortable and will be able to ski in better control, as well as look a lot neater, if you ski with shorter ski poles.

NOTE

◉◉◉ Skiing bumps at speed can be quite exhausting and demanding on your muscles. Tired or poorly conditioned muscles can lead to falls and potential injuries. Thus it's important that you are fit and have good muscle flexibility and tone if you plan on doing a lot of bump skiing.

ADVANCED SKIING

section four

I mentioned in the introduction to Section I that most of the exercises presented are actual ski maneuvers used in advanced skiing. If you've practiced those exercises, as well as the exercises presented in Sections II and III, you should be fully prepared now to become an advanced skier and ski the steeper trails in good control.

The many ski maneuvers presented in this section will enable you to start your turns on the steeper runs more easily and complete them with more control. You will learn how to make use of natural phenomena such as gravity and centrifugal force to help initiate the turns. You will also learn how to ski on ice and hard snow; perform simple acrobatics to improve your coordination and stability; perform jet turns, both to have fun and as a recovery maneuver; and learn to ski the very steep slopes, including gullies and mountain faces.

ANTICIPATION

PHOTOS 86A-D & PHOTOS 87A-C

Anticipation is a maneuver that helps make the initiation of turns easier. This movement is especially useful when skiing on steep slopes. I think that anyone wanting to be an advanced skier should incorporate anticipation into his or her skiing repertoire.

Because it makes the start of turns easier, I try to use anticipation as much as possible when I ski. I use *extreme anticipation* when I am skiing the steepest slopes and gullies.

To ski with anticipation, you must anticipate the turn with your upper body. You do this by turning your chest in the direction of the turn just before you make the turn.

When making medium- or large-radius turns without anticipation, you would normally plant your ski pole at your side, slightly forward of the front of your ski boots. To ski with anticipation you plant your ski pole farther back than that. Exactly where you plant it depends on the slope's steepness and your degree of anticipation. In pictures 86A-D, I demonstrate variations in anticipation.

Picture 86A shows a pole plant with no anticipation. Picture 86B shows the anticipation that would be used on an advanced intermediate slope: the ski pole is planted down the fall-line on a line from the back of the ski boot. Picture 86C shows the anticipation that would be used on an expert slope: the ski pole is planted down the fall-line, approximately 6-12 inches (15-30 cm) behind the ski boot. Picture 86D shows the anticipation used when skiing in a steep, narrow gully to help initiate the turn with very little speed: the ski pole is planted down the fall-line below the tail of the ski.

To learn to ski with anticipation, choose a traverse track on any slope and prepare to make a large-

Anticipation

Anticipation — turn to the left

radius turn. (Sequence 87A-C shows a turn to the left on an advanced intermediate run.) When you are ready to initiate the turn, *turn your body in the direction of the turn* (as shown in picture 87B) and plant your ski pole. Because you turned your upper body in the direction of the turn, you will automatically be planting your ski pole farther back than you have done when skiing without using anticipation. Now make the turn (picture 87C), and you will find that your skis turn more easily than they did doing the same turn without anticipation. Finish the turn in a good traverse position.

Practice making turns to both sides using anticipation, and then link a series of medium- and large-radius turns, anticipating the start of each turn.

NOTE

◎◎◎ When you are skiing short-radius turns in which you are continually facing down the fall-line with a relaxed upper body and with your hands held in front of you in the tray-holding position, you are automatically using anticipation to help start your turns.

BANKING THE TURNS

I am basically a lazy skier and I like to take as much advantage as possible of natural forces to help me turn my skis. Since gravity is always acting to pull a skier down the hill, I sometimes try to use this power

Using gravity to help initiate a turn

to help initiate the turn. I also like to take advantage of momentum and the centrifugal forces that act on the body as the skis sweep through turns at high speed to allow me to ride up the banked sides of trails and up the sides of bumps. In addition to being good fun, riding up the banks and sides of bumps is an excellent way to slow down while turning, without causing you to alter your skiing rhythm.

1) Using gravity to help initiate a turn PHOTOS 88A-B & PHOTOS 89A-D

On a steep slope, if you offset your upper body by leaning it down the fall-line as you plant your ski pole at the start of the turn, then the force of gravity will try to pull you over. (Your pole plant and your

Banking during a turn

Banking around bumps

ski edges digging into the snow prevent you from falling or sideslipping (picture 89B). If you now make the turn, you will find that your skis will turn very easily. You will, in effect, be using the pull of gravity rather than your leg power to start the skis turning.

In pictures 88A and 88B I demonstrate on a steep slope where you should plant the ski pole to use gravity to help start the turn. In picture 88A I plant my ski pole at my side, requiring me to make the turn in the normal manner. In picture 88B, I reach further down the fall-line, offsetting my upper body, so I can use gravity to help start my skis turning, resulting in a much easier turn.

NOTES

⊚⊙⊙ You can use gravity to help start the skis turning on any steep pitch or abrupt change in terrain. Thus, this is a very useful maneuver when carefully skiing big bumps.

⊚⊙⊙ By combining extreme anticipation and banking, you can make a very slow, controlled turn on a steep pitch even from a standstill with essentially no effort. (This is further elaborated in the section on steep gully skiing on pages 109 and 110.)

2) Banking on bumps and ravines
A) Banking around bumps   **PHOTOS 90A-C**

As you ski through a bump field at speed, it is best to turn around the bumps. However, as you rhythmically turn in the troughs between the bumps you will be maintaining a constant speed. Should you decide that you would like to ski more slowly and still maintain the same rhythm, you can do so by steering your skis farther around the bumps, riding up the sides of the neighboring bumps as you complete the turns. The farther up the sides of the bumps you steer your skis, the more you will slow down.

Picture sequence 90A-C shows how to bank turns through a bump field. In picture 90A, I'm initiating a banked turn to the right by leaning my upper body down the fall-line as I plant my ski pole. As I perform the turn, I steer my skis in a very large radius, aiming to ride up the front slope of the neighboring bump (picture 90B). As I slow down, I continue to steer the skis through the turn and complete it in the normal manner (picture 90C) in a good traverse position, with my weight over my new downhill ski.

You should practice banking turns to both sides and then link three or four turns together. Once you have mastered banking turns around bumps, you can ski these turns through the bump fields. Thus you can employ banking to start the turns and you can bank (or incline) your body as you are turning.

NOTE

⊚⊚⊙ Some ski instructors consider banking a turn to be a fault, as this movement, when performed by beginners, can cause them to skid their turns and end the turns with their weight on the wrong (inside) ski. Skiers with more advanced skills should be able to avoid this problem. As you are completing the turn, begin to transfer your weight onto the outside ski and finish the turn in good control, with your weight on your outside ski.

B) Airplane turns on ravine walls   PHOTOS 91A-C

When you are on a ski trail that travels down a ravine with "walls" (steep banks) on both sides, it is exhilarating to ski up and down these walls making *airplane turns*. To perform banked airplane turns, you must build up a fair amount of speed and then ski up one of the sides of the ravine. When you are ready to turn, bank your turn by leaning (inclining) your body toward the valley of the ravine, roll your feet and ankles in the direction of the turn, and then, holding your arms out like the wings of an airplane, steer your skis across the fall-line, turning them on the side of the wall, (pictures 91A and 91C). Even though your body leans towards the horizontal, centrifugal force will prevent you from falling.

As your skis turn across the fall-line, continue to lean your shins against the fronts of the ski boots and accelerate down the side of the ravine, shoot across the middle of the slope, and ski up the other side of the ravine (picture 91B.) Then make another turn, repeating the same banking movements.

Airplane turns on ravine walls

NOTES

⊚⊚⊙ Obviously this maneuver should not be performed on crowded ski trails. Be very alert to the presence of other skiers when shooting across the middle of the run.

Demonstration of a "counter-turn"

◉◎◎ Some people may experience a loss of equilibrium and become dizzy from banking turns on very steep walls.

THE COUNTER-TURN (J- OR S-TURN)

On a steep slope or on a slope with bumps, a very useful maneuver for controlling your speed without losing your smooth rhythm is the *counter-turn* (also known as the *J-turn* or *S-turn*). In this movement you use your feet and ankles to steer your skis up the hill just prior to executing a downhill turn. By turning your skis up the hill, you slow them down. Since the skis are continually turning on their edges, this is a smooth way of controlling your speed without resorting to hard edge-setting or sideslipping. Also, by twisting and untwisting your skis, you use the torsional resistance of the skis to aid the turn.

On a bump field you can control your speed by doing counter-turns around the bumps, losing your speed on the plateau before the bump and turning in the trough around the bump. This is called a counter-turn, because the skis turn uphill away from the turn just before executing the downhill turn, but it is really nothing more than an uphill turn combined with anticipation. Counter-turns can be made with the weight over the outside ski or over both feet.

1) Demonstration of a counter-turn
PHOTOS 92A-E

Before practicing the exercises that teach the counter-turn, it would probably be useful to study picture sequence 92A-E, which shows me performing a counter-turn prior to making a downhill turn to the right.

In picture 92A, I am completing a turn to the left, flexing my hips, and turning my skis uphill. In order to slow my skis down and still maintain my rhythm, I continue to lower my hips to press the ski edges into the snow and continue to roll my feet uphill, bringing my ski pole forward so that I am ready to plant it at the lowest point of my hip flexion (picture 92B). These lower-body actions cause the fronts of my skis to turn farther up the hill (the counter-turn) which slows them down. Note that the snow spray is caused by the ski edges biting into the snow, and there is no sideslipping.

From this position, I extend and turn around my downhill ski pole (picture 92C), and as my skis cross the fall-line I steer them up the hill to the right (pictures 92D and 92E), preparing for another counter-turn.

SPECIAL TIPS

◎ When you are driving your skis up the hill, as in picture 92B, it is very important to keep your upper body turned toward downhill so that your outside hip (right hip in picture) does not swing too far around in the direction of the turn. This will prevent the backs of the skis from sliding away. (In this maneuver the backs of the skis should follow the fronts of the skis up the hill — not sideslip down the hill.)

◎ As you lower your hips at the end of the turn, be sure to keep your weight over the instep of your downhill ski boot (or over the middles of both boots if you have your weight on both feet).

◎ Try to time the pole plant so that you are planting your ski pole as you reach the lowest point of your flexion movement.

◎ Be sure to roll your feet and ankles up the hill as you end the turn, so that the skis are well-edged and can carve into the snow rather than slip around as they turn.

Since the downhill turn part of this maneuver is essentially the same as the downhill turns you have been making during the previous ski maneuvers, it is advisable to start off practicing the "counter" part of the counter-turn and then, when this feels comfortable, practice combining the two parts.

2) Learning the counter movement of the counter-turn   PHOTOS 93A-C

Choose a moderate pitch on an easy intermediate slope and perform the maneuver as shown in picture sequence 93A-C.

Start by traversing (picture 93A), then begin to lower your hips and steer the fronts of your skis up the hill by rolling your feet and ankles up the hill (picture 93B). Continue flexing your hips and steering your skis up the hill. (The more the skis are edged and the more pressure you apply, the more the skis will turn.) Bring your downhill ski pole forward and plant it as you reach the lowest point of your flexion (picture 93C) and stop, making sure that your skis do not sideslide down the hill.

Note how, in picture sequence 93A-C, the upper body *remains still and facing toward the fall-line*. This prevents the outside hip from *over swinging*, and therefore keeps the backs of the skis carving in the snow. Practice this movement to both sides.

3) The counter-turn on smooth slopes

When you feel confident performing the counter movements to both sides with a well-coordinated pole plant, you should practice skiing downhill turns, using the counter movement, to slow down before each turn as in picture sequence 92.

Practice at first on easy intermediate slopes and when you feel comfortable making smooth, controlled counter-turns, perform this maneuver on advanced intermediate slopes.

Learning the counter movement of the counter-turn

94A

94B

94D

94C

94E

Counter-turn around a bump

4) Counter-turn around a bump
PHOTOS 94A-E

When you feel confident making counter-turns on smooth slopes, practice them on a bump field on an easy intermediate slope.

Choose a small bump and ski toward it, as shown in picture 94A. As you approach the bump, start to drive your skis up the hill on the plateau just before the bump in a counter movement (picture 94B). As you reach the lowest part of your flexion, turn your upper body in the direction of the turn (anticipation position) and plant your ski pole on the top of the bump (picture 94C), then extend and turn around your ski pole (picture 94D). Try to turn in the trough around the bump, finishing your turn in a good traverse position (picture 94E), and aim for the next bump.

5) Practice on steeper slopes with bumps

After making a series of slow-speed counter-turns around bumps on the easy intermediate slopes, you should practice these same turns on an advanced intermediate slope, turning around larger bumps.

ICE AND HARD-SNOW CONDITIONS

PHOTOS 95A-B

I grew up skiing at ski areas in the northeastern United States, so I had to learn to ski on ice with good control — the runs are often hard or icy and quite narrow, bordered by pretty, but very solid, trees. In fact, northeastern skiers can handle icy ski runs with the same ease and confidence that skiers in the western United States and Europe have on soft snow slopes. Therefore it is evident that skiing on ice is not so much a question of difficulty as it is a question of training and familiarity.

Almost all skiers will encounter icy snow conditions at some point. The snow which falls at low altitudes is normally very moist, and this snow easily turns to ice when the temperature drops below freezing. The same is true of machine made snow. In the springtime, high-altitude slopes that catch the hot afternoon sun thaw and then freeze during the cold nights. These western- or southwestern-facing slopes (northwestern in the southern hemisphere) are usually still frozen the next morning. Should there be rain followed by the temperature dropping below freezing, the entire mountain may be covered by sheets of ice. Often, during the violent windstorms that occasionally blast very high-altitude ski slopes, all the loose surface snow is blown off the exposed slopes, leaving extremely hard or icy surfaces. This can also occur during very windy snowstorms.

In order to ski on icy slopes you must have sharp ski edges, or you will find your skis slipping out from under you when you try to dig in your edges. You also must modify your body position in order to grip the ice.

Picture 95A demonstrates a normal traverse position. Picture 95B demonstrates a modified traverse position that should be used for skiing icy slopes. Note how much more the lower body is angled in picture 95B than in picture 95A, and how much more the upper body is leaning down the hill. To assume this position, lower your hips and lean your upper body down the fall-line (bending from the waist) in order to keep your weight over the edge

Normal and modified traverse positions for skiing icy slopes

of your downhill ski. In order that you don't fall over you need to roll your feet and ankles uphill. I have found that it also helps to lean your upper body slightly forward.

SPECIAL TIPS

◎ A common fault of skiers trying to ski on ice is to over-edge their skis, rolling their feet and ankles too far uphill. This creates too sharp an edge angle and could result in the skis losing their grip and slipping out from under the skier.

◎ The best body position for controlling your skis on ice depends on the type of skis that you have (different skis have different sidecuts, widths, and cambers), the length of your skis, and your height and body-weight distribution. It is therefore worthwhile to practice traversing and turning on an easy icy slope, angling your lower body and leaning your upper body in various ways so that you are pressing down on different places along the ski edges until you find the body position which gives you the best grip on the ice.

◎ For better stability on the ice it helps to separate the skis more, though you have to be careful to not spread them too far apart, making it difficult to keep your weight over your downhill ski without resorting to using too much angling and upper body lean.

Turning on a hard surface

NOTE **PHOTOS 96A-C**

◎◎◎ I've found that the best type of turn to use for skiing on ice or frozen granular snow is the short-radius turn. Medium- and large-radius turns require holding the edge grip for longer periods, which is more difficult to do on ice.

The modifications required to ski in control on the ice are:

1) Have your weight distributed entirely, or almost entirely, over your downhill foot (in order to control the downhill ski).

2) Eliminate any exaggerated or brusque body movements while skiing so that you do not lose the tenuous contact between the ski edges and the icy snow.

3) Push from ski edge to ski edge using smooth, rapid movements so that the edges bite into the snow very briefly. (If you try to hold the edge too long, the ski may slip away.)

It takes some practice to become proficient at skiing on icy snow, but it is definitely worthwhile putting in the time to learn so that when you do encounter an icy ski slope you will be able to ski it confidently.

Picture sequence 96A-C demonstrates turns at speed on a hard surface, the angling of the lower body being very evident. Notice how still the upper body remains throughout the turn, and how it is constantly leaning forward and down the hill to keep the weight over the edge of the downhill (carving) ski.

Practice short-radius turns on icy slopes
Practice making short-radius turns on an icy, gentle slope. Be sure to modify your body movements as recommended above. When you feel confident on this easy slope, move on to an icy intermediate slope.

SPECIAL TIPS

◎ Although you should not exaggerate your body movements, you must ski aggressively by constantly leaning forward and over the downhill ski. People who ski ice timidly tend to lean backwards and as soon as they do they lose control of their downhill ski and their skis go shooting off, resulting in a hard fall on the ice.

◎ If the icy area is just a small patch or short section of the ski run and you can see that the snow just beyond is softer, ski across the icy section keeping the skis a comfortable distance apart and almost flat on the surface, maintaining your balance over both skis, and then make a turn in the softer snow after the icy patch.

◎ Once you are capable of skiing fast and competently on ice, when you come upon a long, icy section of a slope with good snow just beyond the icy section, an easy way to negotiate the ice is to make your turns keeping the skis almost flat — in other words, using very little edging — and separated so that you have good stability. With your skis almost flat you will not be able to slow yourself down much, but you can still maintain enough control through your turns to steer yourself to the softer snow beyond the icy section. There you can use your edges to slow down.

◎ When coming to a stop on ice, don't try to stop sharply by digging your ski edges into the snow. Instead, allow yourself enough room, initiate the stop and then sideslide to a gradual stop, applying gentle pressure to the ski edges.

THE STEM TURN
(for intermediate and advanced skiers, skiing crusty snow conditions)

This is a maneuver which I find especially valuable when skiing off the packed slopes on crusty snow that has a tendency to break beneath the skis. It enables you to turn your skis with a minimum of extension movements, and uses instead gentle weight transfer which helps prevent the skis from breaking through the crusty snow surface. I also like this maneuver when skiing *off-piste* (off the packed trails) where there are windblown ridges. (A very different way of skiing these crusty conditions is the jump turn, which is explained on pages 101–102.) This turn can also come in handy for skiing on a run where the snow conditions are not smooth.

1) The stem turn for crusty snow conditions PHOTOS 97A-D

The *stem turn* should be practiced first on packed snow and then applied to crusty snow.

Picture sequence 97A-D demonstrates a stem turn on lightly crusted snow. Picture 97A shows the near completion of a turn to the left with the weight just about evenly spread over both skis. To turn in the other direction, place more weight on your downhill ski and slide (or step) the back of your uphill ski out to the side, changing the ski edge by rolling your foot in the direction of the turn. Keep the tips of the skis fairly close together. When you push (or lift) the uphill ski to the side you should have very little weight on it. As this ski crosses the fall-line, begin to shift your weight onto it (picture 97B), testing, as you do so, the firmness of the snow beneath the skis.

If the snow seems capable of supporting you, continue to gently transfer your weight onto this ski and continue steering the ski across the fall-line until it starts to point uphill (picture 97C). When you feel in control, with your weight mostly on the instep of your new downhill ski and your ski turning up the hill, start to slide the uphill ski parallel to the downhill ski and roll your uphill foot onto the new edge. Now distribute your weight evenly over both skis and

The stem turn for crusty snow conditions

finish in a good traverse position (picture 97D).

SPECIAL TIPS

◎ When skiing on the crust, if the snow does not feel firm and starts to break when you begin to shift your weight onto the outside ski, remove the weight from that ski by placing your weight back on your downhill (inside) ski, bring the outside ski back alongside the downhill ski, and continue to traverse, looking for another place to initiate the turn.

◎ Do not be anxious to bring your inside ski parallel to the outside ski, but rather allow it to trail behind in a slight V as your skis cross the fall-line (pictures 97B and 97C). Bring the inside ski parallel to the other one after you've completed the turn (picture 97D), when you feel in good control.

The "jet turn"

NOTES

◎◎◎ The stem turn should be performed only at slow or moderate speeds.

◎◎◎ The standard stem turn was taught by many ski schools to beginners as a step in the progression to learning to ski parallel, and generally emphasizes exaggerated up-unweighting movements. My observation through the years has been that beginners who have had the standard stem turn drilled into them tend to remain stem skiers, and often find it difficult to move on to parallel skiing. While there is nothing potentially dangerous or wrong about skiers using the stem turn as their standard turn, I feel that it is not as graceful as the parallel turn, it cannot safely be performed at high speed, and the body movements required to make the stem turn do not naturally integrate with the movements used in many of the advanced skiing maneuvers. In my opinion, one should already be a reasonably good parallel skier before learning the stem turn, and then should only use the stem turn in particular situations.

THE JET TURN

PHOTOS 98A-B + 101A-E

The *jet turn* is a skiing maneuver developed by ski racers to help them get their skis through the turns faster, and was very popular during the early 1970s as recreational skiers tried to emulate the "sitting-back" styles of the top racers. While the jet turn has lost a lot of its popularity as a racing maneuver, it is extremely useful to advanced and intermediate skiers who, for all sorts of reasons, occasionally find themselves thrown backward against the backs of their boots with a consequent loss of control of their skis. The jet turn enables you to bring your weight forward again and regain control so that you can end the turn in a correct position, leaning against the fronts of the ski boots. The jet turn is also an enjoyable ski maneuver when you're playing around on the bumps.

The major difference between the jet turn and the standard turn is that instead of extending your legs by pushing up off your skis as for the standard turn, for the jet turn you shoot your skis forward and toward the direction of the turn. You do this by thrusting, or accelerating, your legs forward (as can be seen in pictures 101B and 101C).

When you shoot your skis forward, you end up leaning against the backs of the ski boots (picture 101C). Therefore, in order to maintain control as you come out of the turn it is essential that you recover your correct position by pulling with your stomach muscles and pushing hard off your ski pole so that your body returns to a position with your weight over the middle of your ski boots and your shins leaning against the fronts of the boots (picture 101D).

SPECIAL TIP

◎ When skiing on packed slopes, the jet turn is used exclusively for skiing bumps and is not normally employed on the smooth parts of the slope except as a recovery tactic. It is therefore advisable to learn the jet turn on bumps.

Prior to learning the jet turn across the fall-line, it is

best to learn how to accelerate the skis forward. This you can do by traversing across a series of bumps and accelerating your skis off the summit of each bump in the direction of the traverse.

1) Accelerating skis forward while traversing PHOTOS 99A-D

Choose a traverse track that will bring you over a series of small bumps on an easy intermediate slope, as shown in picture 99A. Start traversing, and, as you approach the first bump, start flexing (lowering) your hips and prepare to plant your ski pole at the summit of the bump (picture 99B). From your lowest flexed position at the top of the bump, shoot your skis forward in the same traverse direction.

This will result in your legs extending and being thrust against the backs of your ski boots and you will be supporting yourself momentarily with your ski pole (picture 99C). As soon as you have shot your skis forward, push off your ski pole and pull yourself forward using your stomach muscles, bringing your body forward again so that you end up in the correct traverse position over the middle of your ski boots and leaning against the fronts of the ski boots (picture 99D). Repeat this maneuver as you ski over each bump. Do the same in the opposite direction.

When you have mastered shooting your skis forward and recovering your position you are ready to make jet turns.

2) Jet turn uphill PHOTOS 100A-D

It is usually a good idea to learn to perform new maneuvers by turning uphill before making turns downhill across the fall-line.

On an easy intermediate slope, start off skiing on a steep traverse toward a small bump, as shown in picture 100A. Bring your uphill ski pole vertical and, as you did in the previous exercise, plant it on the summit of the bump as you flex (lower) your hips (picture 100B). Since you want to turn your skis uphill, as you shoot your skis forward steer them uphill by turning your feet and legs uphill (picture 100C). Now push off your ski pole to bring your body forward and continue to keep the skis turning uphill (picture 100D). Finish the uphill turn in a good traverse position with your weight balanced over your instep and your shins leaning against the fronts of your ski boots.

Jet turn uphill

Accelerating skis forward while traversing

Jet turn across the fall-line

SPECIAL TIP

◎ It is easiest to ski jet turns with your weight evenly distributed over both skis at all times.

3) Jet turn across the fall-line
PHOTOS 101A-E

In picture sequence 101A-E I am performing an exaggerated jet turn across the fall-line in order to visually emphasize the extension of the lower body. (When performing the jet turn it is not necessary to exaggerate as much as this.) As recommended for all of the learning sequences dealing with bumps, start with small bumps on easy intermediate slopes and gradually progress to large bumps on advanced intermediate slopes.

Choose an easy intermediate slope and, starting in a good shallow traverse position, ski toward a small bump, as in picture 101A. As you approach the bump, bring your downhill ski pole forward so that it is ready to be planted, and start lowering your hips (picture 101B). As you arrive at the summit of the bump, plant your ski pole and shoot your skis forward (picture 101C). Since you want to turn your skis down the hill, as you shoot your skis forward, roll your feet and ankles in the direction of the turn so that your skis turn across the fall-line. Now push off your ski pole and bring your body forward over your skis so that you are in a good traverse position with your shins against the fronts of your ski boots as you complete the turn (pictures 101D and 101E).

Repeat this maneuver to the opposite side, and then progress to bigger bumps and steeper slopes.

When you can perform jet turns confidently on both sides and can link the turns together, enjoy yourself by skiing down some bump fields, jet-turning off the tops of the bumps.

NOTES

◉◉◎ If you plan on eventually being a powder snow skier, it is a good idea to perfect your jet turn because it is an excellent turn for deep powder snow. In fact, when I'm powder skiing in evergreen glades, I frequently employ jet turns to turn my skis around the trees. Naturally, in deep powder you cannot lean on your ski pole as you can on a packed slope, so you must modify the extension of the lower body as you accelerate the skis into the turn and use more stomach muscle power to help bring your body forward at the end of the turn. Skiing powder snow with the jet turn is covered in Section Five.

◉◉◎ The jet turn is also a very good way to initiate turns in heavy, wet, or crusty snow.

THE JUMP TURN

PHOTOS 102A-D

Perhaps the most natural way to turn your skis is to jump them out of the snow, turn them in the air and land in the new direction. This is the way I was taught to ski and I have been forever grateful to my early instructors. Not only did I learn from the start to turn my skis parallel, but I have also used this turn ever since for getting through difficult snow conditions.

The problem with jump turns is that they are very tiring, since you are jumping against the pull of gravity, and hard on the knees, which absorb and cushion the landings. Also, modern skis are designed to turn so easily that in most snow conditions it is unnecessary to jump your skis around from one traverse to

The jump turn

the next. There are, however, snow conditions in which it is very difficult to turn using any of the previously explained techniques. In such conditions the jump turn can always be employed, so every advanced skier who plans to ski the steep and off-piste snow should be thoroughly familiar and comfortable with the jump turn. The beauty of this turn is that by jumping your skis across the fall-line you don't build up much speed and thus you can ski as slowly as you want to and remain in total control on the steepest of slopes. This turn is one that every aspiring advanced skier should learn and master.

To learn to jump turn, practice on an advanced intermediate packed slope and then practice on a steeper packed slope. To perform the jump turn, execute the extension turn using an explosive up-motion

Traversing on the uphill edge

so that the skis lift off the snow.

On an advanced intermediate slope, begin traversing and start to lower your hips, simultaneously planting your downhill ski pole at your side (as shown in pictures 102A and 102B). Now jump up and around your ski pole, lifting your skis off the snow and turning them while they are in the air (picture 102C). Land in the new traverse position with your skis rolled uphill so that you are landing on their uphill edges, with your hips and knees cushioning the impact of the landing (picture 102D). Now repeat this jump turn to the opposite direction.

When practicing on the steep slopes, keep your upper body facing down the fall-line and plant your ski pole farther back than you did on the advanced intermediate slope, using anticipation to help you jump in a tighter radius.

SIMPLE ACROBATICS

Ballet and acrobatic skiing are disciplines that have lost some of their popularity, but they are still very beautiful to watch and fun to do once you have learned the movements. Many of the ballet and acrobatic maneuvers require lots of practice in order to perform them gracefully and safely. However, there are a number of simple maneuvers that are easy to perform and that I recommend for advanced skiers as, apart from being enjoyable, they help to perfect better balance, stability, and edge control. In addition, a number of the maneuvers require skiing on the uphill edge of the uphill ski,

which is extremely useful to help skiers learn independent leg action. Because a top skier should be equally able to ski on the downhill ski, uphill ski, or both, I recommend that you practice some of these acrobatics.

By practicing some of the simple jumping maneuvers, you will learn to control your skis in the air and help improve your body awareness. Furthermore, you will learn how to land correctly so that should you accidentally be tossed airborne by a bump or an unexpected drop-off, the consequences need not be disastrous.

1) Skiing on the uphill edge of the uphill ski

Since a number of the acrobatics require skiing on the uphill edge of the uphill ski, it is best to start by learning how to do this simple maneuver.

A) Traversing on the uphill edge **PHOTO 103**

Choose a gentle slope that is not crowded. Assume a proper traverse position and begin skiing on a very shallow traverse. As you pick up speed, lean your body up the hill, keep your knees bent, and lift your downhill ski out to the side (holding the ski parallel to the ground) until you have your weight balanced over the uphill edge of the uphill ski (picture 103).

Continue traversing in this manner and stop. Repeat to the opposite side.

B) Sidesliding to a stop on uphill edge **PHOTOS 104A-C**

When you can perform exercise A comfortably on both sides, choose a slightly steeper traverse track on the same slope and repeat the procedure. When you are ready to stop, flatten the uphill ski slightly, turn the ski uphill by steering with your foot, and sideslide to a stop (picture sequence 104A-C). Repeat to the opposite side.

C) Turning uphill on the uphill edge with no sideslip **PHOTOS 105A-C**

On a traverse track similar to that used in exercise B, repeat the same procedure. Instead of sideslipping to a stop, keep your ski on its edge and steer it up the hill to a stop (picture sequence 105A-C). Repeat this traverse and uphill turn on both sides until you have mastered the technique.

Sidsliding to a stop on uphill edge

Turning uphill on the uphill edge with no sideslip

2) The Charleston ski dance

This is a maneuver which Art Furrer, a Swiss ski acrobat, developed in the early 1960s. I've had lots of fun with it through the years. Apart from using it to show off on easy slopes, it is a delightful way to dance down a field of small bumps. Once you can ski on the uphill edge of your uphill ski this maneuver is easy; it is only a matter of learning the timing and rhythm.

106A

106B

106C

Charleston on a smooth slope

107

Charleston around bumps

The benefit of practicing this maneuver is that it sharpens your ability to ski turns on the "wrong inside ski," so that should you make a mistake when skiing either on a smooth slope or on a mogul slope and get thrown onto that ski, you will be able to make a turn on it and regain control.

A) Charleston on a smooth slope PHOTOS 106A-C

Start as I do in picture 106A, in a steep traverse track on a gentle slope, with your weight on your uphill ski and with your downhill ski lifted in the air to the side. Begin to slide, and almost immediately start to swing the downhill ski beneath you (picture 106B) and transfer your weight onto the inside edge of this ski as it makes contact with the snow. *Simultaneously,* swing the other ski off the snow and to the side. As you glide on the edge of the ski, continue to turn

uphill, start swinging your other ski beneath you, and again transfer your weight onto this ski edge as it makes contact with the snow (picture 106C).

SPECIAL TIPS

◎ This is a ski dance and can only be done with a constant, steady rhythm; as one ski swings down, the other ski swings up.

◎ The Charleston can be performed with or without ski poles. When using them, plant your ski pole simultaneously with your ski swing. As the swinging ski makes contact with the snow, plant the ski pole.

◎ Try to keep your upper body fairly still and facing down the fall-line the entire time. Note in picture sequence 106A-C that the upper body remains fixed as the skis swing beneath it.

B) Charleston around bumps PHOTO 107

Once you feel relaxed skiing the Charleston on a smooth slope, it is good fun to Charleston around the bumps. Choose a short series of bumps on a gentle or intermediate slope and practice the same Charleston movements that you did on the smooth slope, making each turn on the uphill edge of your uphill ski and turning around the bumps. Picture 107 shows the Charleston through a bump field.

3) The butterfly (or Royal Christie)

I've heard this maneuver referred to as both the *butterfly* and the *Royal Christie*. Since I learned it as the butterfly, and also because this is a more vivid name, that's what I call it. The butterfly is a very impressive

Practice with ski lifted to the side

maneuver for spectators and yet it's very easy to perform, since it is nothing more than a combination of skiing on the uphill edge of the uphill ski and skating.

NOTES

⊚⊙⊙ As in many of the simple acrobatics, the difficulty is in getting the rhythm started. However, once you get reasonably good at the maneuver, it will become easier to get quickly into the rhythm.

⊚⊙⊙ Prior to learning to place one ski behind your head (picture sequence 109A-C), it is best to first practice skating across the fall-line with your weight on the uphill edge of the uphill ski.

A) Practice with ski lifted to the side PHOTOS 108A-D

Start on a medium traverse track on a gentle slope and traverse with your weight on the uphill edge of

your uphill ski (picture 108A). As you gain momentum, roll onto the downhill edge of this ski (picture 108B) and step across the fall-line onto the inside edge of the opposite ski (picture 108C), leaning your body in the direction of the turn and holding the outside ski horizontally out to the side parallel with the ground. Glide on the new uphill ski as you cross the slope (picture 108D) and come to a stop. Repeat in the opposite direction, and then practice linking the turns without stopping.

B) Butterfly position PHOTOS 109A-C

Once you have mastered skating across the fall-line holding the outside ski horizontally in the air, it is only a matter of courage to place the ski behind your back.

Start performing the maneuver exactly as for

Butterfly position

A sinmple jump turn over a bump

A jump turn over 2 bumps

exercise 3A (as shown in pictures 108A-B and 109A-B). As you step across the fall-line onto the inside edge of the new uphill ski, bend your downhill knee and place this ski behind your back rather than hold-

ing it to the side (picture 109C). Glide across the slope in this butterfly position and steer to a stop.

Repeat to the opposite side, then practice linking the turns without stopping between turns.

SPECIAL TIP

◎ It helps to bend from the waist so that your back is horizontal and parallel to the ground (picture 109C).

NOTES

◎◎◎ When making butterfly turns, hold onto your ski poles for balance, but don't plant them.

◎◎◎ When you feel comfortable skiing butterfly turns on both sides, you can impress your friends by skiing down a gentle slope linking a series of them.

◎◎◎ If you become proficient and are daring, you might want to try skiing a bump field making butterfly turns around the bumps.

4) A simple jump turn over a bump
PHOTOS 110A-C & 111A-C

Jumping off the tops of bumps can be fun and very easy to perform. It's also easy to make a turn during the jump.

Approach a bump on an easy intermediate slope with more speed than you would normally ski if you didn't wish to be thrown airborne. Lower your hips as you would for the normal turn and plant your downhill ski pole on the up-slope of the bump (picture 110A). As you start to ride up the bump, forcefully thrust your legs upward and start your turn around your downhill ski pole.

As you crest the bump you will find that your violent up-thrust motion and your increased speed have caused your skis to fly off the bump so that they are no longer in contact with the snow (picture 110B). Continue turning your skis in the air across the fall-line and land in the new direction in a correct traverse position with your weight over the instep of your downhill ski boot (picture 110C). When you are in the air your legs should be extended, and as you land you should absorb the landing shock by flexing your hips and knees so that you land softly. Now traverse to a stop. Practice jumping off bumps in both directions.

When you feel comfortable jump-turning to both sides, link the jump turns, concentrating on landing

Straight tuck jump

Tuck jump with turns

softly and in control. When this becomes easy, increase your speed and try to jump over two bumps (picture sequence 111A) as you turn your skis in the air. If the bumps are sufficiently close together and you have enough speed, you may even be able to jump over three.

SPECIAL TIP
◎ Survey the jump and time it carefully so that you always land in the trough behind a bump or on its back slope, as it can be quite painful landing on the up-slope or the top of a bump.

5) Two-pole tuck jump over a bump
The *tuck* jump is a simple maneuver to execute and is impressive when performed over large bumps. During this maneuver the legs are tucked up toward

the chest while the skis are in the air, as shown in pictures 112B and 113B. This jump can be executed with or without turns. I enjoy making tuck jump turns on advanced slopes over large bumps at slow speeds. I usually employ the tuck jump without a turn for jumping off cornices and snowdrifts into deep powder snow.

A) Straight tuck jump PHOTOS 112A-C
Practice on an intermediate slope. Ski toward a medium-sized bump on a shallow traverse. As you approach the bump, place your hands on the tops of your ski poles and swing the poles forward (picture 112A). Then, as you flex your hips, plant both ski poles near the top of the bump and spring up with a strong leg extension, pushing off both feet. Simultaneously push down on your ski poles and straighten your arms so that

The split jump (spread eagle)

toward your chest and continue turning your skis in the air across the fall-line (picture 113B). Straighten your legs prior to landing and land in control in the new direction, in a correct traverse position, with your weight on the instep of the downhill ski boot. Absorb the landing impact with flexed knees and hips, and ski to a stop. Practice this on both sides.

When you feel confident making the two-pole tuck jump turn over the medium-sized bumps, gradually choose larger bumps to jump-turn over, and then perform the maneuver on steeper slopes.

SPECIAL TIPS

◎ The trick is to be certain to land in good control and to absorb the landing with flexible knees and hips.

◎ Keep your back straight and relaxed.

◎ Always try to land on the back of a bump, on a steep pitch on a slope, or in the trough between bumps. Never intentionally land on the up-slope nor on the top of a bump.

◎ For all jumps, it is very important that you land with your skis parallel to the slope that you are landing on, so that the skis land flat on the snow.

6) The split jump (spread eagle)
PHOTOS 114A-D

Jumping off big bumps, cornices, and specially prepared jumps has become very popular among young skiers, but there are many acrobatic jumps and flips that are potentially very dangerous if not performed correctly. I prefer to leave all flips to those ski acrobats who are performing in freestyle competitions. (The only flips I have ever done have been unintentional, and I've always managed to land upended!) However, jumping off bumps with your skis beneath you is easy, fun, and safe.

My favorite jump over the years, and also that of many of my students, has been the *split jump*, which looks difficult, but is actually very easy to perform. Once you can execute and land the split jump correctly you will have the basic skill to perform any number of other jumps where you keep your head more or less above your skis. These include the *Daffy, Mulekick, Backscratcher, Twist, Tip Drop, Mute Grab, Japan Air, Huntony and Zudnick*, to name but a few of the more common ones. How big a bump you choose

your arms end up above your ski poles. As you become airborne, lift your knees toward your chest (picture 112B). Start to straighten your legs prior to landing and land in control in a traverse position (picture 112C), flexing your knees and hips to absorb the impact. Practice this maneuver in both directions and jump over progressively larger bumps.

B) Tuck jump with turns PHOTOS 113A-C

On an intermediate slope, ski a shallow traverse track toward a medium-sized bump. As you approach the bump, lower your hips, plant both ski poles near the summit, spring up (in the same way as for the straight tuck jump), and initiate a turn around your downhill ski pole. As you become airborne, tuck your knees up

to jump over depends on your age, courage, and ability.

To perform the split jump, choose a bump that has a smooth, moderately steep pitch behind it, or a small, specially prepared jump with a moderately steep landing pitch.

Ski toward the bump and plant your ski pole as you lower your hips (picture 114A). At the top of the bump, spring off with a strong leg extension, pushing off with both feet, and, as you are going up in the air, spread your skis wide apart (picture 114B). At the same time, spread your arms for balance. As you pass the apex of the jump, bring your legs together and lower your arms to maintain good stability (picture 114C). Keep your legs extended prior to landing and absorb the impact by flexing your knees and lowering your hips (picture 114D).

SPECIAL TIPS

◎ The key to this maneuver is to be sure to bring your legs together as you start your descent toward the snow.
◎ Keep your back vertical and relaxed.
◎ Land with your skis parallel to the slope.

EXTREME SKIING
Skiing steep gullies and mountain faces PHOTOS 115A-D

Skiing gullies and mountain faces is exciting, dangerous, stimulating, challenging, adventurous, and superb fun! Each year, more and more people are venturing off the packed slopes and onto these steep pitches. Two days after a light snowstorm in Tignes/Val d'Isere in France, (one of Europe's top off-piste ski areas), one can see tracks coming down every possible (and seemingly impossible) mountain face and gully. The challenge for the skiers who made these tracks is not speed of descent, but rather to get to their favorite gullies before too many others do. Skiing the mountain faces and gullies is one of my favorite skiing pleasures and can be yours, too, if done with care and safety.

Although one often skis these steep pitches in powder snow over a firm base, it is also common to ski these same pitches on spring snow (also referred to as *transformed* snow due to the changes it under-

Skiing the steep gullies and mountain faces

goes in spring weather). The technique for skiing "the steep" in deep powder snow is covered in Section Five.

Transformed snow can vary from frozen granular (hard and icy), to granular (just soft enough for the ski edges to grip), to sugar (light snow granules on a firm base), to corn (large, slightly wet snow granules on a firm base, also called "ball bearings"), to mashed potatoes or porridge (wet snow on a soggy base), to wet concrete (very heavy, wet snow on a very soft base). Skiing on transformed snow requires nothing more than a refinement of the techniques you have already learned, and a daring nature.

SPECIAL TIP

◎ I strongly recommend that you do not ski the steep slopes on frozen granular, mashed potatoes, or wet concrete snow, as these conditions can all be very dangerous.

Because a fall on many of the steep gullies or mountain faces can be very painful or worse, it is best to practice your technique and control on short, steep pitches on the advanced intermediate or expert slopes.

Obviously, when skiing steep pitchees, control is more important than style; therefore ski with your skis spaced apart at a distance that gives you the most confidence. Some skiers prefer to ski with their feet very close together, but I find that if you ski with independent leg action, with some space between your skis, you can often use the uphill ski to prevent you from falling, should you lose control of your downhill ski.

To learn to ski the very steep slopes, choose a short, steep pitch on a difficult trail and pick a path down the center, so that if you lose control, you will have enough runout to the sides to allow you to regain control. The object of this maneuver is to turn your skis l80 degrees from one traverse to the next without picking up much momentum. There are various ways to accomplish this.

NOTE

◎◎◎ Sylvain Saudan, one of the originators of extreme skiing, has always relied on very powerful thighs to thrust his skis up and across the fall-line. When learning extreme skiing, I was taught to ski in

a similar way, jumping my skis out of the snow, pivoting them in the air, and landing on the edge of the downhill ski, facing in the new direction. (This movement causes the skier to break and then reestablish contact with the snow, and also has the skier working against the pull of gravity.) Although there are certain times that I will use this maneuver, such as in extremely narrow gullies, I find an easier and surer way to turn one's skis in most circumstances is to make a "steep slope turn," combining extreme anticipation (page 88), banking, and knee steering.

To perform this steep slope turn, choose a short, steep pitch on an advanced intermediate slope. Start in a traverse position with your weight on the instep of your downhill ski, your skis sufficiently edged to prevent sideslipping and your upper body facing down the fall-line. Begin traversing (picture 115A), then immediately lower your hips and, using anticipation, plant your ski pole down the hill (picture 115B). (Make sure that both your hands are down the fall-line.)

Now, rather than extending with a strong upthrust, make use of the strong pull of gravity evident on these steep slopes by banking your turn (offsetting your weight by leaning in the direction of the pole plant) and then, using a slight hip extension, roll your knees and feet downhill (picture 115C). As your ski tips begin to swing around, push your inside (pole-planting) arm forward down the hill, transfer your weight to your new downhill ski and continue to roll your knees and feet across the fall-line (picture 115D) to be ready for the next turn. Be sure to press on the instep of the downhill foot to maintain good ski control and keep your upper body facing toward the fall-line. Repeat the turn in the opposite direction.

When you feel comfortable making turns to both sides, choose a narrow path down the center of the slope and imagine that you are in a very narrow gully with walls on each side. Limit yourself to skiing down this narrow width, turning your skis from side to side, gaining as little speed as possible. Perform the same turns on a very steep expert trail, using extreme anticipation.

NOTES

◎◎◎ When you feel confident that you can ski in

total control on a very steep slope, you are probably ready to ski the off-piste gullies and mountain faces. How well you progress from here depends very much on your nature, and even for those of you who are very daring, it is preferable for "students of the steep" to progress gradually if moving on to more dangerous slopes.

◉◉◎ Begin skiing off-piste mountain faces that are wide and free of rocks and lead into snowbowls, so that if you fall you will stop gradually, with little risk of serious injury.

◉◉◎ Gradually choose increasingly steeper slopes to descend.

◉◉◎ Start skiing short gullies that open onto wide slopes or snowbowls, and then gradually progress to longer gullies.

◉◉◎ Only after you have put in lots of ski time on the types of gullies and mountain faces recommended above should you attempt to ski those that cut above cliffs or large drop-offs.

◉◉◎ It is advisable to ski off-piste mountain faces and gullies in the company of ski instructors who specialize in off-piste skiing in that particular area, or with certified mountain guides, since they will be aware of the hazards and inherent dangers of those slopes. These guides can also lead you down safely should the weather turn inclement.

USING SKINS

Skins attached to the bottoms of skis enable a skier to climb up a hill without slipping backward — which is extremely useful for exploring the mountains beyond the limits of the lift-serviced ski areas.

Skins were originally made from seal pelts, on which all the hairs grow in the same direction. Thus, when sealskins are attached to the bottoms of the skis, the skis will slide in one direction and grip in the reverse direction. Modern skins are manufactured using synthetic materials designed to exhibit the same characteristics, and are very efficient. Most modern skins are attached by an adhesive backing.

For steep climbs or when walking long distances, it is much less tiring on your legs to have a ski binding that allows the heel of your boot to lift as you slide your feet backward and forth. There are some excellent ski touring bindings available, and a visit to

Walking on flat terrain using skins

any good ski mountaineering shop will allow you to inspect the various models. With a good ski binding and a good pair of skins, you are ready to walk up the slopes.

1) Walking on flat terrain using skins
PHOTOS 116A-D

Prior to climbing with skins, it is best to learn to walk with them on the flat. Start on level terrain, standing with one foot pushed forward (picture 116A). Plant your ski pole to the side of the foot of your forward ski and lift the heel of the other foot. Now lean your body slightly forward and slide your rear ski forward, simultaneously bringing your rear ski pole forward (picture 116B). Transfer your weight onto this foot as you continue to push it for-

Wlaking up slopes using skins

ward, and allow the heel of your back foot to lift. Now slide your new rear ski forward and repeat the same series of movements (pictures 116C and 116D), so that you are gliding along, placing one foot before the other.

NOTE
◎◎◎ It may seem awkward at first, but with very little practice it will become easy.

2) Walking up slopes using skins
PHOTOS 117A-D
Walking up slopes with skins is essentially the same as walking on the flat with skins. The differences are that your upper body should be leaning slightly up the hill and your legs will have to work harder.

Start on a gentle slope and proceed to walk straight up the fall-line of the hill. Be sure to tilt your upper body slightly forward the entire time you are climbing (picture sequence 117A-D.) Repeat the same weight-shifting and ski-sliding movements that you did while walking with the skins on the flat, concentrating on finding your natural rhythm.

SPECIAL TIPS
◎ At first, you may find your rear ski sliding backward when you are ready to bring it forward. It is only a matter of trial and error to find the right position of your upper body to ensure a grip of the skins on the snow as you transfer your weight from ski to ski. As you continue to practice you should find it easier to prevent the skis from slipping away.

◎ With most ski-touring bindings, you can easily walk up gentle slopes and certain grades of intermediate slopes. A number of companies make bindings with extension devices that permit easy climbing up steeper slopes (picture sequence 117A-D.)

◎ Except on gentle slopes, when climbing up a slope with skins it is usual to walk on a diagonal to the fall-line. The angle of the diagonal depends on the steepness of the slope and the type of ski binding you are using. Bindings that have a steep slope climbing attachment will permit you to climb straighter up the slopes, thereby making the climb easier.

◎ When climbing with skins, always carry a knapsack so that you can tuck the skins away when you are ready for your descent.

◎ Although you can ski tour on any type of ski, there are specialized "back-country" skis that are designed to easily handle the differing types of snow you generally encounter in out-of-bounds areas. These skis normally are shorter, wider, and lighter than standard skis. Many of the major ski manufacturers make a back-country ski.

OFF-PISTE PRECAUTIONS

Since skins are used primarily to gain access to the off-piste, you must be aware of the precautions that should always be taken whenever you ski out of bounds:

◎ Never ski alone.

◎ Always let others who remain behind know where you are planning to go and when you are expecting to return.

◎ Check with knowledgeable persons, such as mountain rangers or the area ski patrol, if it is permissible to ski in the area where you wish to go.

◎ Check with knowledgeable persons as to whether the snow conditions are safe.

◎ Avoid going out of bounds if the weather is bad or unsettled.

◎ It is best to go out of bounds with ski instructors who specialize in this type of skiing and know the area where you are planning on going, or with certified mountain guides.

◎ If going with friends and without a guide, take a topographical map of the area, a heavy-duty needle and thread to repair your skins should they tear, a compass, an altimeter, emergency food and clothing, and a bright, reflecting object that can be seen by res-

cuers, should you become lost or injured. In addition, take a rope, crampons, harnesses and ice axes if the area has crevasses. You should also know how to make emergency splints for injuries. A GPS (global positioning system) unit can be very valuable to have with you.

◎ If there is any chance of avalanches, you should wear a transponder — Arva, Ortovox, Ramer, Tracker, and Pieps make good units — and ascertain that your unit operates on the same frequency as those used by the local rescue services. Have a powder cord attached to your skis, and make sure you are knowledgeable about avalanche slopes, the dangers of avalanches, and the procedures for avalanche rescues. (I never go out of bounds without wearing a transponder.)

◎ Bring along a mobile telephone and the telephone number of the rescue service.

THE ULTIMATE SKIING EXPERIENCE

If you have successfully practiced most of the exercises in Section IV,
then you are now undoubtedly an advanced skier. You should be able
to confidently ski not only all the trails on the mountains, using various
advanced skiing maneuvers, but also lots of the off-piste slopes as well,
on solid snow conditions. You are therefore ready to enter into a new
dimension in skiing, and experience what is for many the ultimate skiing
pleasure: skiing powder snow, which is explained in Section V.

POWDER SKIING

section five

I love skiing powder and take every chance that I have to get into it. In an article I wrote for Skiing magazine, I tried to capture the feeling that I experienced on a steep, newly discovered powder run in Farellones, Chile, as follows:

"Alone — me, my skis, the mountain, and the soft, delicate snow yielding ever so tenderly as my skis pressed from one silent turn to the next. Down, down, down — all I could see was white, fluffy, untracked powder. I was lost in total absorption. I was lost in ecstasy. Mindless of the danger of falling and never being found, I continued on, shooting plumes of fine, white mist behind me until exhaustion and concern broke into my consciousness..."

Through the years I've read and heard other vain efforts by skiers trying to share the joys of their powder descents, and I'm convinced that although powder seems to bring out the poets in skiers, the descriptions fall far short of the reality.

Skiing powder snow is a very personal experience, as the skier develops an intimate relationship with the snow and the mountain. It is exciting, exhilarating, and pleasurable. I feel that powder skiing is to skiing what ballet is to dance, for it requires an artistry and finesse of movement, coupled with body strength and fluidity of motion.

The basic turn for skiing powder snow is the short-radius turn. All that is necessary to use this turn in powder is to modify the body stance and weight distribution. Once this is learned, the next step is to experience the feeling of riding on a soft cushion beneath the skis rather than on a solid surface, and overcoming the fear of not being able to see your skis while they are under the snow. (Except for those instances where snow is flying in your face or you are in "bottomless" powder, you should always be able to see your ski tips.)

To learn how to ski the powder I recommend that you first learn the modified body stance and then practice traversing in deep snow to experience the feeling of riding on a cushiony base.

Shaped skis turn very well in powder. Because of their wide tips and tails they float well in the soft snow, and because of their shape and design they turn very easily. One of the added joys I have with my

Various ski widths

shaped skis is that in many powder conditions I do not have to do exaggerated down-up-down movements. In fact, often I don't do any down-up-down movements. I ski the shaped skis in the powder essentially as I do on firm snow, rolling from one set of edges to the other.

There are, however, powder conditions where you will have to unweight your skis using an up-extension to initiate a turn. It is thus useful to learn and practice the up-unweighting movements.

There are many ways of initiating turns in powder, and in this section I describe a number of them. Skiers eventually develop their own styles and ski the powder in ways that feel most secure and comfortable to them, often combining various aspects of the different powder turns. A very good powder skier will undoubtedly be proficient in many of these turns and will let the type and depth of snow, and the steepness

of the terrain, dictate which turn to utilize.

The most versatile turn emphasizes up-unweighting. I refer to it as the basic down-up-down powder turn. This is the turn that I feel every new powder skier should master, and use. Once you can ski powder confidently with the basic down-up-down powder turn, you will have the ability to safely ski in just about any powder condition that you may encounter.

There are also a large variety of special powder skis which make skiing powder almost as easy as skiing on packed slopes. These skis vary in width and shape, but they are all wider than either traditional skis or shaped skis. The widest of them are generally referred to as fat boys (a name given to the first wide skis by the manufacturer). These skis are very good for people learning how to ski powder because they are more stable than narrower skis and, thanks to their width, do not sink as far into the snow. A person just setting out to learn to ski powder will fall less often on these skis, which makes the learning process less tiring and more enjoyable.

Wide body skis (pictures 118A and 118B) are wider than traditional skis, but not as wide as fat boys. They float better in soft snow than traditional skis and less effort is required to turn them in many powder conditions. They are particularly good in difficult powder conditions, such as crust and heavy snow. Another choice is a so-called cross ski (picture 118C), which combines the best qualities of wide body and shaped skis. These skis look similar to shaped skis but are wider in the waist (the middle of the ski) than standard shaped skis, and often have a softer camber so that they bend well in soft snow. Thanks to their overall width, they float well in powder, and because of their shape, they turn easily.

Because all of these skis make skiing powder easier, I would certainly recommend that you use one of them while you are learning how to ski the powder.

THE POWDER POSITION

PHOTOS 119A-B

Pictures 119A and 119B show the modification of the body stance required to ski powder. Picture 119A shows a normal traverse position. Picture 119B shows the powder traverse position. The key to skiing powder is to move your center of gravity back so that it is over your heels, rather than over the middle of your feet. The way to accomplish this is to sit slightly lower with your hips over your heels and your upper body upright. When you are in the correct position, your toes should be brushing lightly against the upper surface of the inside of the ski boots, rather than resting on the footbed. It is also necessary to keep your weight evenly distributed over both feet. (This is so that you do not sink lower into the snow on one foot than the other, which could easily cause you to topple over.)

SPECIAL TIPS

◎ It is easiest to ski powder with your skis fairly close together. As you get more proficient, you can

Powder position

adjust the space between your skis to your own liking.

◎ Keep your arms held wider apart and slightly higher than you do for skiing packed-snow (pictures 119A and 119B), and roll both feet slightly uphill so that your skis are edged.

◎ A common misconception of many novice powder skiers is thinking that you should always lean backward with your legs against the backs of the boots in order to lighten the pressure on the ski tips. If you ski like that, you will lose control of your skis! To maintain control of your skis in powder, particularly on a steep slope or at speed, you must keep continuous contact between your shins and the fronts of your ski boots. (There are times when you *should* lean back against the backs of the ski boots — when skiing in deep snow on a gentle slope, when skiing up the wall of a steep dip, and when skiing on an intermediate pitch in very wet, heavy snow.)

◎ Notice in pictures 119A and 119B that all parts of the body that are uphill remain slightly in front of their downhill counterparts. During shortswing turns your upper body should, of course, be facing toward the fall-line the entire time.

NOTE

◎◎◎ Although short-radius turns are the most popular powder turns, one can also make medium- and large-radius turns. To do so, you should be standing somewhat squarer on your skis than you are for short-radius turns. This means that while you should

Traversing and up-unweighting

that you feel your heels being pushed into the snow. (When you do that, your ski tips will tilt up.) Then plant your ski pole in the snow, bounce up from your heels, and fully extend your legs (picture 120C). Continue traversing in the same direction and again lower your hips over your heels (picture 120D), plant your pole, and bounce up. Continue across the slope, bouncing up off your heels, and then come to a gradual stop in the same traverse.

Do a kick turn and traverse in the opposite direction, repeating the same motions. Continue these back and forth traverses until you begin to feel comfortable in the powder snow.

SPECIAL TIPS

◎ Try not to jump or hop when you push up off your heels. The motion should be smooth and fluid.
◎ When traversing, keep your arms held wide apart and high enough so that the tips of your ski poles are just out of the snow.
◎ Be sure to keep your weight evenly distributed on both heels at all times.
◎ Keep your feet rolled slightly uphill so that your skis are edged. Do not permit your skis to sideslide.

2) End of turns PHOTOS 121A-C

The end of the turn is the most important part of the turn, since that is where you either gain or lose control. This is especially true in powder. Thus, it would be useful to practice the ends of the turns before you practice making downhill turns.

On a powder slope with the same gradient as that used for the previous exercise, start in a shallow traverse with your body in a neutral, relaxed position (picture 121A). Begin to pick up some speed and then start to roll your feet and ankles more uphill so that your skis become more edged. As you do that, gradually lower your hips so that you are pressing down on both of your heels (picture 121B). Keep rolling your feet and ankles and pressing down until your skis turn up the hill to a stop (picture 121C).

Next, repeat the same ending starting on a steeper traverse. Continue to start on progressively steeper traverse tracks until you are starting just off the fall-line. Repeat the same series to the other side.

still keep your upper body turned toward the fall-line, your shoulders and hips should be facing more toward your ski tips. The uphill parts of your body are therefore more level with the downhill parts.

1) Traversing and up-unweighting
PHOTOS 120A-D

See if you can find a wide stretch of untracked powder on an intermediate-grade slope (you can often find this on the side of a packed intermediate ski trail). Assume the powder position and traverse across the slope in a shallow track, as in picture 120A. You should choose a traverse just steep enough to maintain some speed. Hold your downhill ski pole vertical and ready to be planted. While you are traversing, lower your hips (as in picture 120B) so

End of turns

Downhill turns — starting on the fall-line

NOTES

◉◉◦ Be sure to not swing your upper body in the direction of the turn. (The turn should be made just with your lower body.)

◉◉◦ The ending of the turn is essentially the same as the endings that you made on packed slopes in Section Two. The only difference is that you are in the powder position and you should be pressing down on both heels.

3) Downhill turns

Now that you can turn uphill to a stop, you are ready to make downhill turns across the fall-line. As noted in the introduction to this Section, on shaped skis you can turn in light powder without exaggerated up-unweighting movements. (The way to do that is explained on pages 117-118). However, as you will need to use the basic up-unweighted powder turn in many powder conditions, it is best to start off by learning this turn.

A) Starting on the fall-line PHOTOS 122A-D

Start off on the fall-line (as in picture 122A) on an intermediate-grade powder slope. Begin to slide and gain some momentum with one ski pole held vertical. While gliding, start lowering your hips over your heels, as in picture 122B. Then plant your ski pole, push off your heels as you did in excercise 1, (traversing and up-unweighting), only now extend up around this pole. Your skis will start to turn in the same direction (picture 122C). As you extend up, roll your feet and ankles in the same direction to place both skis on their edges. While the skis are turning uphill, begin lowering your hips over your heels to press down on your skis so that they sink in the powder, and finish the turn exactly as you did in the previous exercise (picture 122D). Repeat this exercise turning to the opposite side.

Starting from a steep traverse

SPECIAL TIPS

◎ At all times, maintain your powder position with your upper body upright, your arms held wide apart and high (your hands should be at about armpit level), your weight evenly distributed on both skis, and sitting slightly so that your weight is over your heels. Your head should be centered and you should watch where you are going. If you bend forward at the waist, you will weight the fronts of your skis and will probably fall over them as the tips catch in the snow.

◎ Be sure to roll your feet across the fall-line during your extension movement and keep them rolling toward the hill until you stop.

◎ Although the skis are edged, you should not ride on the edges as you do on packed snow. When you press down on your heels, the entire width of the ski bottom should compress the snow beneath it. (The reason we keep the skis on their edges is to enable the skis to carve a turn, rather than skid a turn. It also prevents catching the downhill ski edge, which usually leads to an awkward fall.)

◎ Try to flex your hips in a steady, continuous motion so that you do not jerk downward.

◎ Do not put any weight on your ski pole as you place it in the snow. In powder, the ski pole is used primarily to help time and coordinate the turn.

◎ Do not try to hurry your turn; rather, allow your skis to turn in a smooth, large radius. I like to think of a powder turn as the smooth type of turn a sailboat makes when one gently moves the tiller to the side, rather than the abrupt turn made by a small motorboat when the steering wheel is rapidly turned and power applied.

B) Starting from a steep traverse   **PHOTOS 123A-D**
This time, start on a steep traverse and make the same turn as in the previous exercise. Bring your downhill ski pole vertical and turn around this pole.

C) Starting from a shallow traverse   **PHOTOS 124A-E**
Start on a shallow traverse and make a turn across the fall-line. You may find that you need to use a more exaggerated extension to initiate the turn. Try to end all the turns the same way.

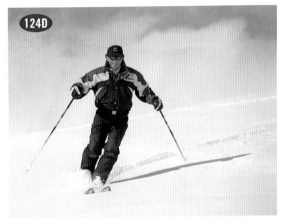

Starting from a shallow traverse

D) Repeat exercises A - C to the other side

E) Linking downhill turns **PHOTOS 125A-E**
Now that you can make a turn to each side, you

should be able to link the turns to ski a continuous series of powder turns. Start off making just two turns. Instead of stopping after the first turn, steer your skis up the hill only enough to slow down. Then, as the skis are slowing down, bring the new downhill ski pole vertical and make a turn around that pole. Then steer your skis to a stop.

When you feel confident linking two turns, try to link four, stopping after the fourth turn. Once you can confidently link four turns in total control, you are ready to ski the powder.

F) Downhill turns on steeper slopes
Skiing in powder is actually easier on steep slopes than on moderately pitched slopes. The steepness allows your skis to slide faster, which enables you to turn more easily (while the powder provides resistance and prevents you from going too fast). Once you can ski the powder on an intermediate-grade

125A

125B

125C

125D

125E

Linking downhill turns

slope, it should be very easy to do so on steeper slopes.

Choose a steeper slope of untracked powder and make three or four turns, then stop. Repeat until you

have mastered this. Then link a long series of turns down the slope, concentrating on skiing slowly and finishing each turn in complete control.

4) Control exercises

I've noticed that some people find it difficult to commit themselves to making a turn in powder because they think that their skis won't get around and they will go shooting off down the fall-line out of control. There are two series of exercises that I have found to be extremely valuable to help overcome this fear. These exercises are worth practicing by every new powder skier, as they will help you become more confident about initiating turns in powder and controlling the turns.

A) Slowing down and gaining control after each turn
  PHOTOS 126A-E
Make one turn and start to steer your skis to a stop (pictures 126A and 126B). But don't actually stop!

Slowing down and gaining control after each turn

Just before you stop, flatten your skis and turn the ski tips toward the fall-line and let them pick up some speed (picture 126C). Then make another turn across the fall-line and steer your skis up the hill almost to a stop (picture 126D) and again flatten the skis and lower the tips to let them gain speed for the next turn (picture 126E). Continue these movements until you feel that you are controlling your skis and not vice versa.

B) Making a turn in segments   **PHOTOS 127A-F**
Start from a very shallow traverse and make a turn in two separate extension movements. Use the first extension to turn the skis just to the fall-line and the second extension to turn the skis across the fall-line.

Start to ski on the shallow traverse and flex your hip and plant your downhill ski pole (picture 127A), and do an extension around the pole rolling your feet and ankles just enough to bring your skis to the fall-line (picture 127B). Then, while you are skiing down the fall-line, flex again and plant the same pole (picture 127C) and extend up around the

Making a turn in segments

pole and roll your feet and ankles up the hill (picture 127D), as you did for exercise 3A. As the skis turn up the hill, bring your other ski pole vertical (picture 127E) and initiate a turn in the other direction (picture 127F), making the turn in two segments.

Link a series of these segmented turns down a powder slope.

NOTE

◉◉◉ When skiing in wet, deep, or heavy powder, or in breakable crust, you may not make it fully around with your first extension. On those occasions, use these segmented turns to complete the turn.

SPECIAL TIPS

◉ An exercise that's both good training and good fun is to follow a friend who is a good powder skier and try to ski exactly to his or her rhythm.

◉ Another good training exercise is to ski behind a good powder skier and try to ski to the same rhythm but out of phase—you start off turning to the left when the other skier turns to the right, so that you constantly cross his or her tracks, making a series of figure 8's.

◉ When you think you are really getting the hang of it, try to ski alongside a good powder skier and match him or her turn for turn. (Warning: Don't get out of rhythm or you will likely collide!)

NOTES

◉◉◉ As mentioned previously, the down-up-down powder turn is useful on practically every type of snow. So practice and perfect this turn on all the powder slopes that you can, and enjoy yourself as you frolic with the other "powder hounds."

◉◉◉ When you feel that you have mastered this turn, you can practice the other ways of initiating turns in powder that are described in this chapter and assimilate those movements that you find the easiest into your own personal powder style.

SKIING POWDER ON SHAPED SKIS

As noted in the introduction to this section, one can ski powder on shaped skis without doing exaggerated up-unweighting movements, especially in light or not very deep powder. These skis float well, thanks to their wide tips and tails, and turn easily because of their shape. I often ski them in the powder the same way that I ski them on the firm slopes. The difference is that I stand on the skis in the powder position, with my weight over my heels. You, too, should be able to ski powder on your shaped skis using the same turns that you practiced in Section Two.

A) Carving turns with foot and ankle roll
PHOTOS 128A-H

Refer to picture sequence 128A-H. With your body in a powder position and your weight over both skis, keep the skis under the snow and start to ski (picture 128A). When you are ready to initiate a turn, merely roll your feet and ankles in the direction of the turn and press down on your heels (picture 128B). Your skis should make an arc across the fall-line (pictures 128C and 128D). After the turn, relax your legs and release the pressure on the skis and let your knees retract back to a neutral position (picture 128E). Then, roll your feet and ankles in the new direction and press down again to make the next turn (pictures 128F,128G and 128H). Continue to link a series of turns down the hill.

NOTE

◉◉◉ I find this method of skiing quite relaxing; it's certainly less tiring than doing exaggerated extension movements to execute each turn.

SPECIAL TIP

◎ When you are carving turns in the powder as explained above, the radius of the turn is governed by the amount of edging, the pressure that you apply to the skis, and the speed with which you release the pressure. If you press and release quickly you can ski

Carving turns with foot and ankle roll

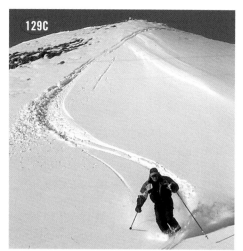

Powder rurns with leg extension

High-energy carving turns

short-radius turns. If you press and release more slow-ly, your turns will be wider. If you press and release very slowly, you can make very wide turns, leaving tracks similar to those made by snowboarders.

B) Powder turns with leg extension **PHOTOS 129A-C**
You can also ski the powder using the same leg exten-sion movements that you do on firm slopes (refer to pages 62–66 Section II). The leg extension move-ments are similar to the leg extensions that you use when you push off your skis to skate. The difference in powder is that you have to push off both skis rather than one ski.

Start skiing and flex your hips to press down on your skis (picture 129A). Then extend your legs and initiate a downhill turn (picture 129B). Roll your feet and ankles to direct the turn, and, as the skis cross the fall-line, lower your hips again in preparation for the next turn (picture 129C). Link a series of these turns down the slope.

C) High-energy carving turns **PHOTOS 130A-D**
You can have a lot of fun on your shaped skis in the powder by skiing dynamically and using the rebound of the skis to spring you into the turns, the same way that you do on the firm slopes for short-radius turns (refer to pages 58–60).

Keep your body facing down the fall-line at all times. As you are skiing, press down on your skis so that they flex under the snow (picutre 130A). Then quickly release the pressure on the skis so that the skis spring up and propel you into the next turn (picture 130B). Of course, you have to roll your feet and ankles to direct the turns. Try to establish a rhythm and link a long series of these turns.

NOTES

⊚⊚⊙ Practice this on gentle-gradient powder slopes or else you may pick up too much speed.

⊚⊚⊙ It requires some practice to learn how much pressure to apply and when to release it so as to get the most spring out of the skis.

⊚⊚⊙ The faster you ski and the more you flex the skis, the more they will rebound when you release the pressure.

⊚⊚⊙ This turn is not recommended when you are skiing in "bottomless powder" (very light, deep, dry powder), as you need to have a layer of resistance under the skis in order for them to rebound.

PUNCHING THROUGH POWDER

PHOTOS 131A-D

"Punching through the powder" helps to pull your skis out of the snow and is very useful when skiing in deep, heavy, or crusty snow. The punching action can be combined with many of the other methods of turning to help make initiating turns easier.

Punching is simply a modification of the basic powder turn. To punch your turns, you continually face downhill, making shortswing turns close to the fall-line while you punch "uppercuts" with your hands, arms, and shoulders. This is usually performed without pole planting.

In picture sequence 131A-D, I am skiing short-swing turns, punching through the powder. Notice how my hands and arms end up above my shoulders and how they coordinate with my extension to help pull my skis out of the snow.

To ski with punching, start on a steep traverse on an intermediate-grade slope of untracked powder. Pick up speed, lower your hips, and, as you start your extension, punch your outside hand, arm, and shoulder up and slightly toward the downhill turn so that you feel a strong pull on the outside of your ribcage

Punching through powder

Jet turn in powder

(as can be seen in pictures 131B). As your skis approach the fall-line, begin lowering your hips and your arm. When your skis cross the fall-line, extend up and punch your new outside hand, arm, and shoulder up and slightly toward the downhill turn (picture 131D). Continue these motions down the slope.

NOTES

◉◉◉ If you punch just your arm, it's unlikely anything will happen. You need to coordinate the arm punch with the extension movement.

◉◉◉ Try to not drop your arm down to your side before punching it — it will likely throw you off balance when you punch up because of the excess movement.

JET TURN IN POWDER AND CRUST

PHOTOS 132A-C + 133A-D

As I mentioned in discussing the jet turn in Section Four, I frequently ski jet turns when skiing through evergreen glades in deep powder. I also use them in heavy snow, in wet snow, and in certain breakable-crust conditions.

The jet turn is very effective for these snow conditions because during the turn the tips of the skis shoot out of the snow (picture 132B). In heavy or wet snow, this breaks the bond between the skis and the snow and makes it easier to turn the skis.

Furthermore, because your ski tips are shot forward, your weight is much farther back on your skis, which prevents the tips from nose-diving — digging into the snow. On breakable crust, the jetting action forces the inside edges of the skis to cut through the surface, reducing the risk of catching the outside edge during the turn, as can be seen in pictures 133B and 133C. In the evergreen glades, shooting the tips out of the snow lessens the danger of catching the ski tips on branches hidden beneath the snow.

Before making jet turns in powder, you should practice the jet turn exercises presented in Section Four. Once you can make correct jet turns on packed slopes, it is simple to use the turn for powder skiing.

Picture sequence 132A-C shows some jet turns in powder. Notice how the skis shoot forward and turn downhill (picture 132B) while the upper body remains quite still. As you are completing the turn, it is very important that you recover your correct powder position with your shins touching the fronts of your ski boots in order to maintain control of your skis (picture 132C).

NOTES

◉◉◉ When you plant your ski pole in deep powder, you cannot lean your weight on it to push off and recover your upper body position at the end of the turn — it will sink into the snow. When performing a jet turn in powder, you do plant the ski pole, but you use the pole plant more as a timing maneuver (picture 132B).

◉◉◉ If the snow is compressible, as it will be in most

snow conditions other than very fine, light, dry powder, your ski-pole baskets will have some resistance as they sink in the snow, which can help you push off to recover your body position. Your recovery must be accomplished mainly by contracting your abdominal muscles in the same way that you would when performing sit-ups. (It is therefore a good idea to tone up your abdominals before the ski season.)

JET TURN PRACTICE

On an intermediate-grade slope of untracked powder, practice making one jet turn across the fall-line and ski to a stop. Repeat on the other side and then link two jet turns. When you feel that you can perform the maneuver in control, link a series of jet turns down the powder slope and then ski them as often as possible until you master this fun way of turning.

SPECIAL TIP

◎ As you jet your skis out, roll your feet so that your skis are well edged throughout the turn. Try to use the entire bottoms of the skis to carve through the snow.

NOTES

◎◎◎ One of my more enjoyable delights when skiing deep powder is to jet turn at speed off the crests of small rolling hills or large mounds and land on the downslopes or in the troughs behind the hills, where blown snow collects. When you jet turn off the crest and land in this deep snow you normally sink quite deep, and the impact often creates an explosion of swirling snow which can be completely enveloping and momentarily blinding. Should you be accompanied by a friend with a camera, this effect makes a great picture.

◎◎◎ The jet turn is a great recovery technique to use anytime you find yourself leaning backward while turning. Instead of shooting off across the hill out of control, looking for a safe place to lose speed, simply jet your skis into a turn and recover your good body position over your skis.

Jet turn in crust

Anticipation — short radius turns

Banking in powder

ANTICIPATION AND BANKING

When you are facing down the hill making short-radius turns, you are automatically skiing with anticipation. If you bank your turns by planting your ski pole further to your side, so that you are leaning in toward the center of the turn, you will find it easier to initiate powder turns.

To learn anticipation and banking, you should practice the exercises described on pages 88–91. Once you can ski with anticipation and banking on a packed slope, it is easy to use these maneuvers in the powder.

1) Anticipation PHOTOS 134A-C

If you are making medium- or large-radius turns or if you are starting a turn from a shallow traverse, to anticipate your turn you must turn your upper body in the direction of the turn as you lower your hips and plant your ski pole. Picture sequence 134A-C demonstrates short radius turns in powder using anticipation (picture 134B) to help initiate the turn.

SPECIAL TIP

◎ Anticipation makes it easier to initiate a turn and is especially useful when skiing in difficult powder.

2) Banking PHOTOS 135A-D & 136A-D

I love banking turns — both on packed runs and in the powder. The reason is that when banking, we let nature's forces help us initiate the turn, thereby saving lots of energy.

Banking requires your upper body to lean to the inside of the turn as you perform your flexion movement at the start of the turn. By leaning your upper body to your side, you are offsetting your weight and center of gravity in the direction of the turn, thereby making it easier to start your skis turning.

To practice banking your turns in the powder, ski with your arms held wide and, as you start your flexion movement, reach far to your side as you plant your ski pole so that you must lean your upper body to the side (picutre 135B). Now spring up with the same movements that you use for the basic powder turn. As your skis turn across the fall-line, roll your feet across the fall-line and bring your upper body over the skis, so that you are in a good powder posi-

Banking in crusted powder

tion at the end of the turn (picture 135C). Repeat this turn in the opposite direction (picture 135D) and when you can make the turn equally well to both sides, ski a series of banked turns down the slope.

SPECIAL TIP

◎ You can bank short-, medium-, or large-radius turns.

Picture sequence 136A-D shows banking and anticipation during large-radius turns in crusted powder. Notice in pictures 136A and 136C how the chest is facing towards the turn at the initiation of the turn and how the body leans in to the center of the turn. These actions help to initiate the turns.

Powder wedeln

POWDER WEDELN

PHOTOS 137A-C

Wedelning on a packed slope is usually performed with the skis kept almost flat to the surface, with very little extension movement and with quick motions of the skis, all of which are contrary to what should normally be done in powder. However, there are times when fine, light powder falls on a solid base, and if a skier is descending a gentle slope it is possible to keep the skis totally in the snow, riding on the hidden base, and powder wedeln down the fall-line.

Before wedelning in powder, you should first practice on the packed slopes some of the wedeln exercises presented on pages 79–80. To wedeln in powder, keep your body in the basic short-radius position, facing constantly down the fall-line, and swing your skis on wider arcs than you would swing on packed snow. Roll your skis from one set of edges to the other (by steering with your feet and ankles) in order not to catch the outside ski edges in the resisting snow.

Picture sequence 137A-C shows a series of powder wedeln turns. Notice how the skis remain in the snow and how little the body moves as the skis swing from one turn to the next.

SPECIAL TIPS

◎ To wedeln in the powder, you should be in the powder position, sitting slightly lower than you do when wedelning on packed runs so that your center of gravity is over your heels rather than over the middle of your feet.

◎ Keep your feet fairly close together and plant your ski poles at your sides.

◎ If you feel that you are going too fast or are starting to lose control, start to exaggerate your flexion-extension movements and swing a few large turns to get back in control. Then either stop or continue on down the slope using the powder wedeln or the basic powder turn.

NOTE

◎◎◎ When I'm skiing powder in the woods, I often powder wedeln to get around closely spaced trees. In fact, I prefer to powder wedeln at every opportunity I can, as this is one of the most efficient means of turning one's skis using the least amount of energy.

THE JUMP TURN

PHOTOS 138A-D

As noted in Section Four, the jump turn is a very useful maneuver to employ to ski down difficult off-piste slopes.

Conditions that can require the jump turn are as follows:

1) Very heavy snow (either moist or wind-packed) on a moderate to steep incline: the jump turn is used to get the skis out of the heavy snow so as to turn them easily in the air;

2) Hard surfaces of wind-packed snow with lots of wind-ridges: the jump turn is used to jump over the ridges and turn in the air;

3) On non-supporting breakable crust over a powder base: this is the trickiest because it requires great strength to break up through the crust and precise edge control when landing, so as to not catch the outside ski edge;

4) In gullies or on mountain faces with difficult conditions (such as crust, heavy powder, protruding rocks, large frozen snow granules, and wind-ridges);

5) In steep, narrow gullies, to turn the skis in a tight radius without gaining momentum; and

6) In spring conditions when the sun has left only a narrow strip of snow remaining.

When you feel that you can safely jump turn on packed slopes, as explained on pages 101–102, practice jump turning in light powder and then jump turn in heavier snow (pictures 138A-D). Next, practice on short stretches of breakable crust close to the packed slopes in order to safely acquire the finesse required to ski in these conditions before venturing off into the back-bowls.

NOTE

◉◉◉ After the wind has blown up, or in the springtime when the hot, blazing sun has altered the texture of the exposed powder faces, it is sometimes necessary to ski through some stretches of very tricky snow to get to a good off-piste powder slope. Knowing how to jump turn can therefore be extremely useful, permitting you to venture on undaunted while other skiers turn back.

The jump turn

DOWN-UNWEIGHTING

German, Austrian, and some American ski schools taught *down-unweighting* for years as the basic means of unweighting the skis when turning across the fall-line. Down-unweighting, which I have also heard referred to as the "magic turn," works, and though I don't feel it should be the basic means of initiating turns, I do feel it is valuable for advanced skiers to know.

Down-unweighting results when the skier rapidly sinks down. The effect of the quick down-movement is to momentarily unweight the skis (a standard visual demonstration is to stand on a scale and rapidly lower your hips and watch the weight indicator drop). To make use of this phenomenon for skiing, at

The stop turn using down-unweighting

the same time that you rapidly lower your hips, you steer your skis across the fall-line.

Down-unweighting is an alternative technique for skiing bumps (you can down-unweight as you turn around them) and is the quickest way to make a *stop turn* (which can be very useful to advanced skiers in areas with cliffs and drop-offs). It is also an alternative way of smoothly skiing an intermediate-grade powder slope.

A) The stop turn using down-unweighting
PHOTOS 139A-C

Start off facing down the fall-line on a packed slope and begin to gather speed (picture 139A). When you wish to stop, rapidly sink your hips down and twist your feet across the fall-line (picture 139B). Continue rolling your feet and ankles so that your skis are well edged, and keep your upper body facing and leaning down the fall-line (picture 139C). Try to come to a stop as quickly as possible. Repeat this maneuver, stopping to the opposite side.

B) Downhill turns   PHOTOS 140A-E

It is best to first learn to make down-unweighted turns on a packed slope and, when you can control your turn and speed, practice on an intermediate-grade powder slope.

Start traversing on an intermediate-grade slope (picture 140A). When you are ready to turn, lower your hips (picture 140B). At the same time, roll your feet across the fall-line and press your skis down into the snow. After your skis cross the fall-line, start to

raise your hips back to a neutral position (picture 140C) and finish the turn in a good traverse position, ready for the next turn (picture 140D). Make a series of turns to gain confidence.

When you feel you can make good down-unweighted turns, seek out an intermediate-grade powder slope and practice making smooth, round turns, down-unweighting at the start of each turn and returning to a neutral position between turns.

Once you feel comfortable down-unweighting, you will have an additional means of turning in powder.

NOTES

◉◉◉ Apart from the quick down-unweighted stop turn, smooth down-unweighting generally produces long, round turns, and therefore you tend to pick up speed during this maneuver. Consequently, you should perform these turns on slopes that are not too steep.

◉◉◉ This turn can be used in most powder conditions.

BREAKABLE CRUST TURNS
(skiing on the uphill edge of the uphill ski)

Skiing breakable crust is an art, and, like any art, requires lots of practice (in addition to basic talent) to achieve a high level of accomplishment. I have

Downhill turns — using down-unweighting

already described a number of different ways of ski-ing breakable crust, namely, the stem turn, the jet turn, and the jump turn. Another way to ski the breakable crust is to make the turns on the inside edge of the inside ski so that you are always skiing on the uphill edge of the uphill ski. (For an understanding of inside/outside ski, refer to Figure 3 and picture sequence 32C-F, page 48.)

The advantage of skiing in this manner is that you can maintain a constant rhythm and make smooth turns while limiting the risk of catching the outside edge in the crust. Because this maneuver is almost acrobatic —it requires very good balance and precise edge control — it is best to first learn the previously mentioned techniques of initiating turns on this type of snow surface. When you have had enough experience skiing breakable crust, so that it is no longer menacing, you should practice turning

on the uphill edge of the uphill ski on a packed slope. Refer back to pages 102–105 and practice exercises 1A, 1B, 1C, 2A and 3A.

Once you have mastered these exercises and can ski and turn on the uphill edge of the uphill ski on the packed slopes, you can practice on the packed slopes making parallel turns on this uphill edge with your skis held together.

A) Downhill turns on the inside edge of the inside ski
1) Turns on packed slopes **PHOTOS 141A-D**
Start skiing in a traverse position on an intermediate-grade packed slope with your weight on the uphill edge of the uphill ski (picture 141A).

SPECIAL TIP
◎ On the packed slopes, your weight should be over the middle of your uphill foot. When you perform

Turns on packed slopes

2) Turns in powder   PHOTOS 142A-D

When you can perform this maneuver on a packed slope, practice turning in shallow powder.

SPECIAL TIP

◎ Assume the powder position, so that your weight is over your heels.

3) Turns on breakable crust   PHOTOS 143A-C

When you can perform this maneuver in the powder, seek out a gentle slope of breakable crust and practice turning in control. Position your body so that your weight has moved back toward your heels in order to keep your ski tips lightly weighted.

When you can safely and confidently ski down this slope, seek out an intermediate-grade slope of breakable crust and perform the same maneuver. Picture sequence 143A-C demonstrates how this turn can be used to ski tricky windblown, breakable crust confidently. Once you can link a series of smooth turns, skiing in complete control, you can venture off into the out-of-bounds areas knowing that you are capable of skiing any condition you may encounter.

SPECIAL TIPS

◎ This maneuver is generally skied quite dynamically, using short-radius turns so that the end of one turn is the start of the next turn. Because breakable crust is so inconsistent, it is best to push off the edge as soon as possible after crossing the fall-line, riding the edge only as long as is necessary to complete the turn.

◎ Try to keep your feet and legs well inclined toward the mountain at the start and end of the turn so that your skis are extensively edged and you don't catch the outside edge.

◎ Your ski boots should fit as snugly as possible so that your skis respond instantly to the movements of your feet.

◎ As this is a fast, delicate maneuver, it is best to use it when skiing gentle or medium-grade slope. Use the stem turn, jet turn or jump turn on steep slopes.

this on the crust, you should have your weight slightly farther backward.

When you are ready to turn, start to lower your hips and plant your downhill ski pole at your side (picure 141B). Extend up and around your ski pole, incline your turn by leaning to the inside of the turn and roll your feet and ankles aross the fall-line (picture 141C). Complete the turn with your weight on the new uphill edge, your hips and knees relaxed and your shins well edged toward the mountain (picture 141D), and ski to a stop.

Repeat this maneuver to the opposite side and when it feels comfortable doing this to both sides, link a series of turns down the fall-line, skiing from the uphill edge of one ski to the uphill edge of the other.

Turns on breakable crust

Turns in powder

THE FINAL WORD

In the Introduction, I stated that the ultimate goal of this book is to help you reach a level of competence that enables you to safely ski every type of snow and slope that you may encounter.

Through the years I've accumulated a great deal of information and a number of ski tips that make skiing easier, and I have tried to pass these on to you as clearly as possible.

In Section II I've explained how to ski on shaped skis, using their design and shape to make the turns with minimum effort. Though these turns are easier to perform on shaped skis, they can also be made on traditional skis.

In Sections III and IV, I've described all those advanced skiing maneuvers which I feel will help you to become a more proficient skier. I do not profess to have explained every last way of initiating a turn, as there are many personalized skiing styles.

In describing powder turns, I haven't discussed a turn once taught in Japan as the porpoise turn, nor what I call the "windshield wiper" technique in which one sits well back against the backs of the boots and flicks the ski tips across the fall-line. Instead, in Section Five I've limited myself to describing the turns that I feel are the most useful to aspiring powder and off-piste skiers. With these turns you should be able to have fun, be safe, and confidently ski anywhere your fancy takes you.

Whereas a poet would try to capture in descriptive and evocative phrases the joys of skiing the off-piste, far from the lifts and crowded slopes, and thus share them with you, I have tried, via the many ski exercises, photographs, and explanations, to teach you the skills you need so that you can experience those joys yourself.

All the topics contained in this book are covered in the "Ski Tips" video series. By studying the book and watching the demonstrations on the videos, you will accelerate your learning experiences.

Copies of the "SKI TIPS" videos
can be obtained from:
Martin Heckelman and Co.
215 Commonwealth Ave.
Massapequa, NY 11758 USA
Tel/Fax: (516) 798-9059
e-mail: mheckelman@aol.com
Website: www.skitips.com

SKI TIPS 1 — Parallel skiing made easy
SKI TIPS 2 — Advanced skiing made easy
SKI TIPS 3 — Powder skiing made easy
SKI TIPS 4 — Mogul skiing made easy
SKI TIPS 5 — Skiing with shaped skis made easy

All the videos are approximately 60 minutes.
Information about ski clinics with Martin Heckelman
can be obtained by contacting the address listed above.

W9-BNS-522

THE *STAR WARS* LIBRARY
PUBLISHED BY DEL REY BOOKS

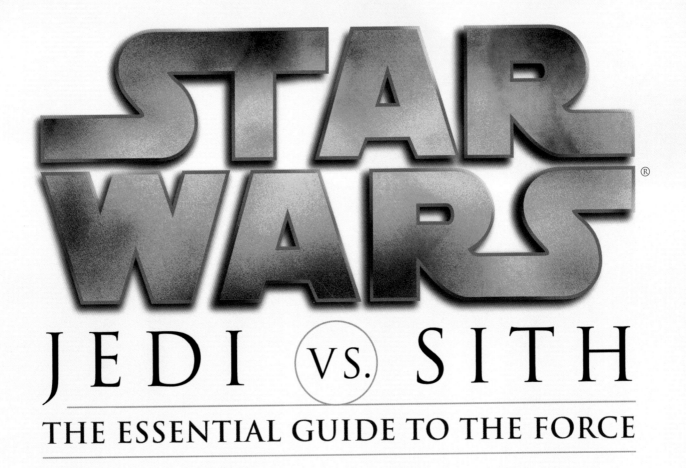

STAR WARS

JEDI vs. SITH

THE ESSENTIAL GUIDE TO THE FORCE

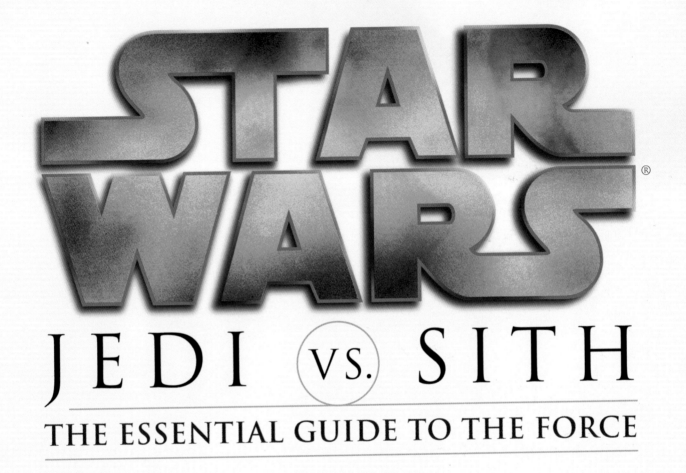

STAR WARS

JEDI vs. SITH

THE ESSENTIAL GUIDE TO THE FORCE

RYDER WINDHAM

ILLUSTRATED THROUGHOUT BY
CHRIS TREVAS AND TOMMY LEE EDWARDS

BALLANTINE BOOKS
NEW YORK

▲ MACE WINDU *(Trevas)*

A Del Rey Books Trade Paperback Original

Copyright © 2007 Lucasfilm Ltd. & ® or ™ where indicated.
All Rights Reserved. Used under authorization.

Published in the United States by Del Rey Books, an imprint of The Random House Publishing Group,
a division of Random House, Inc., New York.

DEL REY is a registered trademark and the Del Rey colophon is a trademark of Random House, Inc.

ISBN 978-0-345-49334-7

Printed in the United States of America

www.starwars.com
www.delreybooks.com

9 8 7 6 5 4 3 2 1

Interior design by Foltz Design

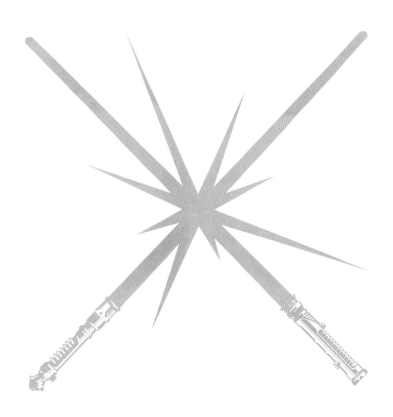

AUTHOR'S ACKNOWLEDGMENTS

The Essential Guide to the Force could not have been assembled without a number of very essential people. Thanks to Keith Clayton, Erich Schoeneweiss, and Brad Foltz at Del Rey; Jonathan Rinzler, Sue Rostoni, Troy Alders, and Leland Chee at Lucasfilm; artists supreme Tommy Lee Edwards and Chris Trevas; and Jean-François Boivin, Abel Peña, and Daniel Wallace of the *Star Wars* Fanboy Association.

This book draws information and dialogue from many *Star Wars* novels, comics, games, and reference books as well the movies and animated cartoons. Thanks to the writers Alice Alfonsi, Aaron Allston, Kevin J. Anderson, Greg Bear, W. Haden Blackman, Craig R. Carey, Andy Collins, Troy Denning, William C. Dietz, Chris Doyle, Mary Jo Duffy, Jason Fry, Jeff Grubb, Pablo Hidalgo, David S. J. Hodgson, Michael Allen Horne, Peet Janes, Drew Karpyshyn, Ann Margaret Lewis, James Luceno, James Maliszewski, Patrick McLaughlin, Zach Meston, David Michelinie, Michael Mikaelian, Steve Miller, Morrie Mullins, John Ostrander, Abel G. Peña, Steve Perry, Jeff Quick, David West Reynolds, Stephen J. Sansweet, Curtis Saxton, Juan Schwartz, Peter Schweighofer, Bill Slavicsek, L. Neil Smith, Michael A. Stackpole, Owen K. C. Stephens, Matthew Stover, Paul Sudlow, John Terra, Rodney Thompson, Karen Traviss, Daniel Wallace (again!), Jude Watson, Robert Wiese, JD Wiker, Tom Veitch, and Timothy Zahn.

For reasons that need no explanation, special thanks to George Lucas, Ralph McQuarrie, and Joe Johnston.

◄ JEDI MASTER YODA.
(Edwards)

▲ JEDI MASTER YARAEL POOF. *(Edwards)*

CONTENTS

EXIS STATION ▲
(Edwards)

INTRODUCTION

Recorded 40 A.B.Y.

Jedi. Hear the words of Tionne Solusar.
It is a dire time.

The Jedi Master Mara Jade Skywalker is dead, killed by an assassin's toxic dart. Abandoning patience and meditation, Luke Skywalker, Mara's husband and current head of the Jedi Order, confronted and killed the primary suspect, Lumiya, the self-proclaimed Dark Lady of the Sith. Afterward, Luke learned that Lumiya's confirmed movements precluded her from being the assassin. Now focus has shifted to the former Jedi Knight Alema Rar, a possible apprentice of Lumiya. While it remains conceivable that Lumiya was an accomplice in Mara's death, the possibility of her innocence has further devastated Luke and divided the Jedi Order.

All Jedi feel the loss of Mara Jade Skywalker, but we are not united by grief. Recent events involving our role in Galactic Alliance policy have prompted many Jedi to question the fabric of our Order, which is strong enough to be considered a threat by outside factions, yet so delicate that it can still be torn from within. Suspicions have led to accusations, and guilt has mixed with anguish to poison our spirits. Despite all the battles that we've fought and won, it seems our greatest enemy is—and always has been—ourselves.

Because Lumiya was trained in the ways of the Sith and has yet to be ruled out as an accessory to Mara's death, some Jedi have come to me with specific questions about Sith history and practices, hoping that such knowledge might help to identify and capture Mara's killer. Many believe that this is a time for urgent action, but it would be negligent of me to hastily divulge answers about the Sith with-

out providing relevant information about the Jedi, as it would seem that the destinies of these two groups will almost always be intertwined.

Younger students, be aware that a great deal of our history has at least twice been lost through the machinations of the Sith: first at the destruction of the original Jedi Temple on Ossus, and second when Emperor Palpatine seized the Jedi Archives on Coruscant. It was no coincidence that the Sith were responsible for both incidents, for their hatred of the Jedi has been established for many thousands of years. However, it should be noted that galactic academia regards these as minor losses compared with the devastation wrought on the library world Obroa-skai, which the Yuuzhan Vong invaded and scoured clean.

Although our knowledge of the Sith remains limited, it is widely agreed that their goal is to eliminate not only the Jedi but all evidence of our existence as well, or at least disgrace our legacy. Because of the possible temptation of the dark side of the Force, the majority of contemporary Jedi have long maintained that ignorance of Sith history and teachings is for the best. This belief is not without merit, as nearly every Jedi who has studied Sith Holocrons and relics has been drawn into darkness. However, belief is not the same thing as knowledge, and by deliberately avoiding comprehension of that which we refuse to understand, we confine ourselves to a darkness of our own design.

Given the Sith's historic propensity to attack, vanish, then reemerge after long periods, it's disturbing that so many Jedi believed the death of Palpatine brought an end to the Sith threat. Likewise, many were subsequently astonished by the return of Lumiya. Despite all concerns regarding the dark side, recent events serve as conclusive proof that ignorance is *not* the solution. As for the current status of the Sith Order, there is no evidence to substantiate that it died with Lumiya on the planet Terephon.

All chroniclers must hope, if not believe, that they will be survived by their recorded accounts and narratives. Had Jedi of yore known with utmost certainty that many of their struggles and achievements would be forgotten and erased, one can only imagine whether they might have chosen different paths, and how those paths would have affected galactic history. I can only speculate how my own work will be perceived in the future, but I consider it my responsibility to ensure that our legacy *will* survive to enable future generations, and *not* be confiscated or obliterated.

Although this historic record may lack objectivity, I do not intend to glorify the Jedi or vilify the Sith, but to present a cohesive account of our origins and encounters, and illustrate our similarities and differences. Our histories are not separate but dangerously entwined, like two branches on a tree that threaten to break each other in their respective attempts to embrace sunlight and shadow. Some have speculated whether the Jedi and Sith can even exist without each other, and most doubt that there will ever be a peaceful resolution to their eternal conflict.

While many aspects of the Sith Order may forever remain a mystery, of this I am certain: as long as Sith knowledge exists, so, too, will the Sith and their pretenders. Furthermore, the Sith know more about the Jedi than we do about them, and unless we examine the history of the Jedi vs. the Sith, the Jedi will remain at a disadvantage.

I must trust that you will use this knowledge wisely and without malice. Under ordinary circumstances, I would urge patience as you study and contemplate this material, but I am compelled to remind you that these are not ordinary times.

It is a very real possibility that Mara Jade Skywalker's killer is not only still at large, but also a Sith.

INTERIOR OF THE JEDI ARCHIVES AT THE ▲
JEDI TEMPLE ON CORUSCANT. *(Trevas)*

TIME LINE

As long as sentient beings have attempted to measure time, there have been disputes over the times by which one measures. The complicated history of the Jedi and the Sith incorporates ancient records from numerous worlds, which—depending on when they were created or whether the creators were citizens of the Old Republic—may or may not have adopted Standard Time Parts as units of measure.

It was the Historical Council of the Galactic Federation of Free Alliances that officially established and popularized the Battle of Yavin as the zero point to mark the beginning of our current society. Despite protests from some younger generations who maintain that subsequent battles were more significant, most educated beings agree that the Battle of Yavin was a hugely pivotal moment in galactic history. In keeping with the conventions established by the Historical Council, the following time line employs Standard Time Parts that hinge Before the Battle of Yavin (B.B.Y.) and After the Battle of Yavin (A.B.Y.).

c. 100,000 B.B.Y.	Dawn of Sith civilization on the planet Korriban.
c. 30,000 B.B.Y.	**The Force-using Rakata tunnel through hyperspace to claim their modest "Infinite Empire."**
c. 28,000 B.B.Y.	Sith ruler King Adas unifies the Sith nations on Korriban.
c. 27,700 B.B.Y.	King Adas defeats the Rakatan invaders and gains Holocron technology; The Sith relocate their capital to the planet Ziost, and Korriban is designated their tombworld.
c. 25,200 B.B.Y.	Rakatan Infinite Empire implodes.
c. 25,000 B.B.Y.	Formation of the Galactic Republic. Creation of the Jedi Order.
24,500 B.B.Y.	First Great Schism: the Legions of Lettow, a faction of Jedi Knights led by General Xendor, rebel against the Jedi Order.

7003 B.B.Y.	Second Great Schism: Dark Jedi declare themselves free from the Jedi Council.
7000 B.B.Y.	Dark Jedi rebel against the Jedi Order; the Hundred-Year Darkness begins.
6900 B.B.Y.	The Hundred-Year Darkness ends with the Battle of Corbos; surviving Dark Jedi, known as the Exiles, are banished to an uncharted region of the Outer Rim Territories and conquer the Sith species to become Sith Lords. A few Sith Lords return to Republic space in a failed effort to conquer the Jedi, but succeed only in revealing that their fellow Exiles have taken control of a region called Sith space, the location of which will remain unknown to the Jedi until the Fall of the Sith Empire.
5000 B.B.Y.	**Jedi Odan-Urr has a vision of the death of Marka Ragnos, the Dark Lord of the Sith, whose passing instigates a schism between rival Sith Lords Naga Sadow and Ludo Kressh.**

The Great Hyperspace War.
Fall of the Sith Empire; Sith Lord Garu dies, losing King Adas's Sith Holocron on the planet Ashas Ree; Odan Urr recovers a different Sith Holocron from the wreckage of Sith Lord Naga Sadow's ship. Naga Sadow arrives on Yavin 4.

4400 B.B.Y. Jedi Freedon Nadd awakens Naga Sadow's spirit and discovers King Adas's Sith Holocron, which he uses to conquer the planet Onderon.

4250 B.B.Y. The Vultar Cataclysm (Dark Jedi annihilate the entire Vultar planetary system).

4200 B.B.Y. The Sith-inspired Mecrosa Order is founded on the planet Nyssa.

3997 B.B.Y. Jedi Exar Kun and Jedi Ulic Qel-Droma become Sith Lords.

3996 B.B.Y. The Sith War; Exar Kun kills Jedi Odan-Urr and takes a Sith Holocron, then kills Jedi Master Vodo-Siosk Baas, gatekeeper of the Tedryn Holocron; Ulic Qel-Droma is stripped of his Force powers; Exar Kun's spirit becomes trapped on Yavin 4.

3993 B.B.Y. The Great Hunt.

3986 B.B.Y. Ulic Qel-Droma dies.

3976 B.B.Y. Mandalorian Wars begin.

3964 B.B.Y. **The Jedi Covenant hunts down Zayne Carrick, hoping to prevent the return of the Sith.**

3961 B.B.Y. Jedi Civil War; Darth Revan and Darth Malak become the new Dark Lords of the Sith.

c. 3956 B.B.Y. Jedi Master and historian Atris amasses a collection of Sith Holocrons at the Telosian Jedi Academy.

3951 B.B.Y. Sith Civil War; Darth Traya attempts to bring an end to the Jedi and Sith Orders.

2000 B.B.Y. Jedi Master Phanius abandons the Jedi Order and becomes the Sith Lord Darth Ruin; Rise of the New Sith.

1000 B.B.Y. New Sith Wars; Battle of Ruusan; Darth Bane's New Sith Order institutes the tradition of the Rule of Two Sith Lords, a Master and an apprentice.

896 B.B.Y. Birth of Yoda.

c. 600 B.B.Y. Jedi Bodo Baas, a descendant of Jedi Vodo-Siosk Baas, inherits the Tedryn Holocron.

132 B.B.Y. **The Jedi Order expels Jedi Leor Hal, founder of the Potentium, a group maintaining that the Force is inherently good and without a dark side.**

102 b.b.y.   Count Dooku born.

92 b.b.y.   Qui-Gon Jinn born.

72 b.b.y.   **Mace Windu born.**

57 b.b.y.   Obi-Wan Kenobi born.

54 b.b.y.   Darth Maul born.

46 b.b.y.   Padmé Amidala born.

44 b.b.y.   Battle at Galidraan.
Qui-Gon Jinn takes Obi-Wan
as his Padawan.

41 b.b.y.   Anakin Skywalker born.

32.5 b.b.y.   Amidala elected Queen of Naboo.

32 b.b.y.   Return of the Sith: Darth Maul;
Deaths of Qui-Gon Jinn and Darth Maul;
Senator Palpatine elected Supreme
Chancellor; Count Dooku leaves the
Jedi Order.

30 b.b.y.   Mace Windu dispatches Jedi Vergere to
the Gardaji Rift; Vergere is captured by the
Yuuzhan Vong.

27 b.b.y.   Jedi Master Yarael Poof dies.

26 b.b.y.   **Jedi Master
Yaddle dies.**

23 b.b.y.   Jedi Quinlan Vos retrieves the Sith Holocron
of Darth Andeddu for Count Dooku.

22 b.b.y.   Count Dooku informs the Jedi that the
Senate is being manipulated by a Sith Lord;
the Clone Wars begin; secret wedding of
Anakin Skywalker and Padmé Amidala.

19 b.b.y.   Death of Dooku;
The Jedi Purge; Palpatine
executes Jedi Master
Ashka Boda and seizes
the Tedryn Holocron;
**Anakin Skywalker
becomes Darth
Vader.**

Creation of the Galactic Empire;
Death of Amidala; Birth of Luke Skywalker
and Leia Organa; Obi-Wan and Yoda go
into hiding; Mecrosa agent Sir Nevil Tritum
recovers King Adas's Sith Holocron.

18 B.B.Y. Darth Vader begins training a secret
apprentice.

17 B.B.Y. Birth of Mara Jade.

0 A.B.Y. Obi-Wan Kenobi introduces Luke Skywalker
to the Force; Luke and Leia meet, but are
initially unaware of their kinship;
Battle of Yavin.

4 A.B.Y. Battle of Endor.
Deaths of Emperor Palpatine and Anakin
Skywalker.
Foundation of the New Republic.
A revived Mecrosa Order gives Sith Lord
Adas's Holocron to Lumiya.

5 A.B.Y. Dark Jedi Jerec and his followers are
defeated by Force-sensitive Republic agent
Kyle Katarn.

8 A.B.Y. Marriage of Leia Organa and Han Solo.

9 A.B.Y. Jaina and Jacen Solo are born to Leia
Organa and Han Solo.

10 A.B.Y. **Palpatine is resurrected as a clone;**
Leia takes the Jedi Tedryn Holocron from
Palpatine.

10+ A.B.Y. Luke discovers Force-sensitive Ysanna on
Ossus; death of Jedi Ood Bnar; Anakin Solo
is born to Leia Organa and
Han Solo; Death of Palpatine's clone.

11 A.B.Y. The Jedi academy established on Yavin 4;
the Tedryn Holocron is destroyed, Exar Kun's
spirit incapacitated.

14 A.B.Y. The spirit of Sith Lord Marka Ragnos inspires
a Sith cult, but is defeated by Jedi trainee
Jaden Korr, a student of Kyle Katarn.

19 A.B.Y. Marriage of Mara Jade and Luke Skywalker.

22 A.B.Y. A Jedi [Tionne?] recovers Obi-Wan Kenobi's
lightsaber and the Holocron of Jedi Master

Asli Krimsan on Vjun.

25 A.B.Y. Yuuzhan Vong War begins.

26.5 A.B.Y. Ben Skywalker is born to Mara and Luke
Skywalker.

27 A.B.Y. Anakin Solo dies on Myrkr.

28 A.B.Y. Yuuzhan Vong War ends; establishment of
new Jedi Council, which includes politicians.

35–36 A.B.Y. Allana is born to Jacen Solo and Tenel Ka;
the Jedi Council severs ties with political
entities, becomes the Masters' Council; the
Jedi academy relocates to Ossus.

40 A.B.Y. Death of Mara Jade Skywalker;
Death of Lumiya, the Dark Lady of the Sith;
Recovery of the alleged Great Holocron and
Telos Holocron.

PART ONE

HISTORY AND HOLOCRONS

RECORDED 40 A.B.Y. · AUTHOR: TIONNE SOLUSAR

The Jedi Order was founded more than twenty-five thousand standard years ago, at the same time as the formation of the Galactic Republic. Although the origins of the early Jedi remain mysterious, ancient texts indicate that they not only shared abilities to manipulate the energy field we call the Force, but were also compelled to use their powers selflessly to help others. This practice became a key foundation of the Jedi Order.

However, as long as there have been Jedi, there have been those who have been tempted to use the Force for selfish and even nefarious purposes; Jedi drawn into the negative side of the Force known as the dark side became referred to as Dark Jedi. Approximately seven thousand years ago, a conflict between Jedi and Dark Jedi led to the latter fleeing to the far reaches of space. Shortly afterward, a few of these Dark Jedi—known as the Exiles—managed to return to Republic space in an attempt to destroy the Jedi. The effort failed, and the Jedi learned that the surviving Exiles had conquered the people of the Sith system and proclaimed themselves Sith Lords.

For nearly two thousand years, the location of the Sith system remained unknown to the Jedi, while the Sith Lords were unable to find their way back to Republic space. The Sith's eventual return initiated what became known as the Great Hyperspace War. It was during a subsequent conflict—the Sith War, which occurred more than four thousand

years ago—that the Sith triggered the explosion of ten suns, causing a shock wave that ravaged the original Jedi Temple and the Great Jedi Library on Ossus. Research has revealed that the Jedi rescued only a fraction of the materials from the Great Jedi Library, and that these items were brought to Exis Station before they were eventually transferred to the Jedi Temple on Coruscant.

Fortunately, all was not lost on Ossus, as the planet's remote location, dry atmosphere, and native Ysanna—descendants of the Jedi who remained on Ossus after the cataclysmic disaster—helped preserve many ancient scrolls and books that remained in the ruins of the library. These texts, along with all known Jedi-related data that survived the Clone Wars, are now held at the new Jedi library on Ossus.

Contemporary Jedi also have two very unusual resources on the history of the Sith: *The Lundi Series,* recorded lectures of Professor Murk Lundi, who was by most accounts a better teacher than researcher; and the Wavlud Manuscript, which was recovered from the personal effects of Ingo Wavlud, a suspected Sith sympathizer from the world of Byss. Although *The Lundi Series* frequently fails to cite specific sources and some data appears to have been invented by Lundi to boost his academic reputation, the heavily annotated Wavlud Manuscript not only corroborates many of Lundi's findings but also provides previously

◀ DARK LORD OF THE SITH NAGA SADOW DIRECTING MASSASSI TO CONSTRUCT TEMPLES ON YAVIN IV *(Edwards)*

unknown information regarding the *Darth* title and the Sith Lord Darth Sidious.

THE HOLOCRONS

The most precious and significant sources of Jedi history are held in Jedi Holocrons. Both compact repositories of knowledge and interactive learning devices, Holocrons employ patterns of organic crystals and hologrammic technology to simulate conversation with long-dead Jedi "gatekeepers," whose teachings infuse particular Holocrons. With few exceptions, Jedi Holocrons are cubes that can easily be held in one's hand. Evidently, Holocrons are partially powered by the Force, as only Force-users can activate them; once activated, anyone—even non-Force-users—can communicate with the gatekeepers. However, not all data is readily ac-

cessible, because Holocrons are engineered to detect students' abilities in order to hold back elements they are not prepared to know.

In addition to the exotic Holocrons, Jedi utilized standard data tapes for some educational aspects. Data tapes lack the archival qualities of books, scrolls, and Holocrons, but it is most fortunate that some have survived, as they've provided many details about the training of Jedi during the Old Republic era. Nearly all of the existing tapes were recovered from a single source: the wreck of the *Chu'unthor,* a mobile training academy for groups of Jedi apprentices, which crashed more than three centuries ago on Dathomir.

Records also indicate that the Jedi Archives on Coruscant once held a collection of Sith Holocrons, most of which were pyramidical and—because they housed information that was dangerous in the wrong hands—off limits to the majority of Jedi.

Like Jedi Holocrons, Sith Holocrons implement restrictive mechanisms to detect whether a student is prepared to receive certain knowledge. The Sith's hologrammic simulacra can exert only verbal influence, but allegedly attempted to corrupt otherwise innocent beings and draw "students" down the path to the dark side. The Jedi Order's earliest known awareness of Sith Holocrons dates back to the end of the Great Hyperspace War, when one was recovered from an abandoned Sith ship by the Jedi Odan-Urr. Odan-Urr kept this Sith Holocron for nearly a millennium before it was stolen by the Jedi Exar Kun, who used it to learn many secrets of the Sith. It is also highly probable that at least one Jedi with the knowledge of Holocron construction was among the Exiles who proclaimed themselves the first Sith Lords.

Although the Jedi once regarded Sith Holocrons as tools and not evil entities, the devices are embodiments of temptation to those who hope to achieve power by way of arcane knowledge. During the Clone Wars, the former Jedi Count Dooku—at the time, one of only twenty Jedi Masters known to have renounced the Jedi Order—stole at least one Sith Holocron from the Archives on Coruscant and also acquired the Sith Holocron of Darth Andeddu. Like Exar Kun, Count Dooku became a Sith Lord; while it is conceivable that the respective experiences and personality traits of both individuals guided their paths to the dark side, the possession of Sith Holocrons certainly directed their courses as well. Records do not reveal the fate of the Sith Holocrons used by Exar Kun and Count Dooku.

Various databases and eyewitnesses testify that the Jedi Archives on Coruscant held scores of Jedi Holocrons. Unfortunately, the ancient technology of the Holocrons, as well as the majority of the devices themselves, may be lost to time. Because Holocrons have been such a significant resource in the creation of this record, descriptions of noteworthy Holocrons precede a detailed time line of events in Jedi and Sith history.

THE TEDRYN HOLOCRON

Leia Organa Solo discovered the existence of Jedi Holocrons during the events of Palpatine's resurrection, six years after the Battle of Endor. After being captured by Palpatine and detained at his citadel on the planet Byss, Leia escaped with a Jedi Holocron—by all appearances a milky jade crystal block—that Palpatine claimed had been given to him by an aged Jedi Master. Subsequent research eventually determined that the Jedi Master was Ashka Boda, who was slain by Palpatine during the Jedi Purge at the end of the Clone Wars.

This Holocron's primary hologrammic gatekeeper was the Jedi Bodo Baas, who'd served in the Adega system six hundred years earlier. Via the Holocron, Bodo Baas revealed many details of the history of the Jedi, including the saga of Exar Kun and his contemporary, the Jedi Ulic Qel-Droma, who also turned to the dark side. Shortly after Leia first activated the Holocron, Bodo Baas recited a prophecy that had been written by his own Master a thousand years earlier:

A brother and sister born to walk the sky,
But reckless brother falls into Dark Side's eye!
Jedi sister carries hope for future in her
* womb.*
Only she can save the Skywalkers from certain
* doom!*
A Jedi-killer wants to tame her.
Now the Dark Side Lord comes to claim her.
She must battle join against this thief,
Or the dynasty of all the Jedi will come to
* grief!*

Leia had no reason to doubt the veracity of the prophecy, for it described her then current

circumstances: Palpatine, the "Jedi-killer," wanted to convert Leia and her expected child to the dark side, while Luke Skywalker had embraced the power of the dark side in an effort to conquer Palpatine. Fortunately, Luke eventually realized that he could not defeat Palpatine alone, and the Dark Lord ultimately failed to seduce Leia or any of her children. Because the Holocron contained other prophecies as well as seemingly infinite data about the Jedi, its value was incalculable.

Although this particular Holocron was sometimes referred to as the Jedi Holocron or Holocron of Bodo Baas, it should be noted that Bodo Baas was merely the last of a long line of Jedi who left their impressions within the device. Originally, it was known as the Tedryn Holocron, named for the Jedi Master Tedryn, who may have been the Holocron's maker as well as its first keeper. More than four thousand years ago, the Tedryn Holocron was kept by Jedi Master Vodo-Siosk Baas, an ancestor of Bodo Baas and the former teacher of Exar Kun. The Holocron not only stored Vodo-Siosk Baas's knowledge but apparently enabled his hologrammic simulacrum to draw from the knowledge of subsequent gatekeepers as well. According to Luke Skywalker, who was the last to converse with this Holocron, Master Vodo's hologram told him, "Exar Kun destroyed me. He slew his own Master."

One might think such a statement could be made only by a spirit or supernatural technology, but holograms are merely recordings of personalities, not thinking beings that can be manipulated by the Force. Although Holocron personalities rarely adapt to requests and problems outside their areas of knowledge, it is assumed that Vodo-Siosk Baas's hologram could relate "his own" demise by accessing data that was later inserted by his descendant Bodo Baas.

To limit confusion over Vodo-Siosk Baas and Bodo Baas, and also to honor their predecessor, this Holocron has long been referred to as the Tedryn Holocron, albeit in the past tense, because it was

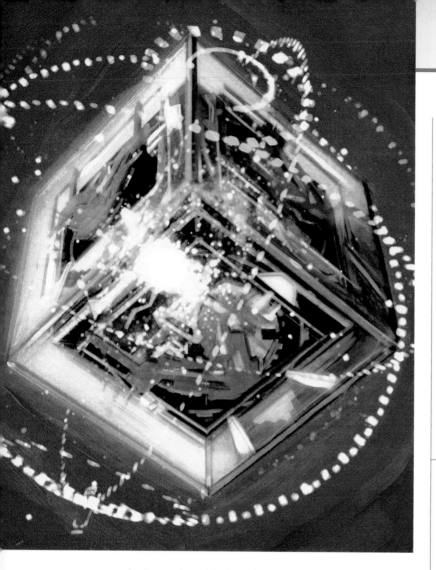

the artifact's uniqueness that hastened my activity; I shuddered at the possibility that the gatekeepers' voices might someday be forever silenced. If my fear was a premonition, I regret that I was not more heedful, for it was only a matter of months before the Tedryn Holocron was destroyed by Exar Kun's spirit, which had long been dormant in the ruins of Yavin 4. Although I suspect I'd barely tapped the Tedryn Holocron, it did yield an enormous amount of information about the origins of the Jedi and Sith and their earliest conflicts. Other Jedi who studied the Tedryn Holocron provided additional data and recollections. Fortunately, the transcriptions and copied data are well maintained at the new Jedi library.

destroyed on Yavin 4 by the resurrected spirit of the Sith Lord Exar Kun.

ADDENDUM BY
TIONNE SOLUSAR

It was in the year following Leia's recovery of the Tedryn Holocron that I joined Luke Skywalker's Jedi academy—then called the praxeum—on Yavin 4. There I began studying the Holocron and transcribing its data with a sense of urgency. Aside from my obvious interest in historic preservation, I cannot entirely explain my almost desperate motivation to comprehend and record its contents on data tapes and holograms. At the time, I convinced myself that it was

THE ASLI KRIMSAN HOLOCRON

Eleven years after the destruction of the Tedryn Holocron, a mission to Bast Castle—once Darth Vader's personal fortress on the planet Vjun—yielded two relics: the lightsaber Obi-Wan Kenobi used in his duel with Vader on the first Death Star, and the Holocron of Jedi Master Asli Krimsan.

Krimsan was a humanoid female with more than two hundred years of teaching experience at the Jedi Temple on Coruscant. It remains unknown how the Holocron that she maintained came into Darth Vader's possession. Although the Asli Krimsan Holocron was primarily conceived for the education of young Jedi, it also contains information on a wide range of ancient events, including tales of the Jedi Knights of the Old Republic and their battles against the Sith. Because Vader's few records make no mention of Asli Krimsan, we can only guess why this particular device was kept at Bast Castle.

THE GREAT HOLOCRON

Overcoming numerous obstacles, the new Jedi Order recovered a dodecahedron Holocron that some Jedi maintain is the Great Holocron, believed to have been lost during the Jedi Purge. Because of this Holocron's uncertain provenance, one cannot dismiss the possibility that it is an extremely well-crafted replica. If it *is* a reproduction, it seems likely that it was created by a Force-sensitive being, as it is inaccessible to all others.

Questions of authenticity aside, this Holocron has provided a staggering amount of information, most of which is profoundly enlightening. Because the Empire destroyed or twisted so many historic resources, verification of the data is sometimes a painstaking process, but eyewitness narratives have helped separate many facts from legends, myths, and outright lies. A computer analysis could not determine the full scope of this Holocron's knowledge, which seems multidimensional and limitless. Unless a contrary origin is revealed by yet-to-be-discovered evidence, this device shall henceforth be referred to as the Great Holocron.

THE TELOS HOLOCRON AND DARTH ANDEDDU'S HOLOCRON

Shortly after the recovery of the Great Holocron, a very different Holocron was discovered on the planet Telos. Although this Holocron is not pyramidal and has no external markings or glyphs, it is unquestionably of Sith origin. Because it may contain previously unknown information about the Sith, this Holocron may prove useful as well as valuable.

A clear crystal is set within the Telos Holocron's apex, which seems to rule out the possibility that it could be Darth Andeddu's Holocron, a description of which was recorded by the Jedi Master Quinlan Vos, who operated as a secret agent during the Clone Wars to infiltrate the Confederacy of Independent Systems. The Clone Wars had been raging for sixteen months when Vos recovered the Holocron from the planet Korriban and delivered it to CIS leader and former Jedi Count Dooku. One month later, at a time when the Jedi still only suspected that Dooku might be a Sith Lord, Vos returned to the Jedi Temple on Coruscant and made the following holocube statement:

give him *"access to the long-dead wisdom of Darth Andeddu, the wisdom and the power of the Sith."* Dooku hasn't told me what he plans to do with this knowledge, but I doubt it's for anything good.

When I held the Holocron, I couldn't feel any obvious release mechanism, but Dooku seemed to know just how to open it, or certainly didn't have any problem doing so. The upper part of the Holocron held a red crystal that—according to Dooku— once powered Darth Andeddu's lightsaber. Dooku gave the crystal to me, told me to use it to power my own lightsaber. Aside from making the blade blaze red, I can't say that the crystal has any other effect. My weapon cuts like it always has.

Still, the way Dooku popped open the Sith Holocron, it seems likely that he had previous experience. Maybe someone in Archives should look into his background a bit more, and also find out if there's anything on Darth Andeddu.

Count Dooku told me that the Holocron had been constructed by an old Sith Lord named Darth Andeddu. I've never touched a Sith Holocron before, but this one didn't feel anything like a Jedi Holocron. It's not just that it's shaped like a pyramid and its surface was etched with unusual markings, apparently Sith hieroglyphs and incantations. The Holocron felt hot and cold at the same time, and I sensed something malevolent about the energy that charged the thing. I only held it briefly, but it made me feel uneasy, even a little queasy. Dooku said the Holocron would

Records indicate that Count Dooku first learned about the existence of Sith Holocrons at age thirteen, shortly after he became the Padawan to Jedi Master Thame Cerulian. Evidently, Dooku and fellow Jedi apprentice Lorian Nod were uninvited when they entered Cerulian's quarters and discovered a datapad that contained information about a Sith Holocron in the Archives. Nod stole the Holocron, but his deed was discovered, and he was conscripted into the Agricultural Corps. Despite the rumors that Dooku studied Sith Holocrons in the years that followed, his actions as a Jedi did not betray any leanings toward the dark side until the Clone Wars, when he revealed himself to be a Sith Lord.

It is probable that Dooku's previous experience and his subsequent conversion to the Sith enabled him to access the Holocron of Darth Andeddu. There has been no account of the Holocron of

Darth Andeddu since the Clone Wars, and as with Quinlan Vos himself its fate remains unknown. However, the Asli Krimsan Holocron has yielded some information about Darth Andeddu, who may have been the first of numerous Sith Lords with the honorific *Darth*.

ADDENDUM BY
KAM SOLUSAR

Because the rediscovery of the alleged Great Holocron almost immediately led to the discovery of the Telos Holocron, I am suspicious of both devices, and will remain so until we learn more about their histories. Because certain enemies may attempt to take the Telos Holocron, many Jedi—including nearly half of the Masters' Council—have endorsed the idea that it should be destroyed.

Despite my own cautions, I acknowledge that the Telos Holocron might contain information that will help the Jedi during any potential future dealings with the Sith, and support Luke Skywalker's decision to let Tionne study it. Luke has insisted that at least four Jedi must be present while Tionne examines both Holocrons, and that she must be simultaneously monitored by medical scanners for any indications of negative physical or psychological response.

Having conversed with the gatekeepers of the Great Holocron myself, I confess my hope that the device is genuine and that its contents are true. The scope of its knowledge is truly overwhelming. It puzzles me why the ancient Jedi poured so much data into the Great Holocron, as I doubt even the longest-lived Jedi could have ever studied it completely. I can only assume they had their reasons.

SIGNIFICANT BATTLES

Throughout history, the Jedi and Sith have nearly annihilated each other on countless occasions, only to survive, adapt, and re-form until their next encounter. In that sense, an objective scholar might think that these adversaries are more alike than most lightsaber-wielding Force-sensitives would care to admit. When one considers that renegade Jedi were responsible for founding the Sith Order, the similarities are ironic as well as logical.

While most historians inevitably compare the Jedi and Sith, the comparisons are rarely unbiased. Although individual Jedi—as well as the Order as a whole—have erred in the past, their intentions were usually regarded as noble, and their overall interest in maintaining galactic peace is rarely disputed. The Sith, however, are almost always depicted as the antagonists, insidious masters of subterfuge and sneak attacks, not only prepared but in fact eager to let innocent blood spill in order to accomplish their goals.

A most complete record of battles between Jedi and Sith can be found in the chronology prepared by Voren Na'al, archivist emeritus of the Historical Council of the Galactic Federation of Free Alliances. For this record, Jedi scholars have selected first-person narratives and eyewitness accounts that offer unique perspectives and illuminate the role of the Force in these historic confrontations. All narratives are drawn from the Great Holocron, the Asli Krimsan Holocron, and recordings of the Tedryn Holocron except where noted.

THE HUNDRED-YEAR DARKNESS

7000–6900 B.B.Y.

Author: Jedi Master Vodo-Siosk Baas, gatekeeper of the Tedryn Holocron, teacher of Exar Kun.

Long before the Great Hyperspace War delivered the Sith to the Jedi, time and again did the Jedi—divided by the light side and the dark side of the Force—cross lightsabers amongst themselves. One of these Great Schisms occurred approximately seven thousand years ago, when a group of Dark Jedi discovered that they could use the Force to transform creatures into mutant warriors, mounts, and spirit-devouring Leviathans. The war that followed lasted more than a century, left many worlds ravaged in its wake, and became known as the Hundred-Year Darkness.

The Jedi all but vanquished these Dark Jedi and their monsters, who made their last stand on the mining world of Corbos. The surviving Dark Jedi were banished to an uncharted region of space, far beyond the boundaries established by the Republic. There they discovered Korriban, a world inhabited by a primitive but Force-sensitive species called the Sith. After conquering the indigenous beings, the Dark Jedi proclaimed themselves Sith Lords. It is believed that one of the founders of the Sith Empire was the Dark Jedi Ajunta Pall.

It would be nearly two thousand years before the Sith Lords rediscovered the path to Republic space.

ADDENDUM BY
TIONNE SOLUSAR

Records indicate that Ajunta Pall, a humanoid Dark Jedi or Exile, personally slew more than a dozen Jedi at the Battle of Corbos. A survey of the Sith tombworld Korriban confirms the existence of Pall's tomb, and scientific analysis

THE DARK JEDI AJUNTA PALL ARRIVES ON ▶ THE SITH HOMEWORLD ZIOST. *(Edwards)*

places this tomb among the earliest burial sites on that planet.

Although most records indicate that lightsaber technology had, by approximately 7000 B.B.Y., progressed to weapons that required plug-in power packs attached to the users' belts, there are contradictory records about whether Jedi and Dark Jedi used lightsabers or ordinary swords during the Hundred-Year Darkness. After their defeat at Corbos, the Exiles were stripped of all their weapons before being banished to a then unexplored region in the Outer Rim Territories; because their descendants did not employ lightsabers during the Great Hyperspace War,

we can surmise that the Exiles were either unable or unwilling to create or re-create lightsaber technology in Sith space.

In the year 12 A.B.Y., the Jedi academy battled enormous creatures that had destroyed a mining colony on Corbos. It was discovered that these creatures were ancient Force-mutated Leviathans that had been abandoned by the Dark Jedi during the Battle of Corbos. Several archaeological teams have since visited Corbos; there have been no subsequent reports of Leviathans, but it is unknown if any more creatures survived beneath the planetary surface. Colonists and miners continue to avoid the world.

THE GREAT HYPERSPACE WAR

5000 B.B.Y.

Author: Jedi Master Odan-Urr, gatekeeper of the Tedryn Holocron and founder of the original Jedi library on Ossus.

Though I am both a Jedi and a historian, I confess a strange discomfort in relaying events in which I participated. It is only at the persistent urging of my students that I feel compelled to record the events of the Great Hyperspace War.

Younger Jedi, you may find this difficult to believe, but the great leaps across space that are now commonplace were not only less frequent, but far more hazardous during my own youth. It was a time when hyperspace routes were still being navigated, and many of the Core Worlds had yet to be unified. I was on a mission to the Koros system, which you now know as the Teta system, when I came to the aid of two hyperspace explorers, Gav and Jori Daragon. They were being threatened by assassins when my Master Memit Nadill and I interceded.

Days later, I was visited by a dark nightmare, a premonition that the banished Jedi of ancient times had become the Lords of the Sith Empire, and that they would soon return to Republic space. So strong was this vision that I knew it was delivered by the Force, and that I could not ignore it. My Master was an adviser to Empress Teta, and I told them both of my nightmare. They listened, and they believed.

Shortly after my premonition, Gav and Jori Daragon inadvertently arrived in Sith space and landed on the Sith tombworld of Korriban. Their arrival coincided with the funeral of the Dark Lord of the Sith Marka Ragnos, whose passing caused a feud between two rival Sith Lords: Naga Sadow, who claimed a long Sith bloodline and aspired to broaden the realm of his power, and Ludo Kressh, who was content with the holdings already controlled by the Sith Order.

The Daragons were captured, but Naga Sadow allowed Jori to escape in her starship. Why? Because he knew that she would return to Republic space, and that the tracking device he'd planted on her ship would lead them back to his ancestors' greatest enemy, the Jedi. How do I know these details? Patience, and I will tell.

Empress Teta informed the Republic Senate of my vision, but many Senators refused to heed her caution. Fortunately, the empress had unified the seven worlds of the Koros system, and the armies under her command were as loyal as they were ready to fight. Our forces were soon scattered. Empress Teta readied her troops on Koros Major while Memit Nadill joined other Jedi Knights on Coruscant. I went to Kirrek, where I'd previously fought during the Unification Wars, to serve alongside the great Jedi Master Ooroo and await the Sith.

And then the Sith came. Wave after wave of spear-wielding Sith poured out from their massive invasion fleet, some riding enormous monsters. Despite my premonition, I was surprised by the sheer viciousness of their attack. Our allies quickly dismissed the possibility of our victory, but continued to fight with great courage despite the apparent odds against us.

After much blood had been spilled, we realized that our enemy had been using illusions conjured by Naga Sadow to make themselves appear innumerable, which they

JEDI DEFEND CORUSCANT AGAINST SITH LORD ▶
NAGA SADOW'S INVASION FLEET. (Trecas)

were not. The battle turned in our favor, and the Sith retreated whence they came. However, they were mistaken in thinking they were safe. Using coordinates provided by Jori Daragon, Empress Teta's armada chased the weakened enemy back to their own shattered empire. Not surprisingly, Naga Sadow refused to surrender. Teta herself witnessed the destruction of Naga Sadow's flagship.

Master Ooroo and Gav Daragon were amongst the many casualties of the battle. Moments before he died, Ooroo told me I would become one of the most ancient Jedi ever, and that I would ultimately die among my precious books and scrolls. I am proof that his prophecy was true. Even a century before this recording, I knew of no Jedi older than I, and my eyes are still not tired of reading.

Regarding the Great Hyperspace War, the knowledge that I did not gain by experience was gleaned from three sources: the explorer Jori Daragon, who granted me several interviews; the Jedi Anavus Svag, who served in the fleet that pursued Naga Sadow back to Sith space; and a Sith Holocron that I recovered from an abandoned Sith starship on Koros Major. Locked within the recesses of this Sith Holocron—the only Sith Holocron, as far as anybody knows—are the forgotten histories and lore of the Sith, dating back a hundred thousand years and more. Both Jori Daragon and Anavus Svag are long gone, and the Holocron—because of the dangerous knowledge it contains—remains off limits to all but a few Jedi Masters.

Now, there is one piece of information from the Sith Holocron that I will share.

According to the Holocron, Naga Sadow escaped Empress Teta's assault and vanished with his followers. It is most puzzling how this information came to be on a Sith Holocron that had been abandoned on Koros Major before Naga Sadow's retreat to Sith space, but then I do not pretend to fully understand the workings of this possibly corrupt device. It is very possible that this Holocron contains an interstellar transmission receiver, the likes of which we cannot detect.

Ludo Kressh was never heard of again. If Naga Sadow survived, is it possible any Sith still exist? We know not, and we can only imagine.

But if you are visited by nightmarish visions, Jedi . . . trust me on this . . . do not dismiss them.

ADDENDUM BY
TIONNE SOLUSAR

On Korriban, the funeral of Dark Lord of the Sith Marka Ragnos is represented by ancient hieroglyphs, which show his spirit appearing before the rival Sith Lords Naga Sadow and Ludo Kressh. Of the various Sith who have demonstrated the power to transcend death, Marka Ragnos is the earliest case on record.

Naga Sadow did indeed survive the Great Hyperspace War, and escaped on his Sith flagship to Yavin 4, where he directed his Massassi warriors to construct many temples. The flagship would later be discovered and utilized by the Jedi Exar Kun, who also transformed the temples into his stronghold and assumed command of the Massassi. Although a tomb for Naga Sadow was discovered on Korriban, it remains unknown whether his body was ever moved there.

After recovering the Sith Holocron, Odan-Urr kept the device at the original Jedi library that he founded on Ossus. It is puzzling that the Sith Holocron could have contained data about Naga Sadow's escape from Empress Teta: this implies that the Holocron's contents were updated by supernatural forces. Although it is not known how extensively Odan-Urr studied the Holocron, it was in his possession for more than a millennium, and records indicate that both he and Jedi Master Vodo-Siosk Baas studied it without any adverse effect. Still, it is possible that some Holocrons may be more than mere repositories of knowledge, and that they attract evil. Because Exar Kun's desire for Sith teachings prompted him to slay Odan-Urr—who was indeed surrounded by his books at the time of his death—and seize the Sith Holocron, the devices themselves have a dangerous reputation that seems well deserved.

It is unfortunate that Odan-Urr is remembered less for his scholarly achievements and preservation efforts than for his role in the development of both the Great Hyperspace War and the Sith War. More than one historian has commented that the Daragons might never have happened upon Sith space—and led the Sith back to the Republic—had Odan-Urr not rescued the siblings from assassins, and that Exar Kun might not have risen to power so quickly had Odan-Urr destroyed the Sith Holocron when he'd had the chance. However, numerous Jedi texts recall Odan-Urr as a Jedi who was especially mindful of the Force; if his actions were guided by the Force itself, he was hardly culpable for the wars.

THE SHADOW OF FREEDON NADD

4400–4000 B.B.Y.
Author: Jedi Master Arca Jeth, teacher of
Ulic Qel-Droma.

Six hundred years after the Great Hyperspace War, the Jedi Freedon Nadd was seduced by the dark side, slew his own Master, and apprenticed himself to a Dark Lord of the Sith. In the tradition of the Sith, there can be only one Dark Lord at a time. Unable to become a Sith Lord as long as his Master lived, Nadd came to the planet Onderon to make himself a king.

Four centuries after Nadd's death, I went to Onderon to bring peace to the divided world. I was preceded by my students Ulic Qel-Droma, his brother Cay, and Tott Doneeta, who had discovered that Queen Amanoa, wife of Onderon's ruler King Ommin, was possessed by the spirit of Freedon Nadd. My students and I tracked Amanoa to the deepest sublevels of her palace and discovered Freedon Nadd's tomb, which had become the focus of dark side energy and enabled his power to pass to his descendants from generation to generation.

Exposed to the light, the dark power that had supported Amanoa abandoned her and left her dead. Nadd transferred his power to King Ommin. I was then attacked by Ommin, who smothered me in dark side energy and attempted to transform me into his own Dark Jedi. After my Jedi students came to my aid, Freedon Nadd realized that King Ommin would fall to the Jedi, so he switched his support to the Krath, a secret society founded by the cousins Satal and Aleema Keto, descendants of Empress Teta.

THE SITH LORD EXAR KUN ATTACKS HIS FORMER ▶
TEACHER, JEDI MASTER VODO-SIOSK BAAS, IN THE
GALACTIC SENATE ON CORUSCANT. *(Edwards)*

The Krath gained knowledge of Sith sorcery from ancient texts and relics. Nadd killed Ommin before his own apparition vanished into thin air, swearing to me that the Jedi had lost the battle.

To prevent Freedon Nadd from ever again exercising his power from beyond the grave, I have transferred his sarcophagus to a great tomb on another world. The tomb is guarded by many beasts. May no one dare to find it.

ADDENDUM BY
TIONNE SOLUSAR

Master Arca transferred the remains of Freedon Nadd, Queen Amanoa, and King Ommin to the moon Dxun, but Nadd's tomb was quickly discovered by Exar Kun. After the Krath grew from a secret society to a galactic threat, Arca was mortally wounded by Krath war droids on the planet Deneba. Arca's death motivated his student Ulic Qel-Droma to form a plan to infiltrate the Krath in order to discover a way to destroy them. Tragically, Qel-Droma's desire for vengeance only led him to the dark side.

According to Sith researcher Murk Lundi, Freedon Nadd gained his knowledge of the Sith not by direct apprenticeship to a living Sith Lord but through the discovery of an abandoned Sith Holocron. Allegedly, this Sith Holocron was originally owned and maintained by King Adas, who had ruled the Sith approximately twenty-three thousand years previously, or three thousand years before the formation of the Galactic Republic. Lore has it that Adas learned about Holocrons from Rakatan soldiers who attempted to conquer Sith space. Around the time of the Great Hyperspace War, a Sith Lord named Garu lost King Adas's Holocron on the planet Ashas Ree, where it remained until it was found centuries later by Freedon Nadd. Other sources suggest that Freedon Nadd's search for Sith knowledge led him to Yavin 4, where he apprenticed with the spirit of Naga Sadow.

Master Arca did not note the existence of King Adas's Holocron, but records indicate the Jedi hid it under millions of tons of water on the remote world Kodai. In 29 B.B.Y., Murk Lundi's student Norval recovered the Holocron, which was subsequently seized by Obi-Wan Kenobi and turned over to the Jedi Council. For reasons that remain unclear, the Council ultimately entrusted the Sith Holocron to Jedi-affiliated House Pelagia's extensive Holocron library in the Tapani sector instead of to the Jedi Archives on Coruscant; this was ultimately unfortunate, as King Adas's Holocron was stolen during the Jedi Purge, and it seems the remaining Holocrons were destroyed before Palpatine or his agents could claim them.

THE SITH WAR

3996 B.B.Y.
Author: Jedi Master Vodo-Siosk Baas

I must tell you of the Great Sith War that occurred four thousand years before your time.

This war was caused by a student of mine, Exar Kun, who found forbidden teachings of the ancient Sith. He imitated the ways of the long-fallen Sith and used them to form his own philosophy of the Jedi Code, a distortion of all we know to be true and right. With this knowledge, Exar Kun established a vast and powerful brotherhood and claimed the title of first Dark Lord of the Sith.

After the war, I had hoped Exar Kun and his kind were defeated once and for all. But Exar Kun joined forces with another

JEDI CONSULARS WHO FOUGHT ▶
DURING THE SITH WARS. (Trevas)

powerful Jedi and great warlord, Ulic Qel-Droma. He worked his invisible threads into the fabric of the Republic, bringing downfall through treachery as well as through his distorted abilities with the Force.

Because I was his Master, I alone of the allied Jedi went to confront him, hoping that I could turn him back. I knew it was a foolish mission, but I had no choice. I had to try.

ADDENDUM BY
TIONNE SOLUSAR

It has already been noted that Vodo-Siosk Baas was slain by his former student Exar Kun. It has also been noted that the consciousness of Vodo-Siosk Baas may have not only survived his death but been contained by the Tedryn Holocron, from which his account of the Sith War was drawn. Given that the Tedryn Holocron allowed Vodo-Siosk Baas to communicate information about his own death, we can only assume that he may have known more than he was telling, for his concise account omits some important details.

Exar Kun was not the first Dark Lord of the Sith, but he was the first Dark Jedi to appropriate that title after the events of the Great Hyperspace War. He was aided not only by Ulic Qel-Droma but by the Krath's founders, Aleema and Satal Keto. Ulic Qel-Droma killed Satal, an action that completed his conversion to the dark side and enabled him to become Exar Kun's apprentice.

Exar Kun masterminded the two most notorious events of the Sith War. The first was to use his Sith powers to recruit Jedi apprentices to the dark side, then dispatch them to assassinate their own Jedi Masters. The second was to use the weaponry on Naga Sadow's ancient Sith flagship to destroy the ten suns of the Cron Cluster, which caused the massive shock wave that destroyed many worlds and left Ossus in ruins.

The Jedi chased Exar Kun to his stronghold on Yavin 4 and used their combined power to strike him down and annhilate his Massassi warriors. However, Exar Kun was able to escape death by using Sith sorcery to preserve his spirit in the Massassi temples. Although the duration of a disembodied consciousness is more often discussed by philosophers than historians and scientists, it is an undisputed fact that Exar Kun's spirit survived more than four millennia, and that he retained more than enough power to attack Luke Skywalker's then fledgling Jedi academy.

The Jedi Nomi Sunrider, who served with Ulic Qel-Droma before his defection to the Krath and the Sith, demonstrated a most unusual Force ability when she stripped Ulic Qel-Droma of his powers, leaving him blind to the Force. According to Sunrider, she learned of this power from Jedi Master Odan-Urr.

THE SECOND SITH WAR

3958–3956 B.B.Y.
Author: Bodo Baas

Two Jedi acquired a taste for rebellion during their victories in the Mandalorian Wars. They discovered pre-Republic Rakatan artifacts that led them to the Sith tombworld of Korriban. Despite their lack of a connection to the Sith species, they drew knowledge from the Sith tombs and declared themselves to be the new Dark Lords of the Sith—Darth Revan and Darth Malak.

Because they were known heroes of the Mandalorian Wars, many Jedi Knights regarded "the revanchist" and his former apprentice Alek as champions, and eagerly joined their cause. A Sith training academy was revitalized on Korriban, and a new corps of Dark Jedi readied to defend their growing Sith Empire. Under the command of Revan and Malak, they seized control of the bulk of the Republic fleet, and it was this act that initiated the Second Sith War.

The Sith Lords recovered an ancient Rakatan device, the Star Forge, which possessed the power to create fully formed machines of destruction. They amassed an even greater fleet and might have brought the Republic to its knees but for the efforts of the Jedi Knight Bastila Shan, a master of battle meditation.

Bastila subdued and captured Revan, and the Jedi Council Force-scoured his memories to learn the location of the Star Forge. In the process, the Jedi removed Revan's memories of his allegiance to the Sith and conscripted him to fight on their behalf. Revan killed Darth Malak and destroyed the Star Forge.

As for the end of this conflict, many records are either unclear or inconsistent. Revan's fate is not documented, but it is known that his defection caused a civil war amongst the Sith, and that a host of potential Sith Lords—including Darth Sion, Darth Kreia, and Darth Nihilus—attempted to take his place. According to one record, Brianna, an attendant to Jedi Master Atris, defeated the Sith Lord Darth Nihilus. Another record indicates that the Miraluka Jedi Visas Marr was involved in killing Nihilus, while still other records suggest that Nihilus slew Marr.

After the Second Sith War, the Jedi hunted down and exterminated the disciples of Darth Revan and Malak, and many other followers of the dark side. The Sith virtually disappeared for centuries, and it was believed the galaxy was at last safe from their dark order. This erroneous belief lasted until the emergence of Darth Ruin.

◄ DARK JEDI MALAK AND REVAN PROCLAIM THEMSELVES THE NEW DARK LORDS OF THE SITH. (Artist)

DARTH RUIN

2000 B.B.Y.
Author: Bodo Baas

A mysterious figure who may have been an Umbaran, Darth Ruin revived the Sith Order and seduced a number of Jedi to his cause. A war with the Jedi Order inevitably followed, but the Sith soon turned the war upon themselves. Ruin was destroyed by his own disciples, who ushered in a millennium-long period of betrayal and darkness amongst the Sith.

ADDENDUM BY
TIONNE SOLUSAR

According to the arcane scholar Murk Lundi, Darth Ruin was previously a Jedi Master named Phanius. A charismatic Jedi of his time, Phanius abandoned the Jedi Order to pursue prohibited teachings. Records list Phanius among the first of the Lost, a roster of Jedi Masters who abandoned the Order and eventually—after the abdication of Jedi Master Count Dooku—became referred to as the Lost Twenty. Unknown to the Jedi Order of the Old Republic, Phanius infiltrated and united various surviving Sith clans, then changed his name to Darth Ruin. A merciless leader with supremely self-centered philosophies, Ruin was known for whims that resulted in countless deaths of his own minions. Evidently, his confidence blinded him to the possibility of being assassinated by his own Sith acolytes.

BATTLE OF RUUSAN

1000 B.B.Y.

The Battle of Ruusan, the notorious conflict in which Jedi recruited novice Force-sensitive youths to battle the Sith, was a series of seven ground battles, and may have been the bloodiest confrontation between Jedi and Sith in history. Casualties on both sides numbered in the thousands, and the planet itself—once lush with life—was decimated. Only a few brief mentions of Ruusan have been found within the Great Holocron; it seems that even the Jedi Order wished to forget the incident.

Luke Skywalker first heard of the Battle of Ruusan from the Jedi Master Yoda. Five years after the Battle of Yavin, the Alliance received a message regarding a place called the Valley of the Jedi on Ruusan, which compelled Luke to share his knowledge with Alliance leaders:

> *Hundreds and hundreds of years ago, a Jedi named Kaan turned away from the light and formed the Brotherhood of Darkness. The Brotherhood used the dark side of the Force to build an empire, and they were well on their way toward expanding it when an army was raised to oppose them.*
>
> *The army of opposition consisted of beings from many species and planets, representing all walks of life. But they had one thing in common. They were Jedi.*
>
> *The two sides came together on a remote and little-known world. Salvos of pure energy were exchanged, storms raged across the land, and lightning flashed from the skies. Entire cities were destroyed, a species was pushed to the edge of extermination, and spirits separated from their bodies.*

> *Finally, after days of mortal combat, the Brotherhood was defeated. Knowing that he had lost but unwilling to accept defeat, Kaan lured his opponents into a valley. And it was there that the Brotherhood of Darkness committed suicide, taking good Jedi with them. Not to the freedom of death but into a state of suspended animation, where they remain trapped.*

The Republic agent Kyle Katarn—before he became a Jedi—gathered additional facts. The renegade Jedi Kaan had become a Sith Lord, and his opposition was the Army of Light, which was led by the Jedi Lord Hoth. To defeat the Jedi, Kaan and his Brotherhood of Darkness—which consisted of thousands of so-called Sith Lords—committed suicide through the use of a Force weapon known as a thought bomb, a volatile cauldron of seething Force energy that consumed all Force-sensitive beings within its blast radius. The disembodied spirits of Jedi and Sith were instantly trapped within a large ovoid of dark energy.

Fortunately, the Jedi Order had not sent all

of the Jedi Knights to Ruusan. As the Order went through a period of re-formation, the Jedi built a monument to their fallen comrades in what became known to them as the Valley of the Jedi, but knowledge of its location became lost over time, and the spirits remained trapped.

The Ruusan natives made a prophecy: "A Knight shall come, a battle will be fought, and the prisoners go free." More than a thousand years after the Battle of Ruusan, the prophecy was fulfilled by Kyle Katarn.

RETURN OF THE SITH

32 B.B.Y.

Author: Obi-Wan Kenobi

It is five days since the death of my Master. At the request of the Jedi Council, I make this report of my encounters with the Sith.

The first encounter was on Tatooine. My Master, Qui-Gon Jinn, and I were escorting Queen Amidala from Naboo to Coruscant when the hyperdrive of the Queen's starship became damaged and we were forced to land on the desert planet. Repairs had just been completed as Qui-Gon was returning to our landing site from the city of Mos Espa. He brought with him the Force-sensitive boy he'd discovered, Anakin Skywalker.

According to Qui-Gon, they were within sight of the ship when a black-clad figure came racing out from the dunes on a repulsorlift speeder. The figure leapt from his speeder, ignited a lightsaber, and attacked, but Qui-Gon managed to instruct Anakin to run for the ship. I was inside the ship's cockpit when the Queen's security head, Captain Panaka, came running in

with Anakin. It disturbs me to realize that I hadn't sensed even the slightest danger before Panaka's alert.

Outside the cockpit viewport, I saw Qui-Gon fighting the dark figure. I directed the ship's captain to fly toward Qui-Gon, who was able to leap on board before we ascended from the planet, leaving the attacker behind. Qui-Gon was winded, but was compelled to note that his opponent was well trained in the Jedi arts.

When Qui-Gon and I next saw this enemy, we were assisting in the defense of Naboo against the Trade Federation's droid armies. Close up, he resembled a male Zabrak, but his face was so completely covered with black and red markings that identification was difficult. He used a double-bladed lightsaber and moved incredibly fast. Just as I sensed that the creature was aware that Qui-Gon and I would beat him, he found a way to divide us. Moments later, we were separated by laser doors in a security hallway. I could do nothing but watch as our enemy struck down Qui-Gon.

When the last laser door lifted, I gave in to my anger as I charged the dark warrior. I absolutely wanted to destroy him. He used my anger against me, actually fed off my fury, gaining strength as I exhausted my own. I lost my lightsaber and he had me. But then I saw my Master's weapon, and as I reached out for it, I heard Qui-Gon's words within me . . .

Be mindful of the living Force.

The Force guided my movements, and it was by Qui-Gon's blade that his killer was felled.

Whether our adversary was stalking us or attempting to assassinate the Queen, we may never know. He was certainly a Sith, but was he Master or apprentice? I believe it is only a matter of time before we find out. Anticipating a future encounter, I am compelled to remind all Jedi of what they have been told since their earliest training: do not lose yourselves to anger, even briefly as I did, for not only is this against our Code, but it will make the enemy stronger.

ADDENDUM BY
TIONNE SOLUSAR

Thanks to the findings of the New Republic Senate Council on Security and Intelligence, research has confirmed that Obi-Wan slew Darth Maul, an Iridonian Zabrak who was an apprentice to the Sith Lord Darth Sidious, the alter ego of Palpatine. Queen Amidala was Maul's probable target on Tatooine and Naboo.

Before Qui-Gon's first encounter with Darth Maul, numerous records indicate that the Jedi of the Old Republic believed the Sith had been extinct for a millennium, apparently since the Battle of Ruusan. The Jedi also had records of separate pre-Ruusan Sith Orders that were led by two Sith Lords, such as Exar Kun and Ulic Qel-Droma, or Darth Malak and Darth Revan. Via the Great Holocron, the Jedi Master Yoda said of the Sith, "Always two there are . . . no more . . . no less. A Master and an apprentice."

But two was not always the standard. According to Luke Skywalker, Yoda knew of the Sith Lord Kaan's Brotherhood of Darkness, an army of thousands who fought at Ruusan. It is not known whether Yoda was aware that all members of the Brotherhood referred to themselves as Sith Lords, but records indicate that most of the Brotherhood was hastily trained; it is probable that Kaan's Force-sensitive minions were "Lords" by name only, and conceivable that the Jedi considered them as such. It remains a mystery why Yoda

and other Jedi—most of whom had believed the Sith were annihilated at the Battle of Ruusan—seemed so certain that the Sith had returned to their Rule of Two, but it is possible they sensed this through the Force.

THE BATTLE OF GEONOSIS

22 B.B.Y.
Author: Obi-Wan Kenobi

At the request of the Jedi Council, I make this report of my confrontation with Count Dooku on Geonosis. I confess, I'm at something of a loss about where to begin. What started as a mission to trace the origin of a Kamino saberdart has led to the death of many Jedi and, even worse, interstellar war.

It seems the seeds for the battle on Geonosis were planted at least a decade ago. Actually, I'm not sure if planted is the right word. Strewn seems more accurate, yet strewn with apparent precision in a star system that someone didn't want us to know existed, like some cosmic sleight of hand that . . .

Please forgive me. My thoughts went to my Padawan, who lost a hand on Geonosis. He's with the surgeons now. I'll continue.

As you know, I traced the saberdart to Kamino, despite the fact that all records of that star system were wiped from the Jedi Archives. To reiterate my report from Kamino, the Kaminoans maintain that Master Sifo-Dyas placed the order for a clone army at the request of the Senate almost ten years ago. I recalled that Sifo-Dyas was killed around that time, so

it seems possible that the Kaminoans dealt with an imposter. According to the Kaminoans, Sifo-Dyas also requested that they keep his involvement a secret until a Jedi arrived to claim the clones, and to expect the arrival of the clone host. The clone host was the bounty hunter Jango Fett, and the Kaminoans introduced us. Fett claimed he'd been recruited not by Sifo-Dyas, but by a man named Tyranus on one of the moons of Bogden. I quickly assessed that Fett was the same hunter who had fired the saberdart that led me to Kamino in the first place.

Fett attempted to escape me on Kamino, but I followed him to Geonosis, where I discovered Count Dooku meeting with the Separatists about combining their forces. After transmitting a message to Anakin, I was captured by the Geonosians and briefly interrogated by Dooku. He was very charming, made it seem like an interview, even though I was trapped in a force field at the time.

Dooku told me that the Republic is under the control of a Dark Lord of the Sith called Darth Sidious. He said that Sidious was once in league with the Trade Federation but betrayed them ten years ago, which is the same year as the Battle of Naboo. Dooku claimed the Trade Federation sought help from the Jedi Council, but they were ignored. He asked me to join him and destroy the Sith.

Obviously, I refused. I sensed the dark side in Dooku. The rest you know better than I: how Anakin relayed my message about the droid armies, how Jedi reinforcements traveled to Geonosis, and how Chancellor Palpatine was granted emergency powers to utilize and activate the clone army. I take no comfort in acknowledging that the Jedi would have lost the battle at Geonosis had the clone troops not arrived when they did.

Count Dooku told me that our vision has become clouded by the dark side of the Force. As Master Yoda will attest, Dooku is himself strong with the dark side, and it may be impossible to unravel any truth from his claims. Still . . .

Perhaps I have become too much of a detective, but I find myself preoccupied by so many references—if not facts—related to events of "ten years ago."

A Sith Lord named Darth Sidious betrayed the Trade Federation.

Sifo-Dyas commissioned the clone army.

The mysterious Tyranus recruited Jango Fett as a genetic template for the clone army.

Sifo-Dyas was killed.

And Count Dooku left the Jedi Order. All ten years ago.

I suspect that only a Jedi—possibly Sifo-Dyas or Count Dooku—could have erased the Kamino system from the Archives. It seems highly likely that this deed was done at a time consistent with the other noted events. Sifo-Dyas strikes me as a more likely suspect if only because I can't imagine why Dooku would have taken measures to build a secret army for the Republic, then allow that army to attack his own forces on Geonosis.

What disturbs me most of all is that the Kaminoans were expecting a Jedi to arrive when I did, as if everything was going according to plan. Could it be that my finding the saberdart was also part of this plan? And sending the clone troops to Geonosis? I thought the Force was guiding me, yet now I wonder whether I was an unwitting pawn in some decade-old scheme.

I will not wonder much. Dooku has caused the death of many Jedi, and must be stopped.

ADDENDUM BY
TIONNE SOLUSAR

According to the Great Holocron, Master Yoda—by the end of the Clone Wars—had gathered most of the facts regarding the Sith's maneuverings ten years prior to the Battle of Geonosis. The events occurred as follows:

1. The Sith Lord Darth Sidious betrayed the Trade Federation at the Battle of Naboo.

2. Count Dooku left the Jedi Order and became Darth Tyranus, an apprentice to Darth Sidious.

3. Acting in secrecy, Sifo-Dyas ordered the clone army from the Kaminoans. Because Sifo-Dyas was a close friend of Count Dooku, Yoda theorized that Sifo-Dyas may have been acting under Dooku's influence.

4. The Kaminoans received payments from Tyranus (Dooku).

5. The Kaminoans never saw either Sifo-Dyas or Tyranus (Dooku).

6. Sifo-Dyas was killed. Yoda theorized he was murdered by Dooku.

7. Dooku erased Kamino from the Jedi Archives.

8. Jango Fett arrived on Kamino, and the Kaminoans began production of the clones.

THE CLONE WARS

22–19 B.B.Y.

Because the Empire had authorization over nearly all existing records of the Clone Wars, many facts were twisted or buried to prevent the public from discovering the truth: The Clone Wars were entirely conceived and orchestrated by Darth Sidious, who—under the guise of Palpatine—used his powers and influence to manipulate the Senate. Darth Sidious's primary goals were both the extermination of the Jedi, and galactic conquest. Because the Jedi did not discover the Sith Lord's identity until it was too late, few Jedi records reveal anything but—in hindsight—how easily they fell victim to the Sith.

Palpatine projected an unassuming manner as he manipulated situations to grant himself additional political authority at every opportunity; few suspected he was seizing power, because virtually everyone was foisting it upon him. All were deceived by Palpatine's modest, reluctant acceptance speeches.

Although the Clone Wars officially began with the Battle of Geonosis, when the Republic's clone army first engaged the Separatists' droid militia, it is difficult to determine exactly when Darth Sidious began setting plans in motion that would lead to this war. His schemes were years in the making, and the fact that he engineered the development of two massive opposing factions without arousing suspicion is a testament to his cunning and patience.

Darth Sidious did not accomplish his goals on his own. After Obi-Wan killed Darth Maul, the then newly appointed Supreme Chancellor Palpatine took on as his next apprentice the renegade Jedi Master Count Dooku, who also operated as Darth Tyranus. Although it is well known that Dooku came to lead the Confederacy, information gathered by the New Republic Senate Council on Security and Intelligence indicates he was also involved in commissioning the Republic's clone army.

Dooku is also credited with teaching lightsaber fighting techniques to two notorious killers of Jedi: General Grievous, the cyborg leader of the Confederacy's droid army, and the Force-sensitive Asajj Ventress, who aspired to being a Sith. Records indicate Grievous was not a Force-user; although he probably knew Dooku was a Sith Lord, he may never have realized that Supreme Chancellor Palpatine—whom Grievous abducted during the Clone Wars—was really Darth Sidious. Whether Dooku was grooming Asajj Ventress as a genuine Sith apprentice remains unknown, as does her fate.

Near the end of the Clone Wars, Anakin Skywalker killed Count Dooku, discovered that Palpatine was a Sith Lord, and was conscripted into the Sith Order as Darth Vader. Recordings sequestered by the droid R2-D2 eventually revealed a possible motivation for Anakin to ally with the Sith. These recordings include conversations between Anakin and his secret love, Senator Padmé Amidala, the former Queen of Naboo. Evidently, Anakin feared that Padmé would die in childbirth, and came to believe he could gain new knowledge of the Force—apparently from Darth Sidious—that would enable him to save her. Also believing that the Jedi had become his enemies, Anakin personally executed many Jedi on Coruscant before Palpatine declared himself Emperor. Ultimately, Anakin/Vader attempted to kill Padmé and continued to serve his Sith Master—although not necessarily with any degree of loyalty—until the Battle of Endor.

The Clone Wars may have truly been the end of the Jedi had Padmé not given birth to the twins Luke and Leia. Leia would be adopted and raised by Senator Bail Organa on Alderaan, while Luke was taken to Anakin's stepbrother Owen Lars on the sand planet Tatooine.

THE GALACTIC CIVIL WAR

2 B.B.Y.–18 A.B.Y.

The war between the Galactic Empire and the Alliance to restore the Republic has been extensively documented, and most young students are aware of the pivotal battles that led to the Alliance's victory and the formation of the New Republic. The following recording was made by Leia Organa Solo in 35 A.B.Y., at the end of the Chiss–Killik border war, and presents a most personal perspective of the events that shaped recent history:

> So much has been written about the Galactic Civil War that I thought there was nothing left to be said, certainly not much more I could add. But recently, I saw a series of recordings that compel me to make one of my own. The recordings were made by R2-D2 more than five decades ago, during the Clone Wars, and show both my biological parents as well as the man who would raise me. As painful as it was to watch these recordings, it was also an incredible experience, as they answered questions I'd had for years about my birth mother and how Luke and I came to be separated from her.
>
> Senator Bail Organa of Alderaan was one of the three founders of the Alliance to Restore the Republic, which was more commonly known as the Rebel Alliance. I knew him as Father, for he adopted me almost immediately after my mother died in childbirth. The last time I saw him, the Alliance was barely two years old and I was leaving Alderaan on a mission to recover plans for the Death Star. It was then that he instructed me to contact Obi-Wan Kenobi on Tatooine. I had no idea it would be the

◀ LUKE SKYWALKER EVADES DARTH VADER'S TIE FIGHTER IN THE DEATH STAR'S TRENCH AT THE BATTLE OF YAVIN. (Trevas)

very last time I saw my father, or the last time I'd ever taste Alderaan's sweet air.

The rest you probably know. It seems as if everybody does. If I had a credit for every academic who wanted me to verify specific details about the events leading up to the destruction of both Death Stars, I could pay for several planetary relief efforts. But for posterity's sake, I want my descendants to know that it was a great turning point for me when I learned that Luke Skywalker was Darth Vader's son, and that Luke was my brother. It's hard to explain to anyone who doesn't comprehend the Force, but when Luke revealed this information, it really did feel as if I'd known about our true relationship all along.

But I was also overwhelmed by the knowledge that Vader was not only Luke's father, but mine, too. My memories raced to my first encounter with Vader. It was during my first trip to Coruscant, when I'd accompanied my father—that is, Bail Organa—to a reception for the Emperor. In hindsight, I'm surprised I was allowed to go, as it exposed me to both the Emperor and Vader. Granted, I'd never demonstrated any Force powers at that point, so perhaps Bail Organa thought it was relatively safe. I never knew anyone who guarded his secrets as well as Bail Organa.

The reception was at the Imperial Palace. As things turned out, it seems neither Sith Lord sensed anything about my true identity, for if they had, surely they would have done something. That's not to say their powers were in any way weak. I'd meant to confront Palpatine and tell him what I thought of his xenophobic Empire, but as he approached me in the reception line, I was struck numb with fear. I remember thinking it was as if he were pitch-black inside. Vader loomed behind

him like a malevolent shadow, and there was no doubt in my mind that if I had found the courage to speak my mind to the Emperor, Vader would have killed me on the spot.

Me. His own daughter, not that he knew it at the time.

It was only a few years after that first encounter that Vader captured me, right after the Alliance had intercepted the Death Star plans. In an effort to locate Alliance headquarters, Vader tortured me. Do I think he would have done so had he known I was his daughter? Yes, and in a heartbeat. Whether he would have tried to lure me to the dark side or just induce pain, I can only imagine, but given how he dealt with Luke on Cloud City, there was nothing stopping him from harming his own offspring.

And yet Luke believed there was still some good in him, just as my mother—as revealed by the old recordings—believed, and after Vader had tried to strangle her! It was beyond difficult for me to believe any goodness could be found within that black armor, even after I'd learned from Anakin's surviving friends about what he'd been like as a boy on Tatooine.

And yet some goodness did remain in Anakin. Luke succeeded where others had failed. I have no illusions that I could have helped save Anakin Skywalker from the dark side. Only Luke could have done that. I wasn't strong enough. Not then.

It disturbs me to have such violent family history. I can forgive Anakin Sky-walker because he could not prevent himself from being seduced by the dark side and transformed by Palpatine. The actions of Darth Vader and the Emperor, however, remain unforgivable.

Am I concerned that I raised my own children to be Jedi? Of course I am. I want *my children to be safe and happy. I worry. I know they have felt the lure of the dark side at various times. I can only trust they know how much I love them, and hope that the lessons they have learned will continue to keep them in the light.*

Standard records indicate the Galactic Civil War ended nineteen years after the Battle of Yavin, with the historic peace accords that were signed aboard the Chimaera *by Admiral Pellaeon and Chief of State and President of the Senate Ponc Gavrisom. For some, like me, the war still rages in my memories and dreams. How can I forget the horrors that claimed Alderaan and pitted a man against his own children?*

For all that I have learned about the balance of nature and the power of the Force, I will probably always have difficulty with the idea that there's enough room in the galaxy for any Sith Lords.

THE DEMISE OF PALPATINE

10–11 A.B.Y.

Author: Luke Skywalker

This record is for my nephew, Anakin Solo.

Anakin, I speak to you from the planet Onderon, where your parents, siblings, and I are the guests of Modon Kira and his warrior clan. At this very moment, you are sleeping peacefully in a crib in your parents' suite. This is a wonderful thing for you to be doing, Anakin. It is how every baby should sleep, softly snoring without fear or concern. And yet yesterday, we came so close to losing you.

I have no doubt that you will grow up good and strong, and that by the time you review this recording, you'll already have heard something about the events of yesterday. Because the Force is so strong in you, I suppose it's possible that your in- choate memory may preserve some aspects of what happened. But I want you to know— know from me—about what happened, as best as I can tell it. And afterward, I'll tell you why I want you to know.

For more than two decades, the galaxy was controlled by Emperor Palpatine, a Sith Lord who had conquered the Republic and virtually destroyed the Jedi Order. To say that Palatine was evil, and would stop at nothing to accomplish his goals, is an understatement. He annihilated entire civilizations and left worlds ravaged beyond salvation, all in his ongoing effort to achieve greater power. He was also responsible for luring my father, the Jedi Knight Anakin Skywalker, to the dark side and transforming him into a Sith apprentice named Darth Vader. I will tell you more of my father another time, but for now, know that he renounced the Sith, and that it was he who killed Palpatine seven years ago at the Battle of Endor. Know that your grand- father, your namesake, died as a Jedi.

And for six years, I believed, as everyone else did, that Palpatine was dead. Only last year did I learn the truth: Palpatine had not been consumed by a blast of energy, but had survived as dark side energy itself. In this bodiless, transitional state, he traveled across the galaxy until he reached his hidden retreat world. There he projected his spirit into the body of a waiting clone, a replica of himself. By this method, he had cheated death. It was not the first time. He had previously utilized clones after he had discovered that the corrupting power of the dark side had a detrimental effect on his physical form. But after the Battle of Endor, he commissioned many more clones of himself to ensure that he would live forever.

And then his reign of terror began again. He developed a loyal military and built a new fleet of warships. Seeking a new apprentice, he set his sights on me, and then your mother. But from the moment that he sensed you inside your mother's womb, you became the greatest object of his desire. Even more so after I destroyed his cloning facility, leaving him with only a single clone to possess. No, he didn't want you as his apprentice. He wanted to possess a genuine Jedi body. Yours.

After you were born, it didn't take Palpatine long to track you and your mother here, to the Kira Fortress on Onderon. He was desperate for a new body, as his own was rapidly deteriorating. As soon as I realized he was heading for the fortress, I raced here with the Jedi Knight Empatojayos Brand, my Jedi apprentice Rayf Ysanna, and your father.

Brand and Rayf found Palpatine first. I was too late to stop Palpatine from unleashing Sith lightning upon them. Rayf was killed instantly, but Brand—possibly because his cybernetic body absorbed most of the energy—was still alive when your father and I arrived in the chamber where Palpatine had cornered you and your mother. I told Palpatine that I would accept his surrender. He lunged for you, trying to tear you from your mother's arms. Your father blasted him, and as he fell, he said it was time for him "to enter the child" as he had vowed.

An instant later, Palpatine's cloak emptied, and both Leia and I sensed that his spirit was about to possess your body. Empatojayos Brand moved faster than

thought. He took you in his robotic arms and used the light side of the Force to shield you from Palpatine. Then he handed you back to your mother, and assured us that he had trapped Palpatine's spirit.

Brand said he could feel himself being eaten alive by the darkness, and he could not stop it. Or maybe he would not stop it. He said that Palpatine would die with him, and that Palpatine would never return. "The Force," he said, "and all the Jedi who went before us will make sure of that." And then Brand died.

Had I known how to contain and destroy Palpatine, I would have done it to save you. Because I did not know this ability, I am grateful that Brand was with us. He was a greater Jedi than I.

So now, Anakin, I shall tell you why it's important to me that I relate this story to you. It's not because I want you to remember your place in history at the moment Palpatine died. I want you to remember Rayf Ysanna and Empatojayos Brand, two men who fought to save you. I also want you to remember Rayf's sister, Jem, who died while defending your mother and me against Palpatine's minions on New Alderaan. I hope you will honor them by living a good, long life, as this is what they would have wanted for you.

Now that Palpatine is finally gone forever, I feel a great relief. I don't know how long this relief will last, and I can only imagine what your future holds. But with the last Sith Lord dead, the future of the Jedi Order has never looked brighter.

May the Force be with you, Anakin.

ADDENDUM BY
TIONNE SOLUSAR

Luke Skywalker and Kam Solusar found Rayf and Jem Ysanna, descendants of Jedi who survived the Cron Supernova, while searching for Jedi artifacts on Ossus in 10 A.B.Y. That same year, the Jedi Knight Empatojayos Brand came to the aid of the New Republic. Brand had escaped the Jedi Purge, but was mortally wounded when Darth Vader hunted him down and destroyed his starship. Rescued by the technologically limited Ganathans, Brand's body was so ravaged that he could only survive as a cyborg, with his head and limbless torso encased in prosthetic machinery. Despite his condition, Brand remained strong with the Force and became the leader of Ganath.

THE RESURRECTION OF EXAR KUN

11 A.B.Y.

Exar Kun's spirit was trapped for four millennia in the temples of Yavin 4 before it was briefly stirred by Luke Skywalker's arrival at the secret Alliance base. Eleven years later, when Luke founded the Jedi academy on Yavin 4, Exar Kun corrupted Luke's most powerful student, Kyp Durron, and attempted to resurrect himself by draining power from Luke and the other trainees. Among the trainees were Streen, a former gas prospector, and Kirana Ti of Dathomir, who eventually became Jedi Masters and—following the war with the Yuuzhan Vong—co-founded a new Jedi praxeum to train Dathomirian Force-sensitives. Nine years after the conflict with Exar Kun, Streen made the following recording:

I'm not much of a storyteller, but after Tionne heard me talking with some youngsters who'd asked me about that business with Exar Kun, she wanted me to tell it again for the record, so here I am. Just so you know, I'm not even going to try for a whole history of Exar Kun or what Kyp Durron went through. There's other records for that, and Tionne can direct you to them. I'm just going to say what I remember about the Dark Man's last day on Yavin 4.

The Dark Man had already caused the death of my friend Gantoris, turned Kyp Durron against Master Skywalker, and put Master Skywalker's body into a state that hovered between life and death before we—the other Jedi apprentices and I—finally realized what we were up against: a spirit who put thoughts into our heads to corrupt us. Sad to say we didn't sort this out until the spirit had gotten his hooks into me. I told my allies that he'd been whispering to me constantly for weeks, just as he'd done to Gantoris, but that didn't stop his prattle. Entered my mind while I was sleeping, he did, and made me think I was having a dream about fighting him, but what he was really doing was making me try to destroy Master Skywalker's unconscious body, which I very nearly did. Fortunately, Leia Organa Solo and my fellow Jedi trainees were able to stop me. I snapped out of the nightmare, and thought Kam Solusar was going to take my head off before Kirana Ti quickly convinced him I didn't know what I was doing. After I recovered, I told everyone what I knew must be done. We had to destroy the Dark Man before he killed us all.

It was Jacen and Jaina Solo who told us the Dark Man was Exar Kun. They'd come to Yavin 4 with their parents to check on their uncle, Master Skywalker that is. The twins were only three years old at the time. Turned out they could communicate with their uncle, who spoke to them from the spirit plane, and told them Exar Kun's name.

Tionne already knew more about Jedi lore than most, and she knew a thing or two about this Sith Lord. After Exar Kun's Master failed to turn his student back to the light side, other Jedi banded together in a massive strike force and followed him back to his stronghold, right here on Yavin 4. The Jedi combined their might, unified their focus of the Force to lay waste to most of the jungles. Exar Kun's body was obliterated, but he must have used some kind of Sith sorcery to preserve his spirit in the temples.

I was entrusted with Master Skywalker's lightsaber and was guarding his body—he was laid out on a stone platform in the grand audience chamber—when the Dark Man returned, and appeared before me as a shadowy figure clad in dark, padded armor. A pulsing tattoo of a black sun burned from his forehead. I told him I wouldn't do his bidding and activated the lightsaber.

Exar Kun taunted me, and it was a struggle to resist the anger he wanted to bring out in me. In the years I'd spent as a prospector at Bespin, I'd come to believe that I wasn't very comfortable around people, but I felt empowered by the arrival of my fellow trainees, who included Kirana Ti, Kam Solusar, Tionne, Cilghal, Dorsk 81,

Kirana Ti had activated her lightsaber, and she and I crossed blades through the middle of Exar Kun's shadowy body. There was a great blaze of light, then darkness flooded out of Exar Kun. The Sith Lord screamed before he vanished forever, then Vodo-Siosk Baas disappeared, too.

And Master Skywalker awakened. Soon he was fully recovered.

It does not pain me to admit that I couldn't have defeated Exar Kun or rescued Master Skywalker on my own. Even Master Skywalker was vulnerable to that Sith fiend! Only proud or overly confident beings think they are completely able to take care of themselves without help at all times. Pride and confidence can make a solid suit of armor, but such armor is weak compared with the power of the Force, especially if it isolates you from other Jedi. Remember the words of Vodo-Siosk Baas: "Together Jedi can overcome their weaknesses."

and Brakiss. They'd been waiting for the right moment to enter the chamber and catch Exar Kun off guard. Present, too, were Jacen and Jaina, who stayed close to Cilghal's side.

Exar Kun was not impressed by our numbers. He taunted us, even seemed confident he might defy us, but then another Jedi appeared. It was the spirit of Master Vodo-Siosk Baas, who said, "Together Jedi can overcome their weaknesses. Exar Kun, my student—you are defeated at last."

Then yet another apparition appeared, that of Master Skywalker, whose physical body remained inert. His apparition said, "The way to extinguish a shadow is to increase the light."

THE YUUZHAN VONG

25–30 A.B.Y.

Jedi scholars have speculated whether the Sith played a part in the war with the Yuuzhan Vong. While investigations have so far been inconclusive, the war is noted here because it was very possibly the greatest challenge ever for the Jedi, and forever changed not only the New Republic, but the known galaxy itself.

Extragalactic invaders whose religious beliefs threatened all, the Yuuzhan Vong considered technology an abomination. In the name of their gods, they performed blood sacrifices and painful rituals with fanatical devotion, and believed it was their holy duty to destroy nonliving architecture, machines, droids, and all "infidels" who opposed them.

The earliest Jedi record of the Yuuzhan Vong's existence dates to 29 B.B.Y., when Obi-Wan Kenobi and his Padawan Anakin Skywalker searched for the mythical "living planet" Zonama Sekot. They learned that a year earlier, another Jedi, Vergere, had surrendered herself to the extragalactic "Far Outsiders"—the Yuuzhan Vong—to prevent them from attacking Zonama Sekot. More than five decades later, Leia Organa Solo's eldest son, Jacen Solo, discovered that Vergere had survived without revealing her Force powers to the Yuuzhan Vong, and that she had provided the Yuuzhan Vong with information that eventually allowed them to infiltrate New Republic space.

Because of a unique genetic sequence, the Yuuzhan Vong seemed to exist completely apart from the Force. This characteristic rendered the Yuuzhan Vong and their living vessels and weapons virtually invisible to the Jedi, who could not use the Force to perceive or influence the invaders. According to Vergere, the apparent invisibility of the Yuuzhan Vong owed not to any inherent failure of the Force, but to the way Luke Skywalker and his fellow Jedi perceived the Force, specifically what Vergere referred to as the unifying Force. Somehow, it seemed the Jedi had failed to grasp that the Force was grander and farther reaching than even they understood it to be.

It was eventually discovered that the Yuuzhan Vong had been severed from the Force by their ancestral living homeworld, Yuuzhan'tar, after an ancient confrontation with a warfaring species left them with a hunger for violence and conquest. The Jedi's apparent inability to deal with the Yuuzhan

Vong by traditional methods prompted the New Republic to consider other options, including extremely hazardous bioweapons.

A mission to infiltrate a Yuuzhan Vong worldship over the forest world Myrkr proved tragic for the Jedi: Leia Organa Solo's youngest son, Anakin Solo, died, and Jacen Solo was abducted by the Yuuzhan Vong. Months later, the Yuuzhan Vong Nom Anor invited Jacen to convert to the invaders' religion; Jacen agreed because he hoped to destroy the Yuuzhan Vong from within, but as events turned out he escaped and returned to his family.

After Coruscant fell to the invaders, the New Republic implemented a daring plan—conceived by the aged Admiral Ackbar—to lure most of the Yuuzhan Vong fleet to the moon Ebaq 9. The battle that ensued brought an effective end to the war, but certain Yuuzhan Vong factions remained outraged by Jacen's false promise to convert and wanted him dead. In a Yuuzhan Vong ship that attempted to escape from Coruscant, Jacen battled the invaders' Supreme Overlord and was briefly transformed into the most powerful manifestation of the Force on record. The duel was

witnessed by Leia Organa Solo and Han Solo, who had boarded the ship with the assistance of the Yuuzhan Vong executor Nom Anor. Leia Organa Solo made the following record:

> The escape ship was still accelerating from Coruscant as I followed Nom Anor and Han into the cavernous chamber that was the bridge. What I saw made me feel as if I were wedged between a dream and a vision, lifted into a realm that was usually denied to mortal beings.
>
> In the center of the bridge, Jacen stood like a pillar of blinding light, feet planted, arms at his sides, chin lifted. The dazzling light seemed to spin outward from his midsection and surround him like an aura. His face was almost frighteningly serene, and also, I thought, a touch sad. The pupils of his eyes were like rising suns. He seemed to age five years—features maturing, complexion softening, body elongating. I felt light-headed, as if I'd forgotten to breathe.
>
> Across the bridge, a male Yuuzhan

Vong—Jacen later identified him as the Supreme Overlord—was pinned to the coarse bulkhead like a captive shadow-moth. Between Jacen and the Supreme Overlord was Jaina, suspended a meter above the deck by horns that protruded from the inner bulkhead. She was paralyzed but conscious, and dangled limply, like a mournful sculpture. Then Jaina's form began to strengthen, and at the same time the Overlord waned. Before our eyes, his disfigured body melted away and the bridge's deck absorbed him like a stain.

Jaina was rescued, but what youth might have remained in my son vanished that day. The sight of him on the bridge is something I will carry with me to my dying day.

The Yuuzhan Vong officially surrendered to the New Republic on the Bothan Assault Cruiser *Ralroost*. The death toll for the Yuuzhan Vong War has been estimated at 365 trillion.

Perhaps the most perplexing aspect of the war is Vergere, who willingly spent fifty years among the Yuuzhan Vong, and who remains something of a mystery. Although records indicate that a Jedi named Vergere *was* sent to Zonama Sekot in 30 B.Y., some Jedi scholars have speculated whether Vergere may have been a Dark Jedi or a failed Sith apprentice to Palpatine.

Is it possible that Vergere deliberately encouraged the Yuuzhan Vong War or used it as a vehicle for the singular purpose of grooming a new Sith Lord? While some Jedi scholars have dismissed this theory, there are precedents for Sith conspiracies that were years in the making, leading to interstellar war and new Sith regimes. All that is certain is that Jacen Solo was heavily influenced and transformed by the being who called herself Vergere, and it is in part because of her that he is the Jedi he is today.

LUKE SKYWALKER VS. LUMIYA: FIRST ENCOUNTER

4 A.B.Y.

It was a long and twisted path that led to Luke Skywalker's first confrontation with Lumiya on the planet Kinooine. This path involved a conspiracy and various levels of deception; because a chronological presentation of events might inaccurately suggest that Luke Skywalker could have foreseen aspects of the conspiracy, this entry begins not at the start of the path but with the Rebel Alliance's earliest awareness of Lumiya.

Following the Battle of Endor, Princess Leia Organa and Mon Mothma were on a diplomatic mission to the planet Herdessa when they were introduced to Lumiya, a female cyborg who wore a face-concealing helmet and presented herself as the head of Herdessan Planetary Security. Leia soon discovered that Lumiya was allied with renegade Imperials who were in partnership with Herdessan slavers. According to Leia, Lumiya displayed no Force powers, and had blaster weapons concealed in her cybernetic hands. Leia shot Lumiya, but Lumiya survived and managed to escape.

Luke Skywalker pursued the deadly fugitive to Kinooine. There Lumiya attacked him with her lightwhip, a whip possessing a combination of energized and corporeal tendrils. Unprepared for the attack, Luke was defeated and captured, but escaped with the assistance of his friend Kiro, a Force-sensitive Chuhkyvi from Iskalon. Luke hastily constructed a red-bladed shoto, a lightsaber with a relatively short beam, which he wielded simultaneously with his own lightsaber to subdue Lumiya. During that duel, Luke shattered Lumiya's helmet to reveal a familiar face: Shira Brie.

Luke had met Shira Brie when she joined the Rebel Alliance after the Battle of Yavin. Brie claimed she was a native of the planet Shalyvane, and that she was among the few members of her tribe to escape an Imperial attack that destroyed the city of Chinshassa. A skilled pilot, she soon became a member of Rogue Squadron. Along with Luke, she was among several pilots who flew in modified TIE fighters on a mission to infiltrate an Imperial armada; although these TIEs had been outfitted with transceivers to prevent the Rebels from targeting their fellow pilots, the Imperials used a powerful frequency jammer that prompted Luke to rely upon the Force when choosing his targets. It was in this capacity that Luke unknowingly fired upon Shira Brie and destroyed her ship, a realization he did not have until after the battle, when Princess Leia showed him a holorecording that displayed Brie's body in the shattered TIE's cockpit.

Luke was devastated that he had killed a close friend. Suddenly regarded as a pariah by many Rebels who openly blamed him for Brie's death, he was also stripped of his rank as commander. However, Luke refused to believe that the Force had failed him when he shot down Brie's ship. With help from Chewbacca, he eventually found information that would vindicate his belief. At an Imperial data vault on Krake's Planet, Chewbacca recovered a recording chip that yielded the following information:

Subject: Shira Elan Colla Brie.

Current rank: Major, Imperial Special Forces.

Personal history judged ideal. Born in Empire capital. Raised in palace of Emperor Palpatine as part of experiment in adolescent indoctrination. Experiment totally successful.

Gained expert rating in all known forms of combat. Intelligence and coordination both extraordinary.

Biologically altered to reject pain, and to accelerate physical healing process.

Graduated with top honors in history of Academy. Record unequaled since.

Personally selected by Lord Darth Vader for infiltration into banned organization known as "Rebel Alliance." See Reference Log #49734.

Vader project required total razing of city of Chinshassa on planet Shalyvane to establish credible background for subject.

Project's purpose: The elimination—either actual or effectual—of Rebel commander Luke Skywalker.

Project status: Open.

End of program.

Although Luke was absolved of blame for shooting down Brie and was reinstated as a commander, he took little consolation as he had been so easily manipulated, and that Darth Vader had gone to such extreme efforts to either destroy or discredit him. The fact that the Empire had razed Chinshassa merely to establish a "credible background" for Brie was enough to remind the Rebels that their fight was far from over.

Luke continued to believe that Shira Brie was dead until he confronted her cybernetic alter ego on Kinooine. Evidently, Darth Vader had recovered Brie's body from the wreckage of her TIE fighter and had her reconstructed as Lumiya. Despite Luke's victory over Lumiya on Kinooine, he was forced to abandon her upon the arrival of her allies, the Nagai invaders. Later that same year, Lumiya sided with the Nagai's enemies, the Tofs, and nearly shot Princess Leia on Saijo before she herself was shot by one of her former Nagai agents. Once again, Lumiya survived and escaped.

In a briefing to Rebel officials in 4 A.B.Y., Luke Skywalker stated:

On Kinooine, after Lumiya was unmasked, she made it clear to me that she not only hates me but also blames me for who and what she is. She claimed she has suffered ever since she was remade as a cyborg, and held me responsible for her condition. She vowed that someday, she would spit on my pyre, after she had seen me bereft of hope and the will to live.

I tried to reason with her, told her that I never intended to harm her when she flew as Shira Brie on that terrible mission. I pointed out that Darth Vader, who was responsible for reconstructing her as a cyborg after he'd molded her into an Imperial agent, was dead, and that before his death he'd reconciled to the good in himself. I told Lumiya that my father wouldn't have wanted her to go on hating as she does, and that I believed she could find goodness in herself, too.

And then the Nagai invasion fleet arrived. I had no choice but to leave Lumiya. I have little doubt that our paths will cross again. Although I acknowledge that she is a disturbed and dangerous individual, and discourage anyone from approaching her without extreme caution, I urge you to consider that she is also a victim of the Empire.

Let it be known that I refuse to believe that the woman I knew as Shira Brie was just an act, and that I am confident she will return to the light.

Years later, Mara Jade Skywalker furnished additional details about Shira Brie's transformation into Lumiya. After Darth Vader supervised Lumiya's reconstruction on his flagship, the *Executor*, he helped her hone her ability with the Force and may have given her some Sith training. Because Vader knew he was unable to keep Lumiya a secret from his own Master, he presented her as a gift: a new Emperor's Hand. The Emperor sequestered Lumiya on the ancient Sith world of Ziost, where she crafted herself a lightwhip from Kaiburr crystal shards and Mandalorian iron. She was still on Ziost when the Emperor died at the Battle of Endor, and she subsequently committed herself to exterminating the Rebels who had ruined what she believed was the "natural order." It was probably during this time that she assumed the mantle of Sith Lord.

LUKE SKYWALKER VS. LUMIYA: FINAL DUEL

40 A.B.Y.

Except for aforementioned information from Mara Jade, there are few records of Lumiya's activities between 4 A.B.Y. and the current year of 40 A.B.Y. Following the Emperor's death, Lumiya was conscripted by Ysanne Isard, the director of Imperial Intelligence. Isard dispatched Lumiya to hunt down fugitive Emperor's Hand Mara Jade, whom Lumiya fought on Caprioril. Mara Jade defeated Lumiya, and yet again Lumiya was assumed dead, an assumption that was only strengthened by the lack of any records of Lumiya after the duel on Caprioril.

In 40 A.B.Y., Luke Skywalker sensed that Lumiya had returned; shortly after this premonition, Lumiya and the renegade Jedi Alema Rar killed Jedi Master Tresina Lobi—who had been searching for Ben Skywalker—at Fellowship Plaza on Coruscant. Ten days later, Luke and Mara dueled Lumiya and Alema at Roqoo Depot, a refueling station in the Hapes Cluster. Both Lumiya and Alema escaped.

It has already been noted that Lumiya was the primary suspect in the death of Mara Jade Skywalker when Luke Skywalker killed Lumiya on the planet Terephon. It has also been noted that Luke subsequently learned Lumiya's confirmed whereabouts precluded her from poisoning Mara. Although both Mara and Lumiya were on Kavan in the Hapes Cluster at the moment Mara died, Ben Skywalker—who was also on Kavan—personally accounts for Lumiya being nowhere near Mara at the time. Lumiya's activities on Kavan and the identity of Mara's killer are still under investigation.

Because of the sensitive nature of the ongoing investigation into the death of Mara Jade Skywalker, further information is currently available only to sanctioned Jedi.

▼ LUKE SKYWALKER DUELS DARK
LADY OF THE SITH LUMIYA. (Edwards)

PART TWO

THE JEDI

RECORDED 40 A.B.Y. ⋅ AUTHOR: TIONNE SOLUSAR

JEDI EVOLUTION

Over many millennia, the Jedi Order has undergone numerous changes, from the semi-organized band of "wizards" in ancient times to the highly disciplined warriors and peacekeepers of the Old Republic. Some changes have been gradual, implemented by the Jedi after much contemplation, while others came in quick response to unanticipated events and political upheavals. Despite such transformation, the most remarkable aspect of Jedi history is the fact that so many powerful beings chose not only to band together but to use their powers in service to others as well. Jedi may share the ability to manipulate the Force, but it is through the Jedi Order that they are truly united.

THE FORCE AND ITS MYTHIC ORIGINS

The Force is an energy field that binds together time, space, and living beings. Although predecessors of the early Jedi are often credited with identifying it, the Force has always existed, and the Jedi were not the first to utilize it as a source of power. Ancient history accounts for many beings who unwittingly discovered and demonstrated special abilities that indicate they were Force-users or Force-adepts. Although such beings have always been in the minority, it is believed that many more are at least Force-sensitive, meaning they have varying degrees of potential to become Force-users.

Approximately thirty thousand years ago, a species known as the Rakata used the Force to power much of their technology, including starship engines that enabled them to travel through hyperspace and visit distant worlds. Despite various ancient glyphs that illustrate the Rakata's claims of scientific invention and dominance of the galaxy, some historians have speculated that the Rakata may have appropriated their technology from the mysterious Architects of the Corellian system, who predated the Rakata by unknown millennia.

Relying upon information found in crumbling history disks, researchers have attempted to trace the Jedi back to several long-lost organizations, including the mystic Order of Dai Bendu, the Followers of Palawa at the legendary Chatos Academy, or the Ashla worshipers of Tython. Although the Great Holocron sheds some light on the Tython-based organization, it seems that all that remains of the other groups is their names.

EARLY JEDI

Approximately twenty-five thousand years ago, the development of hyperspace-travel technology prompted many Core Worlds to form the

light side of the Force was regarded as the essence of creation, balance, and growth that flowed naturally throughout the galaxy. The dark side was believed to be entirely selfish in nature, and embraced negative energy that made one simultaneously more isolated and more destructive.

The Jedi required generations to master the Force, transforming what once had been regarded as wizardry into something of a science. After they learned that the Force was all-encompassing, they ventured to other worlds to recruit and train those with similar powers. Some Jedi chose the path of diplomacy while others became experts at battle, respectively distinguishing themselves as Jedi consulars and Jedi guardians. Those Jedi who served specific sectors of space became known as Jedi Watchmen. According to Sar Agorn, a Jedi consular from the earliest days of the Republic, who speaks from the Great Holocron:

> *The ability to manipulate the Force may be unusual, but it is not unique. Given time and the proper chemistry, almost anyone can learn how to tap into the power of the Force and move small objects or influence weak minds. But this is not the way of the Jedi. The decision to use such powers for the betterment of all, and not for selfish purposes, distinguishes the Jedi from all others.*

Through meditation and practice, the Jedi discovered that avoiding the emotions of hate, anger, and desire could make them grow more powerful in the light side of the Force. The ancient Jedi did not forbid intimate relations or marriage among their Order, but it was understood that the strong emotions associated with such relationships could easily affect the decisions and behavior of most Jedi. The majority led monastic lives. Some legends claim that the first Jedi Knights traveled to the planet Caamas to learn proper moral judgment in an attempt to understand how to use their powers ethically.

democratic union known as the Galactic Republic. According to the Great Holocron, the first society of Force-sensitive beings may have been founded on the dawn world of Tython, where Force-users harnessed a positive energy that they called the Ashla. This energy allowed them to telepathically communicate across vast distances, heighten their senses, heal themselves, and see past the veils of time. Eventually, they learned that this energy was not limited to Tython, but permeated the entire galaxy. It seems that it was these Force-users or their descendants who eventually became known as the Jedi, warriors who obeyed the precepts of harmony, knowledge, serenity, and peace.

The Tython Jedi came to recognize that the Force had two fundamental aspects: the light side, or Ashla, and the dark side that they called the Bogan. The

Study of the Force continued at the school of Jedi philosophy that was founded on Ossus after the Great Hyperspace War. Jedi students trained in the arts of combat, but also learned that patience, humility, and self-sacrifice were paths to enlightenment. According to the Jedi Master Odan-Urr:

> *A Jedi Master always said this to each of his students before their first lesson: "Cross an unfamiliar river without first discerning its depths and shallows, and you will drown in its currents without reaching your goal." Being a Jedi is no different. Identify the pitfalls and learn the proper path, or you fail the Order and sacrifice yourself in no good purpose.*

As the Jedi became celebrated for their actions and achievements throughout Republic space, Jedi Masters remained ever mindful of the dark side. According to the Jedi Master Bodo Baas:

> *A Jedi does not grasp at power. A Jedi is not a dominator, not an oppressor. To grasp for power is to abandon the ways of the Force. Such a one ceases to know the Force, except in his dark side. To grasp at power is to take up the path that leads to destruction. The dominator is the enemy, yes. But the Jedi do not use the dark powers of the dominator against him.*

On Ossus, the Jedi came to understand that both the light side and dark side of the Force reflect aspects of the living Force, the in-the-moment manifestation of life energy, and the unifying Force, the cosmic expression of prophecies and destinies. More precisely, they realized that the light and dark sides are intertwined and necessary to each other, as they form a cosmic balance. A Jedi could avoid embracing the dark side, but could never ignore its power. Over the millennia, awareness of the unifying Force became lost to the Jedi, but it was rediscovered during the New Republic's war with the Yuuzhan Vong.

JEDI KNIGHTS OF THE OLD REPUBLIC

Although the Jedi realized many great achievements during the four-thousand-year-span between the Great Hyperspace War and the Battle of Ruusan, their numbers were decimated during the Second Sith War, and their image became tarnished when they began taking active roles in government; despite the noble intentions and scrupulous behavior of the several Jedi who served as Republic Supreme Chancellor, the general public was never entirely convinced that their influential leaders had won their elections fairly, and came to regard the Jedi as the most powerful of power-mongers. Even more scandalous was the Jedi Order's part in a military strike that left the Ubese homeworld inhospitable, and its desperate recruitment of Force-sensitive children to fight the Sith at the Battle of Ruusan.

No matter the circumstances, Jedi must always remain conscious of how their actions will be perceived. All Jedi would do well to remember the words of Jedi Master Odan-Urr:

> When a Jedi behaves badly in public, an observer might think, If this Jedi is representative of the whole Order, then plainly no Jedi is worthy of respect. *On meeting a second Jedi, who behaves better than the first, that same person might think,* Does this say that half of the Jedi are good, and half bad? *On meeting a third Jedi, who behaves as well as the second, the person thinks,* Was the first

Jedi an exception, then? *In this way, only by the good behavior of several Jedi can the public be certain that the poor behavior of one Jedi was unusual. Thus, it takes many Jedi to undo the mistakes of one.*

In the aftermath of the Battle of Ruusan, the surviving Jedi were forced to reevaluate every aspect of their Order. A twelve-member Jedi Council established new rules, the most radical of which applied to recruitment and training. Via the Tedryn Holocron, they heeded the words of Jedi Master Bodo Baas:

> *Training Jedi is a most rewarding pursuit, but one ringed with many unseen perils. Never, O Master Jedi, rest easy when your pupil begins to grow anxious to learn at a pace greater than that which you have set for him. Such impatience is natural in the young and inexperienced, and a commendable trait in a student. But it also signals a time when the pupil is most open to the temptation of stepping onto the broad path of easy advancement that leads to the dark side. Beware, Jedi Master, lest through carelessness and inattention you loose on the galaxy a monster.*

After the Jedi Masters decided that it was too dangerous to train anyone familiar with fear, anger, and any other emotion that might lead to the dark side, it was agreed that Force-sensitive juveniles, adolescents, and adults would no longer be eligible for enlistment or conscription. Instead, they sought out and adopted Force-sensitive infants who would be raised and trained at the Jedi Temple on Coruscant; to prevent any emotional attachments that might cloud judgment, most recruits would never have any subsequent contact with their families.

Although the method by which the ancient Jedi detected potential Force-users was almost lost to time, records indicate that the Jedi—shortly after the Battle of Ruusan—either discovered or rediscovered the existence of midi-chlorians,

microscopic life-forms that reside within all living cells and communicate with the Force to reveal its will. Midi-chlorians can be detected by a simple blood test, and a high midi-chlorian count indicates great potential as a Jedi. The Great Holocron confirms that the Jedi relied upon this blood-analysis method up until the Jedi Purge.

While some beings considered it an honor to have their child become a member of the Jedi Order, others likened the Jedi to baby snatchers. However, records indicate that most parents—after being educated about the myriad risks and responsibilities of raising Force-sensitive children—were genuinely relieved to relinquish their offspring to the resourceful Jedi.

It also seemed that the new rules worked. The millennium that followed the Battle of Ruusan became known as the Golden Age of the Republic. Many worlds prospered, and the Jedi lived by their ethical code:

> *There is no emotion; there is peace.*
> *There is no ignorance; there is knowledge.*
> *There is no passion; there is serenity.*
> *There is no death; there is the Force.*

But the Golden Age was not to last. It ended with the Rise of the Empire and the Jedi Purge, which nearly succeeded in crushing the Order once and for all.

THE POTENTIUM PERSPECTIVE

As Jedi learn more about the Force, it is not unusual for them to form their own theories about how and why it works. They question how, if the Force creates and sustains life, it can have a dark side. Some arrive at the conclusion that the Force is not divided into dark and light, that its energy is inherently positive, and that there is no "dark side" waiting to corrupt them. Time and again,

this conclusion has been proved erroneous, and the Jedi who felt compelled to test the limits of the Force rarely perceived the dangers of their explorations. As they approached the brink of the dark side, some were rescued by other Jedi or came back willingly when they saw the error of their ways. Those who refused to renounce their mistaken beliefs were either exiled to the farthest reaches of the galaxy, or destroyed.

During the penultimate century of the Old Republic, the Jedi Leor Hal founded a philosophical group that challenged the Jedi Order's perspective of the Force. Hal and his disciples maintained that the Force could not push one into evil; that the universe was infiltrated by a benevolent field of life energy whose instructions were inevitably good. They called this energy field the Potentium, maintaining that it was the beginning and ending of all things, and that one's connection with it should not be mediated or obscured by any sort of training or discipline. Followers of the Potentium

insisted that the Jedi Masters and the Temple hierarchy could not accept the universal good of the Potentium because it meant they were no longer needed. According to Asli Krimsan:

You are not the first student to ask me of the Potentium, and I doubt you'll be the last. It sounds so appealing, the idea that one does not require any study or practice to embrace and be a part of a benevolent energy field. But when one considers the history of the Force, all the many and various reasons why the Jedi understand there are definite divisions and pitfalls in life's tenure in space and time, one realizes that the Potentium view is ultimately selfish. It allows one to believe that one's actions are good and justified simply because there is no evil intent.

If you find any merit in this philosophy, be cautioned. This is not the way of the Jedi.

You might consider yourself a fair

person, even a good person, but do you believe all of your contemporaries consider you the same? Is there not one of your fellows who—from your perspective—has ever acted unkindly? Is it conceivable that at least one of your friends might not regard you as entirely benevolent and with-out any negative qualities?

Do you believe that you're as good as you will ever be? That you know all that you need to know? No, of course you do not, for you are already wise.

There is nothing wrong with questioning authority, history, and the nature of exist-ence. But do not assume that all your ques-tions can be answered by listening only to yourself and an energy field you've just begun to sense. You have much to learn, and much to learn about the Force.

In the end, the Jedi Padawans who had been caught up in the Potentium movement left the Temple or were pushed out, and dispersed around the galaxy. Although records do not reveal that any of the original followers of the Potentium succumbed to the dark side of the Force, their beliefs may have been adopted by Vergere, who twisted the philosophy to suit her own purposes.

It has also been theorized that the Potentium may have originated as a Sith scheme to subvert Jedi teachings; this theory allows for the possibility that Leor Hal was entirely unaware of any Sith influence on his explorations of the Force. The Jedi Order continues to regard the Potentium philosophy as dangerously misguided at the least, and heresy at the worst.

THE LOST

Histpry accounts for numerous Jedi Padawans, Jedi Knights, and Jedi Masters who turned to the dark side and either fled or were banished from the Jedi Order. But according to the Great Holocron, only nineteen Jedi Masters ever officially renounced their commissions to the Jedi Order prior to Jedi Master Dooku in 32 B.B.Y. This group had long been referred to as the Lost, but after Dooku joined their numbers, they became known as the Lost Twenty.

The Holocron's record of the Lost is incomplete, and one can only speculate whether it has been corrupted. The record indicates that most of the Jedi Masters left because of ideological differences with the Order, and did their best to leave on positive terms. Except for Dooku, only one other Jedi Master is identified by name: Phanius, who left the Order circa 2000 B.B.Y. According to Sith scholar Murk Lundi, Phanius became Darth Ruin, a Sith Lord who recruited other Dark Jedi to fight their former allies. No records indicate that the Jedi of the Old Republic were aware Phanius or any other members of the Lost had turned to the dark side, let alone become Sith Lords. The fact that the Jedi may have been completely oblivious to Phanius's conversion, and that few Jedi even suspected that Dooku had joined the dark side until ten years after he had renounced his commission, suggests that other Lost Jedi left the Order without arousing concerns.

Research on the Jedi known as Vergere has revealed that she was a Padawan to Jedi Master Thracia Cho Leem, who left the Jedi Order in 29 B.B.Y. The Great Holocron does not offer any explanation for why Thracia Cho Leem left the Order, but the record suggests that she was not considered among the Lost.

Following the Battle of Geonosis, many Jedi chose to leave the Order rather than serve as generals in the Republic army. Others, such as the Jedi Master Sora Bulq, chose to ally with Count Dooku and fight against the Republic. By the end of the Clone Wars, it seems that the Lost Twenty had been reduced to a footnote in history.

THE DARK TIMES

Following the Jedi Purge, the Empire confiscated or destroyed most Jedi records, and the few remaining Jedi went into hiding on separate, distant worlds. Despite this great darkness, hope had survived, for it was during this period that Obi-Wan Kenobi showed Luke Skywalker the ways of the Force, which led Luke on his path to become a Jedi. Luke eventually learned that Darth Vader had been Anakin Skywalker before being seduced by the dark side of the Force, and he was able to rescue his father from the dark side, at last ending the horrors wreaked by Vader.

Even after the Empire fell and the New Republic reclaimed Coruscant, it seemed unlikely, even impossible, that the Jedi Order could be restored. However, Luke's exploits led him to encounters with other Force-sensitive beings, and he realized that his powers were not altogether unique. These encounters encouraged him to consider training others to become Jedi.

THE JEDI ACADEMY

Eight years after the Battle of Yavin, Luke discovered the nearly three-hundred-and-fifty-year-old wreck of the *Chu'unthor* on Dathomir, which provided him with old data tapes on the subject of training Jedi. Because Luke had never received a traditional Jedi education, he studied the tapes to further his own knowledge and abilities. These tapes—like the Tedryn Holocron and the texts recovered from the Jedi library at Ossus—contained little information about the hierarchy of the Jedi Order during the Golden Age, but there was invaluable data regarding Jedi training, meditation, and lightsaber forms. Although Luke knew the Jedi

Order could not be restored to its former glory, he believed that it could be reinvented.

Three years after the recovery of the data tapes, the New Republic granted permission for Luke to seek out students whom he could train to become new Jedi. Whereas Jedi of the Old Republic had been conscripted as infants into the Jedi Order and were generally forbidden to marry and have children, Luke was willing to consider anyone who demonstrated some ability with the Force. Because Luke believed the galaxy needed a new generation of Jedi and knew firsthand that the Force was strong in certain families, he did not discourage marriage and procreation.

Luke founded his Jedi academy on Yavin 4 in the Great Temple that had once been the secret base of the Rebel Alliance. He considered it an institution established not only for learning but also for discussion; rather than dictate what the new Jedi should think, he encouraged his trainees to arrive at group conclusions. While most students regarded the academy as a place of contemplation where they could learn to use their powers, some saw it as a haven where they could strive to overcome the dark side within them.

Luke's first students included Kam Solusar, who'd been a young Jedi when he escaped the Jedi Purge; Kirana Ti, a Witch of Singing Mountain Clan who had a husband and daughter on Dathomir; Streen, a former recluse and gas prospector at Bespin; Dorsk 81, a humanoid clone from Khomm; Gantoris, a leader of abandoned colonists on the planet Eol Sha; Corran Horn, who'd served as a pilot with Rogue Squadron; Kyle Katarn, a former special operative for the Rebel Alliance; Mara Jade, a former Emperor's Hand; Cilghal of Mon Calamari; Brakiss, who was eventually revealed as an agent of the Imperial Inquisitorius; Kyp Durron, an escapee from the Kessel mines; and myself, Tionne, a historian and minstrel with only a modest amount of Force ability.

The academy's first year was marked by unanticipated events, including the resurrection of Exar Kun's spirit, which resulted in the death of Gantoris and the dark side seduction of Kyp Durron. Mara Jade, Corran Horn, and Kyle Katarn left the praxeum for different reasons, but each eventually returned to resume training. Although critics suggested that Luke Skywalker might have done better to begin with fewer students, all the surviving students were stronger and more united by their experiences, and better prepared for service to the New Republic.

Academy students subscribed to the basic tenets that characterized a balanced approach to their role in galactic affairs:

- **The Force is to be used to save lives, not to take lives.**

- **The Force should never be used for personal gain.**

- **Every Jedi has a vote in making decisions for the group.**

- **The Jedi should work to support and maintain the New Republic—but not at the expense of Jedi ideals.**

- **If the Jedi are called upon to fight, they will defend the helpless without hatred, anger, or thoughts of revenge.**

Using an illusion technique Luke learned from the Fallanassi, Kam Solusar and myself—two of the academy's permanent staff—he kept the Jedi academy relatively safe from casual inspection. Some academy students would eventually see their own Force-sensitive children follow in their footsteps. These offspring included the twins Jaina and Jacen Solo, and their younger brother Anakin; and Ben Skywalker, the son of Luke and Mara Skywalker.

THE NEW JEDI ORDER

In 28 A.B.Y., Luke Skywalker established a new Jedi Council that consisted of politicians as well as Jedi. Like its previous incarnations, this Jedi Order found that its survival depended not only on adherence to rules of conduct but on a certain degree of adaptability as well.

At the outbreak of the war with the Yuuzhan Vong, most Jedi left the academy on Yavin 4 to help with the defense of the New Republic. When a Yuuzhan Vong invasion force arrived at Yavin 4, it signaled the end of the academy. The invaders destroyed the Great Temple and captured several Jedi, including Anakin Solo. After Anakin was rescued, New Republic ally Talon Karrde commanded the destruction of the Yuuzhan Vong–occupied base on Yavin 4.

The Yuuzhan Vong invasion caused some Jedi to question the tenets of their academy. Several Jedi gravitated to Kyp Durron's "radical party," which believed that negotiation was best accomplished from a position of power, and it was foolish not to strike first against a clear enemy. This contingent's philosophy was summed up as follows:

- **Do not be afraid to use the Force—it's a tool, just as a lightsaber is a tool.**

- **Do not wait for others to perceive the danger before acting.**

- **Listen to the Force. It's on your side and will warn you if you're making a mistake.**

- **The Jedi have served the Republic for millennia. They have a proud tradition and should never be perceived as a collection of weaklings or cowards.**

- **The Jedi are the best weapon the galaxy has against the Yuuzhan Vong**

invasion. Waiting for the New Republic to understand this might be self-defeating, if by the time they realize the need for the Jedi there is no more New Republic—or no more Jedi.

Luke Skywalker and Kyp Durron did not resolve all their differences, but worked together to stop the invaders. When the war with the Yuuzhan Vong ended, Skywalker summoned all Jedi to the planet Zonama Sekot, where he made the following address:

If I have learned anything from the events of the past five years, it is that the Force is more all-embracing than I ever realized. Light and dark do not always stand opposed, but mingle with each other in curious ways. More important, the Force seems to have a will, and it's when we're acting against the will of the Force that we can get into trouble. Anger by itself is not of the dark side unless it is accompanied by a desire to dominate.

When we act in harmony with the will of the Force, we disappear into it. When we struggle against it, we not only sever our ties with the Force, but also feed the needs of chaos.

The evolution of sentience reflects the constant movement between those two poles. Evil—the dark side—won't be eradicated until it has been discarded as an option for acquiring power, subjugating would-be opponents, or offsetting feelings of anger, envy, or exclusion. Where victims of injustice exist, the dark side finds initiates. That is the cycle our actions are meant to forestall, and in this battle the Force is both our ally and our guardian. We serve it best by listening to its will, and serving the good with our every action—by personifying the Force.

But I'm no longer convinced that we're meant to police the galaxy. For one thing, we're too few in number. That was made evident early in the war, and it's likely to hold true for whatever conflicts erupt in the coming years. The Jedi began as a meditative order. Our forebears believed that they could balance light and dark by remaining always in the Force, and thereby perfecting themselves. Gradually, however, as the Supreme Chancellors appealed to the Order time and again for advice in resolving disputes, the Jedi became adjuncts of the Old Republic, then marshals and warriors, taking it upon themselves to uphold the peace, and little by little being drawn away from the Force and into the mundane.

I don't propose that we place ourselves in seclusion and pass our days meditating on the Force—though that might be the path for some of us. But I do advocate attuning ourselves to the longer view, and reaching out to others who seek to serve the Force. The genetic makeup of each and every one of us augments our ability to tap the Force, but everyone, regardless of his or her genetics, has the potential to use the Force to one degree or another. Perhaps not to move rocks and take giant strides; but in some sense those physical powers are little more than surface effects. The real powers are more subtle, for they involve adhering to the true path, avoiding the temptation to dominate, sacrificing oneself for those who have less, and living impeccably, by recognizing that the Force doesn't flow from us but through us, ever on the move.

Following the war with the Yuuzhan Vong, the Jedi decided that they should not be affiliated with any political entity that might interfere or restrict their efforts to maintain peace. The Jedi dismissed all politicians from what is now known as the Masters' Council and relocated the Jedi academy to Ossus. Kirana Ti returned to her war-ravaged homeworld Dathomir with Streen, who worked with her to establish a new Jedi praxeum for the Force-senstive Dathomirians.

Luke Skywalker continues to lead the new Jedi Order, but in this current period of darkness it is difficult for anyone to foresee how the Order will evolve and whether it will continue to thrive.

FORCE-SENSITIVE ABILITIES

For all the countless hours that Jedi have spent in meditation and contemplation of the Force, it is not their quiet moments for which they are generally recognized, but rather their special abilities. Popularly regarded as supernatural powers, some of these abilities—including fast reflexes and telepathy—are naturally possessed by various species, but only Force-sensitive beings are known to have mastered such a wide array of paranormal talents.

The Jedi regard their skills as rooted in three areas: Control, Sense, and Alter. According to the Jedi Master Bodo Baas:

> *Control is internal. It is the Jedi's ability to recognize the Force in himself and to use it to his benefit. Sense involves the next step, in which the Jedi recognizes the Force in the universe outside herself. Here she feels the Force and is able to draw upon it for information about the world around her. Through it she is connected to the rest of the universe. Alter is the third and most difficult area to master, for it involves the student's ability to modify the Force and redistribute its energies. Through these skills, the Jedi can influence the universe, making changes as needed to accomplish his or her goals.*
>
> *The power known as Alter Mind bridges all these skill areas. Through it a Jedi can project her perception of reality into the mind of another, or an illusion or conclusion that she needs the other to hold as true. This is a most magnificent and useful power, but it is also one fraught with danger. Bending the will of another for a benign purpose can be noble and good. The dark side lurks nearby in this power, so it should be used with caution.*

Some Jedi are more adept than others at specific Force-related abilities. While such proficiency is often the result of intensive study and practice, genetics and heredity can be a crucial factor in either enhancing or limiting certain abilities. For example, members of the Halcyon Jedi bloodline lack telekinetic powers but excel in other areas of the Force to easily compensate for their "weakness."

SENSE POWERS

Nearly all Force-users are born with heightened sight, hearing, and olfactory senses, allowing them to perceive things that otherwise would be impossible without artificial aids. A Jedi learns to feel the bonds that join all living things and gains the ability to understand how these things are interconnected. Such talents enable the Jedi to gather information about their environment, detect danger and hidden beings, and "see" in total darkness or through barriers.

Although Jedi cannot always easily sense the presence of Sith, they can sense disturbances in the Force that can indicate such a presence. The sensation is mostly instinctive, a bad feeling that should not be dismissed as simply an emotional reaction to a situation. If a Jedi senses that something is amiss, the feeling is almost always justified.

TELEPATHY

Jedi are not telepathic to the extent that they can read minds, but they can read emotions and see images from another's mind. Jedi who are related or share close bonds, such as the relationship between a Master and apprentice, can exchange short four- or five-word sentences with each other, but few can engage in actual telepathic conversations. Generally, Jedi employ telepathy to read *states of minds* and exchange silent communications. This talent is most useful in moderating peace negotiations, but is also used in combat situations to anticipate an opponent's actions. Although Jedi routinely rely upon comlinks for the purposes of standard communication, there have been cases where individuals were able to contact each other over great distances using the Force.

One of the more intriguing Jedi telepaths

on record is the Iktotchi Jedi Master Saesee Tiin, who served on the Jedi Council during the Clone Wars. Like all Iktotchi, Master Tiin was a natural telepath, but his powers were much greater than any other on his homeworld. Interestingly, various records indicate that other Jedi regarded him as something of a loner, an attribute not typical of Council members, but one should keep in mind that verbal communication is almost always a redundant process for an Iktotchi.

Twenty years before the Clone Wars, few were surprised when Master Tiin refrained from speaking at the funeral of his own teacher and mentor, the renowned Jedi Master Omo Bouri. Several months later, Mace Windu encouraged Tiin to consider taking on a Padawan, and Tiin met with a group of Jedi younglings at the Jedi Temple on Coruscant. The following is a recording of his speech—his longest on record—to the younglings, which should enlighten any student about the pitfalls and strengths of telepathic powers:

When I was a Padawan, many of my fellow students believed that my inherited telepathic abilities gave me an unfair advantage in my education. It is true that I never had difficulty in communicating my thoughts or comprehending the thoughts of others, but I do not believe that this made my education any easier. For unlike my peers, I was a natural receiver and transmitter of thoughts, a condition that I—not then able to organize incoming thoughts or consistently contain my own deliberations— often considered a hindrance and, at times, an embarrassment. I will not share details, but allow you to imagine. Had I been raised on Iktotch, where societies are designed to accommodate telepaths, my circumstances still would have been awkward, for my Force sensitivity would have set me apart.

I did my best to seal off my mind from others. I found that I could home in on the minds of specific beings if I maintained eye contact. I also learned to incorporate my abilities during a fight.

In combat, telepaths do have a distinct edge. Even if one fights by instinct and reflex, most cannot stop themselves from emitting monosyllabic thoughts that project their next movement. During my training bouts at the Jedi Temple, my opponents unwittingly revealed their every move, allowing me that crucial fraction of a moment that enabled me to be the one who would remain standing. Understandably, my fellow Jedi students began to keep their distance.

I came to the attention of the Jedi Master Omo Bouri, a Wol Cabbashite who, for reasons I could not fathom, selected me as his Padawan. I had never encountered a Wol Cabbashite before. Master Omo's cognitive brain, as opposed to the one that controlled his digestive tasks, was so highly evolved and alien from mine that his musings were often indecipherable. To communicate, he used phonemic pulses of

*energy with syntactic contours in a mag-
netic field that he exuded and controlled
with his tongue. At first, I couldn't understand his thoughts or a single word he said.
It was a most refreshing experience.*

*I'd thought I knew more than I needed
to know about telepathy, but Master Omo
showed me that I was wrong. He showed me
how to use the Force to isolate my own brain
waves, intercept stray thoughts, and screen
dozens of minds at once. How to whisper
across space, yell without noise, keep secrets,
and sift through layers of lies and buried
memories to uncover the truth. How to seek
out information from the stars themselves,
allowing one to astrogate a starship through
lightspeed without a nav computer.*

*What's more, he taught me the
meaning of conviction and dedication to
the Jedi Order.*

*What path might my life have taken
had not Omo Bouri chosen me as his
Padawan? I do not care to speculate, for I
am certain any other path would have been
far less engaging. And I would have been
less of a Jedi.*

Records indicate that Tiin did not take on a
Padawan. He devoted much time toward an effort
to communicate with his deceased teacher's spirit,
but it is unknown whether he succeeded. He died
during the Jedi Purge on Coruscant.

AFFECT MIND/ JEDI MIND TRICK

A Jedi can use the Force to manipulate the
behavior and perceptions of weak-minded beings.
Essentially, this power—referred to by Jedi as affect
mind and alter mind, but popularly known as Jedi

mind tricks—utilizes a combination of receptive
empathy, projective empathy, and hypnosis. Jedi
mind tricks can stop the understanding of what's
really happening by blocking the senses, and can
also obliterate memories altogether or even replace
them with false ones. Species with highly organized
mental facilities, such as Hutts and Toydarians, are
naturally immune to mind tricks.

The Jedi Master Yarael Poof was a consummate
illusionist, reportedly capable of making himself
invisible to fellow Jedi. He was also able to quickly
determine an opponent's fears through the use
of the Force, and could create illusions that were
perceived by entire armies. In several instances,
his projected mind tricks prompted quick ends to
battles. The Asli Krimsan Holocron provides the
following recording by Master Poof:

JEDI MASTER YARAEL POOF. ▶
(Edwards)

Young Jedi, I know many of you are eager to test your affect mind abilities, and that some have already attempted this power amongst yourselves. While it can be most useful in conflict resolution, affect mind must be used with restraint, almost always as a last resort, after exhausting less dangerous avenues that lead to peace. Yes, less dangerous, say I, for the power can easily cause permanent damage to a relatively innocent subject.

For example, imagine you are on a mission that requires you to discreetly infiltrate a secured building. Despite your efforts at stealth, you are sighted by an armed guard. Ah, an opportunity for affect mind! But with so many opportunities to choose from, what is a Jedi to do?

Before you answer, consider this: While the guard may prove to be an obstacle on your mission, he is also a living being. He may not be menacing by nature, merely an employee or servant. He may have a family, others who care about him. Had you met him under different circumstances, you might have discovered him to be a friend and ally.

What to do, then? Make the guard see you as a small, unthreatening creature? Make him go to sleep, or forget he saw you at all? Hypnotically suggest that you have leapt away from where you are standing, and encourage the guard to chase the apparition you have created? Project a frightening image that will cause him to flee?

All these things could very well work, young Jedi, but have you considered the consequences? What if the guard enjoys shooting at small, unthreatening creatures? What if his species is physically incapable of sleep? What if he forgets he saw you, but the fact that he even unwittingly allowed you to pass will cost him his job or his life? What physical trauma will he suffer if he chases your apparition into a wall of solid rock? What if you strike such fear in him that he dies on the spot, or forgets the nature of gravity as he tries to escape over the edge of the nearest cliff?

I need not lecture that you are responsible for your decisions and actions. However, I will remind you that any course will leave a wake, and that even the smallest ripple can cause death. I also will remind you that you have yet to resolve that problem with the guard.

Makes you wish you had been more stealthy, yes?

I have presented only a few variables for you to consider about the situation with the guard, but this is enough for you to realize that it would be irresponsible of me to encourage any specific utilization of affect mind.

I will make a few suggestions, however.

As a Jedi, you should be able to sense immediately whether the guard is prone to violence or susceptible to fear. This knowledge can be used to your advantage, and may direct your use of affect mind. Also, you must determine whether it is best to divert or subdue your target. Such decisions must often be made instantly, without hesitation.

What would I have done in such a situation, you ask? I really can't say. A Jedi is not proud or boastful, and I trust you will understand I am sincere when I say that it is hard for me to imagine that the guard might have spied me in the first place, had I not wished to be seen.

But if a guard had seen me, I might make him believe I was nothing but a gust of wind, or the shadow of a soaring indigenous avian. A Jedi can do such things, for it is the will of the Force.

TELEKINESIS

Commonly known as a Jedi's object movement power, telekinesis is more accurately described as a manipulation of the Force to control the direction of objects through space. Jedi utilize this talent not only to push, pull, and lift objects, but also to redirect projectiles and guide their starships through combat.

Before Dooku renounced the Jedi Order and reclaimed his family title of *Count,* he was among the most highly regarded lightsaber instructors and made a series of recordings that demonstrated his expertise. These recordings—preserved on the Great Holocron—became required viewing for two generations of Padawan learners during the twilight of the Old Republic. On the Asli Krimsan Holocron, one of Dooku's lesser-known recordings deals with telekinesis, and also suggests that

Dooku was not always as confident as he seemed. Although Dooku ultimately turned to the dark side, a Jedi can still learn from his account of a lesson with Master Yoda:

Hello, younglings. Asli Krimsan has asked me to tell you about using the Force to move objects. Rather than offer specific instruction, I offer you my recollection of the day I learned that this skill was something more than a Jedi's own personal tractor beam.

Unlike many Jedi, my origins were always something of a public record. My homeworld was Serenno, my family wealthy and of noble rank, and they were proud that I had been conscripted into the Jedi Order. In my youth, I believed that my fellow Jedi knew of my background and so looked upon me differently. Not with sympathy, envy, admiration, or disdain, but merely

differently, *as if my being a Jedi was not as remarkable as was my lineage. I stress that this was my perception, and mine alone. I was never treated unfairly.*

And yet, as a child at the Jedi Temple, there were times when I wanted to separate myself from my biological relatives. I thought that if I knew less of my origins, I would not feel as I did, as though I had a greater burden to prove myself. I did my best and pushed myself to be better, as I thought this might alleviate the weight that I felt upon my shoulders.

My self-consciousness did not go unnoticed by Master Yoda. I was just over seven years old on the day that I crossed paths with him at a garden in the Temple, a research laboratory for the Jedi Agricultural Corps. I found him on a stone path, standing beside a potted long-stemmed plant that had broad, translucent yellow leaves. He gazed up at the delicate leaves, and told me the plant was alien, very rare, the only one of its kind on Coruscant. He said some service droids had left the plant on the path, and he wondered if I might move it onto a nearby patch of grass. I bent to pick up the ceramic pot, but before my fingers touched it, Master Yoda encouraged me to use the Force.

Every Jedi learner is trained to move objects, and I had already proved some capability with this skill. I stepped back to examine the rounded shape of the pot and sensed the air around it, then allowed my mind to lock onto the pot. I attempted to visualize it rising from the path, but the pot merely shifted, scraping the surface of the stone that it continued to rest upon.

Collecting myself, I focused on the pot's base, confirmed that it was not vacuum-locked to the path, then pushed upward. The pot wobbled, causing the plant's leaves

to tremble. Using the Force, I touched the leaves and calmed them, and it was then that I felt the plant's own life energy, something a tractor beam could never do. It had been my error to think of the plant as an inanimate object, rather than something linked to the Force itself.

I extended my hold and visualized the pot within a column that extended from the garden floor to the ceiling. Finding myself short of breath, I inhaled, then slowly, slowly, I lifted the pot until it hovered a full meter above the path.

I guided the plant through the air and lowered it upon the grass. Although I'd meant for a soft landing, I was surprised when the pot sank a few millimeters into the ground, the base tearing the blades of grass.

Master Yoda then said, "Incredibly dense alien soil, that plant can only survive in. Very heavy, the pot is. Neglected to tell you of this, I did. No matter. The path it blocks no longer." Then he looked me in the eye and said, "Why our paths cross today, I wonder?"

With some reluctance, I confided my belief that other Jedi regarded me as different because of my heritage. Master Yoda responded with great laughter. When he recovered, he said, "Aware of your family, few Jedi are. For themselves, your skills and behavior speak. Think others look at you differently, do you? Because of your posture, they might. Stand straighter than any other youngling, you do!"

The lesson that I learned from Master Yoda was that burdens are only as heavy as one imagines, and that—with the Force— any weight can be lifted.

LUKE SKYWALKER USES A FORCE-POWERED BURST ▶ OF SPEED TO AVOID ATTACK FROM THE HUMAN-REPLICA DROID GURI ON CORUSCANT. *(Edwards)*

FORCE LEAP

The ability to leap higher and farther comes relatively naturally to Jedi. Among other useful aspects, a well-timed Force leap enables a Jedi to quickly draw within range of a potential enemy. Although the leaping range varies depending on a Jedi's training and physique, most Jedi Masters are easily able to make leaps several times their own height. This skill can also be integrated with acrobatic martial arts, and is essential for Jedi who practice Form IV lightsaber combat.

BURST OF SPEED

By using the Force to attune their entire body with their heightened reflexes, Jedi can use the skill commonly referred to as the burst of speed to sprint with such velocity that they appear to vanish from their starting point. In unarmed combat, this ability can be utilized to bring a rapid end to a fight. More than other Force powers, the burst of speed can have a draining effect on a Jedi's energy and metabolism, and extended use typically requires a recovery period.

Although this power was understood and used by the Jedi of the Old Republic, Luke Skywalker did not discover it until three and a half years after the Battle of Yavin, when he confronted the human replica droid Guri in Prince Xizor's castle on Coruscant. Luke described his experience to his first students at the Jedi academy:

> By all appearances, Guri was human. If Lando Calrissian hadn't told me about her beforehand, I never would have guessed she was a droid, let alone an assassin who served Prince Xizor. It wasn't until Guri demonstrated her supernatural strength and speed that she revealed herself to be inhuman.

In brief, I was in a castle that was only minutes away from obliteration when Guri blocked my exit. She was unarmed, unafraid of death, and because she'd heard about Jedi from Xizor, she wanted to find out whether she could best one in hand-to-hand combat. She leapt at me, and it was only by the Force that I was able to evade her initial attack. Unfortunately, I was momentarily distracted, and that fraction of a second was all she needed to strike me in the stomach and the side of my head, driving me to the floor. I was dazed, and felt I'd lost contact with the Force.

Then I heard Ben Kenobi's voice calling as if from a great distance, echoing across time and space. He said, *The Force. Let it work for you, Luke.*

I had to trust the Force completely.

Guri's hand was coming down like a blade at me. A death strike. I watched her hand descend, saw it moving to smash me, but it seemed so incredibly slow that I was able to roll aside and stand before the blow could land. I felt as if I were moving at normal speed, though there was a crackling feeling to my motions, and a sound like a strong wind whistling about my ears. To me, Guri seemed to be suddenly mired in thickened time. It wasn't any effort to knock her to the floor. As she fell, time seemed to speed up and return to normal. Guri was subdued, and I proceeded to exit the castle.

The burst of speed that I experienced was not a fluke, but unlike other Force powers, I cannot say I felt in complete control of it. All of you should bear in mind that while it often seems we use the Force to achieve our goals, it is ultimately the will of the Force that guides our actions.

HEALING

Ancient Jedi learned that the power of the Force could be used to ease pain, heal wounds, and cure various afflictions, and that these healing arts were effective on ordinary beings as well as Force-users. During the Old Republic era, the Jedi Temple on Coruscant headquartered the Jedi Medical Corps, where young Force-users learned valuable lessons about the frailty of life through their work in a medcenter, training to ease the suffering of others. The Old Republic Jedi also founded a chapter house on Rhinnal, a planet that remains famous for its expertise in medicine. As with other Force powers, some Jedi have a natural ability as healers; such Jedi have never been common, and their kindred guard them carefully.

◀ JEDI MASTER CILGHAL EMPLOYS HEALING POWER. *(Trevas)*

The Jedi Master Cilghal is one of the most celebrated of contemporary Jedi healers. Before becoming a Jedi, Cilghal—a niece of the legendary Admiral Ackbar—was a New Republic ambassador of Mon Calamari. It was during a raid by Imperial forces on Mon Calamari that Leia Organa Solo became aware of Cilghal's ability to predict which casualties would die in battle or survive triage. Realizing that Cilghal was Force-sensitive, Leia sent her to join Luke Skywalker's academy on Yavin 4, where she became one of the first of Luke's students to graduate as a Jedi Knight. Cilghal and her talents achieved renown after she used the Force to cure Mon Mothma of a degenerative molecular poison.

After Mara Jade Skywalker became infected with deadly coomb spores planted by the Yuuzhan Vong agent Nom Anor, she was eventually cured by an antidote from a most unusual source: a vial of tears from the former Jedi Vergere. Cilghal learned that Vergere produced natural antitoxins through a Force technique that Vergere referred to as "making herself small." Through this technique, a Force-user can manipulate and alter things at a molecular level. After meeting with Vergere in the New Republic Fleet Command annex on Mon Calamari, where the New Republic had established a provisional capital during the Yuuzhan Vong war, Cilghal made the following recording:

> Because Vergere was regarded as untrustworthy, I was cautious of her advice and instructions on any subject. However, I could not ignore the fact that it was she who provided the antitoxin that saved Mara's life, nor could I deny that I wished to know how to produce such chemicals myself.
>
> I met with Vergere in her cell, where she had spent many hours being debriefed by Fleet Intelligence. Although she appeared a bit tired, I found her to be entirely cooperative as she explained her healing technique to me. Essentially, she narrows her focus—her mind and Force-awareness—until it becomes microscopic. While her physical body remains unchanged, her projected form shrinks to an infinitesimal size. In that state, she can rearrange molecules, take them apart, and build new ones bit by bit. She maintains that she uses her tears because they are convenient, but that she can accomplish the same thing with other material.
>
> Afterward, I met with Master Skywalker, who had also discussed Vergere's technique with her. I presented my assessment that this skill presents limitless possibilities for healing, and was surprised when Master Skywalker asked me if I had considered alternative uses. I admitted that I had not, and he explained that Vergere had demonstrated how making oneself small could also be used to conceal one's ability with the Force, or render a Force-user invisible. According to Master Skywalker, Vergere claimed that an enemy has the same chance of finding her as of finding one molecule amid billions of others.
>
> Despite my cautions, I endeavor to learn this technique to the best of my abilities, and to share my discoveries with other Jedi.

Vergere died shortly after this recording, but Cilghal was eventually able to master the art of making herself small. Many beings have been healed by the technique, and thus far Cilghal has suffered no ill side effects from its use.

HEALING TRANCE

Some Jedi have learned to place other Force-sensitive beings in healing trances to accelerate their natural healing process. While in a trance, patients' heartbeats slow, their breathing all but ceases, and they appear to be dead. Unconscious of their surroundings, human patients have been known to remain in trances for up to a week in dry climates, and even up to a month in wet climates before there is a risk of them succumbing to dehydration. In cases where water was supplied, patients have remained in trances for as long as three months without requiring further nourishment.

A number of Jedi have also demonstrated the ability to put themselves into trances for long periods of time. Perhaps the most amazing example is the Kushiban Jedi Master Ikrit, who had been trained by Yoda. In 378 B.B.Y., Ikrit traveled to Yavin 4 and discovered the Golden Globe, an ancient device created by the Sith Lord Exar Kun to imprison the souls of Massassi children. Ikrit realized that only Force-sensitive children could break Exar Kun's curse on the Golden Globe to free the captive souls, and went into a trance to wait until help could come. Incredibly, Ikrit was

still in hibernation when he was discovered in 22 A.B.Y. by Jedi trainees Anakin Solo and Tahiri Veila, who soon figured out how to release the souls and destroy the Golden Globe.

FARSIGHT

Through the Force, a Jedi can sense the occurrence of distant events or receive a brief glimpse into the future. This sense sometimes activates at unexpected moments, but can also be achieved through a meditation technique called farsight.

Luke Skywalker's first awareness of farsight occurred while traveling through hyperspace in the *Millennium Falcon* with Obi-Wan Kenobi, who sensed the sudden death of millions before the *Falcon* arrived upon the remains of the planet Alderaan. Roughly three years later, while training with Yoda, Luke himself experienced farsight when he envisioned that Princess Leia Organa and Han Solo were in danger in the Bespin system.

Although Luke's training with Yoda was brief, he could not have learned from a better teacher. One of the greatest practitioners of farsight during the Old Republic era, Yoda's meditations often led to visions that helped guide the Jedi on missions throughout the galaxy. The following recording of Yoda is from the Great Holocron:

> Often difficult to see, the future is, like searching for raindrops beneath the surface of the water. But raindrops do fall, and discerned in depths, they can be. Fleeting can be visions of the future, momentary glimpses of both the familiar and the strange. More dangerous are clear visions, as easy it is to confuse clarity with truth. Truth can be murky, and crucial is perspective to any vision.
>
> See you do from the right angle at the wrong thing, or from the wrong angle at the right thing? No perspective is fixed.

Frequently am I asked if inevitable is the future. Do visions reveal what may be or what will be? Know you will when a vision is what will be. Feel it by the Force you will. Know you will whether to chase raindrops before they fall or remain where you are. Stay where you are, and move you will anyway. Always in motion is the future.

Yoda was also renowned for his sense of precognition, which alerted him to extreme danger in time to avert an immediate threat or take evasive action.

PSYCHOMETRY

Although psychometric talents are limited to a small number of species, and not something inherent in Jedi, there are members of these species who also possess Force powers. Thus these individuals have psychometric abilities that are naturally enhanced through the Force. Psychometry is the ability to "read" inanimate objects psionically, to perceive past events by gathering the tenuous psychic imprints left by living hands. The received perspective is the same as the perspective of the object's original wielder, and a skilled Jedi can also gain an impression of the wielder's emotions in regard to specific events. One of the most accomplished psychometrics was the Jedi Quinlan Vos of Kiffu.

Although the twin planets Kiffu and Kiffex had been part of the Old Republic for thousands of years, they were protected by not only the Jedi but also the Kiffar Guardians, whose commander was known as the Sheyf. For three centuries, members of the Clan Vos held the position of Sheyf. Several Guardians had psychometric talent, but the one who possessed the highest known ability was Quinlan Vos, second cousin of Sheyf Kurlin Vos. The Jedi Master Tholme, Watchman of the sector that included Kiffu and Kiffex, discovered Quinlan's strong affinity to the Force and was granted permission to train him, but because of Quinlan's heritage and potential as a Guardian, Clan Vos insisted that Quinlan's Jedi training would be conducted on Kiffu. After several years, Tholme declared his decision to take Quinlan as his Padawan, but evidently few Jedi knew why Clan Vos agreed to allow Quinlan to leave Kiffu. In the year 28 B.B.Y., shortly before Quinlan Vos became a Jedi Master, Tholme made the following recording, presented here because it sheds light on the dangerous aspects of psychometry:

Recently, Quinlan Vos has overcome the loss of his memory and been restored to the Jedi Order. He has also saved Coruscant from the Witches of Dathomir, recovered his Padawan Aayla Secura from abductors, and defeated the Dark Jedi Volfe Karkko. Though I believe that these

by the Guardians. There were no marks on their bodies, and no cause of death could be determined. Unfortunately, I was occupied with another assignment, and was unable to return to Kiffu until three days later. Shortly afterward, I lay down my Watchman duties and took Quinlan as my Padawan.

I confess there is more to the story, but the details are not on any of the official records because, for Quinlan's sake, I omitted them. Before my return to Kiffu, Tinte Vos—without the consent of her brother—had forced Quinlan to hold an emblem that his mother had been wearing when she died. Tinte Vos told him it was the only way to find out what killed his parents. What she didn't tell him is that death experiences are very vivid, and that touching such objects can be hazardous to psychometrics.

By holding his mother's emblem, Quinlan learned that his parents had intercepted a ship of Anzati who were trying to land on Kiffex. His parents attempted to arrest the Anzati, but despite their Guardian training they were unable to overcome an attack from the thirsty beings. The shock of seeing the Anzati feast on his parents' essence was beyond overwhelming.

By the time I found Quinlan, he'd been screaming for three days. It wasn't until I used Jedi healing techniques that I knew that we could draw his mind back from his mother's grave. The boy was shattered, and Sheyf Kurlin was appalled by what his sister had done. When I told the Sheyf that only Jedi training would enable the boy to face and master his newly and deeply instilled fear of the Anzati, he readily agreed to allow me to bring Quinlan to Coruscant.

Quinlan was my first Padawan. Though I was sometimes at a loss to advise him on the best use of his psychometric talents, I did teach him to be a Jedi. I taught him

accomplishments more than sufficiently qualify Quinlan to be granted the position of Jedi Master, I am aware that some members of the Council have always had misgivings about my training Quinlan, not only because he was already a toddler when I first detected his high midi-chlorian level, but also because—at the request of his clan—the initial training was conducted on Kiffu, not Coruscant. For anyone who ever questioned my reasons for taking him as my Padawan, I urge you to consider certain details of his history.

You will recall that Quinlan's parents were Guardians, and also direct relations of Sheyf Kurlin Vos and his sister Tinte Vos. Several years into his training, Quinlan's parents were found dead within their starship on the surface of Kiffex, the world that contains the prison colonies overseen

to carry the light within him. If one senses a darkness about Quinlan, remember his experience as a child, but trust that I also trained him how to walk in shadows.

Although corpses are essentially objects without sentience, neither Guardians nor Jedi encourage or approve the use of psychometry on the dead. Death experiences are extremely intense; by touching a corpse, a psychometric's own mind can become trapped, possibly causing him or her to follow the subject into death.

FORCE CAMOUFLAGE

Several recordings from the Great Holocron cite a power known as Force camouflage, which renders a Force-user invisible to others. Although specific instructions and insights have yet to be discovered, it seems Force camouflage manipulates light as well as sound waves around a Jedi. Although this ability would be useful on missions requiring stealth, it also demands a greater degree of concentration and energy expenditure than powers such as alter mind, a skill that also enables Jedi to evade enemies. Records indicate that four thousand years before the rise of the Galactic Empire, a Jedi named Juhani—a feline Cathar with natural camouflaging ability—was especially skilled with this power.

BATTLEMIND

A relatively obscure power, battlemind augments Jedi morale and fighting abilities by enhancing concentration and commitment. Jedi Master Mace Windu utilized battlemind in combination with other skills to exercise Vaapad, which Old Republic records indicate is the most challenging and demanding form of lightsaber combat.

BATTLE MEDITATION

Through their study of the Force, ancient Jedi learned to influence battles by envisioning a desired outcome: opposing factions would find themselves compelled to lower their weapons, or one side would be given courage and strength while the other was sapped of its will to fight. Using their skills in battle meditation, powerful Jedi have demonstrated the ability to control entire armies and fleets, directing them to do their bidding. According to the Great Holocron, Jedi Masters Thon, Arca Jeth, and Nomi Sunrider all excelled in this technique. During the Clone Wars, the Jedi Master Oppo Rancisis employed Jedi battle meditation to subtly alter the will of opposing forces, shifting the odds in favor of the Republic.

Luke Skywalker discovered a book about Jedi battle meditation in the ruins of the Jedi library on Ossus. Written in an arcane language, the book was translated by the protocol droid C-3PO.

The following text is an excerpt from the second chapter, which was written by Master Thon:

Why do scholars use the outcome of battles to indicate significant moments in history? Is not every moment significant in some way?

Why do analysts collect data about wars, counting the dead and wounded, and surveying the structures that survive? Do they really believe that if they collate such information, others will better understand why such events take place, and future wars might be prevented?

Then why—even now, as I write this—are so-called intelligent beings dominating and slaughtering others? Why are weapons still readied before peace is considered? Why are so many prepared to kill to achieve power, claim property, or prove that their gods are true?

The answer is simple: beings fight because they can, and sometimes because they must; sometimes by choice, but not always.

So long as there is life, there will be wars. Even the smallest insects can have their armies.

It is not the way of the Jedi to start wars.

It is the way of the Jedi to end wars, and to be aware that this duty is one that never ends.

Jedi battle meditation requires more from a Jedi than other disciplines. It can be most exhausting, and becomes even more challenging with the arrival of unexpected reinforcements for the opposition. But when it works, it works wonders.

If a Jedi's talent is measured by the ability to end battles without activating a lightsaber, then Jedi battle meditation must be counted among the most worthy of skills.

◄ ANAKIN SOLO EMPLOYING BATTLE MELD AGAINST THE YUUZHAN VONG. *(Trevas)*

BATTLE-MELD

By telepathically linking their minds together, Jedi can draw on one another's strength for support. Initially referred to as Force-meld or Jedi meld, the power became most commonly known as battle-meld because of its more frequent use in combat. Battle-meld permits a group of Jedi to become stronger than if each stood alone, while also enabling them to communicate with one another through the Force. Using a combination of the group's minds and perceptions, each individual Jedi gains a sense of the entire battle arena, helping them to better discern where to move tactical elements and when to press an attack, hold back, or withdraw. By narrowing his or her focus, a Jedi can also sense the distinct personalities and feelings of the individuals who make up the meld.

Although earlier Jedi may very well have utilized this power, it was fourteen-year-old Anakin Solo who introduced it to the new Jedi Order during the evacuation of Dubrillion, one of the first New Republic worlds to fall to the Yuuzhan Vong. Shortly after the evacuation, Jaina Solo recalled her brother's actions:

> There are still people on Dubrillion, but it's possible that they've already been overwhelmed by the invaders. The entire planet may be lost to us. Yet something happened during the evacuation that does give me some hope, a power that Anakin somehow discovered. I believe every Jedi should know about this.
>
> After we realized the invaders had targeted Dubrillion, everything happened pretty fast. Anakin, Jacen, and I were piloting Lando's TIE fighters, flying surface patrol and doing our best to keep incoming ships away from friendlies. My tracking screen was already glowing red from the sheer number of enemy fighters when they destroyed Belt-Runner I, which had been providing our only shielding power. There were just too many of them to fight. I ordered Anakin and Jacen to break back to Dubrillion, but Anakin disagreed, and instructed us to follow him into the asteroid belt called Lando's Folly. The enemy pursued us.
>
> It's hard to explain what happened, but Anakin connected with me and Jacen, and then we all linked together. Using telepathy, Anakin said, Join with me. Three as one. Within seconds, it was as if we'd found communion, a telepathic joining and bond. Each of us flew with the added perspectives of, well, of each other. I can only describe it as suddenly having extra eyes and extra perceptions as we all gave in to the Force. Our reactions were transformed into anticipation.
>
> Anakin was the focal point of our symbiosis. We became the perfect squadron, joined in thought and purpose. We weaved through the asteroids and destroyed one enemy fighter after the next. They couldn't keep up with us, at least not until Anakin became overwhelmed and nearly lost consciousness.
>
> I don't think this meld that we experienced was a fluke. If enough Jedi can learn to embrace the Force together as my brothers and I did, I believe this power might be our best weapon against the invaders.

Indeed, the battle-meld was an advantage the enemy couldn't match. The Jedi utilized the power with great success during the Yuuzhan Vong War, including at the Second Battle of Duro, which ended in a nearly bloodless victory for the New Republic. Generally, battle-meld requires more than three Jedi to be particularly effective, but three can be sufficient if the Jedi are well attuned to one another already. The presence of a single additional Jedi greatly increases the power of the meld, but if the individuals aren't in complete agreement, the meld can swiftly fall apart.

Near the end of the war with the Yuuzhan Vong, Luke Skywalker noted that the strength of his battle-meld with Jaina and Jacen Solo was such that the three might have been sharing the same mind, and that mind was the Force itself.

MALACIA

The Asli Krimsan Holocron and the Great Holocron reveal information about the Force technique called Malacia, by which a Jedi turns an opponent's equilibrium against him or her, causing extreme dizziness and nausea without any permanent effects. It seems that this ability was seldom used by Jedi of the Old Republic, as most found it easier to employ affect mind or a simple Force push to achieve similar results, but Malacia's proponents regarded it as a powerful defense. The

Jedi Master Oppo Rancisis was a master of Malacia and taught the technique to a small number of his peers. According to Master Rancisis:

The Force can be used in many ways to subdue an opponent, but the principal quality of Malacia is that the Jedi achieves it not by expending energy but by transforming the energy of the target. Critics always note that Malacia is limited to organic opponents, but there are many situations where it is preferable to other means.

Imagine a sentry guarding a post that you must bypass. The sentry may be standing still, but his mind is alert and his systems are functioning. Everything is in motion. Blood flows, muscles tense, food is digested, and atmospheric gases are inhaled and exhaled. All that motion is enough to make him dizzy and queasy, and by focusing on the flow of blood, you can make that happen. The sentry will be so overwhelmed that he is completely disabled, yet will suffer no permanent side effects.

Now imagine a gang of murderous warriors running toward an intended victim when they are suddenly sickened by their own movements. Robbed of their sense of balance and unable to proceed, the warriors collapse, clutching at the ground as if they might fall from it. There are some Jedi Masters who have contended that such brutes may benefit from Malacia, as it serves to remind them that they are—like their prey—mere mortals.

Malacia requires a direct line of sight between the Jedi and the targets, regardless of distance. However, if the targets begin to retch, you may want to briefly avert your gaze, as this is almost always unpleasant to watch.

According to the Great Holocron, Master Rancisis was killed by the former Jedi Master Sora

◀ JEDI MASTER OPPO RANCISIS.
(Trevas)

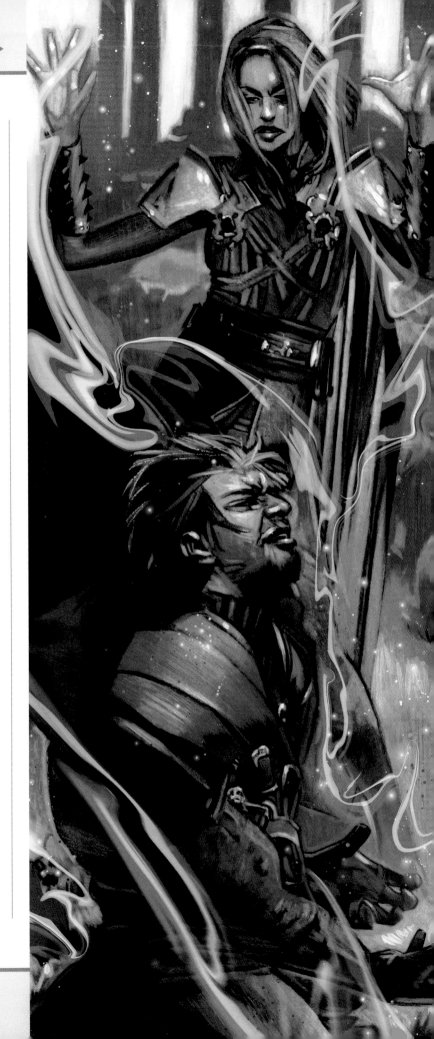

Bulq, who had abandoned the Order and allied with the Confederacy of Independent Systems during the Clone Wars. Soon afterward, Bulq died in a duel with Quinlan Vos.

SEVER FORCE

A powerful Jedi can block a Force-user's access to the Force, preventing him or her from using Force skills or Force feats. The Jedi Nomi Sunrider, who served with Ulic Qel-Droma before he became a Sith Lord, used the skill known as sever Force to strip Ulic Qel-Droma of his powers, leaving him essentially blind to the Force. Nomi Sunrider learned of this power from the Jedi Master Odan-Urr, who speaks of it via the Tedryn Holocron:

> When you feel the dark side energies turned against you, you must use your Jedi abilities to take power away from an opponent, rather than to inflict harm. This technique blinds your enemy to the Force with a wall of light, a permanent blockage if you so choose, rendering him unable to use Jedi powers. It is difficult. And it is the most devastating attack possible using the powers of the light side. To block a Jedi from the Force—even a Dark Jedi—is a terrible thing.

BEAST LANGUAGE

The Force can enable one to communicate with various nonsentient creatures—including herd animals, predators, and scavengers—in a language they understand. Because nonsentients rarely have true languages, the Jedi is actually reading the differences in surface emotions within grunts and growls and cues of body language.

The power is relatively easy to employ if the animal is already domesticated or naturally friendly, and becomes increasingly challenging if a beast is wild and predatory. Communication is most effective when the messages or commands are simple and convey that the animal should trust the Jedi: *Don't be afraid. I won't harm you. Will you carry me?* More intelligent creatures are sometimes capable of following more complex instructions (*Meet me here when the moon is high*) and questions (*Can you help me find my destination?*). A Force-user cannot converse with creatures that do not normally communicate, such as microbes and other simple organisms.

MORICHRO

A forbidden Jedi technique, Morichro works in a way similar to a Force trance. It slows down a being's metabolism, breathing, and heart rate (or similar biological systems). Unlike a Force trance, Morichro can be used to affect beings other than the Jedi employing the technique; a targeted subject can be rendered unconscious for a specific or indefinite period.

The Jedi Master Yaddle was one of the most prominent practitioners of Morichro. While head of the Librarians' Assembly of the Jedi Temple, Yaddle made the following recording for the Great Holocron:

> *Learned of Morichro from a single source, I did not. Barely hinted at it, three holocrons did. Partially described over many ancient scrolls and tomes, it was. Used by Jedi long ago, Morichro was. Used, forbidden, and forgotten.*
>
> *A Force technique, it is. The body functions of targets, it rapidly slows. Most effective for subduing opponents, this is.*
>
> *Yet dangerous, too. Constantly monitored, a target must be. Fail to reverse the process, should the Jedi, and indefinite, the unconsciousness can be. Die of dehydration*

or starvation, can an untended target. Realized this, the ancient Jedi did.

> *Much research into history, I have done. Known to use this technique, dark side Force-users are not. Not malevolent is Morichro. To master Morichro, less malevolent uses of the Force must a student master first.*

Although the Jedi Council of the Old Republic apparently allowed Yaddle to teach some Jedi students about Morichro, the Council ultimately forbade its use because abuse of the technique could prove fatal. It is not known whether any of her students ever actually used Morichro. Four years prior to the Clone Wars, Yaddle died on a mission to the world of Mawan.

FORCE LIGHTNING

At the Battle of Geonosis, the renegade Count Dooku revealed the full measure of his dark nature when he cast lightning from his fingertips in an attack on the Jedi who pursued him. Years later, Emperor Palpatine unleashed this same power on Luke Skywalker during the Battle of Endor. Although the Jedi were long aware of Force lightning, a purely offensive power that often appealed to those who had embraced the dark side, it was so long associated with the Sith that it was often referred to as Sith lightning.

Force lightning causes excruciating pain as it weakens an individual's life, and is nearly impossible to deflect. Because of the power's obvious negative aspects, it is no wonder various Jedi Orders forbade its use. However, some Jedi peacekeepers have refused to dismiss or suppress what they considered to be a natural asset to their arsenal of powers. Before his appointment to the Jedi Council, the Jedi Master Plo Koon left the following record on the Great Holocron:

At the request of the Jedi Council, I submit this report of my actions on the mission to Metellos, specifically my use of Force lightning.

I'd been tracking Dreed Pommel for five days across space before I found him on Metellos. Pommel had taken refuge in an executive suite within the floating city of Ektra. Despite my efforts at stealth, Pommel was somehow alerted to my approach, for when I entered the suite he was already clutching a female human child and holding a blaster to her head.

The suite was spacious, and I was separated from Pommel by a distance of fifteen meters. Keeping his eyes on me, Pommel began pulling the crying girl—I estimated her to be five years old—out through a wide doorway, beyond which I could see a small ship that rested on the suite's private landing pad. Obviously, his intent was to escape, and he considered the child his insurance. I had no reason to doubt that he would ultimately kill her, even if I allowed them to board the escape vessel, for I could see what he'd done to the girl's parents and two siblings, whose bodies lay upon the floor of the inner suite.

In hindsight, there were many possible tactics I might have employed to apprehend Pommel and rescue the child, but I did not consider any options or calculate angles of attack as I watched him drag her toward the ship. I believe I acted entirely instinctively when I extended my right arm toward Pommel and released a barrage of lightning.

I know that the Jedi Council was hesitant to send me on any assignment so soon after the death of Master Tyvokka, but I did not let loose with Force lightning the way undisciplined beings might release stress. Like other Jedi, I learned of Force lightning at the Jedi Temple, and I am well aware that

it is regarded as a dark side power. I never had any special interest in Force lightning, or felt compelled to experiment with it, but I knew it was—at least in me—an innate ability. I did not feel anger as I directed the lightning at Pommel's head, nor did I fear for the girl's safety. I was calm and in control of my faculties. I merely acted to end the situation before any more innocents died.

Upon being struck by the first bolt, Pommel reacted as anticipated as the shock seized his system. His arms flew out and away from his body, releasing both the blaster and the child, who fell to the landing pad. A second bolt ensured that Pommel would remain unconscious until the local authorities arrived. I was never tempted to deal a killing blow.

Upon my return from Metellos, my use of Force lightning was included in my report to the Council. I maintained that I did not embrace the dark side when I used this ability, and that I acted by the will of the Force.

I appreciate the Council's concern with my report. I have not forgotten that it was Master Tyvokka's last wish that I join the Council. I also acknowledge the Council's observation that the Force runs strong in my family. My uncle was a Jedi Knight, as is my niece Sha Koon. While Kel Dors like ourselves have a reputation for seeing moral issues in black and white, I urge the Council to disregard my family in this situation, for I alone am responsible for my actions.

The Council asked me to contemplate whether I would hesitate to use Force lightning again, and whether I was wrong to employ it on Metellos. After much meditation, I believe it would be wrong of me to ignore this power that I might develop into a useful technique for combat. As for whether I was wrong to use it, I believe the only person who can rightfully answer that question is a five-year-old girl. Her name is Claria Labreezle, and she has been placed with relatives at Stratablock 7 on Metellos.

May the Force be with us all.

Plo Koon was not only appointed to the Jedi Council but apparently succeeded in perfecting the technique that he called Electric Judgment. Old Republic records from the Clone Wars place Plo Koon at Cato Neimoidia, where it is believed he was killed during the Jedi Purge.

JEDI SPIRITS

Despite their powers, even the most powerful of Jedi eventually die. For most, death is a release from their physical forms, and allows them to join the totality of the Force. However, encounters with Jedi apparitions indicate that some Jedi have learned how to maintain their identities even after death, so that they linger at the edges of the physical world of the living as Force spirits.

Although these spirits can communicate with the living, the method by which they become spirits has never been documented, and is not completely understood. Being a Jedi does not seem to guarantee one's ability to rematerialize, and it is only assumed that the transition cannot be achieved accidentally, but rather by some deliberate effort or knowledge. In some cases, the Jedi's body dematerializes upon death, but not always. According to Luke Skywalker in a recording he made shortly after founding the Jedi academy:

After my father died on the Death Star his body vanished. I brought his armor, and his mechanical remains to Endor and burned them. It seemed like the right thing to do. Maybe the best thing. The idea of burial just felt wrong. I could only imagine what it must have been like for him, trapped within that armor for so many years, and I guess I hoped the flames would somehow liberate him.

As I joined my friends at the victory celebration, apparitions of Obi-Wan and Yoda appeared before me. Because of my previous encounters with Obi-Wan's spirit at Yavin, Hoth, and Dagobah, I was aware that his spirit could travel across space, so I wasn't surprised to see them so much as I was glad they had endured.

Then a third apparition appeared that I recognized as my father. I cannot express the joy I felt upon seeing his face, unmasked and smiling.

There are many old stories in which a Jedi becomes one with the Force but it seems this phrase could be interpreted as a Jedi euphemism for "dying," as the tales seldom indicated whether a Jedi's corpse actually vanished.

Tionne was able to find numerous records of Jedi that corroborated the fact that I was not the first to witness a Jedi's transition to spiritual form. Two accounts were recorded by the ancient Jedi Nomi Sunrider, who saw the spirit of her husband, the Jedi Knight Andur Sunrider, moments after he was slain by an underworld gang. Years later, she saw the physical body of the mortally wounded Ulic Qel-Droma—like my father, a former Jedi and reformed Sith Lord—disappear on the planet Rhen Var after he'd redeemed himself to the Jedi, yet there is no mention that he reappeared in spiritual form.

Evidently, the ancient Jedi did not regard such spirits as remarkable or accidental occurences, which suggests that they may have been aware of how to survive death, but it seems that this knowledge became lost or forgotten, possibly more than three thousand years ago. Although some texts indicate that only Jedi Masters

could achieve this transition, exceptions such as Jedi Knights Andur Sunrider and Anakin Skywalker indicate that a Force-user's title is not so significant. For now, I can only assume that the survival of a Jedi's consciousness beyond death may have something to do with training, as well as with the will of the Force, or with the individual's openness to the Force.

The ability to transcend death is not exclusive to Jedi: Emperor Palpatine and the ancient Sith Lords Marka Ragnos and Exar Kun managed to preserve their psyches after their deaths, but it seems their spiritual forms were restricted by certain boundaries and limitations. Palpatine's spirit required clone bodies to manifest his powers; Marka Ragnos's and Exar Kun's spirits were essentially trapped within Sith-engineered temples for thousands of years. Although it may never be known why Exar Kun was not able to cause more havoc on Yavin 4, the Jedi Corran Horn offered the following theory:

> The only vaguely positive explanation for Exar Kun's dormancy that I could come up with was that his effort to draw the Sun Crusher from Yavin and to down Luke had tired him out. I had no way to determine how powerful Exar Kun could be, but it struck me as possible that he'd expended a lot of energy to defeat a Jedi Master.

During the Jedi academy's battle with the spirit of Exar Kun, an apparition of Jedi Master Vodo-Siosk Baas—who was slain by Exar Kun on Coruscant—materialized on Yavin 4 and aided the Jedi in bringing an end to the ancient Sith Lord. Given that an earlier effort to materialize might have thwarted Exar Kun from endangering the Jedi in the first place, it is a mystery why Vodo-Siosk Baas appeared when he did. One can only surmise whether he sought or found closure in witnessing the final downfall of his own killer, but his appearance was proof that Jedi spirits—like their Sith counterparts—can endure for many millennia.

DETECTING JEDI POWERS

Prior to the rediscovery that potential Force-users can be detected by a blood test for midi-chlorians, Luke Skywalker—while training his sister Leia Organa Solo in the ways of the Force—stumbled upon a different method for naturally detecting Force-users. He explained this method in a recording made at the former Jedi academy on Yavin 4:

> I was working with Leia on developing her control of the Force, testing her ability to invoke her inner defenses by using the Force to probe her mind. At first, I touched random spots in her mind to try to take her by surprise, but then I reached to the back of her consciousness, to an area of deep primal memories. Her thoughts were like a map laid out in front of me, and I doubted that I could get any defensive reaction there. So I touched inward to an isolated nub in her mind, and I pushed.
>
> What happened next is hard to describe. It felt as if a giant invisible palm had planted itself on my chest and shoved me backward. I actually stumbled to keep my balance. We were both surprised by this, and we weren't even sure of what had just happened, but we decided to try it again. We got the same result. Suspecting the reaction was an instinctive reflex, I encouraged Leia to seek and find the same area at the back of my own mind. Without any conscious effort on my part, Leia was knocked off her feet and landed in a chair.
>
> I need to try this on other people, but if the reaction is a reflex, it could be a very useful test for discovering people who have latent Jedi powers.

Through subsequent experiments, it was determined that a Force-sensitive individual's deep subconscious is shielded by a protective barrier that prevents penetration by another Force-wielder; it is this protective "shield"—an involuntary defense mechanism maintained by every Force-sensitive being—that pushes violently back at an intruder. Some Jedi also learned to anticipate and occasionally resist the reflexive "push" that results from testing Force-sensitive subjects. Although this natural method of detection is not as scientifically accurate as a midi-chlorian count, it has proven a consistently effective technique.

THE FORCE AS A SOURCE OF ENERGY

Through meditation and by remaining calm, Jedi are able to draw power from the light side of the Force to further enhance their abilities. In diametrical fashion, the Sith embrace anger to draw power from the dark side, and also utilize this energy to enhance both vehicles and weapons. Force-users have long known that particular worlds and locations are especially strong with the Force, and that this energy sometimes lingers in places where the Jedi and Sith have fought.

Although the Force exists everywhere and within all living things, certain artifacts have demonstrated the ability to augment it. One such artifact is the Kaiburr crystal of the planet Circarpous V, locally known as Mimban. According to an ancient myth, the god Pomojema, a minor deity of Mimban, used the Kaiburr crystal to heal the wounded. In the year 2 A.B.Y., Luke Skywalker and Leia Organa became stranded on Mimban and met a self-proclaimed "master of the Force" named Halla, who had spent seven years searching for the crystal. Together they found the crystal in the jungle Temple of Pomojema. Thirty-three years after her visit to Mimban, Leia Organa Solo remembered the occasion in a recording made during her induction as a Jedi Knight:

> According to Master Saba, I am now a full Jedi Knight. I first constructed a lightsaber more than twenty years ago, but Master Saba did not need to convince me that my skills needed improvement. However, because she so graciously relieved me of that weapon, I was compelled to make a new one. Although it only took me a few days, it has a history I'd like to share.

> Two years after the Battle of Yavin, Luke and I . . . well, we took a wrong turn and wound up on the swamp planet Mimban. There we met a woman named Halla, who showed us what appeared to be a splinter of red glass that she claimed was a fragment of the Kaiburr crystal. The first time Luke touched it, he quickly drew back his arm as if he'd touched a live current. He said that the crystal caused sensations to course through him, and that the sensations weren't felt so much as experienced. The fragment increased one's perception of the Force, and apparently magnified and clarified in proportion to size and density. Luke believed that anyone in possession of the entire crystal would have such a lock on the Force that he or she could accomplish almost anything. Unfortunately, by the time we found the crystal in the Temple of Pomojema, Darth Vader had found us.

> Keep in mind that Luke and I had no idea of our true lineage at the time of this encounter. I was unaware that I possessed any Force powers, and our proximity to the crystal did nothing to trigger any insights to our relationship with each other or Vader. I'm certain Vader had no idea he was my father, and if he had any inkling that Luke was his son, he didn't mention it. He was too busy trying to kill us both.

> Everything happened so fast. After Vader struck down Luke, I took Luke's lightsaber and . . . I'm afraid I didn't accomplish much. Vader didn't just hurt me. Actually, he killed me. I'd stopped breathing. Incredible as it sounds, Luke used the crystal to revive me and heal my wounds as well as his own. As for Vader, Luke told me he'd fallen into a crumbling well in the temple's floor.

> We left Mimban with the crystal, and soon found that its powers decreased in direct proportion to its distance from the temple. Returning it to Mimban was out of the question, as it would have inevitably become the target of thieves or, worse, been claimed by the Empire. Except for its history, it seemed relatively useless, and over the years I almost forgot about the Kaiburr crystal.

> Eventually, Luke used the crystal as a training aid for students. He did some experiments and found that fragments of the gem could be used as focusing crystals for lightsabers. He said he found the resulting blade to be remarkably energy-efficient and strong. I remembered this when Master Saba advised me to build a new weapon.

> I must say that my new lightsaber is a significant improvement on my old one. But more than that, I feel more connected to this weapon because it carries a part of my history. A long time ago, Luke and I were saved by the Kaiburr crystal. Although I am

prepared to activate my lightsaber in the line of duty, it is my hope to employ the crystal so that it continues to save lives, not take them.

Also known to enhance Force powers are the artusian crystals from the mines of the planet Artus Prime. In 12 A.B.Y., the ex-Jedi-student Desann used Sith alchemy in combination with artusian crystals to artificially imbue human youths with the Force. However, it seems that Desann's knowledge of the Sith was limited to data provided by Lord Hethrir, a former Imperial Procurator of Justice who led the radical movement that he called the Empire Reborn. Aided by Luke Skywalker and Lando Calrissian, Kyle Katarn defeated Desann and his "Reborn" warriors.

During the Sith War in 3996 B.B.Y., Sith Lord Exar Kun constructed the superweapon known as the Dark Reaper. The Dark Reaper was powered by the Force Harvester, which was capable of drawing in the life energies of thousands of combatants within a limited range of kilometers. Exar Kun's lieutenant Ulic Qel-Droma unleashed the Dark Reaper against hundreds of Republic troops on the outpost world of Raxus Prime, but before Ulic could deliver the weapon to Coruscant, he was defeated and captured by Republic forces. Eventually, the Dark Reaper's parts became scattered on various planets, and the Force Harvester was buried on Raxus Prime. During the Clone Wars, Count Dooku unearthed the Force Harvester and used it on Mon Calamari, Bakura, and Agamar. Dooku attempted to assemble the Dark Reaper on the planet Thule, but Anakin Skywalker destroyed the superweapon before it could be properly deployed.

Ten years prior to the Clone Wars, the Sith Lord Darth Maul piloted a unique starship to the planet Naboo, and at least one record suggests that the ship may have been imbued with the power of the dark side. The following recording was made by Jedi Master Saesee Tiin, a member of the Jedi Council who was called in to secure the ship after its automated weapons gunned down the Republic engineers who discovered it on Naboo:

Greetings, Master Yoda. The vehicle

that delivered the Sith Lord to Naboo has been secured. It does not surprise me that the ship was designed to kill intruders, but given its contents, it seems strange that it did not self-destruct when its owner failed to return.

The ship's exterior bears a striking resemblence to an experimental Sienar Design Systems armed star courier, but every aspect of the vessel is either heavily modified or prototypical. It is equipped with a built-in cloaking device, and I've confirmed that the device is fueled by stygium crystals. Various weapons and devices indicate Sith technology.

All the ship's records have been wiped clean. I have found nothing to identify the Sith Lord slain by Obi-Wan. Although I have disabled the ship's weapons, I am compelled to say that it still poses a great danger, and I recommend that this vessel be placed in the Jedi Council's care.

That ship is alive with the dark side, Master Yoda. I can feel it clinging to my robes. And worse, it still tempts me, calling me back with promises of fantastic journeys to the far reaches of the galaxy.

Despite Master Tiin's recommendations, Maul's ship—eventually identified as a Sith Infiltrator dubbed *Scimitar*—disappeared while being transported to a Kuat Drive Yards facility. The ship's fate remains unknown.

The Jedi and Sith are not the only beings who have used the power of the Force as a source of energy. As already noted, the ancient Rakata relied upon Force-powered technology to conquer many worlds. Their most incredible achievement was the Star Forge, a space station that used raw stellar material to build anything its creators desired. Infused with the power of the dark side, the Star Forge was used to mass-produce weapons, droids, and starships. Approximately 25,200 B.B.Y., a plague decimated the Rakatan species; the surviving Rakata devolved into barbarism and eventually forgot how to operate their own technology. After lingering unoccupied and unused for more than twenty millennia in orbit of the Rakatan homeworld, Rakata Prime, the Star Forge was discovered during the Second Sith War by the Sith Lords Darth Revan and Darth Malak. Having learned of the Star Forge's existence from ancient Sith sources, the Sith Lords revived the station and used captive Jedi to fuel the station's dark side power. Fortunately, the Republic was ultimately able to defeat the Sith Lords and destroy the Star Forge.

FORCE ANOMALIES

Anthropologists and xenobiologists have identified various life-forms that have unique and unusual connections with the Force. Among the most deadly of these creatures were the terentateks, alchemically birthed monsters that stood about half the size of a rancor and fed on Force-strong blood. During the Sith War, Exar Kun bred these beasts as "Jedi killers" and distributed them on numerous worlds. Because a single terentatek was a match for an entire squad of Jedi, the extermination of terentateks was the Order's highest priority in 3993, three years after the end of the Sith War. This "dragon quest" became known as the Great Hunt, and led to what is believed to be the extinction of the terentateks.

Ysalamiri are salamander-like, nonsentient creatures native to the planet Myrkr. Sessile, arboreal, and equipped with strong claws that draw nutrients from Myrkr's mineral-rich trees, they cling to their branches with such tenacity that special knowledge is required to remove them without killing them. The ysalamiri's most remarkable characteristic is its ability to create a "bubble" in

indigenous species on Myrkr, the Force-sensitive pack animals called vornskrs. Cunning predators, vornskrs are fur-covered canine animals with sharp teeth and poison-coated, whip-like tails. Their attunement to the Force seems to be tied directly to their hunting instincts, as they are naturally able to detect Force-users, and also use this ability to hunt ysalamiri. They regard any Force-user as prey, and will not hesitate to attack Jedi.

In an article submitted to *Galactic Zoology Monthly,* Karrde offered a concise account of how he domesticated two vornskrs and trained them to serve as his own guard animals. According to Karrde, vornskrs are good company as long as one removes their tails, keeps them well fed, and plays with them regularly. Karrde discouraged inviting Jedi friends over for dinner.

The Yuuzhan Vong are themselves an anomaly in the way they seem to exist apart from the Force, possibly as an ancient consequence of their warfaring heritage. The Yuuzhan Vong genetically engineered vornskr stock to create a new creature, the six-legged voxyn, which was designed to hunt and kill Jedi. Voxyn retained the vornskr's venomous barbed tail but also had sharper, stronger claws and acid-spitting glands. Several Jedi were killed by voxyn before Anakin Solo led a strike team to destroy the voxyn genetic template on *Baanu Rass,* a Yuuzhan Vong worldship in orbit of Myrkr. Tragically, this was Anakin's final mission, for he sacrificed himself so that his team could live, allowing them to destroy the voxyn queen.

Possibly the most bizarre Force anomaly is the taozin, a gigantic, translucent invertebrate that can evade efforts to be detected or located through the Force. Native to the jungle moon of Va'art near the Roche asteroid field, the taozin spews an adhesive substance from its mouth to trap its prey, and it can easily devour a full-grown human. Its flesh is permeated with tiny, crystalline structures that actually diffuse light energy, which makes the creature invulnerable to most blaster weapons and lightsabers. When hit by a lightsaber, the taozin's

which the Force cannot exist. More specifically, the Force cannot be manipulated within such a bubble, which can extend up to ten meters in radius from a single ysalamiri. In groups of ysalamiri, such bubbles can extend and overlap, resulting in vast areas in which the Force cannot be used on Myrkr.

Talon Karrde, the founder of the Smugglers' Alliance, was based on Myrkr when Grand Admiral Thrawn came to acquire ysalamiri, which Thrawn then used to protect himself from Force-users. To prevent the ysalamiri from dying after they were removed from the trees and to allow for their use as a mobile means of defense against Force-users, Imperial engineers fashioned special nutrient-infused pipe frames that could be worn on the backs of individuals.

The ysalamiri's incredible ability to disable or "push back" the Force is part of a natural defensive mechanism that protects them from another

body sends the energy "splashing" outward in all directions. Because the taozin is effectively invisible to the Force, the creature is especially dangerous to Jedi.

Force sensitivity was also found recently in some types of Killik, the sentient insectoid species that inhabited Alderaan many millennia before the arrival of human colonists. Killiks have a pheremonal telepathic connection to one another, and their society is centered on a hive-mind that makes Killik groups act as an individual. Their telepathic connection can extend to other species, including non-insectoids, with the result that these "Joiners" lose their independent will when they are absorbed into the hive-mind. However, Killik Force abilities were due primarily to the absorption of three Force-sensitives in 27 A.B.Y. The Force-sensitives were the Nightsister Lomi Plo, her apprentice Welk, and Jedi Apprentice Raynar Thul, who escaped from Myrkr during the Yuuzhan Vong War. After being absorbed by the Killiks, the transformed Force-sensitives introduced the species to the Galactic Alliance in 35 A.B.Y., and fought their former allies in the conflict that became known as the Swarm War. Of the trio, only Raynar Thul survived; he is the subject of ongoing rehabilitation at the Jedi praxeum on Ossus. By the end of the Swarm War, the Killiks began to revert to their natural state.

Both Hutts and Toydarians possess varying degrees of mental strength that can make them immune to Jedi mind tricks. In an event from the year 4 A.B.Y. that has since become the stuff of legend, Luke Skywalker found himself unable to mentally persuade Jabba the Hutt to release Rebel prisoners, and had to resort to a backup plan.

A personal log of Darth Vader, recovered from his fortress on Vjun, revealed Vader's disturbing perspective regarding Toydarians. It should be noted that Vader's disposition may have been influenced by Anakin Skywalker's relationship to Watto, the Toydarian junk dealer and slaver who was young Anakin's "master" on Tatooine. Although Shmi Skywalker's recovered journal suggests that Watto

was a relatively benevolent master, it is conceivable that Vader's memories of Watto were unfavorable. Furthermore, the identity of the "Toydarian subject" mentioned in Vader's recording remains unknown, but records from Tatooine preclude the possibility that it was Watto.

These creatures have become such an irritation that every time I see one I want to strike it down with my lightsaber. Be that as it may, I interviewed a Toydarian subject who showed a great amount of resistance to Force suggestion, up to the point that I created physical discomfort. I found that they can be easily intimidated by a demonstration of strength. And it proved relatively simple to cause it to expire, merely by making its existence extremely painful. Ultimately, though it showed a great degree of willpower, it was no match for the power of the Force.

It has already been noted that members of the Halcyon Jedi bloodline inherited the inability to use the Force to perform telekinetic feats. Dating back thousands of years, this trait was often mistaken for a weakness, but the Halcyon Jedi so greatly excelled in other areas of the Force that they easily compensated for this "flaw." The Jedi Master Corran Horn is a direct descendant of Keiran Halcyon, a famed Jedi who played a key role in the defeat of the *Afarathu* terrorists on Corellia in 380 B.B.Y. In response to the suggestion that a Jedi was impaired by the lack of telekinetic ability, Corran Horn's grandfather, the Jedi Master Nejaa Halcyon, reportedly quipped, "The starship flies faster and hits harder when you don't need to power up your shields."

LIGHTSABERS

The traditional weapon of the Jedi, the lightsaber is a blade of pure energy that can cut through most materials, with the exceptions of another lightsaber blade, alchemically altered metals used in ancient Sith swords, and a small number of exotic alloys such as cortosis. Although a lightsaber beam radiates no heat, it can easily melt through thick durasteel plating, and—in skilled hands—deflect blaster bolts. It is widely considered the most incredible weapon ever created.

Lightsaber blades operate on the complex principle of tightly controlled arc-wave energy; while the pure energy blade has no mass, the electromagnetically generated arc wave creates a strong gyroscopic effect that makes the lightsaber a distinct challenge to handle. Mastering it requires a lifetime of training. The Jedi Order's affinity for the weapon is such that it was a long-standing tradition for a Jedi to construct a lightsaber before being promoted to Jedi Knight. However, urgent situations sometimes encouraged the Jedi Knights of the Old Republic to issue prefabricated emergency lightsabers. In other cases, lightsabers were handed down from one generation of Jedi to the next, or gifted, as was Anakin Skywalker's lightsaber, which Obi-Wan gave to Luke Skywalker.

The close association of the Jedi, the Force, and lightsabers has led to the misconception that Jedi channel the Force through their weapons. Although Jedi can become more attuned to the Force through lightsaber exercises and rely upon the Force to construct lightsabers, the weapons are not in any way a direct link to the power of the Force.

There are numerous documented cases of Jedi who served the Order without ever igniting their lightsabers, but relatively few Jedi refused to carry the weapon at all. According to Luke Skywalker:

The lightsaber is the weapon of a Jedi Knight, though a true Jedi rarely uses it

to settle a dispute. It is better to outthink and outmaneuver your opponent. But when forced, a Jedi strikes quickly and decisively. In peaceful times, the lightsaber is only a symbol of the fight we wage within ourselves—to keep us from taking the wrong path.

LIGHTSABER CONSTRUCTION

For centuries, the construction of a new lightsaber was a rite of passage accompanied by ritual ceremonies. On the planet Ilum, where generations of Jedi went to build their lightsabers, a lone Padawan was sometimes expected to enter the Force-permeated crystal caves and not emerge until his or her lightsaber was finished, although Jedi Masters were also known to serve as witnesses. While watching a Padawan complete the lightsaber, a Jedi Master sometimes recited the following words:

The crystal is the heart of the blade.
The heart is the crystal of the Jedi.
The Jedi is the crystal of the Force.
The Force is the blade of the heart.
All are intertwined.
The crystal, the blade, the Jedi.
You are one.

Twenty-three years after the Battle of Yavin, Luke Skywalker instructed a small group of young Jedi—including Jaina and Jacen Solo, Lowbacca, Tenel Ka, and Raynar Thul—on the construction of lightsabers. The following is an abridgement of his presentation:

You may have heard about Jedi Masters during the Clone Wars who were able to

fashion lightsabers in only a day or two, using whatever raw materials were at hand. But don't get the idea that your weapon is a quick little project to be slapped together. Ideally, a Jedi took many months to construct a single perfect weapon that he or she would keep and use for a lifetime. Once you build it, the lightsaber will become your constant companion, your tool, and a ready means of defense.

The components are fairly simple. Every lightsaber has a standard power source, the same type used in small blasters, even in glow panels. They last a long time, though, because Jedi should rarely use their weapons.

One of the other crucial pieces is a focusing crystal. The most powerful and sought-after gems are rare Kaiburr crystals. However, though lightsabers are powerful weapons, their design is so flexible that practically any kind of crystal can be used. And since I don't happen to have a stash of Kaiburr crystals, you'll have to make do with something else of your own choosing.

One of my students, Cilghal, a Mon Calamari like Admiral Ackbar, made her lightsaber with smooth curves and protrusions, as if the handle had been grown from metallic coral. Inside, she used a rare Ultima-Pearl, one of the treasures found in the seabeds of her watery planet.

My first true failure as a teacher was another student named Gantoris. He built his lightsaber in only a few intense days, following instructions given to him by the evil spirit of Exar Kun. Gantoris thought he was ready, and my mistake was not seeing what he was up to.

You, my young Jedi Knights, must be different. I can't wait any longer to train you. You must learn how to build your lightsabers—and how to use them—in the

right way. The galaxy has changed, and you must meet the challenge. A true Jedi is forced to adapt or be destroyed.

I'd like you to start on your lightsabers immediately. But I hope you'll need to use your weapon only rarely . . . if ever.

A standard lightsaber consists of a compact handle—generally twenty-four to thirty centimeters long—with a diatium power cell and one to three multifaceted crystals. Contrary to the popular notion that a lightsaber blade's color changes to match its wielder's personality, it is the crystals that determine the blade's color. These crystals also focus energy from the power source through a concave disk atop the handle, resulting in a blade about a meter in length.

Only Force-users are capable of building lightsabers, as it is by the Force that the power cell is initially charged. There is no exact formula for the crucial alignment of the irregular crystals, but they must be aligned by hand or extremely precise telekinesis, and builders are cautioned that the slightest misalignment will cause the weapon to detonate on activation. Documented attempts to mechanize the assembly process were unsuccessful.

Prior to the Battle of Ruusan, the Jedi used crystals from many different sources, and ignited lightsabers in every known hue, including purple, orange, and gold. Toward the end of the Old Republic era, Ilum was the primary source of most crystals used for lightsabers; this dramatically limited the color range, as the crystals harvested from Ilum produce only green or blue blades. Most sources for lightsaber crystals were razed or quarantined during the reign of Emperor Palpatine, but when the New Republic was established following the Battle of Endor, a number of crystal caches were regained. Luke Skywalker and his followers have since drawn from these caches to construct new lightsabers.

The exact connection between the Jedi and certain crystals is not completely understood, but it is known that a Jedi can enhance the properties of

◄ ANAKIN SKYWALKER CONSTRUCTS HIS
FIRST LIGHTSABER ON ILUM. *(Trevas)*

some crystals by imbuing them with Force energy. As noted in *The Galactic Encyclopedia,* "The oldest lightsabers use jewels formed by natural processes. But the Jedi can forge synthetic jewels with a small furnace, a few basic elements . . . and the power of the Force."

IMPROVISED LIGHTSABERS

Unusual circumstances have led to innovative construction techniques for lightsabers. When Corran Horn required a lightsaber after he had infiltrated a pirate gang, he demonstrated great ingenuity by crafting his weapon from various salvaged parts, including exotic gems—a diamond, an emerald, and a durindfire jewel—that had decorated an old bottle of Savareen brandy, a dynoric laser feed line from a broken laser cannon, and a throttle assembly and handlebar tube from a junked speeder bike. Working from instructions that had been recorded by his grandfather, the Jedi Master Nejaa Halcyon, Horn found the assembly process relatively easy. According to Horn:

> The most difficult part of creating a lightsaber was producing a power cell that stored and discharged the amount of energy necessary to energize a lightsaber blade. That said, the parts list called for a pretty basic power cell—in fact, because of the age of the instructions, I had a hard time locating one that ancient. Newer power cells were more efficient than the one my grandfather had specified, but I didn't think that would present a problem.

After all, as I read the instructions I came to realize that the nature of the battery was not as important as how it was integrated with the rest of the components.

The core of the Jedi ritual for creating a lightsaber came down to charging the power cell that first time. My grandfather ridiculed the popular superstition stating a Jedi channeled the Force through his lightsaber. He suggested that this was a misunderstanding of what it took to charge it initially and tie it to the rest of the weapon. The Jedi, carefully manipulating the Force, bound the components together—linking them on something more than a mechanical or material level, so they worked with unimagined efficiency. Without this careful seasoning and conditioning of the lightsaber, the blade would be flawed and would fail the Jedi.

After assembling the components, I prepared to charge the power cell for the very first time. With my finger poised on the transformer button that would start the energy flowing, I drew in a deep breath and lowered myself into a trance. I knew that manipulating matter sufficiently to meld the part and forge the weapon would have been all but impossible for anyone but a Jedi Master like Yoda, but doing just that as part of the construction of a lightsaber had been studied and ritualized so even a student could manage it. It was very much a lost art, a link to a past that had been all but wiped out, and by performing it I completed my inheritance of my Jedi legacy.

I hit the button, allowing the slow trickle of energy to fill the battery. I opened myself to the Force and with the hand I had touching the lightsaber's hilt, I bathed the lightsaber with the Force. As I did so, subtle transformations took place in the weapon. Elemental bonds shifted, allowing more and more energy to flow into the cell and throughout the weapon. I was not certain how the changes were being made, but I knew that at the same time they were being made in the lightsaber, they were being made in me also.

And I was Jedi.

During the war with the Yuuzhan Vong, Anakin Solo was searching for the Jedi student Tahiri Veila on Yuuzhan Vong–occupied Yavin 4 when his lightsaber's focusing crystals became damaged. Anakin disguised himself as a slave to infiltrate a Yuuzhan Vong compound and was assigned to harvest Yuuzhan Vong lambents, living crystals that provide illumination when stimulated by something similar to telepathic energy. After two days of meditation, Anakin attuned himself to a lambent crystal, which he used to repair his lightsaber. He soon discovered that his attunement to this crystal enabled a vague awareness of any nearby Yuuzhan Vong, who had been previously undetectable to any Jedi's Force powers.

ARCHAIC LIGHTSABERS

According to the Holocrons, the earliest lightsabers were crude devices that utilized an experimental "frozen blaster" technology to create an energy beam of a fixed length. Designed primarily for siege warfare, these archaic lightsabers were barely portable; their energy requirements necessitated a flexible cable that connected a lightsaber's handle to a power pack worn on a Jedi's belt. Because the cable was not shielded and literally tied a Jedi to the lightsaber, the limitations in battle were obvious. Over time, emerging technologies allowed the Jedi to miniaturize the parts and pack more power output into a smaller energy cell that could be set within a lightsaber's handle.

JEDI TRAINEE CORRAN HORN CONSTRUCTING A LIGHTSABER FROM JUNKED MACHINERY. *(Edwards)*

WATERPROOF LIGHTSABERS

After the Battle of Yavin, during a mission in the Circarpous system, Luke Skywalker learned that his lightsaber—the one that had previously belonged to his father—was capable of functioning underwater. It was subsequently discovered that not all lightsabers were waterproof, as some were noted to short out if not properly insulated. The Jedi Kit Fisto, an amphibious native of Glee Anselm and a member of the Jedi Council during the Clone Wars, recorded the following information about his lightsaber via the Great Holocron:

> When I first learned the principals of lightsaber construction at the Jedi Temple, I was surprised that most instructors considered waterproofing as an option for customization. My own lightsaber has two crystals that work on a bifurcating cyclical-ignition pulse, which allows for continuous operation in rainfall as well as underwater. I will provide detailed instructions for all who wish to similarly construct or modify their own lightsabers.

Close examination of various historic light-sabers suggests that Kit Fisto's innovation was widely adopted by the Jedi Knights during the Clone Wars, in which Jedi saw combat on the water worlds Kamino and Mon Calamari, and the rain-drenched planet Jabiim.

TRAINING LIGHTSABERS

Lightsaber blades are inherently dangerous and can easily maim young or inexperienced Jedi, but nonlethal training lightsabers, which do not focus their power strongly enough to cut through objects, are a relatively new invention in the long history of the Jedi. It was not until approximately a thousand years ago, after the Jedi Order sustained heavy losses at the Battle of Ruusan, that the Jedi developed training lightsabers for Padawan learners. Although most training lightsabers were destroyed during the Jedi Purge, a number have been recovered from various sources.

Standard lightsabers may be used for training if they are equipped with a control device that adjusts the blade's energy, but such weapons were not available to the first students at Luke Skywalker's Jedi academy on Yavin 4. Instead, students used padded wooden practice swords for combat exercises, and were instructed by Kam Solusar. One of Solusar's students was former Corellian Security officer Corran Horn, who also helped develop the training program and served as Kam's co-instructor for self-defense techniques. Horn provided the following account:

> Kam Solusar taught us well the three rings of defense. The outermost ring consisted of four guard positions: upper right, upper left, lower right, and lower left. The lightsaber's hilt would end up wide of the body, with the tip coming back toward the middle to pick up the grand sweeping blows that are very powerful, but also take longer to deliver.
>
> The middle ring also involved four guard positions: high, low, left, and right. Whereas in the outer ring the blade tended to be held at a diagonal, in the middle ring up and down were parallel to the ground at head and knee height, while left and right were perpendicular to it. The idea with the middle ring was to pick up quicker blows and stop them before they could intersect with the body. Luke also noted that the middle ring was effective against picking off blaster bolts.
>
> The inner ring involved parries instead of blocks and was proof against lunging attacks. For this third line of defense, the lightsaber was kept in close, with the hilt covering the navel. By angling the blade's tip and picking up attacks on the lower third of the blade, attacks could be shunted aside, and a riposte to the opponent's chest or stomach became a very real possibility. The inner ring was the last line of defense, dangerous to be defending from, and dangerous to be attacking from.
>
> During a basic sparring match that pitted me against Gantoris, I learned an important lesson. I'd made the mistake of thinking that my CorSec experience would give me an edge over my opponent, and also believed it was important to convince the other students of my abilities as an instructor. I didn't anticipate Gantoris's speed, and actually felt shame when his blade struck me again and again. He was about to strike a blow to my head when I abandoned conscious thought and felt the Force flow through me. An instant later, I sent Gantoris to the ground.
>
> What surprised me was that my access to the Force had come at a point when I had been forced to abandon the image I had been trying to present to others. Once I got past pretense and was just what I was, the Force flowed more freely. It was as if the role I had created for myself had inhibited the flow, whereas abandoning the role brought me closer to it.
>
> I realized that it was not for me to sculpt the Force's flow to my purposes, but for me to be sculpted into that which more easily works with the Force.

DUAL-PHASE LIGHTSABERS

Lightsabers with dual-phase focusing crystals can be adjusted to variable lengths and widths, granting a deceptive and highly effective tactic against unwary opponents. Records from circa 400 B.B.Y. indicate that Keiran Halcyon constructed a special dual-phase lightsaber that could go from standard length (1.3 meters) to a length of 3 meters with the flick of a switch. Most dual-phase lightsabers date from an earlier period in Republic history, when lightsaber duels were more common and the Sith were at the height of their power. As more beings became aware of Jedi fighting skills, and the Jedi themselves endeavored to end disputes without drawing their weapons, duels grew less frequent and the need for adjustable blades essentially ended. However, lightsaber dueling techniques remained part of Jedi training well into the Golden Age, with Jedi Knights and Masters clashing using lightsabers set to a nonlethal "sparring mode," and Luke Skywalker continues to emphasize lightsaber training within the ranks of his new Jedi Order. The craft of dual-phase lightsabers also continued, as many Jedi prefer the option of the short-bladed adjustment that serves as a more precise cutting tool in emergency situations.

ILLUSTRIOUS LIGHTSABERS

Over time, certain lightsabers have taken on legendary status. In the twilight of the Old Republic, one such lightsaber belonged to the Jedi Knight Sharad Hett. After serving as a Padawan to Jedi Master Eeth Koth, Sharad Hett was assigned to the most malignant corners of the galaxy to defend the weak and uphold the law of the Republic. For his continual acts of daring, he earned a reputation as the most fearless and dedicated Jedi Knight of his time. He also earned many epithets, including the Howlrunner, the Champion of Krmar, the Defender of Kamparus, the Hound of Worlds, the Nemesis of the Kimm, and Tamer of Tyrants. To many Jedi and their Padawans, his lightsaber became a symbol of his valor.

In 47 B.B.Y., Sharad Hett disappeared after taking a leave of absence. Fifteen years later, shortly after the Battle of Naboo, Hett resurfaced on Tatooine as the leader of a group of Tusken warriors. The Jedi Master Ki-Adi-Mundi was dispatched to learn whether Hett had embraced the dark side, and he made the following recording after returning from his mission:

I regret to announce that Sharad Hett is dead. Even though I witnessed his passing,

I admit it is hard for me to believe he is gone. Every living Jedi knows his name, and any Jedi born within the last thirty years would recognize his weapon. I have presented my full report of his activities on Tatooine to the Jedi Council, but feel compelled to notify every Jedi that Sharad Hett lived and died a Jedi.

I also declare my decision to take Sharad Hett's son, A'Sharad Hett, as my Padawan. Since birth, A'Sharad was raised by his father as a Jedi, and the Force is strong in him. He built his own lightsaber, and has inherited his father's weapon. Although I know not whether A'Sharad will choose one weapon over the other, I am certain that he will honor his father and the Jedi Order.

A'Sharad Hett became a Jedi Knight and served during the Clone Wars. According to various records, he utilized both the lightsaber he'd crafted and the one he'd inherited from his father, which placed him among the few Jedi who simultaneously wielded two lightsabers. His fate remains unknown. Records indicate that Ki-Adi-Mundi was slain by his own troops on the InterGalactic Banking Clan stronghold world of Mygeeto near the end of the Clone Wars.

Many contemporary Jedi have expressed interest in the history of Luke Skywalker's first lightsaber, which originally belonged to his father, Anakin Skywalker. According to datafiles, this weapon was actually the second lightsaber made by Anakin, who'd lost his first lightsaber—made on Ilum when he was thirteen years old—during the Battle of Geonosis. It is unknown whether Anakin returned to Ilum to make his second lightsaber, but Ilum crystals were used to create the blue-bladed weapon that he used throughout the Clone Wars.

The astromech R2-D2 eventually yielded

holorecordings that revealed previously unknown details about Anakin's transformation into Darth Vader, including the fact that he slaughtered many Jedi on Coruscant before Obi-Wan Kenobi tracked him to the planet Mustafar. Vader was mortally wounded in the resulting duel with Kenobi, who left Mustafar with his former Padawan's lightsaber. The weapon would remain in Kenobi's possession for nineteen years, until he presented it to Luke Skywalker on Tatooine.

In 3 A.B.Y., Luke lost both the lightsaber and his right hand in his own duel with Vader on Cloud City. Luke's right hand was replaced with a cybernetic prosthetic, and he followed instructions from a book he'd found in Obi-Wan Kenobi's abandoned home on Tatooine to construct a new lightsaber. Eight years later, Luke related this experience to his first students at the Jedi praxeum on Yavin 4:

I not only lost my lightsaber and right hand on Cloud City, but lost a friend, too. Darth Vader had Han Solo frozen in carbonite, then released Han's frozen form to the bounty hunter Boba Fett. After my hand had been replaced with this prosthetic, I eventually went to Tatooine, where I hoped to intercept Boba Fett before he delivered Han to Jabba the Hutt, the gangster who had placed the bounty on Han. While on Tatooine, I hid out in the small house where Obi-Wan Kenobi had lived as Ben Kenobi.

Obi-Wan hadn't left much behind, which is only appropriate. It is not the way of the Jedi to accumulate possessions. Still, given the number of scavengers on Tatooine, I was surprised to find anything still in his home, which seemed to have gone unoccupied since his departure. One thing I found was what appeared to be an old and intricately carved boa-wood trunk, but was actually a keypad safe box. It's a good thing no one else ever attempted to open

the box. Somehow Obi-Wan had rigged it with a thumbprint clasp that would only yield to my touch, along with a flashpacket that would have caused the box to burst into flame and explode if anyone else had tried.

The box held Obi-Wan's journal and an ancient leather-bound book that contained, among other things, plans for building a lightsaber. I hadn't had any communication with Obi-Wan's spirit since I'd left Dagobah, just before my duel with Vader on Cloud City, so I was astonished to find this book when I did. It was as if Obi-Wan had anticipated that I would lose my lightsaber, and had left this book behind to help me.

According to Obi-Wan's book, the best lightsabers used natural jewels, preferably three jewels with different densities and facets to construct a fully adjustable blade. Because there weren't a lot of natural jewels lying around where I could find them on Tatooine, I realized I would have to keep the construction as simple as possible and limit my new lightsaber to a single jewel.

I followed the book's instructions to the letter. I managed to collect most of the electronic and mechanical parts—power cells, controls, a high-energy reflector cup—from merchants in Mos Eisley. The text maintained that building a personal lightsaber was a rite of passage for a Jedi, and that a Jedi Master could construct a new lightsaber in a couple of days.

I was hardly a Jedi Master. I triple-checked each step, doing my best to ensure that when I finally pressed the switch to activate the weapon, it would work. My greatest concern was that I would press that switch and the lightsaber would blow up, vaporizing me, all because I hadn't tuned it quite right. After nearly a month of

tinkering and checking, I still had to make my own focusing jewel.

I used a little furnace to heat and pressurize the jewel. When it was done, I had to cut the jewel, polish and install it, and tune the photoharmonics. The cuts were tricky. One wrong tap with the shearing tool and I could have shattered the jewel, and then I'd have to cook another one and start over.

When I finally completed the lightsaber, I took it outside Obi-Wan's house. Only R2-D2 was with me at the time, and I told him to go back inside. It may sound ridiculous, but I thought if something went wrong, I needed someone to tell Leia that Luke Skywalker, the galaxy's biggest idiot, had flash-flamed himself into a black crisp because he couldn't follow an elementary circuit diagram.

[Laughter from some Jedi trainees]

I waited until R2 was out of sight before I pushed the control button. I felt both relief and satisfaction when the blade ignited as expected. I waved it experimentally to find that it had a good balance, maybe even better than my first one. Holding one hand near the blade, I felt no sensation of heat, which meant the conductors were working. I tested the blade by whipping it down at an angle to cleave through a wrist-thick chunk of rock. It passed through the rock easily, leaving a smooth cut.

And so it was that I carried this lightsaber with me when I next confronted Darth Vader. Except for the color of his lightsaber's blade, I don't know that there were any significant differences between his weapon and mine. My only advantage in that duel was that I knew there was still goodness in my father.

I hope my account conveys that no one should construct a lightsaber in haste.

To those of you who have yet to wield a lightsaber, I urge you to be patient. After using training sabers to learn the basics of lightsaber combat, you will examine our collection of ancient lightsabers that were recovered from Ossus last year. Soon you will learn to build your own.

In 9 A.B.Y., Luke discovered that Palpatine had recovered Luke's severed hand and lightsaber, and that the demented Jedi Master Joruus C'baoth had used genetic material from the hand to grow a mindless clone of Luke. Armed with Luke's also-recovered lightsaber, this clone fought Luke at the Emperor's stronghold at Mount Tantiss on the planet Wayland. This duel ended when Mara Jade—a former Imperial agent who'd been assigned to kill Luke—killed both the clone and C'baoth.

Luke recovered his first lightsaber and gave it to Mara Jade. In 10 A.B.Y., Mara constructed a new violet-bladed lightsaber for herself as part of her training to become a Jedi Knight. Luke has retired his first lightsaber, and continues to use the second one that he made for himself.

SITH LIGHTSABERS

As previously noted, the original Sith Lords—the Jedi Exiles who survived the Hundred-Year Darkness, and their descendants—apparently abandoned the use of lightsabers in favor of other weapons, as the Sith did not use lightsabers during the Hyperspace War. The earliest record of a Jedi-expatriate-turned-Sith using a lightsaber was Freedon Nadd in 4400 B.B.Y.

The construction and use of the first double-bladed lightsaber is sometimes credited to Jedi-turned-Sith Exar Kun, but according to the Tedryn Holocron, Exar Kun assembled his weapon by following instructions from a Sith Holocron, possibly

◀ GENERAL GRIEVOUS RECEIVING LIGHTSABER INSTRUCTION FROM COUNT DOOKU. (Edwards)

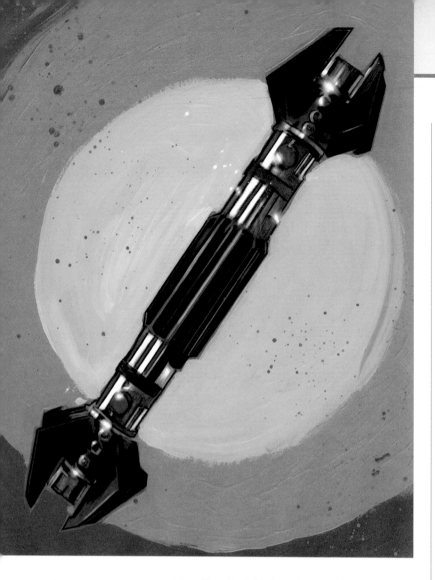

qualities of red crystals, the Jedi Holocron yields
the following information:

c. 1010 B.B.Y.
Author: Jedi Master Pernicar

*In our most recent confrontation with
the Sith, I finally met up with my former
Padawan, Wud Mortull, who went missing
more than eight years ago. I had just slain
three Sith soldiers when he called out
to me. I turned to see an armored figure
among many others on the battlefield,
only this one was running at me with open
arms and a broad smile on his face. I didn't
recognize Wud at first, he'd grown so
much. His face had broadened, and his chin
seemed sharper. He laughed as he came at
me, running as if to embrace me the way
a son might embrace his long-lost father.
And then a lightsaber suddenly appeared
in his right hand and a red blade ignited.*

*Wud was still smiling when I cut him
down.*

*Still smiling when I removed his weapon
from his dead fingers.*

*Still smiling as I stood there, momen-
tarily oblivious to the chaos around, and I
wondered,* Why red?

*Surely I've seen enough Sith lightsabers
in my lifetime that I should have wondered
this before. But for some reason, I'd never
pondered this question until the moment
I realized Wud had forsaken the green-
bladed lightsaber that he'd made for
himself a decade ago. At the time, after
he'd constructed that first lightsaber,
he confided that he felt such a strong
connection to it.*

*What had caused him to ally with the
Sith, I cannot say. But as I held his Sith
lightsaber, this poorly crafted insult to
his heritage, it was hard for me to believe*

prepared by the Jedi Exiles themselves. Because
the singular purpose of a double-bladed lightsaber
is to enable its wielder to make more effective
kills, the Jedi have long regarded it as an offensive
weapon, and Jedi students are discouraged from
attempting to create or train with one.

For more than a thousand years, nearly every
record of lightsaber-wielding Dark Jedi or Sith
Lords indicates their predilection for red-bladed
lightsabers, usually made with synthetic crystals.
The exact origin of this apparent standard remains
unknown, but may be the result of non-Jedi being
forced to use crystals or gems from worlds other
than Ilum. It is also conceivable that the Sith Lord
Kaan's Brotherhood of Darkness adopted red
lightsabers to distinguish their army from their
enemy at the Battle of Ruusan, and that subsequent
Sith Lords maintained this tradition. As for the

that he could have joined the Sith entirely willingly. I know it sounds ludicrous, but I wondered if the Sith lightsaber had been somehow responsible for his conversion. Was there anything in the Sith weapon's properties that might have made him want to relinquish his Jedi lightsaber?

I consulted our armorer, asking if she had any knowledge about whether any properties of Sith lightsabers affected the behavior or disposition of the user. She answered, "I know they affect me, because whenever I see a Sith holding one, I'm inclined to kill the Sith." Then she referred me to a holobook entry on the subject of crystals. Here is an excerpt:

Red crystals are ordinarily unsuitable for lightsabers, since they are less stable than the customary green and blue crystals Jedi use for the blade generators in their lightsabers. However, red crystals—both genuine and synthetic—glow in harmonic vibration when energized by the dark side of the Force. When energized this way, red "Sith" crystals, as they are sometimes called, can actually produce a stronger blade that has the rare potential to "break the blade" of Jedi lightsabers, overloading the energy matrix and instantly burning out the opponent's weapon. Although this rarely happens, it is a known and frightening possibility in combat.

Indeed, this is rare, as I have only seen a Sith lightsaber "break" a Jedi lightsaber on one occasion, something I believed, at the time, was a defect in the Jedi weapon. At my request, the armorer analyzed the Sith lightsaber that I'd recovered from Wud Mortull. She confirmed that his lightsaber contained synthetic crystals, as did every other Sith lightsaber she ever examined.

Still, when I think of that wicked smile on Wud's face, I have difficulty dismissing the feeling that his weapon exerted some kind of control over him, driving him to do terrible things. I suspect I am guilty of wishful thinking. It is easier for me to believe that a red crystal turned Wud to evil than that he took that path all by himself.

When Darth Maul revealed the return of the Sith in 32 B.B.Y., he used a double-bladed lightsaber to duel Qui-Gon Jinn and Obi-Wan Kenobi. Ten years later, Count Dooku—the alter ego of Darth Tyranus—used a curved-handled lightsaber when he dueled with Kenobi and Anakin Skywalker on Geonosis. Like their predecessors, Maul and Dooku wielded red-bladed weapons. Various records note that Dooku's protégée, the Sith aspirant Asajj Ventress, may have gained possession of the two curved-handled lightsabers once possessed by Dooku's last Padawan, Komari Vosa. This theory is given credence by reports that, like Komari Vosa's weapons, Asajj Ventress's lightsabers were red-bladed and featured similar hilts. Records initially indicated that Komari Vosa perished on an ill-fated rescue mission to Baltizaar in 39 B.B.Y.

Interestingly, Anakin Skywalker did not immediately adopt a red-bladed lightsaber when he became Darth Vader in 19 B.B.Y., but initially used the blue-bladed lightsaber that was subsequently taken by Kenobi and passed on to Luke Skywalker. Hologrammic records from the astromech R2-D2 attest to Vader's use of this blue-bladed weapon when he slaughtered Jedi at the Temple. We can surmise that Vader did not have sufficient time to construct a red-bladed lightsaber before the slaughter, but it is equally possible that he used his original Jedi weapon to avoid alerting any of his victims that he had gone to the dark side.

THE SEVEN FORMS

The Great Holocron has yielded a most enlightening recording by the Jedi Knight Cin Drallig, who served as a lightsaber instructor at the Jedi Temple on Coruscant during the final years of the Old Republic. In his recording, made in 31 B.B.Y., Drallig discusses the seven forms: seven fighting disciplines that were studied by the Jedi of his era.

Greeting, Padawans. I am Cin Drallig, your instructor in lightsaber discipline.

I have no doubt that you all believe you know something of the seven forms of lightsaber combat. All of you spent your first years studying Form I, and most of you have spent a year or two studying each additional form up through Form V. Some of you may be undecided about whether to now dedicate yourself to one particular form, and some of you may choose to build your own fighting style. Whether you have gained additional knowledge on lightsaber combat from databooks, seen or participated in demonstrations, or discovered and experimented with certain techniques on your own, I assure you that you have much to learn about the seven forms.

As you know, each form represents differing styles and philosophies, and each has its respective merits. For those of you who are unaware of the unique and subtle differences of the forms, allow me to provide brief descriptions.

Form I, also called Shii-Cho, *requires little explanation, as every Jedi youngling learns the basics of attack, parry, body target zones, and the practice drills called velocities. Form I was created by the an-cient Jedi during the transition from metal swords to energy beam lightsabers, and the principles of blade contact remain essentially the same. Because the ancient Jedi did not have lightsaber-wielding enemies, Form I does not address the lightsaber-to-lightsaber combat.*

Form II, also called Makashi, *represents the ultimate refinement of lightsaber-to-lightsaber combat. It evolved during an era when battles between Jedi and Dark Jedi had become expected, if not routine, and may have produced the greatest dueling masters the galaxy had ever seen. Masters of Form II developed unique offenses and defenses, and trained studiously against having their weapons taken or damaged.*

Following the Battle of Ruusan, Form II became an archaism, for there were few situations in which Jedi fought lightsaber-wielding enemies. However, the former Jedi learner Aurra Sing resurfaced more than a decade ago as a bounty hunter and assassin, and has developed a reputation for taking lightsabers as trophies from her Jedi victims. Furthermore, it is now nearly a year since Obi-Wan Kenobi slew the Sith Lord who killed Qui-Gon Jinn at the Battle of Naboo, and some Jedi Masters have suggested that the Order should reexamine the requirements of Form II. Other Masters have countered that such confrontations will remain exceedingly rare so long as the Jedi remain mindful of the Force and the Sith limit their numbers to two. As long as Aurra Sing and any Sith Lords remain at large, it is the opinion of this instructor that the study of Form II should not be dismissed as impractical.

Form III, also called Soresu, *was first developed in response to the advancement of blaster technology in the galaxy. As an ever-increasing variety of blaster weapons* became available to military factions as well as criminals, Jedi had to revise their lightsaber skills to defend themselves. Originally, the basic principle of Form III was "laserblast" deflection training. This Form maximizes defensive protection in a style characterized by tight, efficient movements that expose minimal target areas when compared with the relatively open style of some other forms. Over many centuries, Form III has evolved into a highly refined expression of nonaggressive Jedi philosophy. True masters of Form III have long been considered invincible; although not always able to overcome their adversaries, no Form III masters have ever been defeated.

Form IV, also called Ataru, is the most acrobatic Form, filled with numerous elaborate moves, and relies heavily upon a Jedi's ability to run, jump, and spin using the Force. Form IV can be astonishing to watch. By incorporating all the Force powers that enable one to exceed standard norms of physical possibilities, Jedi may resemble nothing less than a blur when they utilize Form IV. Yes, it is true that Yoda is a Form IV master. Although it has been many years since Yoda has graced us with a demonstration, the Jedi Archives holds a collection of databooks that are testament to his mastery and prowess.

Form V, which has two distinct variations, Shien and Djem So, was developed alongside Form IV, during an era when Jedi were called upon to more actively maintain the peace in the galaxy, and when purely defensive combat skills—such as those of Form III—were deemed insufficient. Form V focuses on strength and lightsaber attack moves. Form V's Shien variation exploits the ability of the lightsaber to block a blaster bolt, and turns this defensive move into an offensive attack by deflecting the bolt deliberately toward an opponent. Form V's Djem So variation is devoted specifically to lightsaber dueling. A dedication to the power and strength necessary to defeat an opponent characterizes the philosophy of Form V, which some Jedi describe by the maxim "Peace through superior firepower." While proponents of Form V regard it as a worthwhile discipline to prepare a Jedi for any threat, there are others who maintain that Form V fosters an inappropriate focus on dominating others.

You ask for my opinion on Form V? I am neither a proponent nor a detractor. One must question any discipline that has lethal potential. However, if it serves to suppress violent opposition and preserve peace, I believe it is a discipline worth knowing.

Form VI, also called Niman, is the current standard in lightsaber training. This form balances the emphases of other forms with overall moderation. Through Form VI, a Jedi may achieve true harmony and justice without resorting to the rule of power. It is often referred to as the diplomat's form because it is less intensive in its demands than the other disciplines, allowing Jedi to spend more time developing their skills in perception, political strategy, and negotiation. The Jedi Council maintains that Form VI best suits the role of contemporary Jedi Knights. After all, a Jedi Knight who is overly trained in martial combat might be at a loss to resolve a complex political conflict or a sensitive trade disagreement.

How long can you expect to study Form VI before you master it? If you dedicate yourself only to Form VI, you will study for at least ten years.

Is Form VI the most worthy of study? No, but in general it is the most practical.

I would be negligent if I refrained from noting that full masters of other forms have come to consider Form VI as insufficiently demanding.

Form VII, also called Juyo, is the most difficult and demanding of all forms. Only high-level masters of multiple forms can achieve and control this discipline, which can lead to fantastic power and skill. Form VII employs bold, direct movements, more open and kinetic than Form V, but not so elaborate in appearance as the acrobatic Form IV. Unlike Form V, Form VII requires greater energy because the focus is wielded more broadly, and draws upon a deeper well of emotion; while the outward bearing of a Form VII practitioner is one of calm, the inner pressure verges on explosion. And unlike the graceful, linked movement sequences of Form IV, Form VII tactics overwhelm opponents with seemingly unconnected staccato sequences. This combination of traits makes Form VII highly unpredictable in battle.

Because so few have achieved the necessary mastery to advance to Form VII, this discipline can only be regarded as under development by a select few, and forbidden to all others. Mace Windu and his former Padawan Depa Billaba are among the only current practitioners of Form VII, and even they acknowledge that it is a dangerous regimen that may cut close to the Sith intensity of focus on physical combat ability.

And now let us meditate before we begin basic exercises for Form VI.

VAAPAD

Recovered from the Great Holocron, the following recording by Jedi Master Mace Windu provides information about a specific variation on Form VII, and its dangerous connection to the dark side. Made in 22 B.B.Y., the recording also reveals previously unknown details about certain events during the Clone Wars.

Master Ki-Adi-Mundi and Master Kolar. This data tape has been sent directly to you as a precaution against Separatist spies who have been attempting to intercept Republic transmissions.

All members of the Council are aware that we've lost a great many Jedi in the three months since the Republic declared war against the Separatists. Not only those who died in combat, but also those who have refused to serve as generals, instead choosing to abandon the Order. Most recently, Sora Bulq, who fought by our side on Geonosis, chose to leave for his family's estate on Ruul, a moon of the Weequay homeworld Sriluur.

As a lightsaber instructor at the Temple, Sora trained and influenced many, many Jedi. When Quinlan Vos had to be retrained after the events that left his memory impaired, it was Sora who helped Quinlan regain his focus with a lightsaber. But on our recent mission to Lianna, Masters Tholme, Yoda, and I learned that Sora had taught Quinlan a maneuver from a Form VII variation known as Vaapad. Obviously, I recognized Vaapad because I developed it. Quinlan claimed that Sora said nothing about Vaapad, and told me that he will not use the maneuver again.

I sensed Quinlan spoke without deceit, but his awareness of Vaapad is disturbing, particularly since Sora Bulq helped me develop the maneuver. Except for Depa Billaba, I have never encouraged any other Jedi to adopt Vaapad.

Ki-Adi-Mundi, you are aware that for me, Vaapad is . . . personal. To Agen Kolar, I shall explain.

I developed Vaapad to answer my own weakness, and channel my inner darkness into a weapon of the light. To use Vaapad, a Jedi must give himself over to the thrill of battle, enjoying the fight and the satisfaction of winning. A Jedi must also accept and embrace the fury of his opponent. This transforms a Jedi into half of a superconducting loop, the other half being the power of darkness, which passes in and out of the Jedi without touching him.

Vaapad is more than a fighting style. It is a state of mind, a path that leads through the penumbra of the dark side.

It is also not meant for any Jedi without my approval.

Shortly after this, Quinlan discovered that four leaders of dissident Jedi—Master K'Kruhk, Master Sian Jeisel, the Jedi Knight Rhad Tarn, and Sora's former Padawan Mira—had gathered on Ruul. All these Jedi had different reasons for renouncing their commissions. Sora Bulq invited me to Ruul to meet with the other Jedi and discuss the possibility of preventing a schism within the Order.

Soon after I arrived on Ruul, I confronted Sora about whether he had indeed taught a move from Vaapad to Quinlan Vos. Sora answered that he had been testing Quinlan, and that he pursued it no further after Quinlan passed the test.

But the meeting on Ruul turned out to be a trap. We were attacked by a female assassin, possibly a Rattataki, who wielded two red-bladed lightsabers with curved hilts. Her weapons were not unlike the one used by Count Dooku on Geonosis, or the pair used by his failed Padawan, Komari Vosa.

I regret I was slow to ascertain that this assassin had been contracted by Sora Bulq, who identified her as Asajj Ventress. Even worse, I failed to foresee that Sora had gone to the dark side.

Sora claimed that he was long fascinated by the dark side, and by our work on Vaapad. He had intended to kill the other Jedi on Ruul and blame me for their deaths in order to widen the schism that divides our Order. He also claimed to be a true master of Vaapad. It is my contention that Vaapad has mastered Sora Bulq.

Ventress killed Mira and quickly conscripted Rhad Tarn before she escaped. Tarn was slain by Jeisel, who left Ruul with K'Kruhk and myself because we were too badly outnumbered by the droids that Sora Bulq unleashed upon us.

It is imperative to alert all Jedi that Sora Bulq has gone to the dark side. We must also learn more about this Asajj Ventress. The Archives yielded no information about her, and it may be pure speculation that her lightsabers indicate any alliance with Count Dooku. There is an undeniable darkness about her, but I sensed she was not a Sith.

Given that Sora Bulq is no longer trustworthy, we must allow for the possibility that Quinlan Vos knows more of Vaapad than he admits. Quinlan is currently on a mission to Brentaal IV. Let us be mindful of him. I now know that it was a mistake to expose Sora Bulq to Vaapad, and hope the mistake will not extend to Quinlan.

I look forward to your return to Coruscant. May the Force be with you.

There is no record of whether Mace Windu chose the name *Vaapad* for his combat style, but the name is shared by a creature that is indigenous to the moons of Sarapin. A notoriously dangerous predator, a vaapad attacks its prey with whipping strikes of its tentacles. Most vaapad have at least seven tentacles, but one confirmed report proves that the number can be as high as twenty-three. Because vaapad move with incredible speed, it is a commonly held observation that their tentacles cannot be counted until the creature is dead. It is easily conceivable that Mace Windu took inspiration from the vaapad when he developed his lightsaber discipline.

THE MARKS OF CONTACT

31 B.B.Y.

Author: Cin Drallig

Greeting, Padawans.

All lightsaber combat forms involve the same marks of contact, target objectives organized as categories of damage that you can inflict on your opponents. These marks help focus your offense and defense on a few clear categories rather than diffusing awareness across an infinite number of possibilities. The names of these marks remain unaltered from the language of the earliest Jedi sages.

Sun djem is the ancient term for "disarming." Because relieving an opponent of his weapon or destroying it could win victory without causing injury, sun djem was especially consistent with Jedi conduct and was the primary goal of early Form I masters. However, advances in Form II made sun djem extremely difficult in lightsaber-to-lightsaber combat, as all Form II masters trained to prevent themselves from being disarmed.

Shiim is any kind of wound that is made with the edge of a lightsaber blade.

An inconclusive mark of contact, shiim is considered inferior to other marks that decisively end a battle. Thus, its appearance expresses nothing more than a struggle with a powerful opponent. According to Jedi Archives, it was not unusual for some ancient combat veterans—Jedi and Dark Jedi alike—to forgo corrective surgery for wounds so that they might wear their lightsaber-induced scars as a badge of honor. Not surprisingly, this tradition began to die out about the same time as the discovery of bacta.

Shiak is "stabbing." Jedi tradition holds that shiak is an honorable method of inflicting serious injury because it causes the least visible injury to the opponent's body. Thus, shiak can express a Jedi's respect for an opponent and the living Force even as it delivers a fatal blow.

Cho mai translates as "to cut off the weapon hand." Because this strike instantly ends an opponent's ability to use a weapon but does not kill, cho mai is always a preferred move in combat. The precision of cutting off only a hand is considered the mark of a superior lightsaber master.

Cho sun is "to dismember," but the term is used specifically in reference to removing an opponent's entire weapon arm. This move lacks the precision and elegance of cho mai, but cho sun is the move most often necessary in the heat of conflict or where no chances can be taken.

Cho mok translates as "to otherwise maim," targeting legs, limbs, or appendages that will disable your opponent. Although emergency situations may sometimes leave you with few options, I discourage cho mok unless you have an essential comprehension of your opponent's physiology. Obviously, it is crucial that you know the location of vital organs before you strike.

Sai cha *comes from the ancient words for "separate" and "head," and as you might expect it describes the act of using a lightsaber to behead an opponent. Jedi commit* sai cha *only when battle is at its most deadly serious and threatening, or when an opponent is considered extremely dangerous even to a fully trained Jedi.*

You ask for an example of such a situation? Six years ago, the Jedi Knight Qui-Gon Jinn and his then Padawan, Obi-Wan Kenobi, encountered Baroness Omnino of Vena on the planet Ord Mantell. Guilty of trafficking savrips, abducting Chancellor Valorum, and murder—among other things—Omnino wore a psychic augmenter, a sophisticated device that enabled her to control the minds and actions of virtually anyone she wished. Although the device did not work against Jedi, Omnino had manipulated savrips to seize Obi-Wan while she also made two Senate Guards aim their blasters at Chancellor Valorum's head. Understand, Padawans, that with but a fleeting thought, Omnino could have urged the guards to pull the triggers of their blasters and made the savrips tear Obi-Wan to pieces. Qui-Gon knew that the only way to prevent Omnino from harming any more victims was to stop her from projecting any more thoughts, and that knocking her unconscious was not an *option, because her dangerous mind might have remained active. It was under these circumstances that Qui-Gon distracted Omnino and resorted to* sai cha.

Sai tok *roughly translates as "to cut body in half." Jedi have long considered the bisection of a living opponent's body as a form of butchery, a desecration to be avoided if possible.* Sai tok *represents a potentially Sith-like desire to destroy one's enemy, whereas the Jedi goal in combat is an inner focus on defeating the danger of opponents, not striking with hate or wishing utter destruction upon them.* Sai tok *is generally used only against enemy droids.*

Should a Jedi hesitate to use sai tok *to kill a Sith Lord? An interesting question, and one you might better direct to Obi-Wan Kenobi, who used* sai tok *to fell the Sith on Naboo. But because he is not present, I shall take it upon myself to answer the question.*

No. A Jedi should not hesitate to use any combat technique to kill a Sith Lord. Again, I stress the goal is not to wish destruction on the Sith, but to defeat the danger they pose.

ON WINNING AND LOSING

The Jedi Master Rekpa De taught basic lightsaber training at the Jedi Temple while Yoda was still just a Jedi Knight. Of his many statements on lightsaber duels, this is perhaps Rekpa De's most influential:

Do not see a lightsaber duel as a choice between winning and losing. Every duel can have many, many outcomes. When you concentrate solely on winning—in lightsaber duels as in everything else—you sully your victory. Winning becomes worse than losing. It is better to lose well than to win badly. And it is always better to end a duel peacefully than to win or lose.

The Seven Forms of Lightsaber Combat

Each form represents differing styles and philosophies, and each has its respective merits. For those of you who are unaware of the unique and subtle differences of the forms, allow me to provide brief descriptions.

Form I, Shii-Cho

Form I requires little explanation, as every Jedi youngling learns the basics of attack, parry, body target zones, and the practice drills called velocities.

Form II represents the ultimate refinement of lightsaber-to-lightsaber combat. Masters of Form II develope unique offenses and defenses, and train studiously against having their weapons taken or damaged.

Form II, Makashi

Form III, Soresu

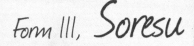

Form III was first developed in response to the advancement of blaster technology in the galaxy. This Form maximizes defensive protection in a style characterized by tight, efficient movements that expose minimal target areas when compared with the relatively open style of some other forms.

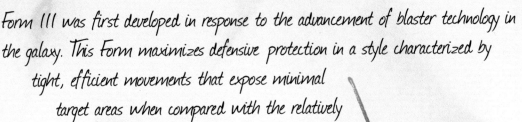

Form IV is the most acrobatic Form, filled with numerous elaborate moves, and relies heavily upon a Jedi's ability to run, jump, and spin using the Force. By incorporating all the Force powers that enable one to exceed standard norms of physical possibilities, Jedi may resemble nothing less than a blur when they utilize Form IV.

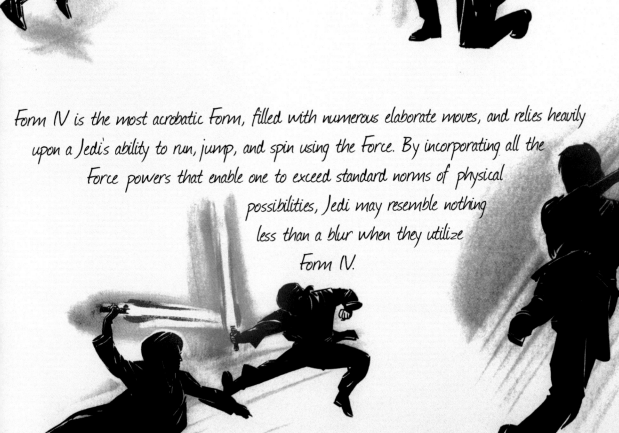

Form IV, Ataru

Form V's Shien variation exploits the ability of the lightsaber to block a blaster bolt, and turns this defensive move into an offensive attack by deflecting the bolt deliberately toward an opponent.

Form V,

Shien

Form VI,

Niman

Form VI balances the emphases of other forms with overall moderation. Through Form VI, a Jedi may achieve true harmony and justice without resorting to the rule of power.

Form VII,

Juyo

Form VII employs bold, direct movements,
more open and kinetic than Form V, but not
so elaborate in appearance as the acrobatic Form IV.
Unlike Form V, Form VII requires greater
energy because the focus is wielded more
broadly, and draws upon a deeper well of
emotion; while the outward bearing of a
Form VII practitioner is one of calm,
the inner pressure verges on explosion.

PART THREE

THE DARK SIDE

RECORDED 40 A.B.Y. ᐧ AUTHOR: TIONNE SOLUSAR.

For nearly as long as the Jedi have used their abilities to manipulate the Force, they have understood the dark side as a power that can influence and seduce even the most dedicated members of the Order. Existing records indicate that Jedi who were drawn to the dark side but returned to the light are greatly outnumbered by those who were unable or unwilling to leave the dark path. It is further stressed that no Jedi has ever emerged from this journey entirely unscathed.

Jedi are hardly the only Force-sensitive beings vulnerable to the dark side. There are numerous cases of Force-users—mostly from very remote worlds—who developed their powers with little or no knowledge of the Jedi and Sith. Some even cultivated their own traditions that were passed on to subsequent generations. However, few of these individuals and factions were as altruistic with their abilities as the Jedi; not surprisingly, selfish and competitive beings were especially inclined to use their powers to dominate others.

Because even cautious examination of the dark side can have dire consequences, the Jedi Order has long forbidden such study by all but the most highly disciplined Jedi Masters. It may be impossible to discourage those who are naturally inclined to explore that which is forbidden, but contemporary Jedi scholars hope to at least diminish curiosity by presenting the following information and case studies that offer unique and even practical insights into the dark side.

DARK JEDI

Those who embrace the dark side have either claimed or been ascribed various titles. Perhaps the best known is *Dark Jedi*, something of a blanket term to describe anyone who is skilled at using the dark side of the Force. Dark Jedi are historically distinguished from Sith and dark side Force-users by heritage and experience; more specifically, Jedi of the Old Republic regarded Dark Jedi as Jedi-trained individuals who had abandoned their Order's way to pursue a selfish and malicious agenda of their own design, and only those with direct Sith influence might be considered as Sith or Sith Lords. Because of these distinctions, two more accurate terms for a non-Jedi who wields dark side powers are *dark sider,* which dates back over many millennia, and *Dark Side Adept*. Both terms were used by Palpatine to describe many of his dark side servants. Still, the term *Dark Jedi* remains most prevalent.

Ancient records indicate a separate term for what a Force-sensitive being can become if he or she turns to the dark side early on: a *dark side devotee*. Unlike Jedi who began their training during infancy or have a mature awareness of the Force, dark side devotees regard the Force as something supernatural, and foster that image in the minds of others to make themselves appear more mysterious and powerful. Because their belief system may not recognize the Force as the same tool used by the Jedi or the Sith, they pursue a different path or develop their own traditions. Historically, not all dark side devotees were obsessed with power, but most did use their abilities to manipulate the environment and exploit the weak. Many took up careers as wanderers and adventurers. Although it is not known whether dark side devotees ever outnumbered more benevolent Force-adepts, they have certainly outnumbered the Sith ever since the Sith Order limited themselves to one Master and one apprentice.

One of the oldest records of a Dark Jedi—and possibly a dark side devotee—comes to us via the Great Holocron from the Jedi consular Sar Agorn. As previously noted, Sar Agorn was counted among the earliest Jedi during the dawn of the Republic. Upon first sight of Agorn's hologrammic representation, most assume that his appearance is the result of a degraded image, but light wave analysis indicates otherwise. It seems he was a most unusual being, an apparently bulbous, soft creature who lacked limbs or facial features, and had greenish gases continually surrounding his form, wholly unlike any species known today.

The following recording dates back to approximately 500 years before the First Great Schism that divided the Jedi, and 18,100 years before the exiled Dark Jedi arrived in Sith space, at a time when the Jedi may have still been developing their terminology for the Force. Although the dark side is not mentioned by name in Sar Agorn's record, his descriptions leave little doubt about the nature of the "shadows."

You ask of my first awareness of evil? That is difficult for me to say. It is not that my memory fails me, but that memories are based on our perceptions at specific moments. Are there not beings, things, or places that you regarded as evil when you were young, but that you subsequently determined were not evil at all? Did you

eventually forgive the inconsiderate relative, the howling wind, and the ominous structures that never really posed a threat to you except in your own imagination?

Furthermore, how shall we define evil? The common definition is that which is profoundly immoral or wrong, such as the desire to deliberately cause great harm, pain, or upset. But let me ask . . . if I told you that right now, at this very moment, your involuntary breathing was killing sentient microscopic innocents, would you choose to continue breathing? And even if you found a way to end the massacre, would it disturb you if you were unable to convince the microscopic survivors that you never meant them harm, and that they and their descendants would consider you evil and wish you dead for the devastation you brought to their loved ones and civilization?

You say that I tend to answer questions with too many questions in return? Well, how else will you learn to think for yourself?

Oh. So you wanted to know if I have ever known of a Jedi who turned to evil. You might have asked that in the first place. For that question, I have a most specific answer: the Jedi Cope Shykrill.

First, let me say that this is a most unusual case. As Jedi, we are bonded by our agreement to use our powers for the goodness of all beings, not for personal gain or to exploit others. Yes, there are times when one is tempted to use the Force simply because one can, but if one does not know when and where to draw the line, then ask more questions, and I shall draw it for you.

Now, about Cope Shykrill . . .

My fellow Jedi and I had been searching for Force-users like ourselves in the outlying systems of the Corellian sector when we found young Shykrill on Sarcophagus, the graveyard moon of Sacorria. At the time, the boy was living with his family, who were groundskeepers. We had not found him by accident, but by way of a report from a Selonian widower, who claimed to have witnessed Shykrill using telekinesis to lower his wife's coffin into an open grave. Shykrill seemed like a most unassuming child, but was indeed able to move objects through the air with little difficulty.

Although some families had been reluctant to allow their children to join the Jedi, Shykrill's parents were most accommodating, and even seemed genuinely grateful to us for granting their son the opportunity to rise above his station on Sarcophagus. And so the boy left with us to train as a Jedi. He was such a bright child. Always displayed a pleasant disposition when he asked for more lessons. Never asked a wrong question or gave a wrong answer. Always helped with chores. Never complained. In fact, over the course of eight years of training, he never gave us any cause for caution, or reason to imagine why his parents might have been eager for him to leave Sarcophagus.

Ah. I am getting ahead of myself.

The Jedi Watchman Nuck Lyu of Esseles was the first of my peers to express some concern about Shykrill. Nuck Lyu had been instructing a group of Jedi, including Shykrill, in how to use the Force to throw a new bladed weapon of his own design at wooden targets. After the lesson was over, Nuck Lyu confided to me that Shykrill repeatedly hit his targets with extreme precision. I conveyed to Nuck Lyu that I was not surprised, as Shykrill was one of our most promising Jedi.

But Nuck Lyu said to me, "You do not understand. I designed the weapon, and

it still took me nearly two months to throw it with consistent accuracy. Cope Shykrill's ability is not merely uncanny. It is unnatural."

Nuck Lyu returned to Esseles, leaving us with samples of his new blade, and leaving me with some inclination to pay closer attention to Shykrill, who was still training to be a Jedi Watchman himself. In the weeks that followed, I noticed no significant change in Shykrill's behavior. Then one night, I found him entertaining a trio of younger trainees—a Fia, a human, and a Nosaurian—with a shadowplay near a campfire. Shykrill stood between the fire and a stone wall, using hand gestures to make lively silhouettes that told a story against the wall's surface. It was a very compelling tale about two brothers, one good and one bad. The good brother wanted to plant seeds and grow vegetables, but the bad brother wanted to eat all the seeds. Lending his voice to the narration, Shykrill made the good brother sound very noble and scholarly, and the bad brother sound like an illiterate oaf. The bad brother made the trainees laugh.

Now, you may have noticed by my hologrammic representation that I am unlike most common species, as I'm without appendages or a complex physiognomy. Although I had always believed that my natural condition did not in any way impede my abilities as a Jedi, I suddenly felt something I had never felt before as I watched Shykrill's hands flutter and dance and cast shadows.

Envy.

I wished I had hands so that I might tell such a story, too, with the skill and grace of the young Shykrill. And then I felt something else.

Shame.

Confused, I returned to my quarters to contemplate what had transpired, and to meditate. Twenty-three minutes later, my meditation was interrupted by the sound of screaming. The screaming attracted all the Jedi in our camp, and we raced to the area where I'd left Shykrill and his small audience. There we found Shykrill and two of the trainees lying on the ground, covered in blood. The third trainee, the Nosaurian, was standing amidst the bodies, gripping one of Nuck Lyu's weapons in his hands. It was the Nosaurian who was screaming, and it appeared that he had used the weapon's blade to slash the others. He bellowed, "The shadows are in my head! Get them out!" And then he slit his own throat and collapsed.

Our medics did what they could. The three trainees died. Only Shykrill survived.

The weeks passed. Shykrill was still in bandages when I encouraged him to join me for a constitutional. He did not seem puzzled or surprised when I brought him to the site where the trainees had perished. There I conveyed to him that I had witnessed part of his shadowplay, and that I had no idea he was such an accomplished storyteller. And with some boldness, I inquired if the shadows ever spoke to him.

He answered, "You know they speak to me. They spoke to you, too. I heard them. They made you wish you had hands of your own."

I asked him how long he had been listening to the shadows. He said, "If you want to know whether the shadows spoke to me before or after I became a Jedi, I can't say."

I asked if he controlled the shadows, or if they controlled him. He said, "The shadows and I are the two brothers. One wants to plant the seeds, one wants to eat the seeds."

Remembering his shadowplay, I asked him whether he was the good brother or the bad brother. He said, "I am the brother who lived. And now, it is time for you to join the shadows."

I suddenly realized that I felt quite cold. Dread flooded over me, and a sickness spread within, but these feelings ended with supreme quickness as Shykrill's head separated from his body, having met the honed edge of Nuck Lyu's blade. It was Nuck Lyu himself who'd thrown the weapon from his hiding spot, for I had summoned him from Esseles when we buried the trainees. Somehow, both of us instinctively knew that Shykrill was responsible for the trainees' deaths, and that the only way to end his evil ways was to end his very life.

I traveled to Sarcophagus to inform Shykrill's parents that their son was dead, allowing them to believe that he had died honorably. But yes, I had another motive for meeting the parents. I wanted to find out if the evil that seemed to possess Shykrill had preceded his recruitment to the Jedi. As delicately as I could, I inquired as to whether Shykrill had a brother. Indeed, I learned that they had had another son, but he had died three years before Cope was born. I asked if young Cope had ever talked to an imaginary friend, or if he had ever shared his shadow stories with them. The parents were polite, but seemed altogether baffled by these questions. And so I left them on their tombworld.

Just as the Force flows through us all, so do we all have aspects that are positive and negative. But a Jedi knows the difference between light, darkness, and the shadows in between. Jedi cannot wrestle with decisions or struggle to uphold our ideals. We must know that what we do is good and just, and should we make mistakes, we must rectify those mistakes.

What made Shykrill's innards so different, so wretched and weak, that he would yield to shadows, embrace them, let them overwhelm him? Why would he live amongst us for more than nine years, learn our ways and methods, only to eventually kill those unfortunate trainees? Did these shadows he spoke of come from within himself, and did they die with him, or do they continue to exist beyond his death? I do not know, and I have no desire to venture into the shadows where one might find the answers.

But I do know that we, the Jedi, must be better and stronger than killers of children. We must be more. It is not our purpose to understand such shadows, but it is our purpose to use our light to extinguish them.

THE FIRST DARK LEGION

Facts are few about the events that led to the First Schism, when the relatively young Jedi Order went up against the first organized band of Dark Jedi. We know that it was in approximately 24,500 B.B.Y. that a faction of Jedi Knights renounced the ancient Jedi Masters and experimented with new ways to use the Force. Apparently frustrated by the rigid teachings of their former teachers, these rebels celebrated their freedom by giving in to their passions and emotions, and touching the power of the dark side. They called themselves the Legions of Lettow, and they were led by General Xendor, a powerful Force-using humanoid whose origins remain unknown. The Jedi Council, enraged at this act of disobedience, declared war on the general and his followers. The Jedi emerged victorious.

A data card provides the following account by a Jedi Padawan who died on Columus during the First Schism, after a battle with the Legions of Lettow. Popularly known as the Columus Data Card, it inspired at least three operas on Coruscant. Although the suspected Sith sympathizer Ingo Wavlud once noted his belief that this particular account was nothing less than Jedi propaganda, tests indicate the data card is authentic to the period.

c. 24,500 B.B.Y.
Author: Jedi apprentice Danzigorro Potts

I have received the transmission, the news that General Xendor is dead. At last, we have prevailed over the Legions of Lettow. I know it may be wrong of me, but I am relieved by his death, as I trust it brings an end to this awful war. For the first time in months, I look forward to tomorrow.

I wonder . . . I wonder if I might find a spot of sunshine before morning. Better yet, I might find a familiar, friendly face . . . one that's still breathing.

Forgive me, my Masters. My thoughts go astray. I do not mean to dishonor your teachings by babbling. You know I was never good with words. I always wished I could make them flow better. My throat is so dry.

And I'm bleeding something awful.

I hope I'm holding this audiocard right. [Static.]

Hear my words, fellow Jedi. I, the Jedi apprentice Danzigorro Potts, am the last survivor of the conflict on Columus. There were nearly thirty Dark Jedi, so we were fairly evenly matched. Tried to trap us in this ravine, they did. The battle was fierce and fast. It's so quiet now, peaceful even, but we can thank the Force for all we . . .

We can thank the Force for . . .

So sorry. I want to leave you with some important words. I guess I'm at a loss.

[Static.]

I'm dying. I'm just going to say whatever I want to say.

I killed my friend Blendri and her apprentice Cuthallox today, right here on the battlefield. Hadn't seen them since they ran off with my old Master, Jook-jook H'broozin, to join up with Xendor. Caught up with H'broozin on Corulag and ran him through, I did, but Blendri and Cuthallox kept getting away, one world to the next. All the way to here. Not that I wanted revenge, of course, but . . . well, all the rebels had to be stopped, did they not?

I loved being a Jedi. Loved it. Wouldn't have changed a thing. But to be honest, after Blendri joined up with the Legions of Lettow, I started thinking. About how long she'd been complaining about the Jedi Order being so sterile. About how bored she was by all that endless meditation.

Understand . . . I was never tempted by the dark side. Being in the light was never a dangerous balancing act for me, it wasn't. Maybe it's because I'm simpler than some, or so Blendri says. I mean, that's what she used to say. But I never ducked a battle, and I never betrayed the Jedi, and I never wanted to do bad things.

To the Jedi who finds this data card, I'm hoping you'll remember this about Blendri. You see, Blendri was my best friend when we were children. She was the one who showed me how to use the Force, even before we knew what the Force was. She was a good girl, Blendri was. A really good person. Maybe she teased me a few times when she became a Jedi Knight and I was still an apprentice, but I knew she was just joking. The reason I mention this is because I don't think she joined the dark side and the Legions of Lettow because she was evil. I think she just got tired of all the Jedi rules, being told what to do, how to behave, how not to behave, all the time. I think it crushed her a bit.

As for all the other Jedi who left the Order to join the legions . . . I don't know. It seems too easy to blame everything on Xendor and the dark side. Maybe we . . . maybe the Jedi were partly to blame, too. I'm not good with history, but I know that for more than five centuries the Jedi didn't have much trouble with anyone. Sure, a dark Jedi here and there, I heard tell. But then along came Xendor, telling Jedi they didn't have to obey orders all the time.

I know it sounds crazy, but I wonder . . . maybe the Jedi need an enemy. I think . . . without a common enemy, we . . . we'll just wind up fighting each other . . . and ourselves. Does that make sense?

It's getting really cold. I only wish—

[End of recording.]

ULIC QEL-DROMA'S RETURN TO THE LIGHT

Recorded 3980 B.B.Y. on the Great Holocron.
Author: Vima Sunrider

My mother, the Jedi Nomi Sunrider, kept two holograms for as long as I could remember. One hologram was of my father Andur, who was killed when I was just a baby. The other was of Ulic Qel-Droma. I was still a child when my mother and I watched Ulic's ship leave Ossus, and I knew even then that he had been my mother's second great love. Because I remembered him so well as he was, it was difficult for me to associate him with the man he became,

described by other Jedi as a tragic and despicable figure.

The story is known by most Jedi. Ulic Qel-Droma, the great Jedi who attempted to destroy a Sith sect from within but succumbed to the dark side instead. After joining forces with Exar Kun, a renegade Jedi who had embraced the dark side for purely selfish reasons, Ulic became a Dark Lord of the Sith, and killed his own brother during the interstellar conflict known as the Sith War. The Sith War concluded when my mother stripped Ulic of his Force powers, and Exar Kun was destroyed on Yavin 4. Many Jedi would prefer that the story ended there, so that it might continue to serve as a perfect cautionary tale for those who consider walking the dark path. However, Ulic's story did continue.

A decade after the Sith War, during the Jedi Convocation at Exis Station, I was a rebellious teenager and eager to learn the ways of the Jedi. Although my mother had insisted that I apprentice to her, she was often preoccupied by her duties as a leader in the Republic and a spokesperson for the Jedi Knights. I admit I felt neglected, but I was also determined to become a Jedi. I cannot explain my reasoning, but when I overheard the Jedi Sylvar remark that Ulic Qel-Droma had gone from being the greatest Jedi Knight of his era to—in Sylvar's opinion—a war criminal who wandered free and unpunished, I realized that I wanted to be trained by Ulic.

I was not so desperate to gain knowledge that I would seek it from the man who had killed so many—including Sylvar's mate, the Jedi Crado—during the Sith War. Nor was I trying to spurn my mother or attract her attention. I maintain it was something in the Force that compelled me to locate Ulic. Although I knew he was no longer the man

I remembered from my childhood, I sensed that I would find there was still goodness in him, and that he would be a great teacher.

A spacer named Hoggon delivered me to the frozen, desolate world Rhen Var, where I found Ulic in an abandoned city. The lost look in his gaze would have been an obvious sign to anyone that he was a shattered being, ravaged by guilt and regret. I imagined his only reason for being on Rhen Var was that he found it a suitable place to die. After I identified myself and explained why I'd sought him out, he told me to go home. Soon afterward, I became lost in a blizzard, but Ulic saved me. As much as he believed he had nothing to offer me, I was convinced that he had to be my teacher. With great reluctance, he finally accepted.

And despite his inability to feel the Force, he taught me how to understand it. Although he was no longer capable of building a lightsaber, he instructed me to construct my own. From him, I learned that there isn't a rule book or a simple test to take to become a Jedi Master; one can only achieve this by facing ordeals, making life-and-death choices, and then facing more ordeals. I believe my time with Ulic gave him a sense of purpose he had not felt since he was a Jedi. By the time my anxious mother tracked us to Rhen Var, I was a Jedi.

Unfortunately, Hoggon had identified Ulic, and he alerted the vengeful Sylvar; together they arrived shortly after my mother. Sylvar attacked Ulic, but he refused to fight her, and his example convinced her that she had, over the years, become a pawn of her own emotions. Although Ulic freed Sylvar of her anger, he was unable to anticipate or dodge the blaster fired by the glory-seeking Hoggon.

My mother held Ulic as he died, and to our astonishment his body vanished, leaving my mother clutching at his empty, ragged clothes. Ulic may no longer have been able to touch the Force, but he understood it more than any of us.

He had the heart of a Jedi.

FOUR STAGES OF THE DARK SIDE

Despite Vima Sunrider's convictions, not all Jedi agreed with her assessment that Ulic Qel-Droma had redeemed himself. One such Jedi was Master Tolaris Shim, a contemporary of Qel-Droma, who made the following recording ten years prior to Qel-Droma's death:

I have been asked to provide an explanation for how Ulic Qel-Droma, who sought to destroy the Krath and the Sith, became a Sith Lord and a committer of fratricide. While certain influences and circumstances may have seemed specific to Qel-Droma's transition from Jedi to Sith Lord, an objective analysis suggests that his transition to the dark side was not so unique.

Whether by accident, inclination, or misdirection from others, even the most disciplined Force-user eventually steps onto the path that leads to the dark side. This gateway to corruption is paved with good intentions, more frequently traveled as a means to efficiently achieve a desired result than to accomplish deliberate evil.

Because Force-users who crave power, embrace hatred, seek revenge, and suffer tragedy are especially susceptible to being lured toward the dark side, some members of our Order have proposed that Force-sensitive beings should somehow be identified and conscripted at infancy, so that they might begin Jedi training without exposure to negative influences. Although such training might produce stronger and more reliable Jedi, the notion of recruiting babies to our cause is obviously controversial. Opponents to the proposal are quick to note that the historic record lists numerous Jedi who raised their own children in the Jedi ways with mixed results. Because even these Jedi-trained offspring were not entirely immune to the lure of the dark side, it seems that even a lifetime of training is no guarantee to prevent casualties.

The dark path is experienced in four stages: temptation, imperilment, sub-mission, and atonement or redemption. To those who believe they are immune to any of these stages, just as Ulic Qel-Droma may have believed himself immune, I say you are already victim to the dark side's seductive tendrils, and urge you to listen as you have never listened before.

First stage: temptation. Because you are a Jedi and possess Force powers, you will find yourself in situations in which you may be tempted to use or demonstrate your abilities, to rush to the aid of an ally, confront apparent dangers, or resolve differences hastily. But if you are prone to action before patience, to draw blood first and ask questions later, you will step onto the dark path.

Second stage: imperilment. A Jedi must know when to act and when to wait. A Jedi cannot be indecisive, nor can a Jedi take a detour onto the dark path and expect to find a guidepost that will return him to the light. If you obsess about doing the right thing no matter what the cost may be, and believe you can maintain at least some semblance of the light when you finally make your decision, you are imperiled to remain upon or revisit the dark path. If you accept the dark side of the Force as a means to power, you are most likely not concerned about taking the next step.

Third stage: submission. Once you accept the dark path, you may no longer believe there is any need to justify your actions. If you are at all aware of how far you have strayed from the ways of the Jedi, you may be merely tainted by the dark side but might still find a way to return to the light. If you find it liberating and exhilarating to give yourself fully to the dark side, then you are a Dark Jedi, and it is the responsibility of your former allies to either stop you or attempt to bring you back to the light.

Fourth stage: atonement or redemption. Through a period of meditation, reflection, and absolution, a Jedi who is tainted by the dark side can atone for her actions. A Dark Jedi cannot atone, but may find redemption by turning away from the dark side and performing a selfless act of heroism without calling upon the dark side of the Force. A Dark Jedi who has no desire to relinquish the power of the dark side and return to the light cannot be redeemed.

The possibility of atonement or redemp-tion has led various Jedi to believe that they could control their journey on the dark path in order to conquer evil. None has ever succeeded.

Do I encourage that you avert your gaze from the shadows? No, I do not! Nor do I suggest that you blind yourself by the light. I merely say that one cannot avoid the darkness unless one knows where it lies and the routes that lead to it, and that a Jedi is ultimately responsible for his powers. Trust that even the most learned Jedi Master must always be mindful of the dark path.

May the Force be with you.

ADDENDUM BY
TIONNE SOLUSAR

If Tolaris Shim ever made a statement re-garding Ulic Qel-Droma's alleged redemption and subsequent death, it has yet to be found. But the conviction of Jedi Master Tolaris Shim's words on the subject of redemption prompted me to reconsider the reputations of several Jedi who traveled over to the dark side, apparently returned to the light, and were eventually considered "redeemed" by some Jedi, if not all. Of particular interest to me was how Tolaris Shim might have regarded the actions of Anakin Skywalker, Luke Skywalker, and Kyp Durron. After I provided what I considered to

be an accurate and objective account of each Jedi's dark side experiences and revelations, Shim's interactive hologrammic simulacrum offered the same judgment upon all: "Any Jedi who kills innocents while under sway of the dark side cannot be redeemed. She can only atone, or attempt to atone."

While most would agree that some actions are entirely unforgivable, it is possible that redemption may be, like so many other things in life, a matter of perspective.

THE REFORMATION OF REVAN

c. 3951 B.B.Y.

Author: Deesra Luur Jada

It has been five long years since the destruction of the Jedi enclave on Dantooine, and only now am I able to return. It grieves me to see what remains of the enclave. Ruins and rubble. What wasn't leveled by Darth Malak has been plundered by the now vanquished Sith occupiers and the less reputable of the surviving natives. Although I trust that my predecessor, Master Dorak, the former official chronicler of the enclave, would have looked upon these remains without a pained expression, I wonder if it is not for the best that he did not live to see this. It was no secret how much he considered the enclave a part of himself.

When I became a Jedi historian, I expected my days would be filled with the study of ancient mediations and battles, not as a chronicler of current events or an archaeologist of recent history. Increasingly, I feel like nothing more than a necrologist, dispatching weekly obituaries to the archives on Ossus. I remain conscientious of my work, for all the good it has done. Just today, I found myself correcting a young Padawan and some locals who were speaking of "the day the Sith Lords Malak and Revan assaulted Dantooine." Perhaps it really doesn't matter to the locals whether only Malak was responsible, but it should matter to the Jedi.

I never foresaw that I would live in such times. But then there has been much in the past five decades that our Order did not foresee. First the Jedi Knights Exar Kun and Ulic Qel-Droma proclaimed themselves Sith Lords, then—some thirty-six years later—Revan and Malak did the same. Besides the fact that all were Jedi, it may be noteworthy that Exar Kun, Revan, and Malak all trained on Dantooine.

Was history repeating itself? No, I think not, as these men had different motives for becoming Sith Lords. Exar Kun craved forbidden knowledge, and the misguided Qel-Droma sought to destroy the Sith from within; they forged an alliance with the Mandalorian warriors and started a war with the Jedi. Revan and Malak, on the other hand, were at war with the Mandalorians after Exar Kun and Qel-Droma had been defeated, and . . . well, Revan and Malak were frustrated soldiers. I knew they were restless in their desires to defend the Republic, and when they attempted to stop the Mandalorians from conquering more fringe worlds, they were outraged by the Jedi Council's instructions to use caution and meditate on the situation.

Did anyone foresee that they would openly defy the Council, use the Mandalorians' own tactics to defeat them, then become warlords? That they would lead not only the surviving Mandalorians, but also many of the Republic crewers and Jedi Knights who had served with them throughout the Mandalorian Wars? Or that they would discover relics created by the pre-Republic Rakata civilization as well as numerous Sith artifacts, and use these in combination with their dark side powers to very nearly crush the Republic? That they would proclaim themselves the new Dark Lords of the Sith—Darth Revan and Darth Malak—and revive a Sith Academy on the Sith tombworld of Korriban?

◄ THE JEDI TRAINEE KYP DURRON PILOTING THE SUN CRUSHER. *(Trevas)*

No. No one foresaw this. All that we, the Jedi, could do was try to stop the Sith Lords after the fact.

Bastila Shan was the only survivor of the Jedi strike team that apprehended Revan. Forgoing the options to imprison or execute the captive Sith Lord, the Council used the Force to scour Revan's memories, leaving him something of a blank slate. Masters Dorak and Zhar Lestin were able to mend Revan's damaged mind and retrain him in the ways of the Jedi. Yes, there was a purpose to all this. The Council had decided that the amnesiac Revan, reconditioned with a new identity as a Force-using soldier of the Republic, would be their best chance to defeat Malak. And they were right.

Paired with Bastila Shan, this altogether new incarnation of Revan went hunting for Malak and the Star Forge, an ancient Rakatan space station and manufacturing facility that Malak used to create an endless supply of vessels and weapons. Soon after the Jedi began their hunt, Malak razed the planets Taris and Dantooine.

Malak captured both Revan and Bastila, but Revan escaped and killed Malak's apprentice, the former Jedi student Bandon. However, Revan had discovered what the Council had done to him, and regained the memories the Council had erased.

Did he seek revenge against the Jedi? No, for he was not the same Revan he had been. Whether his revised self-awareness and ethics were the result of his reconditioning or of his new persona's unique experience and insight remains unknown, but we can be thankful that his transformation was for the better. He chose to rescue Bastila, whom Malak had tortured and transformed into his new apprentice. Revan not only brought Bastila back from the dark side, but killed Darth Malak and destroyed the Star Forge as well.

If only the Sith threat had ended there. Since the destuction of the Star Forge, there have been reports of the existence of others, Sith calling themselves Darth Traya, Darth Sion, and Darth Nihilus. An unconfirmed report suggests that Nihilus was responsible for the catastrophe that killed all life on the planet Katarr last year, including the entire Jedi Convocation that had gathered there to discuss the future of our Order. It was there that Master Dorak perished, along with Zhar Lestin, Vandar Dokar, and so many, many others. Here, on Dantooine, Masters Zez-Kai Ell, Kavar, and Vrook Lamar all fell to Darth Traya.

Do I think Revan redeemed himself? I don't know that it is the place of a historian to make such a judgment, and I shall leave this to the philosophers. I will say this. By erasing Revan's memory, the Council ensured that Revan could never entirely be the same man who conquered the Mandalorians and became a Sith Lord. But it was this new Revan, when he chose not to return to the dark side, who ultimately chose to reform on his own terms.

We will never be able to restore the Jedi enclave that was on Dantooine, but Revan's example encourages me to rebuild.

ADDENDUM BY
TIONNE SOLUSAR

Today only ruins remain of the enclave on Dantooine. Carbon tests have determined that some structures were built more than a century after Deesra Luur Jada's recording, indicating that the enclave was rebuilt, but eventually fell into disuse.

THE DARK JEDI CONFLICT

The Great Holocron indicates the existence of an ancient Sith fortress on the planet Almas in the Cularin system, which was also the site of a Jedi academy. Evidently, the Jedi first became aware of this fortress during the New Sith Wars, when they tracked Darth Rivan to Almas. Rivan had used the Force to begin terraforming the previously poisonous world, and also created an alchemical bond between his commanders and their troops. The Jedi hunted Rivan down and killed him, but abandoned Almas and left the Sith fortress standing. They may not have had much choice: the fortress was and is impervious to blasterfire.

It seems the Jedi and the Republic forgot about the Cularin system until nearly three centuries ago, when the near-human explorer Reidi Artom rediscovered Cularin and visited Almas. An entry from Artom's logbook, dated 232 B.B.Y., provides a vivid description of her view of the Sith fortress from orbit:

Circling over the fourth planet, I am coming toward a devastated wasteland. A few greenish purple plants grow here, but that's it. In the center, part of a building protrudes from the ground. The exposed portion is about thirty meters tall with a dome on the top. Sensors say there's more of the structure below the ground. There's something strange about the place. I can feel it, even from here. A Jedi would say that the Force is strong in this place. I don't know about that, but it sure is creepy. The green-purple grasses don't grow anywhere near it.

The structure is made from some kind of stone, all black. There aren't any entrances or windows of any kind as far as I can see. Sensors cannot penetrate the interior.

Whatever it is, someone else is going to have to find out. I'm going to follow a hunch and not land.

Eventually, more spacers learned of the Cularin system, and colonization began. By 188 B.B.Y., a team of Jedi noted that they, too, had sensed the powerful infection of the dark side surrounding the fortress on Almas. That same year, the Jedi Council dispatched two Jedi to investigate. What happened next became a tale told to each new generation of Jedi at the Almas academy, which was founded eleven years after the arrival of the Jedi investigators.

53 B.B.Y.
Author: Jedi Master Lanius Qel-Bertuk

Greetings, my friends.

As you know, it has been two weeks since academy headmaster Nerra Ziveri disappeared. His last known position was on the far side of Almas, at the Sith temple. What you may not know is that for some years, Master Nerra had turned much of his attention to probing the fortress's dark side aura in earnest. His final communication was with me, telling me to take charge of the academy.

Yes. Yes, I know what many of you are thinking. You are recalling an earlier disappearance, and you are imagining the worst. But we have several new students in our presence, students who are unfamiliar with the precedent, and must now know the story of Kibh Jeen.

One hundred thirty-five years ago, the Council sent the Jedi Qornah and his Padawan, the Jedi consular Kibh Jeen, to Almas. They traveled by shuttle, with Qornah as the pilot. Their mission was to examine and explore the Sith temple, which—though long dormant—continued to radiate evil. There was some urgency to the mission, because many colonists were arriving in the Cularin system at the time. But the same day that Qornah and Kibh Jeen touched down on Almas, Qornah died and Kibh Jeen vanished.

Months later, another Jedi team discovered Qornah's remains. There was no sign of Kibh Jeen or the shuttle. Because there were no known eyewitnesses to whatever had transpired on Almas, the Jedi Council sent the most powerful psychometrics to trace the paths and reconstruct the actions of both the dead and missing Jedi. What these psychometrics learned was shocking.

After Qornah and Kibh Jeen had landed their shuttle on Almas, they walked toward the half-buried fortress. As Qornah probed the area with the Force, he did not hear the whispers that pressed against his apprentice's mind. Kibh Jeen succumbed to these whispered temptations, cutting his Master down from behind. Then, stepping over Qornah's corpse, Kibh Jeen approached the walls of the fortress and disappeared.

Jeen rematerialized shortly before the arrival of the Jedi team who found Qornah's body. Evidently he had accessed the Sith fortress, and gained much knowledge. Taking the shuttle, he set off across space. There, the psychometrics account ends, but Kibh Jeen was just getting started.

Searching for minions who would make useful tools, Jeen found pirates in the Cularin asteroid belt who suited his purposes admirably. He dominated their minds and, through them, attracted others to his service. Soon he had built an army, and he unleashed his forces on the floating cities of Genarius, the third planet in the Cularin system. Thousands died. This assault launched the Dark Jedi Conflict.

For seven years, Kibh Jeen and his mindless soldiers dominated the Cularin system. Their warships stopped or attacked all incoming transports, then disappeared to their hiding places in the asteroid belt. No one could find them, let alone eliminate them.

Finally, a Jedi Knight and her Padawan came to Cularin. After they organized the system's inhabitants and trading companies to build an armada, the Jedi used the Force to locate the pirates and lure them into a trap. The pirate fleet was crushed, and Kibh Jeen did not escape. Before he died, he was heard spouting gibberish about there always being no more or less than two Sith.

After this regrettable incident, the Jedi decided to maintain a permanent presence near the fortress to study it and attempt to ward off its evil. Our academy is now over 130 years old, and from what I have gathered the fortress remains, as ever, a malevolent entity that we can only continue to monitor from a distance.

I know some of you may be eager to find out what happened to Master Nerra Ziveri. There is often more satisfaction in knowing than wondering, and it is discomforting that we are left with so many questions. Was the power of the dark side strong on this world before the arrival of the Sith Lord who built the fortress? Was the fortress entirely responsible for transforming Kibh Jeen into a Dark Jedi, or was there already a darkness lurking within him? Were Kibh Jeen's dying words about the Sith a threat or a warning? Should we expect the return of Master Nerra Ziveri, or count him among the dead?

Only this I know for certain. Although the answers may be found within that fortress, these are not answers we should pursue without extreme caution.

Let us not consider Master Nerra a casualty, and let us be patient. For though patience can be difficult, it is by the will of the Force that we shall wait.

Jedi Master Lanius Qel-Bertuk retained his position as headmaster at the Almas academy during the Clone Wars after he relinquished his lightsaber and refused to serve in the Republic army. The academy was destroyed during the Jedi Purge, and it is presumed that Master Lanius was killed. The Sith fortress remains standing, and Jedi are prohibited from venturing near it. The fate of Jedi Master Nerra Ziveri remains a mystery.

THE CONVERSION OF COUNT DOOKU

When the Jedi Master Count Dooku renounced the Jedi Order in 32 B.B.Y., he made a brief official statement, which is preserved on the Great Holocron:

For many years, I have served the Jedi Order and done my best to honor the traditions of the Jedi. Today I am compelled to announce that I am leaving the Order.

It is not unreasonable for anyone to wonder why I have decided to leave at this time. Yes, I am aware of various allegedly discreet queries from those searching for a reason. The recent, tragic loss of my former pupil, Qui-Gon Jinn? The debacle on Baltizaar? My highly publicized criticisms of an increasingly corrupt Senate? Some of my contemporaries have suggested that seeds of discontent were planted twelve years ago, at the Battle of Galidraan. While I cannot deny that these events have left their mark on me, I will only allow that the time has come that I can no longer be a Jedi.

As most of you are aware, financial resources are at my disposal on my homeworld, Serenno. While I would like to think my many years of devoted service to the Order disavows any notions that I am yielding to economic circumstances, I will enlighten those who don't know me so well with a certain piece of wisdom that I have always found true: money creates as many problems as it does opportunities.

It is my plan to return to Serenno and serve my people as a philanthropist. It is my last request as a Jedi Master that you respect my decision, as well as my privacy.

Good-bye, old friends, and may the Force be with you.

Following Count Dooku's announcement, the recently elected Supreme Chancellor Palpatine sent the following message to the Jedi Council:

Forgive me, members of the Council, for I fear I may be overstepping the boundaries of proper protocol. I have learned that Jedi Master Dooku intends to leave the Jedi Order. I only wish to express that I am saddened to learn of his decision, and hope that his departure is not a painful one. I regret I only met him a few times, but certainly knew his reputation and even admired him, even if I didn't entirely agree with his criticisms of the Senate. Because Dooku has become something of a public figure, I've been asked by a media representative for a comment on his announcement, but I think it may be best if I make no comment. I don't know if there is anything my office can do to help the Order at this time, but please know that I'd be happy to do whatever I can.

It remains unknown whether Palpatine's alter ego, the Sith Lord Darth Sidious, recruited Count Dooku as his apprentice before or after Dooku left the Jedi Order. And unlike other Jedi who have taken the path to the dark side, Dooku remains something of an enigma. If he craved power in his youth, he was extremely discreet. According to various records, it seems most Jedi were unaware of his astronomical wealth until after he left the Order. After his long tenure as a Jedi Master, he was well past middle age when he became a Sith apprentice. Was Dooku merely a very powerful man who wanted more power, or did he have a secret agenda?

Despite Dooku's dismissal of any specific factors that may have contributed to his decision to leave the Order, one can assume that the death of Qui-Gon Jinn did not weigh heavily on his decision. Because Dooku was undoubtedly aware of the report that Qui-Gon Jinn had been slain by a Sith Lord, one can conclude that he chose to become an apprentice to Darth Sidious *despite* the way Qui-Gon died. As for his public criticisms of the Senate, these were stated shortly after the Battle of Naboo, when Dooku probably had already joined forces with Darth Sidious. However, if one is to search for any seeds of discontent that may have led Dooku to the dark side, the conflicts on both Galidraan and Baltizaar bear some examination.

According to records from 44 B.B.Y., the incident on Galidraan began when the Jedi Council received an urgent message from the governor of Galidraan, who claimed that an army of Mandalorian mercenaries was slaughtering political prisoners, women, and children on his world. Master Dooku led a contingent of twenty Jedi to Galidraan and commanded the Mandalorians to surrender. The Mandalorians refused and a melee ensued, leaving eleven Jedi and all but one of the Mandalorians dead. The surviving Mandalorian was Jango Fett, who was turned over to the governor of Galidraan.

One of the surviving Jedi at Galidraan was Dooku's final Padawan, a female human named Komari Vosa. According to an official report, Komari Vosa personally vanquished twenty Mandalorians on Galidraan, and Dooku praised her openly, predicting an eventful future for her. However, Vosa's fighting skills were not yet sufficient to guarantee her promotion to Jedi Knight, and shortly after the Battle of Galidraan it was Dooku himself who denied Vosa the opportunity to take the trials for Jedi Knighthood.

Although Komari Vosa was released from the Jedi Order, she somehow joined a group of Jedi on a rescue mission to Baltizaar in the year 39 B.B.Y., after the world had come under attack by the cult of criminals known as the Bando Gora. Like the mission to Galidraan, many Jedi perished on Baltizaar, and it is believed that Vosa was among the casualties. It is not known whether Dooku was aware of his former Padawan's actions on Baltizaar, but he did submit a protest with the Jedi Council.

An excerpt follows:

With all due respect, I urge the Council to consider our responsibility to the Jedi as well as to the Republic. To send our brethren to any world at a moment's notice may bring approval from the Senate, but does it honor those who fell at Galidraan? I am not a fatalist, nor am I suggesting that we embrace the bureaucracy of the Senate as a means to determine whom we can and cannot save, but I am concerned that we allow ourselves to serve without question. Yes, the Bando Gora are criminals, but is it not criminal to squander the lives of Jedi on missions that are so obviously doomed from the start?

As passionately sincere as this protest may sound, it may be nothing more than a testament to Dooku's legendary charisma. At some point, he began to reconsider the value of Jedi lives, for twelve years after the Battle of Galidraan he conscripted Jango Fett as the template for the clone army that virtually eliminated the Jedi Order.

Some scholars have suggested that it was by the will of the Force that the lives of Dooku and Fett intersected as they did, but it should be noted that Darth Sidious also played a crucial role in their alliance. Had not Darth Sidious conscripted such a wealthy and influential apprentice when he did, it seems doubtful that he could have orchestrated a galactic war within such a relatively short period of time. Although it can be surmised that Darth Sidious needed Dooku much more than Dooku needed Darth Sidious, the historical record shows that the needs of Darth Sidious—while acting as Palpatine—had changed by the time he manipulated events to test Count Dooku against Anakin Skywalker.

Still, many questions remain. Why did Dooku, an idealist with considerable wealth and power, and a Jedi who had studied the ways of the Force for almost eight decades, ally himself with Darth Sidious? Was Dooku ever sincere about his outrage over the loss of Jedi at Galidraan and Baltizaar, or was he preparing for an eventual scheme to exterminate the Jedi long before he left the Order? And if Dooku even slightly foresaw that he might be replaced by Anakin Skywalker, did he accept this fate for the glory of the Sith? The answers may always remain a mystery.

DARK SIDE DISCIPLES

As Darth Sidious's Sith apprentice, Darth Tyranus was compelled to abide by the Rule of Two and did not have a Sith apprentice of his own. However, Tyranus trained at least one disciple, Asajj Ventress, in the ways of the dark side, and also instructed the cyborg General Grievous in the art of lightsaber combat. Before his Sith identity became known to the Jedi, Tyranus—maintaining his public persona of Count Dooku—also attempted to corrupt the Jedi Master Quinlan Vos. Obi-Wan Kenobi encountered all of these individuals, and wrote of them in a book that Luke Skywalker recovered from Kenobi's home on Tatooine.

16 B.B.Y.
Author: Obi-Wan Kenobi

___

Two days ago, on one of my walks, I came across the twisted, withered husk of a short desert plant that had grown in the shadows of a dusty rock formation. Yesterday I passed the same plant again and noticed it had flowered small white petals, flecked with dark gray. This morning, I was surprised to find the entire plant had vanished. Even though I knew some creature had probably eaten it, I felt a sense of loss that surprised me. And I thought of Asajj Ventress.

I've already written instructions for how to build a lightsaber. Now I find myself compelled to write something of the enemies who use them.

From what I remember from the history databooks, the Sith have wielded light-sabers for at least four thousand years. They

SITH ASPIRANT ASAJJ VENTRESS DUELING ▲
ANAKIN SKYWALKER ON YAVIN 4. *(Trevas)*

were long believed to have been extinct until just sixteen years ago, when my Master and I dueled with an Iridonian Zabrak who used a double-bladed lightsaber. This Sith killed my Master, and then I killed him in self-defense.

Ten years later, my apprentice Anakin Skywalker and I dueled Count Dooku at the Battle of Geonosis. The leader of the Separatist movement, Dooku was a former Jedi Master who—we realized too late—had turned to the dark side. This was most unfortunate, not only because Dooku had been a revered Jedi, but also because he was a master swordsman. Dooku escaped at the Battle of Geonosis, but not before he informed me that a Sith Lord was manipulating the Galactic Senate. Three devastating years later, I would learn that he was telling the truth. The Sith Lord was Supreme Chancellor Palpatine.

About ten weeks after the Battle of Geonosis, Anakin and I had our first encounter with Asajj Ventress. She was a humanoid, hairless with pale skin, who wielded two lightsabers simultaneously. These lightsabers could also be joined at the handles to create a double-bladed weapon. Before she attacked, she told me that she had emerged from misery and suffering, only to find the Jedi she had once worshiped were nothing but "weak, misguided fools." She added that she agreed with Count Dooku: the galaxy was in need of a Jedi purge.

Asajj Ventress escaped that day, but not before she killed one Jedi and maimed his apprentice. It was obvious by her technique that she had received training from Dooku. Over the course of the Clone Wars, Anakin and I faced off against Ventress on other worlds. But despite all her fury and murderous inclinations, I always sensed something within her that distinguished her from the Sith Lords: an underlying fear. Mostly, it was a fear of being alone. And I sensed that there was some good in her, some part that had not been corrupted by Dooku. Where the Sith Lords were unquestionably evil, Ventress was simply a slave to the dark side.

Eventually, I learned some details of Ventress's history. She was born on Rattatak, an Outer Rim world so remote that it was unknown to the Republic. She was still a child when her parents were killed by one of the many local warlords. After a Jedi named Ky Narec became stranded on Rattatak, he found the orphaned Ventress and realized she was Force-sensitive. Narec trained Ventress as his apprentice, and apparently trained her relatively well, for together they defeated many criminals. Tragically, a group of warlords killed Narec, and rather than honoring the ways of the Jedi, Ventress sought vengeance. And once again, she was alone. Is it any wonder that she developed such a supreme hatred for the Jedi Order that "abandoned" her Master?

At some point, Dooku recruited Ventress as his enforcer for the Confederacy of Independent Systems. Even though Ventress had killed Jedi and other innocents, I managed to convey my hope that she might listen to reason and stop using fear to fuel her anger. She refused to listen. And I was still trying to reason with her when she nearly killed me on Boz Pity. She would have, too, had not Anakin's lightsaber dealt her a mortal blow. Her death, roughly five months before the Jedi Purge, did nothing to slow the Clone Wars, for by that time General Grievous—another of Dooku's disciples in lightsaber combat, if not the dark side—was already in command of the Confederacy's droid armies.

I'd thought that Ventress would use her dying breath to curse me and the Jedi Order. Instead she cautioned me to defend Coruscant from Dooku, for that was the key to victory. Indeed, Dooku and Grievous would assault Coruscant. She even allowed that I might have been right about her all along. And then she was gone.

Five months after Ventress's death, Anakin defeated Dooku in orbit of Coruscant, but we were unable to stop Grievous from fleeing into space. I neglected to mention that Grievous was a cyborg who had killed a number of Jedi and taken their lightsabers as trophies. He was capable of wielding four lightsabers simultaneously. All in all, a most unpleasant fellow. I defeated him on Utapau.

And then the Purge began. I would soon learn that I was among the few Jedi to survive, and that Palpatine had taken a new apprentice: Darth Vader.

In hindsight, Vader and Ventress had some similar characteristics. Both knew the loss of loved ones, and had reason to distrust the Republic and the Jedi Order. But when I finally caught up with Vader, I sensed nothing but pure evil about him. For unlike Ventress, Vader was not a victim of unfortunate circumstances. Yes, he had his struggles and his shortcomings, but he was not a weak being who feared abandonment. He was a powerful man who had been given opportunities to better himself, yet he only craved more power, and chose his own path, betraying the Jedi and becoming a Sith. He was my greatest failure.

My duel with Vader was awful in its savagery. In the end, he was more determined to kill me than defend himself, and was blind with fury when I felled him. I left him maimed and burning on the shores of a lava river. To have dealt him a killing blow might have been the merciful thing to do, but because I am a Jedi and not a cold-blooded murderer, all I could do was leave Vader to his fate. Had I killed him then and there, I believe I would have taken a step onto the same dark path that he had found so impossible to resist. But by leaving him for dead, I fear I failed yet again, for

I soon learned that Vader had survived, in a fashion. Like the late General Grievous, he is mostly machine now, a malevolent construct of pistons and gears, plastoid and wires, his mortal remains fueled by the dark side. The galaxy will never know peace until Darth Vader and the Emperor breathe their last.

It is hard for me to see what the future holds. Fortunately, I have my mission and my ongoing studies of the Force to help me be mindful of the present, as well as the daily rigors of survival on Tatooine. Whatever tomorrow may bring, I must be ready for it.

I have collected a small number of seeds from my desert walks. I think I will plant them and see what they will grow, in memory of Asajj Ventress.

ADDENDUM BY
TIONNE SOLUSAR

Records indicate that Obi-Wan Kenobi ordered Ventress's corpse transported from Boz Pity to Coruscant for a Jedi cremation. However, the ship bearing Ventress never arrived at its destination. Investigators subsequently realized that she had used a Force technique to muffle her life signs and achieve a state of near-death stasis. Her fate remains unknown.

IMPERIAL INQUISITORS

Following the Jedi Purge, Emperor Palpatine created the role of Imperial Inquisitors, men and women loyal to him and tasked with hunting down the remaining Jedi in the galaxy. If a captured Jedi would not turn to the dark side and join Palpatine's New Order, it was the Inquisitor's duty to eradicate him. Inquisitors also sought out non-Jedi Force-users who might be turned to the service of the Emperor. To accomplish their objectives, they were provided with tools and resources, including ships, troops, weapons, credits, Force detectors, and torture devices.

Potential Inquisitors were carefully tested and examined, first by Imperial Intelligence, then by the Grand Inquisitor, and finally by the Emperor himself. Applicants had to convince the Emperor of their ability with the Force without seeming either too powerful or too critical of the Emperor's cause, as such extremes indicated that an applicant might be no different from his or her quarry, and could prove unreliable.

Following the death of Palpatine, most Imperial Inquisitors—bereft of support and resources—gradually disappeared from the galaxy.

THE EMPEROR'S HANDS

During his reign, Emperor Palpatine retained Mara Jade as an elite Force-trained assassin who was known to a select few as the Emperor's Hand. The New Republic was unaware of the existence of the Emperor's Hand until 9 A.B.Y., when Mara Jade met Luke Skywalker. Mara made the following recording three years later, when she visited the Jedi academy on Yavin 4 while Luke was on a mission with Corran Horn in the Suarbi system. The recording serves as a reminder that even the most dangerous servants of the Empire have the capacity for change:

This is for you, Tionne. I left you in the lurch at the commissary this afternoon. I'm sorry. If you weren't so busy right now, I'd tell you in person. I'm not much for apologies or storytelling, but feel like I owe you some kind of explanation.

Just before you found me in the commissary, I'd experienced an awkward moment with some new Jedi trainees. I'd noticed three of them doing a lousy job of pretending that they weren't looking at me. I walked over to their table and said, "Something on your minds?" Not really a question on my part. Thanks to the Force, I knew what was coming.

"Is it true," one of them said, "that you used to be Palpatine's personal assassin?"

All right, so my history is no longer a secret. But how many times have I been asked that question at the praxeum? Enough, Tionne. Enough so that each time I hear it, I realize that some people aren't satisfied with whatever knowledge they have. They want more. And they feel like they have to hear it from me.

I said, "Yeah, it's true. Now tell me who blabbed so I can go cut his head off."

Well, I thought it was funny. Not the trainees, though. No, they just cringed and looked a bit scared. Not a good look for prospective Jedi.

So then I grabbed some food, sat down at a bench by myself, and tried to think if there was some better answer I could have given. Better yet, some response to make people just stop asking.

What's kind of funny about all this is that when I was Palpatine's assassin, no one ever asked about my vocation. Most people who saw me around the Imperial Palace just assumed I was there for decoration. Except for Darth Vader, Grand Moff Tarkin, Ysanne Isard, and a few other mostly dead Imperials, no one had any idea of what I did. Maybe some of my targets figured it out at the last moment. But only some.

I was still working on my food when you joined me. You said you sensed something was wrong, and asked if I was all right. I told you everything was just terrific, but I acknowledge that I wasn't very convincing. You said if I ever wanted to talk, you'd be happy to listen, and it might make me feel better.

I shot you a nasty look as I left the bench. You didn't deserve that look. I know you meant well. Again, I'm sorry. I hope you understand when I say that talking rarely makes me feel better. Talking doesn't change the past. But for some fool reason, I want to set the record straight with you.

I don't know how much you know about me, or how much you think you know about me, but here's the short version. From infancy, I was trained in the Force at what was then the Imperial Palace on Coruscant. I have no memories of my parents. The Emperor's advisers taught me the art of political intrigue. His spymasters taught me infiltration techniques. I got my combat training alongside the Imperial Royal Guard. The Emperor himself trained me to develop my Force powers, specifically from the dark side of the Force. I learned to listen for his telepathic "voice," which I could hear across the galaxy, and to draw strength from his own vast reserves of power.

The purpose of all this training was, as everyone now seems to be aware, that I would become an assassin. And that is exactly what I became. To a very select few, I was known as the Emperor's Hand. Got that moniker after I broke into Tarkin's private quarters. It was a breeze.

Who were my targets? You name 'em. Ambitious planetary governors, greedy crime lords, disloyal Imperial officers. Did I believe they were threats to the general public? Most of them.

Did I ever feel sorry for them? Emotions were never part of the job. I was sworn to do the Emperor's bidding. I couldn't even feel sorry for myself if I'd tried.

Did I ever miss a target? Yeah. A guy named Skywalker on Tatooine. You had to be there.

After I failed that assignment, the Emperor ordered me to give up the chase for the time being, tackle something else. Days later, I received his final command: You will kill Luke Skywalker.

I knew Palpatine was dead. Can't explain how much rage I felt. Some people get steamed if they lose a hand. I was the hand, severed but still twitching, and I'd lost the one person who'd ever controlled me.

Didn't have much time to sulk. Isard knew about me, saw me as a threat, and imprisoned me on Coruscant. I escaped. She sent her best after me. I sent them back as best I could.

Went to the Outer Rim Territories. Hopped around from world to world. Worked under various identities. I was Merellis, a come-up flector for a swoop gang on Caprioril. That's where I was when a female cyborg found me. She wanted to bring me back to Isard. I didn't want to go. So I didn't. Cyborg got my lightsaber but not me. Better luck next time.

Kicked around some more, wound up working with Talon Karrde. Finally got Palpatine's last command out of my system when I killed an ill-mannered clone who was derived, so I'm told, from the cells of a certain hand lost on Cloud City. Eventually got an invitation to learn the ways of the Jedi. I'm still considering it.

But let's face it. It's hard to fit in when you're consistently pegged as the evil Emperor's former hit lady. And despite Luke's ongoing invitation to learn the ways of the Jedi here, I'm not really sure I want to fit in.

And here I thought I was going to give you the short version.

I'm taking off now, Tionne. Going back to my job with Karrde. Nothing personal, but I know myself well enough to know I need to put some distance between me and Yavin 4 for a while. You can share this with Luke if you want. As for any new trainees, let them think what they will.

Next time we meet, maybe you'll tell me about yourself. I'll just listen. Take care.

A few weeks after making this recording, Mara learned that she had not been the *only* Emperor's Hand. Roganda Ismaren, long rumored to have been one of Palpatine's concubines, had also served as a Force-trained assassin who operated under the same secret appellation. Unlike Mara, Roganda claimed a Jedi lineage. Barely escaping the Jedi Purge, Roganda used her Force powers not only to survive the Inquisitors but also to achieve high social status within the Empire. She died in 27 A.B.Y., slain by her own mentally unstable son.

After Mara learned about Roganda Ismaren, I urged her to help us anticipate future dangers by recalling others who might have served as Emperor's Hands. At our next meeting, she allowed me to record her statement:

Now that I know I wasn't the only Hand, a lot of my memories feel like they've taken a good kick. For all I know, every courier and courtesan who visited the palace was a Hand, and every one of them was unaware of the fact that the Emperor had more Hands than a dianoga has tentacles.

But I can recall one particular encounter with absolute clarity. Remember the female cyborg I mentioned, the one I fought on Caprioril? I'd seen her once before, a few months before Palpatine died. At Endor, that is. I was with Palpatine in his chamber at the Imperial Palace when she was ushered in by Darth Vader. She was covered head-to-heel in metallic circuitry, and I thought she and Vader made quite a pair. Hard to forget a build like that. Her eyes were a cold gray and might have been the original items, but her head was so shiny, I could see myself reflected back off her skull.

The Emperor had asked me to leave then. Being merely an extension of his will, I obeyed. But as I passed the woman, I felt an immediate, inexplicable, and to-tal animosity for her, and I also sensed the feeling was mutual. And behind that cyborg's transparisteel gaze . . . I could tell she was mocking me, silently laughing at me. Like she knew something that I didn't, and the joke was on me.

And as I stepped out of the chamber, I peripherally heard Palpatine cackle: "Come, Lumiya. You will be an extension of my will . . ."

Seems pretty obvious now, doesn't it.

Subsequent research has determined there were at least five more Emperor's Hands, some of whom may have also been under the impression that they were unique in their relationship to Palpatine. They include the resurrected leader of the Legions of Lettow (following Xendor's death), Arden Lyn; the failed Jedi student Sarcev Quest; the hulking Jeng Droga, who piloted the Emperor's shuttle; Maarek Stele, the former swoop pilot who became a TIE fighter ace; and Cronal, the former Prophet of the Dark Side who became the Imperial Intelligence agent Blackhole.

While there has been no account of Maarek Stele or Blackhole in decades, five of the seven aforementioned Emperor's Hands are dead. Arden Lyn was killed by the resurrected Palpatine in 10 A.B.Y. Sarcev Quest was reportedly executed by Jeng Droga in 23 A.B.Y.; that same year, Jeng Droga was slain by Kyle Katarn. And most recently, Luke Skywalker killed Lumiya after the unsolved murder of Mara Jade.

UNDER EXAR KUN'S INFLUENCE

Recorded at the Jedi praxeum on Yavin 4 in 11 A.B.Y.
Author: Kyp Durron

Master Skywalker asked me to talk about my experience with the dark side. I guess he's hoping that other students, if they hear me tell about what happened, they might not go down the dark path like I did. If anyone can learn from me, that's great, but to be honest, I think it's . . . well, it's probably very unlikely that anyone can make the same mistakes I made. I mean, how often does a Jedi get possessed by a

Sith spirit and get his hands on a weapon like the Sun Crusher?

Sorry, possessed *isn't totally right*, at least that's not how it was at first. Maybe I should back up a bit, talk about what happened before I became a Jedi.

My parents were political resisters. The Empire put my parents and me in the correctional facility on Kessel, and stuck my brother in the Imperial Military Academy on Carida.

I recognized the dark side when Exar Kun whispered in my ear, but I was so overconfident, I thought I could resist where even Anakin Skywalker had failed. But the dark side swallowed me whole, and left me wishing I could just be free of my Jedi talent so I wouldn't have to fear what I might do with it.

LUKE SKYWALKER ON THE DARK SIDE

Recorded at the Jedi praxeum on Yavin 4 in 11 A.B.Y.
Author: Luke Skywalker

During my training with my Master, Yoda, on Dagobah, I had a vision of Leia, Han, and Chewbacca in a city in the clouds. They were in pain. Yoda told me it was the future I'd seen, and that if I left Dagobah, I might help my friends or possibly destroy all for which they had fought and suffered. I chose to leave against the advice of both Yoda and the spirit of Obi-Wan Kenobi, who told me I would be tempted by the dark side. Somehow they sensed I would confront Darth Vader at Cloud City. Obi-Wan had told me that Vader killed my father, so I believed he thought I might be seeking revenge.

I regret that I did not heed my Masters' cautions, that I took the situation personally, and regarded it as something like a challenge. No matter what my Masters said, I actually believed that Han and Leia would die if I didn't go to them immediately. There was also the matter of dealing with Vader. It was so hard not to feel fear and anger at the thought of facing him. I didn't know if I could stop Vader, but I was prepared to sacrifice myself to save my friends. I thought the dark side was something I could handle, an adversary that I could ultimately conquer.

I was wrong. And I walked right into Vader's trap.

Vader had captured my friends to lure me to Cloud City. He was waiting for me, and I was unprepared for our duel. He didn't just beat me. He ruined me. And when he was done, he told me that he was not the man who'd killed my father; he was my father. He tempted me with the power of the dark side, invited me to join with him against the Emperor so that we could rule the galaxy together.

And even though I was still in shock from the physical wounds inflicted by Vader as well as his monstrous claim, I sensed he was telling me the truth about our relationship. I also knew his invitation was legitimate. To my horror, it seemed, for a moment, that accepting his offer would be a logical move, the only one that might ensure I'd survive the hour. It even flashed through my mind that I could pretend to ally with him, then attempt to escape at a later time. Yet somehow, instinctively, I knew such a desperate plan would fail, and that I could never join him. I also knew that I had to get away from him immediately.

Back on Dagobah, I'd never envisioned that I would be the one who needed to be rescued. I barely managed to escape Vader, and would have died if Leia—who'd already gotten away on the Millennium Falcon—hadn't responded to my telepathic plea.

What did I accomplish at Cloud City? Except for gaining devastating knowledge about my lineage and the dark side's hold on my father, practically nothing. I didn't save Han, and I only further endangered Leia and the others on the Falcon by urging them return to Cloud City to get me. In hindsight, I believe there was only one thing I'd done right: I'd refused Vader's offer. But there was little satisfaction in that at the time, for I had also learned that my Masters were right, that my Jedi training was far from over . . . and that I was not immune to the dark side.

Just as those who are not predisposed to dishonesty might fleetingly consider the thoughts of thieves, the noblest of Force-users are vulnerable to the dark side. You may not think yourself especially curious, easily angered, or envious, but the dark side is a strong seducer. It is a power that draws from subconscious fears, plays off innocent desires, and feeds off selfish thoughts to transform one into a living nightmare.

You will find, at some point, that the dark side will speak to you. It is seductive, offering you everything with little effort on your part. But you can identify it by your own emotions. If you use the knowledge of its presence for enlightenment, to help others, it may be from the light side. But if you use it for your own advancement, out of anger or revenge, then the power is tainted. Don't use it. You will know when you are calm, passive.

Master Yoda said that once you start down the dark path, it will forever dominate your destiny. And yet during the time of Palpatine's return as a clone, I went over to the dark side. I did so for a variety of reasons, some of which seemed to make sense at the time, and many of which still cause me difficulty. But I had to do it. I had to know my father. I had to know why he chose the dark side.

The powers of control and destruction weren't the only things I found in the dark side. I also found great isolation and sadness. I found fear. These are the feelings my father felt, the feelings even the Emperor felt, in his moments of darkest triumph.

What I experienced has given me an understanding of the dark side that is vital to the fight against it. More importantly, the love of my sister and my friends drew me back. It redeemed me. Even the foulest victim of the dark side can be redeemed.

My experience also taught me that the dark side cannot be conquered, no more than the light side can be extinguished. You can fight the dark side and even have victories, but the battle itself can never really end. Learn from the lessons others have endured, so their strength can become your strength.

ADDENDUM BY
TIONNE SOLUSAR

During the period he spent with Palpatine's clone, Luke Skywalker also gained insights into the dark side by reading Palpatine's books. It was not until 35 A.B.Y. that he learned that Anakin Skywalker had feared for the life of his wife, Padmé Amidala, and had become convinced by Palpatine that knowledge of the dark side was the key to learning to achieve immortality. Although Luke maintains that "even the foulest victim of the dark side" can find redemption, it should be noted that various Jedi do not share this belief.

EMPEROR PALPATINE WATCHES DARTH VADER DUEL ▶
LUKE SKYWALKER ON THE SECOND DEATH STAR. (Trevas)

PART FOUR

THE SITH

RECORDED 40 A.B.Y. ' AUTHOR: TIONNE SOLUSAR.

Today the Sith are regarded as their own Order, but the word *Sith* has changed in meaning over the millennia. Before the Dark Jedi known as the Exiles arrived on the planet Korriban in Sith space and proclaimed themselves Sith Lords, the original Sith were a species of proud, violent warriors. Characterized by crimson hides, glowing yellow eyes, and fierce, predatory profiles, the Sith otherwise appeared as fairly typical humanoids. Primitive, superstitious, and barely civilized, the Sith readily accepted the Exiles as gods but also maintained a crude caste system based on their many subspecies; the warrior caste, known as the Massassi, became the foot soldiers of the Sith Empire.

The Sith devoted themselves to worshiping their new masters, who honed their battle arts and expanded their empire to neighboring worlds and star systems. Because the renegade Jedi were exiled from the Old Republic before the development of personal blaster technology, it is only natural that weapons of the Sith Empire would take a different course of evolution. Scholars continue to dispute whether the Exiles arrived in Sith space with archaic lightsabers, but it is understood that the Sith Empire explored alchemical metallurgy to produce mystically honed Sith swords, which—like lightsabers—could deflect energized beams and bolts, but did not require power packs or energy cells.

Ever since the Sith Lord Naga Sadow led the Sith armies back to Republic space to launch the Great Hyperspace War, there have been many battles between the Jedi and the Sith. History is most often written or rewritten by the victors of such battles, and most can only imagine how the Sith might have chronicled their confrontations with the Jedi. Although it is hoped that the recently discovered Telos Holocron might reveal previously unknown details about the Sith, the device's contents remain inaccessible to contemporary Jedi. Because other Holocrons can be accessed by any Force-sensitive being, we must consider the possibility that this is not an ordinary Holocron, and that it is locked to those who might use it to undermine the Sith.

I know the Telos Holocron is more than a tantalizing puzzle, and it may prove more hazardous than valuable. If it was engineered to yield information only to a Jedi who craves the power of the dark side, we may be left with no other option but to destroy it.

THE *DARTH* TITLE

Recorded 40 A.B.Y.
Author: Agent Gannod Chant, special investigatory agent for the Council on Security and Intelligence, translator of the Ingo Wavlud Manuscript.

Many of the Dark Lords of the Sith chose to add the Darth honorific to their name. The very word has become synonymous with the wondrous power of the dark side. However, the origins of the word are unclear. While many see Darth as nothing

◀ THE SITH APPRENTICE PALPATINE TESTS HIS LIGHT-
SABER BEFORE HIS MASTER, DARTH PLAGUEIS. *(Trevas)*

more than a contraction of *Dar*k Lord of the Si*th*, there is some evidence for a deeper interpretation of the term.

Darth Revan and Darth Malak are generally believed to be the first Dark Lords to have used the title. Given that much of their power was derived from the Star Forge, a creation of the extinct Rakata species, some historians see Darth as a corruption of *Daritha,* the Rakatan word for "emperor." Similarly, others note that the word for "triumph" or "conquest" in Rakatan is *darr,* and the word for "death" is *tah.* This has led to theories that Darth is derived from *darr tah* and means "triumph over death" or "immortal." A competing theory asserts that the true meaning of *darr tah* is "conquest *through* death" . . . of one's enemies.

Numerous other cultures or species can—and do—make similar claims to the etymology of the Darth title. In the end, however, there is no definitive answer.

Following Revan and Malak, there was something of a flurry of so-called Dark Lords who took the Darth title. These included Darth Bandon, a former Jedi who was Malak's apprentice, and Darth Traya, formerly a Jedi Master named Kreia, who was cast out and succeeded by her apprentices Darth Sion and Darth Nihilus. Although the Wavlud Manuscript is unclear on details, text indicates that all of these Dark Lords died in the year 3951 B.B.Y.

The Darth title does not surface again until approximately 2000 B.B.Y., with the emergence of Darth Ruin. It is now believed that Ruin was the former Jedi Master Phanius, who was long counted among a relatively small number of "Lost" Jedi Masters. Darth Ruin was ultimately killed by his own followers. A millennia later came Darth Rivan, a Zelosian who took his name from a corrupted Sith manuscript that misidentified Darth Revan as "Darth Rivan, the most powerful Dark Lord of the Jedi Civil War." Darth Rivan fled into space at the end of the New Sith Wars, but the Jedi eventually killed him.

In approximately 1000 B.B.Y., the Darth title was resurrected by Darth Bane, who established the Rule of Two, and his apprentice, Darth Zannah. A date of death for Bane and Zannah has yet to be determined, but it is known that they were succeeded by Darth Cognus and her apprentice Darth Millennial. Allegedly, Millennial's repeated questioning of the Rule of Two and other laws of the Sith Order prompted Cognus to end Millennial's training; because Millennial went on to found the Prophets of the Dark Side, we can assume that it was Cognus who was a direct antecedent of those who maintained the Rule of Two.

Approximately one hundred years ago, the reigning Sith Lord was a Muun known as Darth Plagueis. Little is known of Plagueis, and it is easily conceivable that his apprentice, Darth Sidious, alter ego of the notorious Palpatine, destroyed all information about him. Darth Sidious proved to be the grim culmination of a thousand years of Sith philosophy and teachings. Research indicates that Sidious served for many decades as the apprentice of Darth Plagueis, learning diligently at the feet of his Master.

Sidious also selected a young Iridonian Zabrak named Darth Maul to become his apprentice. Little is known about the early years of Maul, though it was clear that he trained for years toward a single purpose: to become a living weapon that could be unleashed against the Jedi. When Maul died at the hands of Obi-Wan Kenobi, however, Sidious was forced to find another to join him in the service of the dark side.

For his second apprentice, he chose Count Dooku, the last of the infamous Lost Twenty. While Sidious remained hidden behind the mask of a politician loyal to the Republic, Dooku became the sometimes visible face of the Sith, taking the name Darth Tyranus and leading a violent Separatist movement that dragged the Republic into civil war—all part of Sidious's grand scheme to bring himself to power.

During the war against the Separatists, a fiery young Jedi named Anakin Skywalker rose to prominence. Having long recognized Skywalker's potential, Sidious, after elevating himself to Supreme Chancellor in his role as Palpatine, betrayed Darth Tyranus, allowing him to be executed by Skywalker. This paved the way for Sidious to take Anakin as his apprentice, corrupting the idealistic youth until he was transformed into the monstrous Lord Vader.

With the deaths of both Sidious and Vader, some thought the teachings of the Sith would be lost forever. However, based on my investigation—and our experiences with Sidious—it is clear that this is not the case. It is only a matter of time before the agents of the dark side rise up and threaten our beloved New Republic once again.

ADDENDUM BY
TIONNE SOLUSAR

Although Agent Gannod Chant should be commended for his investigation and analysis of the Wavlud Manuscript, it should be noted that his mention of Count Dooku as Darth Sidious's "second apprentice" may be erroneous: our limited information about Darth Sidious does not preclude the possibility that he had another apprentice before Darth Maul.

GATEKEEPER OF THE TELOS HOLOCRON

Greetings, my curious friend. Long have I hoped that someone would activate this Holocron, seeking information that you have been unable to discover elsewhere. I would not be surprised if some alleged advisers have suggested that such knowledge is dangerous, and that you are too young or inexperienced to learn the teachings of the ancients. I assure you, these naysayers are in error, and have gravely misjudged you. The simple fact that you hear my words now is proof that you are worthy.

No, I am not the first keeper of this Holocron. It has been passed down through the ages by many Sith Lords, most of whom left records for your erudition. All that we know, we shall share freely with you. All we ask in return is that you keep an open mind, and use this knowledge for the benefit of only one being: yourself. It is not out of greed that we ask this of you, but out of respect. Of all those who might have stumbled upon this device, no one is more deserving of our knowledge than you.

Though you are wise beyond your years, I would not be dismayed if you do not recognize my simulacrum. You see, I have chosen to appear before you not as I have come to be, but as I was long ago, when I was young. A vanity perhaps, but I know from experience that a much older teacher, no matter how gifted, can appear antiquated, or even obsolete, and I would be remiss to encourage you to believe I am or ever was your superior. After all, you are full of life, and I . . . Well, because the Holocron is now in your hands, I must assume that I am but a whisper from the past.

So please forgive my youthful façade, which I hope will only serve you to more readily accept me as an equal, an ally, and as a friend.

My name is Palpatine.

There are so many things we must discuss, but first let us be certain that we share a true understanding of our history, for only then can we move on to the future.

THE CONQUEST OF SITH SPACE

Author: Ajunta Pall

To my descendants and those of my brethren . . . When you survey the greatness of our Sith Empire, you may find it pleasing to gaze down from the highest spires of our fortresses on Ziost, or to travel from one already conquered world to the next, receiving tribute from the subjects you inherited from your forefathers. But if you find yourself content to rule in this manner, I promise that your rule will be a short one. It is not enough to be powerful or mindful of the Force to survive. You must also be ambitious. And while you plan for future conquests, I urge you to examine the foundations of your fortresses, for these structures did not spring up from the ground on their own.

And for all the things you have and all that you covet, thank not just your forefathers. Thank the Jedi Knights, for it is because of them that you now enjoy our achievements.

It is likely you are aware of our long, terrible war with the Jedi Knights, which lasted more than a century. Yes, I was once a Jedi, a defender of the Republic, as were most of my brethren, but one must learn to crawl before learning to walk. Unfortunately, the Jedi have been walking on their treadmill of contentment for so long that most had forgotten what it was like to leap. When a cadre of more ambitious Jedi opened themselves to the dark side, they discovered the Force could be used to bend life itself . . . well, that was the leap we had to take.

So envious were the Jedi Knights of our ability to transform creatures into improved manifestations, they made it their ongoing duty to hunt us—the Dark Jedi—wherever we attempted to experiment and practice our knowledge. It is regrettable that we could not persuade more of our persecutors to join us in darkness, and it was most disillusioning to be so overwhelmed on that mining world. Yes . . . yes, we were forced to surrender.

Predictably, our benevolent captors had not been able bring themselves to kill us directly, and so chose to remove us symbolically, purging our names and all evidence of our existence from galactic records. And so we were herded onto a drone starship and banished—without any weapons or navigational instruments of any kind—to this previously unexplored region of the Outer Rim. Yes, there was some slight satisfaction in that we left behind some of our precious Leviathans on Corbos, which should prove to be most inconvenient for future generations, but make no mistake: we had no reason to believe we would survive.

As our defenseless ship traveled into the uncharted space, guided only by the dark side, our thoughts were heavy with the losses we had suffered. But after our ship emerged from hyperspace, we soon arrived upon the world you know as Korriban. We were astonished to find that the native Sith were Force-sensitive. Certainly our so-called banishment was not the consequence of Jedi whim but the will of the Force.

The Sith attempted to terrify us with crude but imaginative illusions, some of which were reasonably impressive. Although we lacked weapons, we were obviously stronger and more intelligent than they, and yet they were still eager to prove themselves and prevent us from appropriating their alchemical secrets. It was almost immediately clear that even their most talented sorcerers were no match for us, but they demonstrated honor when they yielded.

Eventually, all of the Sith—especially their Massassi warriors—lived only to serve their new masters. They really are amazingly malleable, the Massassi. New starships were constructed, weapons were fashioned, and more remarkable beasts were conceived. Although I personally prefer to rely upon the Force to create organic wonders, numerous offspring are living proof that the Massassi are biologically compatible with various members of my brethren.

And so we . . . we who were the fallen Jedi, the fallen become dark, the dark become exiles . . . we became Dark Lords of the Sith. The Jedi Knights intended to let us fall like a single raindrop into an endless desert, but they only sent us to a greater

glory. While they decay in their stodgy trappings and power-inhibiting rules of conduct, we grow stronger every day. It is only a matter of time before we shall thank them in an appropriate manner.

Unfortunately, a few Sith Lords—I maintain they were too ambitious, for there is such a thing—were impatient to give thanks. They analyzed a nav computer from the ship that had brought us to Sith space, then reprogrammed it for a return trip through hyperspace. Obviously, I tried to discourage them. Even if they had retraced the same route, there was no way to calculate or even imagine whether the path had remained clear with the passage of time. With their newly gained knowledge of Sith alchemy and numerous weapons and warriors, they left Korriban despite my cautions. That was the last we saw or heard of them. Because so many years have transpired since their departure, it

is reasonable to suspect that they neither accomplished their objective nor revealed our location to anyone in the Republic.

Will there be another confrontation with the Jedi? As I said, it is only a matter of time.

Allow me to introduce one of the earliest Sith Lords, Ajunta Pall, who fought in the final battle of what became known as the Hundred-Year War.

THE SITH CODE

Author: Lord Qordis, founder and master of the Sith Academy on Korriban.

Over many millennia, since the Exiles became Sith Lords, the Sith Code has served as the backbone of our Order. The tenets of the Sith are more than just words to be memorized. Learn them, understand them. They will lead you to the true power of the Force: the power of the dark side.

Peace is a lie. There is only passion.
Through passion, I gain strength.
Through strength, I gain power.
Through power, I gain victory.
Through victory my chains are broken.

ADDENDUM BY
PALPATINE

Lord Qordis was one of the more powerful Sith Lords to serve in Lord Kaan's Brotherhood of Darkness. He was killed by Darth Bane prior to the final Battle of Ruusan.

SITH WORLDS

Author: Seviss Vaa

I am Seviss Vaa, Sith Lord and trusted servant of Lord Kaan. I have studied many ancient texts, including Naga Sadow's writings on Sith alchemy, and have visited the ruins of several Sith temples.

You wish to know about the worlds of the Sith Empire? There were many, well over one hundred that were habitable, and the Sith controlled the riches of a thousand species. Under Lord Kaan's guidance, we shall undoubtedly reclaim all these planets, and many more! My research is ongoing, but I will share what I know of the major worlds.

The best-known planet is Korriban in the Horuset system, the ancestral home of

◄ SITH SCHOLAR MURK LUNDI.
(Edwards)

the Sith. An arid, desert planet, Korriban is the tombworld of Sith Lords and the former power base of the Sith Order. The massive temples that were carved out of the rocky cliff walls of Korriban's Valley of the Dark Lords contain the mummified remains of the most illustrious Sith Lords, as well as treasures that remain well protected by ferocious creatures and intricate traps. Because the power of the dark side transcends the simple biological functions and spatial fluctuations of existence, it is not surprising that Korriban is home to many restless spirits.

But Korriban was not always a necropolis. Long before the arrival of the Jedi Exiles, it was the homeworld of the ancient Sith civilization. More than twenty-five thousand years ago, the Sith were unified by the long-lived King Adas, who led the revolt against Rakata invaders and subsequently acquired Rakatan technology. Although the Sith were victorious under King Adas's rule, Korriban was so devastated by the Rakata that most Sith chose to relocate to Ziost.

During the relocation, Ziost was a thickly forested world, but it eventually yielded to an ice age that leveled the vast woodlands as well as most evidence of civilization. The towering Sith Citadel is among the few remaining structures, and it was adopted as the central meeting place for the original Sith Lords, those Exiles of the Jedi Order who found their way to Sith space following the Hundred-Year War.

According to records, the Sith Lords might have gained greater knowledge of their subjects from an ancient Sith library temple on Krayiss II. Apparently, this library housed Holocrons and artifacts about the Sith species, but ruins on Krayiss II have yet to be identified as a library, and its collections may have long turned to dust.

Would Lord Kaan have allowed that? I think not!

Although the Sith species were experienced builders of monumental architecture, they certainly benefited from the instruction of the Sith Lords. Travelers of Sith space will find significant Sith temples on various worlds, including some in the Thule and Thurra systems. So far, I have shared my knowledge of these temples with only Lord Kaan. If you can convince me of your sincere devotion to the Sith, I might be persuaded to provide coordinates for one of these temples, but be advised that most expeditions result in fatalities.

The Sith Lord Ludo Kressh's private fortress was on the Sith world Rhelg. Kressh's rival for the title of Dark Lord of the Sith was Naga Sadow, who had a fortress on Khar Delba, but also kept a secret stronghold in a crater on Khar Delba's moon, Khar Shian. According to legend, Sadow's lunar stronghold was his primary fortress, and the Khar Delba structure merely served as a decoy to Kressh's attacking forces. Sadow must have preferred locations where sunlight never reached, for both his former properties can only be visited with an ample supply of glow rods. Those who venture to explore these dark environs may gain nothing more than a better appreciation for ancient construction methods, but I personally found the Khar Shian ruins to be extremely enlightening.

Just prior to the Great Hyperspace War, the Sith Lord Garu lost or abandoned the Holocron of King Adas on the planet Ashas Ree. This was the same Holocron that was eventually recovered by the renegade Jedi Freedon Nadd, and which helped him conquer the planet Onderon. I have yet to visit Ashas Ree, but various Sith texts stress that it is an insignificant world. Tragically, many once prominent Sith worlds—including Ziost, Khar Delba, and Khar Shian—went the way of Ashas Ree, as all were largely stripped of their relics by Republic forces after the Great Hyperspace War. Perhaps the greatest loss during that period was Veeshas Tuwan, an ancient Sith library on the Sith world Arkania. For destroying our history, all Jedi deserve the most painful death Lord Kaan can conceive!

Since the formation of the Brotherhood of Darkness, many worlds have become sites for Sith training. Those with noticeable but limited ability in the Force are sent to Honoghr, Gentes, or Gamorr to become Sith Warriors or Marauders. There they learn to channel their emotions into mindless rage and battle fury. Our alchemists transform them into ravaging beasts of destruction to let loose upon our enemies.

Those with greater ability are sent to Ryloth, Umbara, and Nar Shaddaa. These students learn to use the dark side for secrecy, deception, and manipulation. Those who survive the intense training become unstoppable assassins who can use the dark side to kill their targets without moving a muscle.

Both Dathomir and Iridonia currently have Sith academies where apprentices study under Sith Masters. Successful trainees become the counterparts to the Jedi Knights, and swell the ranks of our armies. But just as the Jedi Knights must answer to their Jedi Masters, so do our own adepts and acolytes answer to the Sith Lords. Those with the potential to become Sith Lords are trained on Korriban.

Duty calls, but I will speak of more worlds at my earliest opportunity. Long live the Brotherhood!

ADDENDUM BY
PALPATINE

For his loyalty to Lord Kaan, Seviss Vaa perished with the rest of the Brotherhood of Darkness at the Battle of Ruusan. Seviss Vaa was justified in hating the Jedi for laying waste to so many Sith artifacts, but he overlooks the fact that countless treasures were destroyed during civil wars among the Sith Lords. Had Lord Kaan and his disciples survived the Battle of Ruusan, it is probable that infighting or betrayal would have brought an end to their conspicuous Brotherhood. Seviss Vaa does not mention the destruction of the planet Malachor V and its Sith academy some four thousand years ago, but even if he was aware of those details, it is doubtful that he would have arrived at the same conclusion as Darth

Bane: more than two Sith Lords do not equal a stronger Sith Order.

Regarding Seviss Vaa's descriptions of the worlds in Sith space, I can only assume he either lied about his visits to Khar Delba and Khar Shian or that his powers of observation were sorely lacking, as I recovered valuable relics on both worlds. The Sith temples he mentioned in the Thule and Thurra systems are on Thule and Dromund Kaas, respectively, and were relatively easy to find despite Seviss Vaa's cautions.

But I do acknowledge some debt to Seviss Vaa for bringing the temple on Dromund Kaas to my attention. The temple's foundation dates back to the original Sith Empire, but seems to have been abandoned after the Great Hyperspace War. After Darth Bane initiated the Rule of Two, the temple was rediscovered and expanded by Darth Millennial, the failed apprentice of Darth Cognus. Millennial founded the Prophets of the Dark Side, a sect that not only survived but in fact anticipated my arrival on Dromund Kaas. Because the Prophets can predict the outcome of specific events, they have proved most useful as my personal advisers.

Seviss Vaa might have also observed that most worlds associated with the Sith are characterized by barren terrain. The best example of this may be the Sith space world of Vjun, where frequent acid rainfalls prevents the growth of any vegetation, and where Darth Vader chose to build his retreat, Bast Castle. Even if Sith worlds were not desolate to begin with, most were by the time the Sith finished building their fortresses. This is only natural, given how the dark side drains energy from living things.

Personally, I prefer the tranquillity of my personal retreat on Byss, which has many lake chains that are not unlike those on Naboo. I also believe in encouraging the growth and development of some life-forms, if only to enjoy the eventual pleasure of guiding them toward their deaths. The only negative aspect of Byss is a relatively small population and a certain lack of culture.

I am looking forward to reclaiming Coruscant.

THE FALL OF THE SITH EMPIRE

An ancient Jedi consular named Kla turned to the ways of the Sith and became the gatekeeper for a most enlightening Holocron, which found its way to my possession. Kla had an encyclopedic knowledge of the Sith Empire under Naga Sadow. Although Kla did not always cite his sources, some of his knowledge may have been gained from a Sith Holocron kept by the Jedi Master Odan-Urr on Ossus. Kla's account of the Fall of the Sith Empire is more opinionated than objective, but his insights as a former Jedi are most valuable.

Author: Kla

Once, the Sith Empire ruled over 120 habitable worlds across an expansive area of the Outer Rim. Founded by a relatively small group of exiled Dark Jedi, who arrived in Sith space without weapons and in a single starship, this Empire was a testament to the greatness of the ancient Sith Lords. Unfortunately, less than two thousand years after it began, the Sith Empire was brought to ruin because of a single Sith Lord's impatience.

The tale begins with the death of Marka Ragnos. A half-breed Sith and warlord descended from the original Jedi

Exiles, Ragnos had tremendous power and a frightening grasp of the dark side of the Force. Through a series of short, ruthless campaigns against his enemies, he had risen to prominence, claiming the exalted title Dark Lord of the Sith. Ragnos maintained dominance by pitting his detractors against one another, manipulating them into challenging him or simply assassinating them. During his reign, he was one of the few Sith alive who knew of the Republic and its defenders, the Jedi Order. Feared, admired, and obeyed, he ruled the Sith Empire for more than a century. The cause of his death remains unknown, but may have been the result of old age.

Only minutes after Ragnos's corpse was interred within a great tomb, two Sith Lords began vying for the title of Dark Lord: Ludo Kressh, a half-breed Sith who was determined to maintain the Empire that Marka Ragnos had built, and the more ambitious Naga Sadow, who claimed a "pure blood" lineage to the Jedi Exiles and wanted to expand the Sith Empire. So great was their animosity that it roused the spirit of Marka Ragnos, who informed the antagonists of their ancient ties to the Republic and the Jedi. He urged them to choose their battles wisely, as the fate of the Sith Empire hung in the balance. Evidently, after Ragnos's spirit faded away, Ludo Kressh offered to make peace with Sadow, but Sadow refused to consider Kressh anything other than his sworn enemy.

If Marka Ragnos—or, more precisely, his spirit—knew exactly what was in store for Kressh and Sadow, he did not say. By all accounts, Ragnos was as shrewd as he was cunning, and he must have recognized the possibility that the Jedi remained as strong as they had been when they defeated his ancestors. We may never know whether Ragnos had believed the Sith were not yet ready to expand toward Republic space and enter into a protracted war against the Jedi, or if he hoped Kressh and Sadow might resolve their differences without bloodshed. But we do know what happened next.

A pair of hyperspace explorers from the Republic blundered upon Korriban. Oblivious of Sith history, they claimed they came in peace, and were interested in establishing a trade relationship. Ludo Kressh suspected the alleged explorers were precursors to an invasion and wanted to kill them at once, but Naga Sadow insisted that the pair be interrogated, as they might lead the Sith Lords to new worlds to conquer. And there was the fundamental difference between Kressh and Sadow: where Kressh was cautious and saw potential danger, Sadow was determined and saw opportunity.

Subsequently, the Sith Lords became divided into factions devoted respectively to Kressh and Sadow. Sadow allowed one of the explorers to flee so that he could track the interloper back to Republic space, and used his dark side powers to create the illusion of an even more enormous army for the Sith than actually existed. Sadow's eventual assault on Republic space instigated the Great Hyperspace War.

Only a few details of this war are important. The Jedi and the Republic repelled Naga Sadow's invasion. Sadow returned to Sith space, only to be confronted by Kressh's armada. Sadow killed Kressh, but the Republic fleet had followed Sadow to Sith space and forced him to flee. Defeated by the Republic and banished by Kressh's survivors, Sadow took refuge on the fourth moon in the Yavin system, where he commanded his Massassi warriors to build a series of great temples.

There, Sadow would die, never forgetting the Empire he had lost.

When I first learned of Naga Sadow's role in the Fall of the Sith Empire, all I could think of was how events might have unfolded differently, had Sadow been less brash. Some Sith scholars have faulted Kressh for his lack of daring and unwillingness to endorse and support Sadow's schemes of conquest, but I am quick to slap these scholars down. Although I renounced the Jedi Order for the Sith, I gained much from Jedi patience exercises, and maintain that every Sith could benefit from such discipline.

Seize the day, and you have the day. But wait for the right day to seize, and you will seize entire lifetimes.

DARTH REVAN'S SITH HOLOCRON

Darth Revan's words were preserved by Darth Bane, who transcribed them from his memory of Revan's Holocron. The Holocron was three thousand years old when Bane discovered and studied it on Korriban. To prevent anyone else from studying the Holocron, Bane destroyed it shortly before the final Battle of Ruusan.

Author: Darth Revan

I am Darth Revan, Dark Lord of the Sith.

Those who use the dark side are also bound to serve it. To understand this is to understand the underlying philosophy of the Sith.

The dark side offers power for power's sake. You must crave it. Covet it. You must seek power above all else, with no reservation or hesitation.

The Force will change you. It will transform you. Some fear this change. The teachings of the Jedi are focused on fighting and controlling this transformation. That is why those who serve the light are limited in what they can accomplish.

True power can come only to those who embrace the transformation. There can be no compromise. Mercy, compassion, loyalty: all these things will prevent you from claiming what is rightfully yours. Those who follow the dark side must cast aside these conceits. Those who do not—those who try to walk the path of moderation—will fail, dragged down by their own weakness.

Those who accept the power of the dark side must also accept the challenge of holding on to it. By its very nature, the dark side invites rivalry and strife. This is the greatest strength of the Sith; it culls the weak from our order. Yet this rivalry can also be our greatest weakness. The strong must be careful lest they be overwhelmed by the ambitions of those beneath them working in concert. Any Master who instructs more than one apprentice in the ways of the dark side is a fool. In time, the apprentices will unite their strength and overthrow the Master. It is inevitable. Axiomatic. That is why each Master must have only one student.

This is also the reason there can only be one Dark Lord. The Sith must be ruled by a single leader: the very embodiment of the strength and power of the dark side. If the leader grows weak, another must rise to seize the mantle. The strong rule; the weak are meant to serve. This is the way it must be.

My time here is ended. Take what I have taught you and use it well.

THE RULE OF TWO

Author: Darth Bane

I am not a man of words. But I respect the power of words, for that is what transformed me. The words of the Sith Code. Others had heard them, contemplated them, and so on. But I understood them, and they changed me. For what was I before I heard those words?

Nothing.

Just another miner on Apatros. Just a target for my father's rage. My name was Dessel, but because my father regarded me as the bane of his existence, he called me Bane.

I was eighteen years of age when he last unleashed himself on me. Broke my nose, my father did. Also knocked out two teeth, blackened both of my eyes, and cracked my ribs. I took it all without a word. Only after he passed out in a drunken stupor did I have the strength to wish him dead. But oh, how I wished so strongly. And then I passed out myself.

I awoke to find my wish had come true. The authorities ruled it a natural death. A heart attack, brought on by a combination of too much alcohol, a life working in the mines, and the overexertion of nearly beating his own son to death with his bare hands. I didn't realize at the time that my wish had been granted by the power of the dark side, by way of the darkness within myself. For then, I did not know of the dark side, and barely knew of the Force. I did not have that knowledge. I did not have those words.

But I did have the power.

I was twenty-three, working as a miner on Apatros for the Outer Rim Oreworks

Company, when one night I fell into a card game with spacers at a cantina. They talked of the war between the Jedi and the Sith, the Jedi general Hoth against the Brotherhood of Darkness. I had heard plenty of wild tales of Jedi performing extraordinary feats through the mystical power of the Force. I figured they were legend and myth, or at least exaggerations. Granted, I had had premonitions in my youth, visions that came true, so I knew there were powers that transcended the physical world. But the stories of what the Jedi could do seemed too impossible to believe.

Listening to those spacers, I wasn't convinced that the Sith were monsters. Bad things happen on both sides during any war. As far as I knew, the Sith were people, just like you. Just like me. And I didn't go along with the Jedi belief that all beings are created equal. After all, some beings are smarter or stronger than others. And for all that Jedi talk about helping those in need, it didn't change the fact that a Jedi had never saved me from any injustice.

That same night, I played sabacc with a Republic ensign who turned out to be a bad loser. When I left the cantina, the ensign and two naval soldiers attacked me. It was dark, so dark that I could barely see a thing, but I somehow saw the vibroblade coming at me. I saw it clearly, as if it glowed with an inner fire. I knew this was strange, because vibroblades don't emit light. It was the ensign who was holding the weapon. I grabbed his wrist and forced the blade straight into his chest.

The two soldiers fled. I knew they would report me to the authorities, that it would be their word against mine, and that no one would believe I had acted in self-defense. I had no interest in going to prison. I left Apatros immediately, and I joined the Brotherhood of Darkness.

I started off as a Sith trooper with the Gloom Walkers unit. I first saw action on Kashyyyk, and was promoted to sergeant after we conquered the planet. On Kashyyyk, and later on Trandosha and Phaseera, I became more aware of my special abilities that enabled me to survive against apparently impossible odds, but I did not know the source of these abilities. I also became aware that my superior officer was a coward and a fool.

After a year of service, my talents came to the attention of the leaders of the Brotherhood of Darkness, and I was transferred to the Sith Academy on Korriban to learn the ways of the Sith. It was there that I first learned that the Sith, like the Jedi, also drew power from the Force, and that it was this power that had sustained me through so many battles.

Many students took new names for themselves on Korriban, leaving their old lives behind. I took what had once made me weak and used it to make myself strong. I took the name Bane.

At the Sith Academy, I learned the Code of the Sith. Others may have spoken the words with conviction, but I found meaning in them that others could not even imagine. At times, I believed the words were meant for me alone. Eventually, my belief would prove valid.

When I wasn't learning from the Masters and training with weapons, I visited what passed for the Sith archives, housed in a crumbling temple. The Jedi had long ago eradicated many teaching tools of the dark side, and the library was limited to scrolls, tomes, and manuals. I spent several hours each day studying these records. I found them fascinating, and felt that the ancient knowledge would be the key to unlocking my full potential.

Through these works, my understanding of the Force took shape.

Kaan, the founder of the Brotherhood of Darkness, believed that strength lay in numbers. But as our war against the Jedi continued, my studies led to the conclusion that the Brotherhood, having amassed an army of thousands, had thinned the power of the dark side. When Kaan, hoping to heighten morale and increase solidarity, conferred the title of Dark Lord to all the Sith Masters, I was the only one who protested. These so-called Lords could no more be equals than the billions of beings whom the Jedi were unable to protect.

Because the title of Dark Lord had been trivialized, I proclaimed myself Darth Bane. I had been told that the Darth title was no longer used because it promoted rivalry among the Sith and gave the Jedi an easy target. Obviously, Kaan and his minions were all cowards.

And so I gave Lord Kaan a detailed description of one of the most fearsome creations of the ancient Sith: the thought bomb, a ritual that would unleash the pure destructive energy of the dark side to consume all Force-users within a wide radius, trapping their energy within an ovoid shell. I gave instructions for the thought bomb to Kaan because I knew he would eventually use it against the Jedi, even though it would also mean an end to the Brotherhood. Aided by his fellow Lords, Kaan created and detonated the thought bomb at the final Battle of Ruusan.

I was the only Sith to survive the cataclysm, but not the only Force-user. Zannah was a young girl, one of the many children whom the Jedi had brought to Ruusan in their last, desperate efforts to vanquish the Sith. She would become my apprentice, Darth Zannah.

The power of the dark side cannot be dispersed among the masses. It must be concentrated in the few who are worthy of the honor. The Sith must be ruled by a single leader: the very embodiment of the strength and power of the dark side. If the leader grows weak, another must rise to seize the mantle. To serve this one true Sith Master, there can be only one true apprentice.

Two there should be; no more, no less. One to embody the power, the other to crave it.

The Rule of Two.

ON SELECTING APPRENTICES

The relationship between a Sith Lord Master and apprentice is far more powerful than any other teacher and student, a duality greater than the fundamental entities of mind and matter. It is vital that neither believes there is greater strength in a single Sith Lord, or in an Order that exceeds two.

Because you are not yet a Master yourself, you might assume that it is the Master's duty to bestow all of his knowledge of the dark side to his apprentice. You could not be more mistaken. It is the apprentice's duty to learn all that he can from the Master, and the Master's right to refrain from revealing all of his secrets. My own Master, Darth Plagueis, made the grave error of teaching me too much, at which point he became unnecessary.

Choosing an apprentice can be a strenuous endeavor. The most important thing to remember is that the apprentice's purpose is to serve the Master. Only when you consider how few beings are worthy of becoming a Sith Lord can you begin to understand the enormity of your responsibility.

You want someone capable of carrying out your orders, but not someone who has every intention of killing you before you can accomplish your goals. And you can expect that your apprentice will come to want your life, for it is only natural for the apprentice to aspire for more. An apprentice should be ambitious, but if your own ambition is to live, you must be mindful.

Choose someone as a successor and you will inevitably be succeeded.

Choose someone hungrier and you will be devoured.

Choose someone quicker and you won't dodge the blade at your back.

Choose someone with more patience and you won't block the blade at your throat.

Choose someone more devious and you'll hold the blade that kills you.

Choose someone more clever and you'll never know your end.

Despite these cautions, an apprentice is essential. A Master without an apprentice is a Master of nothing.

I took inspiration from the Jedi tradition of indoctrinating Force-sensitive infants when I selected one apprentice, whom I named Darth Maul. I took him from his homeworld, Iridonia, and raised him as I would construct the perfect weapon. I trained him in numerous exotic and forbidden martial arts, disciplined him constantly, and personally applied the Sith tattoos that were evidence of his complete dedication to the dark side. Maul had but one reason for being: to exact vengeance against the Jedi Order for the decimation of the Sith ranks. Oh, how he dreamed of burning the Jedi Temple to the ground. I know, for I gave him that dream repeatedly.

Maul completed his basic training several years before the Battle of Naboo, and served me well as an assassin and extension of my will. As loyal as he was, I made no effort to caution him when I foresaw his death in a duel with the Jedi on Naboo, for by that time, the Jedi had already become aware of their "Chosen One," the remarkably powerful Anakin Skywalker. I had foreseen that young Skywalker would eventually become my apprentice, but that I would have to wait for him. Ultimately, Maul was nothing more than a tool, and despite his sense of purpose he never realized that it was not *his* destiny to raze the Jedi Temple. But by slaying Qui-Gon Jinn before he was in turn killed by Obi-Wan Kenobi, that tool accomplished a different goal: he rattled the Jedi Order's long-complacent attitude regarding the existence of the Sith, making many of them nervous and paranoid, and also created a path for Skywalker to be trained in the ways of the Force by Kenobi, a Jedi with relatively limited experience.

To those who do not know me, my actions—or apparent inactions—during the Battle of Naboo may have seemed less like a calculated risk than a gross exercise in wishful thinking. I'm sure you will agree that such suggestions are insulting. No, I knew exactly what I was doing when I allowed events to happen as they did. Why train an apprentice to hate the Jedi when the Jedi can train him for you?

I did not wait long to appoint my next apprentice. I had had my eye on the Jedi Master Count Dooku for quite some time, and had even met with him on several occasions when I was a Senator to discuss his ideologies. Dooku's infinite charm, impeccable manners, and powers of influence were precisely what I needed to accelerate my goals for galactic conquest. Despite his many years of service to the Jedi Order, it was refreshingly easy to convince him to ally with me. Of course, it helped that I knew of his slight fascination with Sith Holocrons when he was but a Jedi Padawan. And so Dooku became Darth Tyranus.

Both Darth Tyranus and his alter ego accomplished a great deal in the years that he served me. As Tyranus, he arranged for the creation of the clone army for the Republic, and as Dooku, he became the leader of the Republic's opposition, the Confederacy of Independent Systems.

Tyranus also enlisted Asajj Ventress to our cause. If ever there were a Sith aspirant, it was Ventress, but her hatred of the Jedi was so intense that it frequently blinded her and made her tactless. She may have deluded herself into believing she was Tyranus's apprentice, especially after he bestowed upon her a pair of lightsabers that had once belonged to Dooku's last Padawan, Komari Vosa. Perhaps Ventress deserved them, for she was an occasionally capable warrior, nothing more or less. The report of her death on Boz Pity hardly came as a surprise.

But as with Darth Maul, Darth Tyranus's tenure was not indefinite. When the opportunity finally came for Anakin Skywalker to take his place beside me, it was imperative to end Tyranus's apprenticeship. Skywalker himself did the deed, which came as a complete surprise to Tyranus. It still amuses me that the old scoundrel never foresaw that my goals might hinge on his death.

And so Anakin Skywalker, hopelessly entranced by my promise to show him the secrets to eternal life, became Darth Vader. Although he fulfilled Darth Maul's dream of bringing down the Jedi Temple and also killed the leaders of the Confederacy, I regret Vader disappointed me early on when he allowed himself to be mutilated by Kenobi. Yes, Vader remained strong in the Force, but strong enough to succeed me? Never. Granted, he *was* strong enough to kill me. But that only lasted for so long.

It has been six years since the Battle of Endor. As leader of my Dark Side Adepts, Military Executor Sedriss has been most loyal, and is commended for reviving me here on Byss. But for all his usefulness, Sedriss is only a moderate Force-sensitive, a capable errand boy but hardly the stuff of a Sith apprentice. No, it is only appropriate that my next apprentice must be someone with more unique qualities.

It must be Luke Skywalker or his kin.

THE CONFESSION OF DARTH TYRANUS

Author: Darth Tyranus

I, Darth Tyranus, make this recording for no other reason than that it will edify future Sith Lords.

It has been twelve years since my former incarnation, the Jedi Master Dooku, voluntarily renounced his commission to the Jedi Order. The years have been fruitful. After leaving the Jedi, I returned to Serenno and claimed my family title of Count, *which gave me access to and control over vast fortunes. This allowed the financing of plans conceived by Master Darth Sidious, plans designed to bring about chaos, dividing the Republic as well as the Jedi.*

My Master's strategy involved many protracted schedules and labyrinthine details, but I shall summarize my most significant accomplishments: as Darth Tyranus, I took measures to secure what would become an eventual army for the Republic, and as Dooku, I founded and organized the Confederacy of Independent Systems to fight this same army. At present, war rages across the galaxy, and the Jedi do not realize they have been manipulated. In the end, the Jedi will be remembered, if at all, as nothing more than an embarrassing footnote in history, and the Sith will rule, at last bringing structure to the galaxy.

Although the Jedi do currently suspect that I—or more precisely, Count Dooku—have allied myself with the dark side, it is with some satisfaction that I can claim they remain ignorant of my alliance to the Sith. No, I am not surprised that they are so slow to connect the dots. My satisfaction lies in the knowledge that the longer they remain ignorant, the stronger my Master and I grow.

According to the Jedi Archives, at the time I abandoned the Order, I was only the twentieth Jedi Master to do so. It still amuses me to recall the Jedi Council's response when I notified them of my decision to leave. I had already prepared a recorded statement, but they insisted that I come before them. I acquiesced, and Mace Windu greeted me with a single word: "Why?"

Not feeling in any way compelled to reiterate the vague explanations I had already offered in my prepared statement, I looked at Windu quizzically. Not more than three seconds of silence passed when Yoda took it upon himself to answer on my behalf. He said, "Because time it is for him to go." And indeed it was.

But why was the time then, and not years earlier? Why not while I was a youth at the Jedi Temple on Coruscant, when I first became aware of the Sith? Why not when I first realized that the Senate was corrupt beyond salvation, and that the Jedi were nothing more than servants to that corruption? To answer this, I must first tell you something of the Jedi that I was.

Like most Jedi, I was brought to the Jedi Temple at a very early age. I spent years training with Yoda. Although Jedi younglings were not permitted to have contact with their biological families, we were allowed to know of our lineage. By the time I learned of my heritage on Serenno, I was already so committed to learning the ways of the Force and becoming a Jedi that I had no interest in whether my relations had any love for me. I could not have cared less if their vaults contained any reserves in my name, which might provide for me in the unlikely event that I failed to become a Jedi Knight. A true Jedi, I believed, did not think in terms of power.

At the age of thirteen, Jedi Master Thame Cerulian chose me as his Padawan apprentice. Cerulian was a member of the Jedi Council and had an avid interest in history, which included the study of ancient Sith Holocrons. Cerulian never gave me any indication that his interest in the Sith was anything but scholarly; I believe he may have been more intrigued by the provenance and mechanics of the devices than he was ever curious about their contents. But in choosing me as his apprentice, Cerulian aroused the envy of one of my contemporaries, a Jedi learner named Lorian Nod. Nod stole a Sith Holocron from the Jedi Archives and blamed it on me. I had considered Nod a friend, but when the Council questioned me about the allegations, I was compelled by my own sense of honor—as a Jedi—to tell the truth. And so Nod was expelled from the Order.

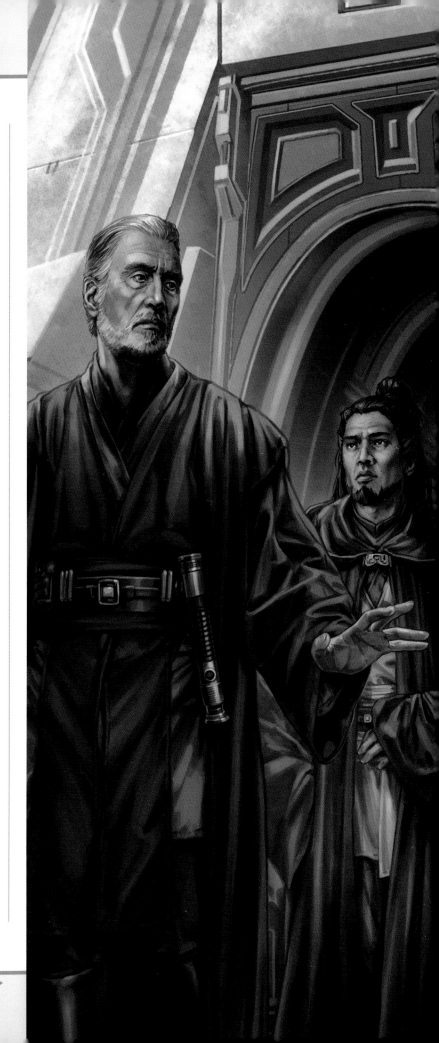

I found it interesting that the Council stressed that Nod was expelled not for stealing the Sith Holocron, but for lying and implicating me. Although I did not contemplate the Council's reasoning much at the time, I am certain I came away from the experience with the impression that Jedi Masters were more concerned with loyalty and honesty than with the temporary loss of a Sith Holocron. I also learned that friendship was a bond that had its limits, and I made my first enemy.

What became of Lorian Nod, you wonder? Not much, really. He spent some years in and out of prisons, but eventually became something of a leader on Junction 5, his homeworld. I met with him just last year, when I invited the Junction system to join the Confederacy. Nod declined. He's dead now.

I will not inundate you with too much minutiae of my years with the Jedi Order, but eventually I became a Jedi Knight. I was in my early twenties when I took on my first Padawan learner, Qui-Gon Jinn, a rebellious spirit with a deep connection to the living Force. Eventually, I became a Jedi Master. Let it be said that I was a good Jedi. I never shirked from duty, nor was I tempted by the dark side. Was I occasionally outspoken? Yes. And did I prefer some semblance of independence that allowed me to operate beyond the confines of the Jedi Temple? Yes. There was a minor commotion when I turned down an invitation to join the Council, but the Council finally conceded that I better served the Force as a proactive peacekeeper. After all, my proficiency with a lightsaber made me most useful in the field.

And so it was as a Jedi Master, some twenty-four years ago, that I led my Padawan Komari Vosa and a Jedi task force to Galidraan, a snow-covered planet in the Outer Rim. We had been summoned by Galidraan's governor, who claimed that Mandalorians were committing atrocities against his people.

Thanks to Master Thame Cerulian, I had some knowledge of the history of the Mandalorians, a nomadic group of mercenary warriors with origins that date back many thousand of years. I was also aware that there had been decades of infighting between two Mandalorian factions, but they operated primarily on lawless worlds outside Republic space, rarely drawing attention to themselves as they almost never left any evidence of their handiwork. By all accounts, they were the epitome of professional soldiers.

Because Galidraan was a Republic world and the Mandalorians' alleged actions were as brazen as they were barbaric, I allowed two possibilities: either the butchers on Galidraan were imposters, or something had caused the Mandalorians—whichever faction they were—to change their ways. Tragically, I did not allow for a third possibility: Galidraan's governor had lied, and the Jedi Council had believed him.

Five Consular-class cruisers delivered our task force to Galidraan. Komari Vosa and I traveled on the Acceptance. Our entire task force totaled twenty Jedi, all hastily withdrawn from various respective assignments for this emergency. The Jedi Council had selected us not because of our combat experience but because of our proximity to Galidraan and how fast we could get there. I was the senior Jedi Master, and when I realized that most of my comrades' awareness of the Mandalorians was . . . shall we say . . . limited, I was beyond chagrined.

Yes, the situation was urgent. Innocent people really were being slaughtered on Galidraan. Against any other small army, twenty Jedi would have been more than enough. But based on what I knew of the Mandalorians, I did not hesitate to request reinforcements from the Jedi Council. In hindsight, I should have insisted. But reinforcements could only travel so fast through hyperspace, and, as I said, innocents were dying.

We located the Mandalorians in a small valley, and had the high ground when we surrounded them. I wasn't surprised when they refused to surrender.

Galidraan was a bloodbath.

When the conflict ended, eleven Jedi and all but one of the Mandalorians lay dead in the snow. Komari Vosa was still standing, having slain twenty Mandalorians single-handedly. The surviving Mandalorian, I soon learned, was named Jango Fett. He'd killed three Jedi with his bare hands. As a Jedi, I could neither hate nor fear Fett, but I did feel something for him that surprised me. I felt respect.

Had Fett and I been the only survivors of that battle, I would have lowered my lightsaber and bid him safe journey. He was the last of his kind, and I'd never known another being who so thoroughly deserved to go wherever he pleased. But other Jedi had survived, and I doubted that we were unanimous in our regard for Fett. In the end, it was the Council who decided his fate, for via transmission they ordered me to turn him over to Galidraan's governor. And like a gutless animal, I obeyed.

The governor remained in power, and Fett was sold into slavery. Although Jedi lives had been lost, it was quickly concluded that we had accomplished our mission, and there was no subsequent investigation.

Eventually, I learned the entire fiasco had been a setup. The civilians had been killed not by Fett's faction, the True Mandalorians, but by the Mandalorian Death Watch. Hoping to crush the True Mandalorians, Death Watch's leader had collaborated with Galidraan's governor to lure Fett's faction with a false assignment, then summoned the Jedi for help.

Even though I knew that the Senate was corrupt, the Council was fallible, and Jedi training methods were far from perfect, I remained with the Jedi Order for twelve years after Galidraan. Why? Because I still believed that I could accomplish some good as a Jedi. I thought I could bring about some positive changes, right certain wrongs, and do better than maintain the status quo. In short, I was an utter fool. Even worse, and I confess this with some degree of shame, I could not imagine a life beyond the Order. I was weak.

But then I met Darth Sidious. He showed me the way to the dark side, and he made me strong.

SITH ALCHEMY

Although the indigenous Sith people practiced alchemy long before the Jedi Exiles conquered their worlds, it was the Exiles *cum* Sith Lords who refined and perfected these dark arts. One of the most powerful Sith alchemists was Naga Sadow, who left detailed records of his work within a Sith Holocron I came across some years ago.

Author: Naga Sadow

Ask me of my heritage, and I shall tell you. Ask me of my ambitions, and you shall know them. Ask me for my hand in battle, and I shall likely lend you both.

But ask me the secrets of Sith alchemy, and I would ask you for three measures of blood: one from a person you love, one from

a person you hate, and one from yourself. A triangle do these measures form, and a powerful triangle it is, so long as your own bloodline is strong with dark side energy and not rife with foreign impurities. If your bloodline reveals that you are merely a spy or pretender to Sith knowledge, may my words reach out to tear your eyes and tongue from your head, and may you drown in your loved one's blood while your enemies look upon your wretched form and laugh.

Because you have not already succumbed to the defenses that guard this record, I will assume you have already prepared the triangle of blood. Now fill the triangle with the sacred words, and brace yourself for death.

You know the sacred words. Welcome, my apprentice. Yes, I shall grant you knowledge despite your imperfections, for you have passed my test, but barely.

As you are already aware, Sith alchemy gives one the power to alter the molecular composition of living beings and reshape inanimate matter. First, you will learn how to construct the equipment required to create such alterations. I will then teach you how to produce weapons and armor that are impervious to all others, and poisons that will convert the noblest of beings to your dark causes. Finally, you will create mutants steeped in the dark side and bound to your will.

Let us begin . . .

Ah, but Naga Sadow was too generous with his knowledge. Far more generous than I. Also, despite his powers, he was ultimately undone by his own impatience to expand the Sith Empire. After his death, Sadow's secrets were gained by Freedon Nadd, who passed them on to Exar Kun. Because none of them came to a glorious end, I think it's best that I guard Sadow's teachings a bit longer. However,

I am tempted to incorporate some of his findings into my own book, *The Creation of Monsters*.

SITH WEAPONS

Author: Komok-Da

I am Komok-Da, direct descendant of the original Sith, and Master of weapons and armor. I will tell you of Sith weapons, but only if you vow to use them, for nothing displeases me more than to know that a weapon gathers dust.

The earliest Sith weapon was the Sith sword. When the exiled Jedi first arrived in Sith space, it was with these blades that my ancestors greeted them. The Sith sword is an alchemically altered blade attached to an ordinary sword hilt. The alterations enable the blade to deflect blaster bolts, just as lightsabers do. The blade also focuses the Force energy of the user, giving the edge an unnatural sharpness. As the wielder grows more proficient in the power of the dark side, the blade becomes more deadly.

Sith swords are effective against lightsabers not only because of the way their alchemically altered metal refracts the lightsaber's energy, but also because they retain their rigidity and sharpness against such energy weapons. And unlike ancient lightsabers, Sith swords do not require power packs or energy cells. Despite the fact that a Sith sword was often a match for a lightsaber when wielded by a trained Sith warrior, they are seldom used by contemporary Sith. Although lightsabers are a superior weapon, there is still nothing quite as satisfying as feeling the warm spray of blood when one cleaves through one's enemy with a metal sword.

There are no records that tell whether the earliest Sith Lords had any knowledge of lightsaber technology, which the Jedi were still refining when they banished the Dark Jedi to the Unknown Regions. The earliest existing record of a Sith who used a lightsaber was the self-proclaimed Dark Lord of the Sith, Freedon Nadd, a former Jedi apprentice who learned the ways of the Sith from the spirit of Naga Sadow. Despite Nadd's complete lack of Sith lineage, it is a testament to his powers that he conquered Onderon and transformed it into a prosperous world.

More than three hundred years after Nadd's death, his spirit trained another renegade Jedi, Exar Kun, who modified his own lightsaber into a double-bladed weapon. Since adopted by other Sith warriors, the double-bladed lightsaber can be ignited from either end or both ends simultaneously. On some models, the handle can be disconnected at the middle to become two separate weapons. The design of the double-bladed lightsaber maximizes the weapon's potential and provides an added surprise in duels with Jedi.

Armor and talismans can be alchemically treated during construction to tip the scales of battle. Dark armor is almost always created to meet the specific needs of the wearer, and generally provides additional protection against blasters and lightsabers, or extra resistance against certain forms of attack. Sith talismans are less restrictive physically, and can provide the wearer with an extra defense against blaster bolts, lightsaber blades, and even the Force itself. I will advise anyone that it is best to craft one's own personal armor and talismans without assistants, as assistants cannot always be trusted to serve one's best interests.

The Sith lanvarok is a short-range

weapon worn on the forearm and designed to hurl thin, solid disks in an unpredictable spray pattern. My ancient ancestors developed the lanvarok as a hunting weapon, and those who are strong with the Force will have little difficulty guiding the disks to their targets. The lanvarok is specifically designed for either the right or left forearm, and few are interchangeable from right to left. Although the lanvarok is time-consuming to reload, it is well worth the wait when one sees the fear and surprise in the eyes of one's enemies as they receive a sudden hail of whirling projectiles.

Although edged and projectile weapons are designed to kill on contact, some targets are most resilient, and one should never dismiss the use of Sith poison. Created by means of Sith alchemy, this toxin is more accurately described as a disease; once in the system of a Force-using being, it remains there, gradually weakening the enemy's resistance to the dark side of the Force. Sith poison can be introduced into a victim's system by ingestion, but I admit a preference for using a long-range dart for injection. The poison feeds victims' anger, drawing them closer to the dark side. A strong dose can overcome those who have already embraced the dark side, and even the most powerful Sith are usually unable to heal themselves after the poison sets in.

I am more than willing to provide detailed instructions on building any Sith weapon or concocting Sith poison. However, you must first demonstrate your ability to kill without mercy. Return to me with proof of your kill and you shall be rewarded. But be warned: I will not be impressed if you return with small prey.

FORCE LIGHTNING

Those who follow the dark side may learn to release pure energy from their fingertips. This Force lightning can be directed at a target and cause great pain as it siphons off the living energy and eventually kills its victim. Knowledge of this power has long been limited to the Sith Lords. No, you are not prepared for any more information at this time.

SITH SPIRITS

There is a long history of Sith Lords and dark siders who abandoned their physical forms upon death to become one with the Force, and return to the material realm as ghostly incarnations. Some of these spirits were lost forever, but others found ways to attach their essence to objects and locations strong in dark power. The Necropolis on Korriban is especially strong with the dark side, and numerous dark siders have sought out spirits there, often with disastrous results. Bear in mind, my curious friend, that few spirits are content to remain as such, and most aspire to live again in some corporeal form.

My study of Sith history has revealed several instances in which Sith spirits dramatically shaped events and influenced aspiring Sith Lords. The first such case occurred more than five thousand years ago on the planet Korriban, during the funeral for the reigning Dark Lord of the Sith, Marka Ragnos. This was revealed to me by way of the Holocron kept by Kla.

Author: Kla

The Dark Lord of the Sith Marka Ragnos had been dead for only a brief period of time when his spirit halted a duel between the rival Sith Lords Ludo Kressh and Naga Sadow, both of whom sought to claim the exalted title of Dark Lord of the Sith. Ragnos did not tell Kressh and Sadow of his beliefs or give them specific direction. He only informed them of the existence of the Jedi, and cautioned them to make their decisions for the future wisely. As I have previously noted, the debacle that followed brought about the death of Kressh, the Fall of the Sith Empire, and Sadow's relocation to Yavin 4, where his spirit was ultimately interred.

Approximately fourteen hundred years later, the Dark Jedi Freedon Nadd followed rumors about the Sith until he arrived at Yavin 4 and discovered the descendants of Sadow's Massassi. These Massassi delivered Nadd to a temple, where he awakened Naga Sadow's spirit. After gleaning information about Sith sorcery and plundering Sadow's vaults for Sith artifacts, Nadd traveled to the planet Onderon, which he conquered and made his own; there he proclaimed himself the new Dark Lord of the Sith.

Freedon Nadd ruled over Onderon for over a century. Following his death, his spirit possessed a series of his descendants for more than 350 years, until Jedi arrived on Onderon and terminated his possession of King Ommin. But Nadd's spirit hardly became inactive, nor was his range limited to a single world. The Jedi were still dealing with Ommin on Onderon when Nadd contacted Satal and Aleema Keto, the founders of the Krath, and told them they were the future of his work. Even after the Jedi transferred his remains to Onderon's moon, Dxun, Nadd's spirit remained on Onderon long enough to appear before the Jedi Knight Ulic Qel-Droma, and foretell that Qel-Droma would become a Sith Lord.

Although the Jedi had designed and built Freedon Nadd's new tomb on Dxun to withstand the ages, it was not long before the Dark Jedi Exar Kun infiltrated the structure and found Nadd's remains. Nadd's spirit awakened yet again, and directed Exar Kun to Naga Sadow's fortress on Yavin 4.

Nadd had hoped to utilize Sadow's ancient alchemical laboratory to accomplish his own rebirth in a new body, but his spirit was vanquished by the power-hungry Exar Kun. Before Nadd's spirit surrendered to utter annihilation, he reached out to the Krath on the planet Koros Major, and told them to beware of Exar Kun. However, Kun sensed Nadd's communication with the Krath, and became determined to destroy his Sith-influenced rivals.

By the time Kun arrived at the city of Cinnagar on Koros Major, Ulic Qel-Droma had killed Satal Keto and joined Aleema to lead the Krath. Kun and Qel-Droma dueled but were stopped by the spirit of Marka Ragnos, who told them that they would restore the Sith Empire to its former glory. Ragnos proclaimed Kun the new Dark Lord of the Sith, and Qel-Droma his first and foremost apprentice.

Although Exar Kun and Ulic Qel-Droma assembled a vast army and corrupted many Jedi students, Qel-Droma was ultimately stripped of his powers and Kun was defeated by the Jedi on Yavin 4. As of yet, there are no records of any further appearances by Marka Ragnos or other significant Sith spirits, but most believe that Ragnos's return is only a matter of time.

Having survived the destruction of the second Death Star as a ghostly manifestation, I can assure you that it is a most wearisome state to be in. It is not enough to retain one's powers beyond death, for a noncorporeal avatar can only do so much. The primary advantage of becoming a Sith spirit is that it allows one the opportunity to return in a new body, so that one might again enjoy the pleasures of the flesh. Because the flesh *is* weak, and can be severely ravaged by the dark side, one must take care when choosing a body.

Yes, this is the essential paradox of the dark side: the more successful the dark sider, the more quickly that dark sider's body decays.

How do I retain my youthful countenance? You flatter me. Read on, my friend. Read on.

IMMORTALITY THROUGH CLONING

As practically everyone knows, cloning is the science of taking a cell from a living organism, duplicating the genetic code, and growing the cell into an exact duplicate of the cell donor. While the achievements made by Kaminoan cloners should not be overlooked, an undeniable problem with Kaminoan-engineered clones is that they can require longer periods of gestation before they arrive at maturity. While this may be suitable for some long-term plans, such as raising a secret army, such time-consuming technology is generally inconvenient for those who may find themselves in need of a body sooner than they expected.

Seeking an alternative, Imperial scientists utilized Spaarti cylinders, which are refinements of Kaminoan technology developed on Cartao during the Clone Wars. These four-meter-tall tanks are mechanical wombs filled with nutrient chemicals and organic catalyzers. While the clone body matures, special polymer chains are introduced to the nutrient cylinder. These polymers combine with the skin to form a tough fibrous membrane that covers and protects the body during the decanting phase. From start to finish, the procedure results in an adult clone within a few weeks.

As one's body is consumed by the power of the dark side, the key to immortality is the growth of new bodies into which one can project one's life essence. Unfortunately, because the clones are one step removed from the natural life process itself, they are much more vulnerable to the effects of the dark side, and age at an extremely accelerated rate. The only logical solution is to grow many more clones at the same time as backups.

How do you go about transferring your life essence into another body? Patience, my friend. Patience. I don't know you that well.

Yet.

ADDENDUM BY
TIONNE SOLUSAR (40 B.B.Y.)

Although these insights from the mind of Darth Sidious are nearly priceless in their historical value, it is important to point out the fact that Palpatine's numerous clones were indeed just that—clones. The possibility remains that the former Emperor's clones only believed themselves to be the real Palpatine. Regardless, they brought imminent danger to the galaxy, and we are fortunate these clones were stopped before they wrought any further destruction.

THE DARK SIDE COMPENDIUM

Author: Palpatine

Because I have no intention of dying, I do not feel any compulsion to create some work of art to survive me. However, I am not so selfish that I am unwilling to share my various thoughts and experiences regarding the dark side. And so I now present to you excerpts from what may well be my masterpiece, the three books that make up *The Dark Side Compendium*.

THE BOOK OF ANGER

Many Jedi claim to have found serenity, and that through serenity they have overcome anger. Such arrogance is astounding. These fools have never faced their anger, and thus have no idea whether they have truly overcome it or not. True calm is only achieved through testing the limits of one's anger and passing through unscathed. The capacity for this ability lies within everyone, though most fear to test their own strength, and are thus considered at best weaklings, and at worst irresponsible.

When the Force is sensed and moved by emotion, from the very center of the body, and meditated from the lower vital centers of the being, it acts with the destructive power of a storm . . . and the savagery of a beast.

Anger is the most potent catalyst to this kind of power. And anger that becomes rage, when channeled through the "vital gate" in the center of the body, can unleash absolutely unstoppable potency through the body.

Add the exquisite control of a fine intelligence standing watch over anger, and one has aggression that can kill with precision, crush cartilage from afar . . . or murder opponents from a great distance.

I have learned that Anger and Will joined together are the greatest power.

I have learned to meditate Anger and Will with clarity and precision, and I have learned to open the hidden reservoirs of dark side Power.

Anger concentrated by Will in the vital center of the body creates a portal through which vast energies are released—the energies of the dark side of the Force.

Standing watch with the mind, in my meditation of Anger, I have slain my enemies from great distances through the dark side Power that permeates the galaxy. I have created lightning, and unleashed its destructive fire.

Using this knowledge, I can unleash the dark side energies that are all around us, even to shatter the fabric of space itself. In this way, I have created *storms.*

Through a simple act of Will, I can generate Force Storms, energy storms that are vastly destructive and virtually unstoppable. Although triggering such storms requires mere thought and inclination, I admit I am not yet able to completely control the phenomenon. Among my goals is to perfect this control.

THE WEAKNESS OF INFERIORS

Inferiors continually endanger their own lives and the lives of others through poor decisions, reckless behavior, and simple inability to engineer the reality of their ambitious dreams. They are like children, crying in frustration because they do not comprehend their own limitations. These weaklings need structure—to be shown their place in the existing social order. It is left to the wise and powerful to provide that structure in order for civilization to survive and thrive in the galaxy. Those who cannot—or will not—accept that peace and order are far more important than their own selfish desires must be removed from society before they can inflict any lasting damage.

1. **All power comes from outside the weak.** The weak have *never* been known to believe in themselves or in their ability to wield power.

2. **The face of authority.** The weak live as in a dream. All their thoughts, actions, and urges are governed by the face and the voice that controls this dream. The face and voice they have learned to obey. The face and voice of *Authority*.

3. **The law of fear.** A consequence of the first two tenets is that the weak live in *fear*. The mere *suggestion of violence* from one in authority is enough to inspire their obedience. How can one who doesn't believe in his own powers stand against the power of another? It is impossible.

4. **The weak do not understand the Force.** The Force is the ultimate means to gain authority over the weak. The weak do not understand the Force. The weak do not

sense the Force, therefore how can they understand or use the Force? So it is that the weak are at the mercy of those who know and use the power of the Force. The proper use of the Force can inspire awe and obedience in the weak.

It has been said that *anyone* who knows the ways of the Force can set her- or himself up as a King on any world where only she or he knows the ways of the Force. *Any* Jedi could do this. But the Jedi, fools that they are, adhere to a religion in which the Force is used only in the service of others.

How shortsighted of them. Is that not why they lost the galaxy to the dark side?

THE CREATION OF MONSTERS

Although the Force can be used to create terrifying illusions, it is sometimes more satisfying to create actual creatures that are willing and eager to shred and devour one's enemies on command. Such monsters are most useful when maintaining discipline and anxiety among subjects and enemies while one's attention is required elsewhere. These creations must be able to follow basic commands, but should not be designed with too much intelligence or self-awareness. Their function is first and foremost to serve their master.

A novice might begin with a small herbivore that appears relatively defenseless, some simple-minded thing at or near the bottom of the food chain. The goal is to transform the creature into something higher on the evolutionary ladder and considerably more ferocious.

Examine the creature for any natural attributes and abilities that can be augmented for maximum destructive potential. If the creature lacks teeth and claws, do not refrain from adding such features. If its eyes are set on either side of its head, revise the configuration to enable them to face their prey head-on, or add an entirely new set of eyes.

Strengthen muscles and bones, especially the jaw and along the spine.

Conquer the temptation to create specimens that are superior in every way. The danger of such monstrosities being turned against you is too great. Instead, focus on instituting controlling weaknesses into each and every beast you construct. Make it strong where you are weak, but weak where you are strong. It must have a fatal flaw that you—and only you—know how to exploit. And always, without fail, be prepared to destroy your most valued creation . . . or be prepared to be destroyed by it.

Do not disregard such practical aspects as whether the monster will be required to access standard doorways or travel upon floors that can support only a limited amount of weight. A large beast is a wondrous thing to behold, but it can also make an easy target.

Alterations should not be merely cosmetic. A monster is most effective when it is hungry and in some degree of pain. Selectively sever or expose nerve endings and alter the creature's internal organs so it has the energy to maintain itself and can digest what it consumes.

Training is also essential. To test your creature, set it loose in a pit or cage with at least a dozen members of its original species, preferably blood relatives. Should it fail to meet one's expectations, either in the categories of efficiency or ferocity, yet manage to emerge from the test relatively undamaged, you do not need to begin from scratch. Monsters can learn from experience, and can be fine-tuned by further enhancements and torture.

Of all the monsters I have created, I still regard Darth Vader as something of a minor masterpiece. No, he was not an entirely alchemical creation, but he was *my* monster nevertheless. Even though he failed to live up to his full potential, there was much pleasure in transforming Anakin Skywalker from a bright-eyed, tousle-headed youth into the greatest Jedi killer of all time. Yes, he ultimately turned against his Master, as monsters sometimes do, but that was my fault, not his. Given the opportunity to create Vader again, I would, and with zeal.

PART FIVE

OTHER FORCE-USING ORGANAZATIONS

RECORDED 40 B.B.Y. • AUTHOR: TIONNE SOLUSAR

Since the Battle of Endor, Luke Skywalker and other Jedi have encountered several Force-using organizations, and discovered evidence of similar groups that date back to antiquity. Some of these groups evolved entirely on their own, while others developed after some initial contact with—or influence by—the Jedi or Sith. This chapter offers concise histories of the more significant Force-using organizations and their respective philosophies on the Force.

FOLLOWERS OF PALAWA

A secretive group of hermits on Bunduki, a world in the Pacanth Reach, the Followers of Palawa was an ancient group of Force-users that may have predated the Jedi Order. Records suggest that they relocated to Bunduki after their homeworld, Palawa, was destroyed in a war that may have involved the Jedi Order. The Followers studied the Force and the science behind midi-chlorians, and also mastered a technique for falling into a deep trance that enabled them to sleep for decades without aging. Although the hermits were highly revered

by natives of Pacanth Reach, records indicate that many of the Followers turned to the dark side. The Followers developed their own martial art, teräs käsi—a term that translates as "steel hands"—to combat the Jedi.

One of the Followers of Palawa and a master of teräs käsi was Arden Lyn, the lover of the commander of the Legions of Lettow, General Xendor. After Xendor's death, Arden Lyn briefly assumed leadership of the Legions of Lettow until she dueled with the Jedi Master Awdrysta Pina. Allegedly, Lyn used a powerful talisman to annihilate Pina, but before the Jedi died he used the horrific technique of Morichro to arrest Lyn's body functions, stopping her heart. Although details remain unknown, it seems Lyn used the Palawa trance technique in combination with her talisman to survive in a suspended state for roughly twenty-five millennia.

SORCERERS OF TUND

Today the planet Tund in the Outer Rim is an uninhabited, irradiated wasteland, but for

◁ THE YSANNA OF OSSUS.
(Edwards)

thousands of years the once lush world was home to a group of Force-users known as the Sorcerers of Tund. The Sorcerers saw their abilities as a kind of magic, and presented themselves to the galaxy at large as powerful wizards.

The Jedi Order was long aware of the sorcerers' existence, and recognized their field of study as training in the Force. According to the Great Holocron, the Jedi Council periodically sent representatives to Tund; at first, these representatives attempted to persuade the sorcerers to join the Jedi Order so they might study the Force without the trappings of magic and mysticism, but the sorcerers—some of whom demonstrated powers at least as great as those of the Jedi recruiters—repeatedly declined. Eventually, the Jedi Council discreetly opted to allow the sorcerers to study the Force in their own fashion, but the Jedi continued to visit Tund to make sure that the sorcerers did not delve into the teachings of the dark side. Apparently, the sorcerers gave the Jedi no cause for concern, for it seems the two groups came to coexist without any tensions.

The Jedi Order's last official visit to Tund was well over a thousand years ago, before the New Sith Wars that eventually ended at the Battle of Ruusan. It is unknown whether the ancient Jedi attempted to enlist the sorcerers to join them in their fight against the Sith, but it seems they eventually forgot about the sorcerers altogether.

Imperial-era records indicate that Emperor Palpatine had a strong interest in the sorcerers, and allege that their religious teachings were based on an archaic interpretation of original Sith doctrine. Although these records are vague, it is known that the last Sorcerer of Tund, Rokur Gepta, allied himself with the Empire and acquired the *Wennis,* a decommissioned Imperial cruiser, along with an Imperial-trained crew that he commanded at his own discretion. The infamous smuggler-turned-entrepreneur Lando Calrissian had a series of encounters with Rokur Gepta, and mentioned the Sorcerer in his bestselling 22 A.B.Y. memoir, *How to Succeed in Everything.* An excerpt follows.

To tell the truth, even though the last Sorcerer of Tund is long dead, I'm not very keen on talking about him. Mind you, my disinclination isn't out of any respect. It's because he was the kind of scary that doesn't die easily, and not talking about him is the way I prefer to keep him dead.

His name was Rokur Gepta. The first time I saw him was in the Rafa system. I was sitting in an office, having a little chat with the colonial governor, when there was this small explosion. The blast formed a blue-black smoke column that evaporated into tiny orange sparks, and when the sparks winked out, there was this vaguely humanoid man standing there, wearing heavy, deep gray robes and a turban-like headdress that ended in bands of opaque cloth across his face.

To the best of my knowledge, nobody was ever quite sure what species the Tund wizards were, or even if they were all members of the same species. But I knew a thing or two about the sorcerers, like that they're boringly mysterious and given to flashy entrances. I wasn't immediately impressed. I figured this one had used a flash-bomb to make his big debut.

Then I noticed his eyes. They were like twin whirling pools of insane hunger of some sort. It was hard to look into those eyes without feeling like they would drive you mad, and I realized I may have misjudged his abilities. What did Gepta want? He'd been searching for a legendary treasure, the Mindharp of Sharu, in various ruins throughout the Rafa system, and after his hunts repeatedly came up empty, he decided to forcibly enlist me to do the job. As every archaeologist and anthropologist knows, I did find the Mindharp, but it was engineered to help restore the native Toka to their glory as the Sharu, and its power was more than Gepta could handle. I thought he died during the subsequent uprising on Rafa IV, but I'd misjudged him again.

A year later, I traveled to Oseon 5792, a planetoid that belonged to the trillionaire Bohhuah Mutdah, and was greeted by the impossibly corpulent Mutdah himself. At least that's who I thought *was* greeting me until my host transformed before my eyes into Rokur Gepta, who'd killed the real Mutdah. What happened next was most unpleasant. Gepta used his powers to manipulate my memories and torture me. At one point, he took a break to drone on about how after what happened in the Rafa system, his whole purpose for being was to make life miserable for me.

Fortunately, a squadron of Renatasian starfighters just happened to pick that particular moment to blast away at Oseon 5792, and I was able to escape. It was only as I was breaking free from the table that Gepta had secured me to that I realized his so-called powers involved some complex electronic equipment that he'd attached to the back of my head, which left me wondering about the limitations of the sorcerer's magic. I can thank my droid pal Vuffi Raa for the Renatasians coming when they did, even though he might have told me in advance why they were looking for him in the first place.

A few months after that, Gepta caught up with me at ThonBoka, where I was helping the Oswaft defend themselves against an Imperial armada. Gepta arrived in his warship and ordered the Imperial fleet to stand down. He gave me an ultimatum: Don space suits and go one-on-one in a duel to the death in the vacuum of space. If I won, the Imperials would leave. If he won, the Oswaft would become extinct and . . . well, I wasn't going to let that happen, was I?

I was allowed one weapon and Vuffi Raa's assistance. The latter was Gepta's idea. He said the droid could help make the fight fairer because I lacked "magic powers." Gepta was under the impression that Vuffi Raa's programming made him incapable of fighting. He didn't know that Vuffi Raa's tentacles could think for themselves.

The duel didn't last long. While Vuffi Raa kept Gepta busy, I blasted away at him, though he initially seemed immune. It wasn't until I squeezed off a shot that tore through the left ankle of his space suit that I did any real damage. Gepta's form withered and faded, leaving his space suit empty. Only I had a hunch it wasn't entirely empty.

I pawed through the suit until I found something down in the left leg. It was a small bundle of ugly, slimy tissue, resembling a half-cooked slug with a dozen skinny, hairy black legs. I recognized it as a Croke, an intelligent but remarkably nasty species, all masters of camouflage and illusion. Crokes are nearly impervious to hard vacuum, and this particular Croke was still alive. He was also responsible for more murders than you can count, friend, so no, I did not hesitate to squeeze that vicious thing to death, even though I knew it would be quite a chore to get the mess off my gloves.

The Imperials hadn't expected the Sorcerer of Tund to die, but they had no intention of honoring his deal. They opened fire on the Oswaft, but then Vuffi Raa's progenitors showed up. They were fifty-kilometer-wide metallic spheres, and there were thousands of them. They were . . . awesome. They only had to destroy one Imperial cruiser before the rest of the fleet withdrew.

If you want to watch the duel yourself,

the Star Destroyer Eminence's *holo-grammic log recorder caught the whole thing, and copies can now be found in most New Republic libraries. Parents be warned: the sight of all that slime on my gloves may not be suitable for small children.*

Although Rokur Gepta was able to use his innate powers to disguise himself, his use of technology to invade Lando Calrissian's mind suggests that his mastery of dark magic was incomplete. However, his skills were apparently adequate to permit him to infiltrate the Sorcerers of Tund, learn many of their secrets, and then annihilate them along with all life on their planet. Soil samples confirm that Gepta used a unique bioweapon—not the Force or "magic"—to lay waste to Tund. It remains unknown whether Emperor Palpatine was aware of Gepta's limitations as a sorcerer, but given the amount of Imperial power that Gepta had at his disposal, it seems that Palpatine had some degree of respect for the Croke.

BARAN DO SAGES

Thousands of years before the planet Dorin joined the Galactic Republic in 5975 B.B.Y., the native Kel Dor species identified the power of the Force and developed their own Force tradition. Known as the Baran Do Sages, this group of Force-sensitive Kel Dors studied the Force to expand their already exceptional senses as a means of predicting danger for their people. By using their powers to foresee the future, the past, and places far away, they not only proved an invaluable resource for investigating crimes and discovering the truth about mysterious events, but also succeeded in averting everything from natural disasters to wars. Because the Baran Do's predictions proved consistently reliable, they acted as advisers and seers for the leaders of Dorin. They eventually became so integrated into

society that various government institutions and businesses employed them as a part of their daily operations.

After Dorin joined the Republic, the Jedi welcomed the Force-sensitive Kel Dors to enter their ranks, and the Baran Do dwindled. However, those who were discounted by the Jedi or discovered too late to begin Jedi training continued to train under the remaining Baran Do Sages, who passed down their eons-old tradition as it was before the coming of the Jedi. Still, the Baran Do members became so few that their order faded into relative obscurity on their own world until Kel Doran society came to regard them as little more than wizards and prophets. By the time of the Clone Wars, the Baran Do were almost completely forgotten. As a result, they went virtually unnoticed when Darth Vader and the Imperial Inquisitors began hunting Force-sensitives, and they still exist today.

After the formation of the new Jedi Order, the Baran Do Sages contacted the Jedi and offered their help as well as their insights into the Force. In the following recording, made in 30 A.B.Y., the Baran Do Dorn Tlo explains the Baran Do philosophy and training methods:

Dear Jedi Masters,

The Baran Do Sages are aware that you know little of our order. We have attached records of Old Republic–era Jedi that attest to our long history, and welcome any questions you may have.

We have chosen to contact you now because we anticipate that the Jedi are evolving toward a different view of the Force. This view will regard the dark side as an essential part of the Force, something incapable of being completely shunned or conquered. The Baran Do have long maintained that the dark side is a necessary evil, as essential to the Force as death is to life. However, we also stress the importance of distinguishing between the light and the darkness. We anticipate that this evolving view will cause confusion, anxiety, and danger within the Jedi Order. All Jedi may not find solutions to their concerns in the ways of the Baran Do, but all will find we are very good listeners.

As you may know, the Kel Dors tend to see all moral issues in terms of black and white, and since our earliest civilization our judicial systems have advocated executions and punitive amputations for criminals. Although the Baran Do have never harmed an innocent or protected a murderer, the Kel Dors have gained an undeserved reputation as bloodthirsty executioners. This is unwarranted, for like the Jedi we kill only when we think, feel, and believe it necessary. But unlike the Jedi, we have a greater safety net for apprentices and members of the Baran Do. Because we can predict whether a Baran Do Sage might be drawn to the dark side, we have always been able to prevent this from happening.

The Baran Do philosophy revolves around quieting the mind and listening to the environment. It was this quiet, meditative outlook that led our ancestors into the study of the Force as a sensory aid. The ancient Baran Do learned to shut out the noise and clutter of the world around them and instead listen to the guidance of the Force. Our training focuses on meditative practices as well as the interpretations of sensations and visions. Many aspects of the training involve some form of sensory deprivation or sensory overload. An apprentice might be placed in a lightproof, soundproof chamber for hours or days, then be transferred to a loud, crowded room where the goal is to establish and maintain communication with a sage on the far side of the room. The training regimen is neither rigorous nor physically taxing, but encourages introspection and thoughtfulness at all times.

In short, the Baran Do listen, watch, and learn. When at peace, we are at our strongest. Generally, we take action only when we are sure of our path. Because we are not quick to act unless extremely pressed for time or reacting to some immediate threat, the ancient Jedi, as well our fellow Kel Dors, sometimes viewed us as inactive in our ways. However, we have seldom been inactive. Even during the Jedi Purge, we continued to help our people, usually discreetly and without their knowledge. We predicted and altered weather patterns, acted as foretellers and diviners, and protected the Kel Dors however we could.

For all our abilities at foresight, we were as stunned and surprised by the events that concluded the Clone Wars as the greatest Jedi Masters. We anticipate that some Jedi will now wonder why the Baran Do did not attempt to fight the Empire. The answer is simple: the Force told us that we were too few, and that we would be exterminated. And so we chose the path of patience, and so we endured.

We expect to hear from you. Trust that we will listen, and are willing to help the new Jedi Order to the best of our abilities.

Following the war with the Yuuzhan Vong, Jacen Solo traveled to Dorin and studied briefly with the Baran Do Sages. Jacen has yet to make a report on this experience.

MECROSA ORDER

Originally sworn to defend and protect the House Meceti, a coalition of noble families in the Tapani sector, the Mecrosa Order was founded in

approximately 4200 B.B.Y. by Viscountess Mireya, a native of Vjun who had married into the Meceti family. At some point over the next two centuries, the Mecrosa Order was corrupted, allegedly by Mireya herself, who had brought Sith teachings with her from Vjun. The Tapani sector was terrorized by the Sith-influenced Mecrosa Order for decades until the Jedi—soon after defeating Exar Kun in the Great Sith War—used their collective might to eliminate the Mecrosa in what came to be known as the Cleansing of the Nine Houses. Despite occasional rumors, it is believed that the Mecrosa Order was completely crushed.

THE KRATH

Founded by Aleema Keto and her cousin Satal Keto, son of the ruler of the Empress Teta system, the Krath began as a secret group with a fascination for artifacts from the time of the Great Hyperspace War. They dabbled in Sith magic and eventually came into contact with the spirit of Freedon Nadd, who offered to guide them in their study of the dark side. Soon Aleema and Satal used their newfound abilities to lead a rebellion against the government of the Empress Teta system.

The Jedi Ulic Qel-Droma led a small group of Jedi to deal with the Krath. After Ulic's master Arca Jeth was killed by a Krath-constructed war droid, Ulic swore to infiltrate the Krath and destroy them from within. Unfortunately, Ulic became the victim of Sith poison and was unable to stop himself from joining the dark side. Ulic killed Satal and joined Aleema to lead the Krath, but the Krath's power essentially came to an end when the Dark Jedi Exar Kun became the first Dark Lord of the Sith and Ulic became his first apprentice.

YSANNA

In 10 A.B.Y., Luke Skywalker and Kam Solusar discovered the Ysanna, a tribe of Force-sensitive humans on the planet Ossus in the Adega system. The Ysanna are the descendants of the Jedi who could not escape Ossus during the Sith-triggered Cron Supernova more than four thousand years earlier, but managed to survive in the vast subterranean caverns that run beneath the mountain ranges northwest of the ancient Jedi library.

Luke had learned of Ossus from the Tedryn Holocron, which identified the planet as a center of Jedi learning for thousands of years. Shortly after Luke and Kam arrived on Ossus, the Ysanna attempted to defend their world by attacking with projectile weapons that were enhanced through weak implementation of the Force. Over the course of generations, the Ysanna forgot their Jedi heritage and used their latent Force abilities as a form of atavistic magic. But when the Ysanna realized that Luke was a Jedi Master and understood his reasons for traveling to Ossus, they yielded and welcomed him.

Luke left Ossus with two Ysanna, a young woman named Jem and her brother Rayf, and began training them in the ways of the Force. The following year, Jem died while defending Luke from the reborn Emperor Palpatine's minions on New Alderaan. Shortly afterward, Rayf died while defending Anakin Solo from Palpatine on Nespis VIII.

Although the tragic deaths of Jem and Rayf left Luke justifiably hesitant to train more Ysanna, the Ysanna themselves fully supported his effort to rebuild the Jedi Order, and welcomed the new Jedi Order's decision to relocate its academy to Ossus.

PROPHETS OF THE DARK SIDE

In 9 A.B.Y., Kyle Katarn was helping to defend a New Republic outpost on Altyr V when he discovered ancient inscriptions that revealed the location of the Dark Force Temple on the swamp world Dromund Kaas, which lies in the Dromund system in Sith space. To learn whether the Empire had any awareness of this temple, Katarn traveled to Dromund Kaas to investigate, only to temporarily succumb to the pure Sith evil that permeated the place. When he was later found by Mara Jade, he engaged her in a duel, but Mara brought him back to the light by deactivating her lightsaber and surrendering, forcing him to choose between the darkness and her own life. Their discoveries at the temple allowed Jedi scholars to piece together parts of Dromund Kaas's history.

More than a thousand years ago, Dromund Kaas was the site of a battle between Sith and Jedi during the New Sith Wars, the interstellar conflict that ultimately ended when the Sith Lord Kaan detonated a thought bomb at the Battle of Ruusan. Years later, after Darth Bane had instituted the Rule of Two, the Sith Lord Darth Cognus either drove off or was abandoned by her apprentice, the three-eyed mutant Darth Millennial, who rejected the Rule of Two in favor of Lord Kaan's philosophy of Rule by the Strong. Fleeing to Dromund Kaas to escape the wrath of Darth Cognus, Darth Millennial meditated on Sith teachings and combined them with the theories of early and pre-Republic thinkers such as Plaristes and Dak Ramis to create a religion that he called the Dark Force. Millennial hailed himself as a prophet chosen by the will of the Force, and attracted many Force-users from across space.

The practitioners of the Dark Force became known as the Prophets of the Dark Side, and the most powerful members of their order were adept at using the Force to predict the outcome of future events. Although they continued to accept additional adherents to their religion, the Prophets took measures to ensure that Millennial's legacy remained unknown to the Sith—as well as the Jedi Order—for centuries.

Eventually, sometime before the Clone Wars, Palpatine's alter ego Darth Sidious discovered the Prophets and conscripted them as his advisers. Apparently, Darth Sidious consulted the Prophets almost as often as he looked into the dark side himself, making sure that all that he had foreseen would occur. He also entrusted them with the training of Dark Side Adepts, including the Force-sensitive Grand Admiral Nial Declann, and recruited the Prophet Cronal as one of his secret operatives.

Shortly after the Clone Wars began, the Jedi Master Yoda discovered that the Dromund system was one of some three dozen star systems—including Kamino—that had been deleted from the Jedi Archives and was missing from commonly used star charts. Evidently, the Jedi-turned-Sith Count Dooku was responsible for expunging this data from the Archives. So far, no records have revealed whether Yoda ever visited the Dromund system.

After Palpatine became Emperor, he brought to Coruscant the two most powerful Prophets of the Dark Side, the Supreme Prophet Kadann and the High Prophet Jedgar. Before the Clone Wars, Kadann had been a Jedi Knight, and Jedgar—disturbed by intense nightmares of future events throughout his childhood—abandoned the Jedi Order at age thirteen, after no Jedi Knight would accept him as a Padawan. According to Mara Jade, the Prophets and their loyal assistants reportedly fled Coruscant shortly after Palpatine left for the Endor system. Whether the Prophets of the Dark Side had foreseen the end of the Empire remains a mystery, as does their fate.

ZEISON SHA

Almost two thousand years before the rise of the Empire, a group of families and friends of the Jedi fled to the remote Outer Rim planet Yanibar to escape the initial conflicts that led to the New Sith Wars. The group's plan had been to establish a temporary refuge and wait for their Jedi relatives and allies to come for them when it was safe. However, it seems that all the Jedi who knew the location of this refuge were killed in battle, and the colony on Yanibar was forgotten.

Yanibar was a harsh world of seasonal extremes, and the original colonists might have perished had not some of them been Force-sensitive. Over the following centuries, their descendants developed a new Force tradition, the Zeison Sha, whose members used their talents to deal with the dangers native to Yanibar and defend the otherwise defenseless. The Zeison Sha came to regard their isolation as abandonment by the Jedi, and they focused their teachings on self-reliance and independence.

A few centuries after the formation of the original colony, fringe traders visited Yanibar and were surprised to find a relatively thriving settlement. The planet's inhabitants—a mix of humans and nonhumans including Duros, Twi'leks, and Rodians—maintained a relative measure of anonymity until the end of the New Sith Wars. Some Zeison Sha returned to the galaxy at large, but after the Jedi learned of their existence, they were alarmed that the Jedi were all too eager to appropriate their Force-sensitive children so that they might be raised as Jedi disciples on Coruscant. This only bolstered anti-Jedi sentiments among the Zeison Sha. The Jedi Bodo Baas, former keeper of the Tedryn Holocron, provided the following information:

580 B.B.Y.
Author: Bodo Baas

After many years of planning and preparations, I regret our diplomatic mission to Yanibar failed to convince the Zeison Sha of the Jedi Order's sincere hope that we might join forces. They remain cautious and distrustful of us, and only reluctantly welcomed us after we agreed that we would not attempt to meet their children unless adult Zeison Sha were present.

In fact, the Zeison Sha made it quite clear that they oppose the concept of separating Force-sensitive infants and children from their families. Their philosophy is so centered on being able to take care of oneself and one's family, and even I must admit that most Jedi, myself included, cannot entirely comprehend this form of devotion.

They did allow us to observe a Zeison Sha training session. I had heard that Zeison Sha are masters of the telekinetic powers, but I was astonished to see that their abilities in this area far surpass those of many Jedi. Not only do they use their telekinetic powers with apparently effortless ease, but they are also able to somehow wrap the Force around their bodies so that they can resist damage from harmful objects. Most remarkable.

Interestingly, they eschew energy weapons for something they call a discblade, a small metal circle with handgrips on the top and bottom; four thin, curved blades protrude from the circle's sides. The Zeison Sha warriors throw their discblades with extreme precision, and use the Force to return the weapon to their waiting hands.

I inquired whether their philosophy of self-reliance caused any losses to the dark side, and the Zeison Sha representatives acknowledged there had been some.

With all respect to their order, I pointed out that self-sufficiency can quickly turn to selfishness, and that incredible feats of telekinetic skill more often lend themselves well to attack rather than defense. Hearing my words, one of the of the younger Zeison Sha warriors, a Twi'lek female, stepped forward and said, "If not for self-reliance, our ancestors would have died shortly after your ancestors left them here."

Because this warrior's elders did not reprimand her, I could only assume they agreed with her assessment. Despite the Jedi Order's hope to reconcile, it seems that the Zeison Sha are determined to remain independent.

JENSAARAI

In 11 A.B.Y., Corran Horn and Luke Skywalker discovered the existence of the *Jensaarai*, Force-users who trained much as the Jedi did, even to the point of constructing and using lightsabers. Although the two Jedi perceived that the *Jensaarai* were not evil, they were astonished to learn that the *Jensaarai* had a strangely twisted view of history; for example, they equated Obi-Wan Kenobi with Darth Vader in terms of being a Jedi exterminator. It was eventually determined that the *Jensaarai* order was founded on various misconceptions and erroneous beliefs about the Jedi and Sith.

Subsequent research has revealed the following details about origins and evolution of the *Jensaarai*. During Exar Kun's reign as a Sith Lord more than four thousand years ago, Kun corrupted the Jedi Larad Noon to join the Brotherhood of the Sith. After Kun was defeated, Noon—apparently scarred by Sith ideology and the countless deaths he had caused—fled to the moon Susevfi, where he discovered a peculiar ore called cortosis. Cortosis was capable of rendering lightsabers inoperative

on contact, and Noon fashioned a suit of armor for himself, hoping it might protect him against any Jedi who might track him down. Despite this precaution, Noon was never found by the Jedi and died alone on Susevfi, survived only by his journal, which went unread for thousands of years.

During the Clone Wars, an Anzati Jedi named Nikkos Tyris left the Jedi Order, allegedly after studying a Sith Holocron he may have obtained from Count Dooku. Evidently, it was from this Holocron that Tyris falsely learned that Jedi had stolen their discipline from the Sith, and had perverted Sith teaching to prevent Force-users from following the true way to the Force. Tyris claimed he had found the *Saarai*, which translates from Sith as the "true way," and he attracted other Jedi as his followers. Tyris's pupils became known as *Jensaarai*, or "the hidden followers of truth," and they were united by their belief that the Jedi were evil.

In 19.5 B.B.Y., Corran Horn's grandfather, the Corellian Jedi Nejaa Halcyon, found Tyris and his pupils on Susevfi. Halcyon's duel with Tyris left both men dead, and most of Tyris's pupils were slain by other Jedi. The few surviving *Jensaarai*—whose incomplete training had left them ignorant of many facts but relatively uncorrupted—escaped and began searching for Sith texts that might help them defeat their "evil" adversaries. It was Tyris's primary apprentice who discovered Larad Noon's journal on Susevfi.

Noon's journal described his theory of *Jiaasjen*, a Sith word that translates as "integrating the shadow," which was an amalgamation of Noon's Jedi learning with his Sith experiences. Some scholars have since suggested that Noon may have developed his theory to keep himself from going insane with guilt and to justify the atrocities he committed during the Sith War. In any case, Tyris's primary apprentice drew from Noon's journal to create a new Force tradition, a unique blend of Sith and Jedi teachings. Shortly after Luke Skywalker's first encounter with the *Jensaarai*, the Jedi arrived at the following conclusion:

The Jensaarai were being taught the Jedi way by people who had accepted Sith thoughts and philosophies, but they themselves were not sufficiently developed to be initiated into them. Their masters had not yet found the hooks by which they could be opened to the dark side. And then, after the deaths of their masters, they continued learning, but did so with the orientation of protecting themselves from the Jedi. They dedicated themselves to defense—choosing the correct path for the wrong reasons.

After realizing that Luke Skywalker and his allies were not their enemies, Tyris's former primary apprentice, the *Saarai-kaar* or "keeper of the truth," and the *Jensaarai* made peace with the Jedi. The *Jensaarai* continue to exist as a small but separate organization, and have long enjoyed a student exchange program with the Jedi academy.

KORUNNAI

Less than a week after the Jedi Purge left the Jedi Temple in ruins, various Coruscant-based media outlets began distributing *The Private Journals of Mace Windu;* the contents of these journals readily convinced the general public that the Jedi Order had been scheming for years to conquer the Republic. In fact, Emperor Palpatine's propaganda architects were responsible for these particular *Journals,* but some scholars believe that the propagandists utilized actual recordings by Mace Windu to lend credence to their fabrications. Although the authorship of the following entry remains in question, the information is consistent with records of the planet Haruun Kal, and remains the best known account of the Korunnai.

215 B.B.Y.
Author (alleged): Mace Windu

The Al'Har system—of which Haruun Kal is the sole planet—lies on the nexus of several hyperspace lanes: the hub of a wheel called the Gevarno Loop, whose spokes join the Separatist systems of Killisu, Jutrand, Loposi, and the Gevarno Cluster with Opari, Ventran, and Ch'manss—all loyalist. Due to local stellar configurations and the mass sensitivities of modern hyperdrives, any ship traveling from one of these systems to another can cut several standard days off its journey by coming through Al'Har, even counting the daylong realspace transit of the system itself.

None of these systems has any vast strategic value—but the Republic has lost too many systems to secession to risk losing any to conquest. Control of the Al'Har nexus offers control of the whole region. It was decided that Haruun Kal is worth the Council's attention—and not solely for its military uses.

In the Temple Archives are reports of the Jedi anthropologists who studied the Korun tribes. They have a theory that a Jedi spacecraft may have made a forced landing there, perhaps thousands of years ago during the turmoil of the Sith War, when so many Jedi were lost to history. There are several varieties of fungi native to the jungles of Haruun Kal that eat metals and silicates; a ship that could not lift off again immediately would be grounded forever, and comm equipment would be equally vulnerable. The ancestors of the Korunnai, the anthropologists believe, were these shipwrecked Jedi.

This is their best explanation for a curious genetic fact: all Korunnai can touch the Force.

The true explanation may be simpler: we have to. Those who cannot use the Force do not long survive. Humans can't live in those jungles; the Korunnai survive by following their grasser herds. Grassers, great six-limbed behemoths, tear down the jungle with their forehands and massive jaws. Their name comes from the grassy meadows that are left in their wake. It is in those meadows that the Korunnai make their precarious lives. The grassers protect the Korunnai from the jungle; the Korunnai, in turn—with their Force-bonded companions, the fierce akk dogs—protect the grassers.

When the Jedi anthropologists were ready to depart, they had asked the elders of ghôsh Windu if they might take with them a child to train in the Jedi arts, thus recovering the Force talents of the Korunnai to serve the peace of the galaxy.

That would be me.

I was an infant, an orphan, called by the name of my ghôsh, for my parents had been taken by the jungle before my naming day. I was six months old. The choice was made for me.

I've never minded.

In 22 B.B.Y., a Coruscant spaceport came under siege by terrorists who claimed to be from Haruun Kal. The terrorists demanded that the Republic leave their planet because they did not want to enter the war between the Republic and the Confederacy of Independent Systems. All the terrorists were killed by a squad of clone commandos. Subsequently, an Imperial armada laid waste to Haruun Kal. If any Korunnai survived, their whereabouts remain unknown.

AING-TII

There are few records of the Aing-Tii, a group of Force-sensitive monks who live near the Kathol Rift. For decades, spacers only hinted at their existence, steering clear of the Aing-Tii's mammoth cigarra-shaped starships, which are etched with millions of glyphs and symbols. Rare images and holoclips reveal the Aing-Tii as two-meter-tall edentate mammals with jointed protective coverings of bony plates that are decorated with painted symbols; these markings resemble the ones that appear on the hulls of their ships. Some spacers say the Aing-Tii are waiting for an answer from "the Ones Who Dwell Beyond the Veil," presumably the area beyond the Kathol Rift.

Talon Karrde learned valuable information about the Aing-Tii in 19 A.B.Y. when he was searching for the Caamas Document, the notorious record that identified a group of Bothans who had participated in the devastation of the planet Caamas shortly after the end of the Clone Wars.

Like most spacers, I'd heard stories about the Aing-Tii, but I was as surprised as anyone when I saw their ships materialize in the Exocron system. I'd gone there looking for my former boss, Jorj Car'das, and the Caamas Document, but I'd been followed by the crime lord and slaver Rei'kas and his fleet.

I was with Admiral Trey David of the Exocron Combined Air–Space Fleet when the Aing-Tii ships arrived. Huge ovoid things, covered with thick hull plates that made them look like some sort of armored sea creature. No symmetry at all to the conical projections—I figured they were exhaust ports or thruster pods—that jutted from the hull. And when I say the ships materialized, I mean just that. There was no flicker of motion to indicate a normal hyperspace jump. They just appeared.

One of the Aing-Tii ships opened fire on one of Rei'kas's ships. Cut the thing in half. The slavers returned fire but didn't even scratch the Aing-Tii. David said that the Aing-Tii hated slavers, which soon became pretty obvious. The Aing-Tii blew away the rest of Rei'kas's fleet, then vanished just as quickly as they'd materialized.

On Exocron, my former boss, Jorj Car'das, told me more about the Aing-Tii. To make a long story short, he said he was dying when he'd had a run-in with Yoda on Dagobah years ago, and that Yoda told him that his only chance to postpone his death was to seek out the Aing-Tii monks of the Kathol Rift. Car'das wound up learning the ways of the Force from the Aing-Tii, which was a surprise to me because Car'das, by his own admission, wasn't a born Force-sensitive. He said the Aing-Tii have a different view of the Force, not in terms of black and white, like we think of Jedi and Dark Jedi, but more like a full-color rainbow. However, their actions against the slavers certainly proved that their view isn't so objective that it stops them from blowing up bad guys.

Car'das gave a demonstration of a very unusual skill he'd learned from the Aing-Tii. We were sitting around a table in his conversation room, and he made a decanter appear on the table. There was a sharp pop of displaced air as the decanter materialized. Said he'd "merely moved it" from his cooking area in an adjoining room, that all he had to do was envision that the decanter was already on the table in front of us. I've seen Skywalker and Mara do a lot of amazing things, but never anything like that.

Jacen Solo studied with the Aing-Tii, and confirmed that their ships do not travel through hyperspace but instantaneously materialize at any desired destination from one point of the galaxy to the next. While the technology behind this fantastic method of teleportation is barely comprehensible to anyone but the Aing-Tii, it is probable that they incorporate the power of the Force. According to Jacen, the Aing-Tii may have a symbiotic connection with their ships, yet have not developed their own Force abilities to any great effect. He added that they seem indifferent to Jedi, and refer to the Force as "a Gift from Those Beyond the Veil."

MATUKAI

Originating in the days of the Old Republic, the Matukai developed their Force tradition many years before the rise of Darth Bane and the New Sith Order. At that time in history, the Jedi Council was relatively lax with its views on Force-users and did not attempt to indoctrinate Force-sensitive children shortly after birth. What distinguished the Matukai from other organizations was the way by which they made their own bodies the primary focus for their abilities. While the Jedi traditionally meditated when they were not physically exercising, the Matukai used physical exercise as a form of meditation. In this capacity, all Matukai are masters of their own bodies.

Various records note that the first Matukai was a human female from the world of Karvoss II who discovered her ability to touch the Force while practicing a form of meditative martial arts. Although existing records have yet to reveal this woman's name, they indicate that she became a relatively strong presence in the Force and began teaching other Force-sensitive students, who in turn followed her example. The unique aspect of Matukai training is that it allows any beings with otherwise negligible inherent strength in the Force to develop it into something formidable using their bodies as a focus. Through basic meditative martial arts, physical exercises, and somatic rituals, they fan the spark of the Force inside them, hoping the spark will one day become a flame.

The basic philosophies of the Matukai revolve around a balance and harmony between the spiritual aspects of the Force and the physical aspects of the body. The general tenets of the Matukai include keeping the body clean and strong, purifying themselves through physical activity, focusing on the Force through exercise and ceremony, and avoiding any taint of the dark side. They also teach a sort of flexibility of spirit that entails never allowing oneself to become flustered or upset, and to always remain relaxed and stress-free. This enables their bodies to channel the Force with greater efficiency.

The Matukai never grew beyond fifty or sixty members at any given time, and were somewhat nomadic, without any base of operations. Still, the Jedi Council eventually recognized the growing power of the Matukai tradition and sent representatives to discuss a possible affiliation.

580 B.B.Y.
Author: Bodo Baas

Shortly after our failed diplomatic mission to Yanibar, we learned that a Matukai named Mendor Typhoons and two of his apprentices had defeated a gang of pirates near Ord Radama. A meeting was arranged in Ord Radama's orbit, and upon meeting Typhoons, I sensed he was a being with a good sense of humor. The way he smiled when he said that he felt that the Jedi method of teaching the Force was both elitist and ineffectual, and that he thought he could do a better job of training students than the Jedi Order could, he was so inoffensive and charming that I thought he was making himself the object of a self-deprecating joke. But he wasn't. He was serious. And I suddenly realized that he and his apprentices were even less interested in

allying with the Jedi than the Zeison Sha.

Because the Matukai generally draw from a pool of Force-users who would not qualify for Jedi training in the first place, I believe we should be content to let the Matukai exist as an autonomous organization, provided that they continue to steer clear of the dark side.

Like the Zeison Sha, the Matukai do not use lightsabers. Their weapon of choice is the wan-shen, a tall polearm with a single-edged blade on one end. The blade is forged and molded with the aid of the Force, making it exceptionally hard. The Matukai use the wan-shen as their external focus for the Force and can manipulate the weapon with great speed, using their bodies as the central axis to create a whirlwind of metal and blade.

Many Matukai were hunted down and killed by Imperial Inquisitors after the Jedi Purge, but the few survivors were able to preserve their Force tradition and pass it on to apprentices in secret. Some of these Matukai have chosen to join Luke Skywalker's Jedi academy, which has less stringent standards for admission than the old Jedi Council.

FORCE WITCHES

In the Old Republic era, countless primitive worlds boasted enclaves of Force-users known as Force witches, who—as their name indicates—drew their power from the Force. Because their worlds typically had low levels of technology, Force witches were isolated from Republic space, and many generations of witches were unaware of the existence and formalized training of the Jedi and the Sith. Therefore, most Force witches believed themselves to be unique in their special abilities, and developed their own traditions. The most dangerous were those who drew their power chiefly from the dark side; these dark Force witches preyed upon the weak to rule their respective worlds, which they were unlikely to leave unless they seized a starship from an unfortunate visitor.

Of all these cultures, the Force witches on the planet Dathomir in the Outer Rim are among the most noteworthy. Represented by matriarchal clans, they generally took their clan names from the locations that they respectively ruled. These eponymous clans included the Singing Mountain, Great Canyon, and Misty Falls clans. The original Dathomir Witches drew their power from the light side of the Force, and from exiled Witches who embraced the dark side. Unfortunately, the exiles eventually created their own clan, the Nightsisters, and frequently opposed their light-side rivals. The Nightsisters also splintered into various sects, and each took perverse pleasure in enslaving males and competing to determine who was the most brutal and dominant.

Records indicate that the earliest formation of Witch clans on Dathomir occurred in approximately 600 B.B.Y., after the Jedi Council banished a fallen Jedi Knight named Allya to Dathomir so that she might contemplate the living Force. At that time in history, Dathomir had long served as a prison colony for some of the Republic's worst criminals, who spent their every moment struggling to survive the monstrous rancors that roamed the planet's forests and plains. Allya used her Force abilities to subjugate the exiles and other desperate life forms, and constructed the foundation of a female-dominated society in which men had little or no power. She also tamed the rancors to do her bidding, and initiated a symbiotic relationship between rancors and Witches that continues to this day. A rancor named Tosh, herd leader of the Singing Mountain Clan's rancors, provided (in 6 A.B.Y.) the following narrative, which had been passed down over many generations:

> Listen, children, to the story of how our ancestors first met the Witches.
>
> A sickly female rancor met a Witch who healed her, and the Witch rode on the rancor's back, and learned to speak the rancor's tongue. By riding the rancor's back, the Witch was able to spot food better with her sharp eyes that see well even in the daylight, and the rancor thrived and became huge. In time, she became a herd mother, and her herds prospered while others died out.
>
> Back then, the rancors did not know how to make fine weapons like spears or nets. They did not know how to protect themselves with armor. Because the Witches have taught them such great things, the rancors must always love the Witches and serve them, even when they make unreasonable demands to give them rides through the wilderness or ask us to fight the Nightsisters.
>
> Never serve the Nightsisters, children. They'll treat you badly, as if you were mere slaves. Their taste is foul, so it is best to crush them. If you cannot crush them, then escape from them, for then you can continue to serve the good Witches, and hope to crush the Nightsisters another day.

Allya wrote her "spells" in *The Book of Law,* a text that was based loosely on the Jedi Code. Originally, this book of advice was intended to guide Allya's female children in the safe and sane use of their "magic." Over many generations, Allya's descendants scattered and created new clans, but each clan made a copy of *The Book of Law.* Kirana Ti, a Dathomir Witch of the Singing Mountain Clan who became one of the first students at Luke Skywalker's Jedi academy on Yavin 4, provided the following excerpt to illustrate Allya's central message:

> Daughters of Allya,
> Learn these words and learn them well, for they are the foundation that will increase your strength and keep you safe from harm.
>
> Those who suffer emotion will never enjoy peace.
>
> Those who choose ignorance will never know their own greatness.

Those who yield to passion will fail to dominate.

Those who fear death will never achieve pure power.

Never forget that your magic must always be used wisely.

Never concede to evil, lest you be consumed by it.

Although Allya's message is similarly transcribed in other copies of *The Book of Law,* it should be noted that each clan subsequently added its own discoveries and spells to its respective books, and that Allya's original text has been largely replaced by various interpretations. Allya's descendants further corrupted the Force into something that resembled a form of shamanistic magic.

Apparently, the Jedi Council made no effort to monitor Allya's progress or legacy, for the Witches of Dathomir did not come to the Old Republic's attention until approximately 340 B.B.Y., when the massive Jedi training vessel *Chu'unthor* crashed on the planet. The Jedi Masters Yoda, Gra'aton, and Vulatan led a team of Jedi Knights to rescue the ship's passengers and fought the "spell-casting" natives, but the Witches and their rancors sent the Jedi fleeing back into orbit. Yoda eventually negotiated a settlement with Rell of the Singing Mountain Clan: Yoda promised that the Republic would stay away from Dathomir until, he prophesied, a future Jedi would come to defeat the Nightsisters. Yoda left the *Chu'unthor* behind along with reader disks about the Jedi, but would not give the Witches the technology to access them because, according to Rell, "the teachings were too powerful." Yoda assured Rell that the Jedi who defeated the Nightsisters would share the recorded data with the surviving clans.

The Great Holocron yields no information about the fate of the *Chu'unthor,* and has so far revealed no data whatsoever about Dathomir. In fact, if the Old Republic had *any* records of Dathomir, it seems that all but one—a damaged computer cylinder that Luke Skywalker discovered in the ruins of an unknown Jedi Master's post-Purge hideout on the planet Toola in 8 A.B.Y.—were deliberately deleted. Evidently, the Jedi erased the records to maintain their centuries-long interdiction of Dathomir. Although the deletion of records may have seemed the best way to prevent others from falling into the Witches' clutches, it is disturbing to current scholars that this action also served to conveniently cover up the fact that a preceding Jedi Council had been responsible for banishing Allya to Dathomir in the first place.

Fortunately for historians, the Jedi Witches of Dathomir kept oral as well as written records. Despite the pact that assured the Jedi would stay away from Dathomir, there are several Dathomirian accounts that describe a Jedi-like warrior—*not* the one of Yoda's prophecy—who arrived on Dathomir and fought a clan of Nightsisters around 30 B.B.Y. According to Voren Na'al, archivist emeritus of the Historical Council, the Jedi was Quinlan Vos, who prevented a Nightsister named Zalem from using an ancient teleportation device called the Infinity Gate—allegedly built by the pre-Republic Kwa species—to obliterate Coruscant. However, Voren Na'al acknowledges that virtually all the information related to this mission was drawn from a single source: a woman named Ros Lai, who claimed to be a former Nightsister in a memoir she apparently self-published in 28 B.B.Y. Efforts to confirm Ros Lai's identity or fate have so far been unsuccessful.

In 8 A.B.Y., Luke Skywalker learned of the *Chu'unthor* and Dathomir from the aforementioned record found on Toola. He traveled to Dathomir, where he quickly realized that the Witches were Force-users, and ultimately assisted the beleaguered clans to temporarily defeat the Nightsisters. Since the founding of the Jedi academy on Yavin 4, several Witches of Dathomir have successfully trained to become Jedi.

THE REBORN

In 12 A.B.Y., the Chistori Jedi student Desann killed Havet Storm, a fellow Jedi apprentice, and fled Yavin 4. Allying with Imperial admiral Galak Fyyar, Desann began experimenting with Sith alchemy and artusian crystals to artificially imbue human Empire Youths—who had previously displayed little or no talent in the Force—with dark side powers. Brought to Ruusan, the Empire Youths found that their innate powers had quadrupled. Desann named this new militia the Reborn.

Soon the Reborn came to the attention of the Jedi academy. Despite magnified Force powers, the barely trained Reborn were no match for the more disciplined Jedi. Aided by Luke Skywalker and Lando Calrissian, Kyle Katarn defeated Admiral Fyyar before he confronted and killed Desann on Yavin 4.

DISCIPLES OF RAGNOS

Three years after the defeat of Exar Kun's spirit on Yavin 4, Kyle Katarn and Jedi academy trainee Jaden Korr learned of a new Sith cult, and that the spirit of Dark Lord of the Sith Marka Ragnos had survived in the tombs of Korriban. The cult, known as the Disciples of Ragnos, was founded by the Dark Jedi Tavion Axmis, who had discovered the Scepter of Ragnos, a Sith relic that was strong with Force energy and housed Marka Ragnos's ancient Sith sword. Tavion resurrected and was quickly possessed by Ragnos's spirit, but Jaden Korr defeated them and brought an end to the cult.

SHADOW ACADEMY

In 23 A.B.Y., four years after the Pellaeon–Gavrisom treaty officially ended the war between the Empire and the New Republic, the Jedi became aware of a new threat: the Dark Jedi Brakiss, a failed student of Luke Skywalker's Jedi academy, had founded the Shadow Academy, a mobile, hyperdrive-capable, torus-shaped battle station with a cloaking device. Brakiss headed the Shadow Academy on behalf of the Second Imperium, a radical group headed by four of the late Emperor Palpatine's most loyal personal guards, who refused to recognize the peace accords and used the station as a training center for a new legion of Dark Jedi and stormtroopers. Initial Force-using recruits came from the Nightsisters of Dathomir, and the Nightsister Tamith Kai assisted Brakiss as an instructor.

The leaders of the Second Imperium had outfitted the cloaked battle station with chain-reaction explosives, which they promised to detonate if they ever became displeased with the Shadow Academy's progress. After Brakiss and Tamith Kai failed to destroy the Jedi academy on Yavin 4, the Shadow Academy was destroyed along with its leaders.

FALLANASSI

In 16 A.B.Y., Luke Skywalker met the Force-sensitive Akanah Norand Pell and became aware of her affiliation with the Fallanassi. Also known as Adepts of the White Current, the Fallanassi are a mysterious religious order made up of Force-using females who can manipulate reality. Like the Witches of Dathomir, the reclusive Fallanassi have developed their own traditions over time, but rather than using their powers to dominate, they practice pacifism and submit to the source of their power, the "White Current." Although Luke observed that the White Current and the Force were one and the same, the Fallanassi maintain that their own religion more truly embraces the light, and they do not approve of how Jedi use the Force to accomplish their goals.

If the Fallanassi themselves know anything of the origins of their order, they have yet to disclose significant details. Imperial-era records indicate that they may have existed for many years in secret on the planet Lucazec until one of the order's members—Akanah's mother, Isela Talsava Norand—revealed their existence to Lucazec's Imperial governor. Hoping to utilize the Fallanassi and their powers, the Empire offered its protection to the Fallanassi in exchange for an oath of loyalty. The Fallanassi refused and fled.

After hiding on various worlds, the Fallanassi finally settled in the Koornacht Cluster on the planet Doornik-628E, which had been renamed J't'p'tan by peaceful H'kig pilgrims. The H'kig had fled their own homeworld to escape religious persecution and build the Temple of the Infinite Spirit on J't'p'tan, where they welcomed the Fallanassi. In 17 A.B.Y., both the Fallanassi and H'kig nearly met their doom when the genocidal Yevetha began exterminating all non-Yevethan settlements in the Koornacht Cluster. Instead of using their formidable powers as a weapon against the Yevetha, the Fallanassi merged the H'kig temple with the White Current to create an illusion of a great ruin; when the Yevetha arrived in J't'p'tan's orbit, the illusion deceived them into believing the H'kig were already destroyed.

Luke persuaded the Fallanassi leader, Wialu, to create an illusion of a New Republic "phantom fleet" that ultimately helped bring an end to the Yevethan threat at the Battle of N'zoth. With the Yevetha defeated, the Fallanassi felt they were no longer needed on J't'p'tan. Eventually, they relocated to Pydyr, a moon of Almania, which had been decimated by the Dark Jedi Kueller.

In 35 A.B.Y., Jacen Solo traveled to Pydyr to study the White Current in order to gain a greater understanding of the Force, and received some training from Akanah. The following recording was sent to Luke Skywalker shortly after Jacen left Pydyr. Although Akanah expressed concern about Jacen leaving the moon before his training was complete, it should be noted that Luke had reason to be cautious of Akanah, which is why he turned this recording over to me for analysis. According to Luke, after he met Akanah, she deliberately misled him about the identity of his mother in an apparently desperate effort to enlist him to help her find her own missing parents and the relocated Fallanassi. Evidently, he has not communicated with her since the Battle of N'Zoth.

Luke Skywalker. It is I, Akanah of the Fallanassi.

Nearly two decades ago, I lied to you about the identity of your mother. My motives were selfish and unpardonable. Despite my apologies and that I have strived ever since to uphold the values of the Fallanassi, I feel—even from far across the galaxy—that you still and always will distrust me. This remains my greatest regret.

I must assume you are aware that your nephew, Jacen Solo, has spent the past five years searching for, as he puts it, "the true nature of the Force." His search brought him to Pydyr. Although I sensed that he was more interested in gaining knowledge of the White Current than immersing himself in it, I granted his request to study with us out of respect to you, because I still feel I am in your debt.

The Fallanassi had heard that since the war against the Yuuzhan Vong, the Jedi have developed a new view of the Force, that you now believe that it embraces more than simply light or darkness. I admit, I have difficulty understanding this. With all respect, if the Jedi no longer look to the light, how can they serve it? You once told me that the White Current was not unlike the Force, but our philosophies are so very different. It troubles me to think that the Jedi now regard themselves as beyond light and dark, beyond good and evil.

I told Jacen that it was an error of pride that Jedi believe they can use the Force instead of submitting to it, and in this pride they have caused more suffering than they have prevented. With so much power and without a guiding light, might the Jedi cause more harm than good?

I acknowledge that I have limited understanding of Jedi, and that Jacen may have decided to end his training on Pydyr because of our disparate beliefs. But you said once that the Force is a river from which many can drink, and the training of the Jedi is not the only cup that can catch it. Because you may still believe this, I hope you will at least respect my concern for Jacen and also for you. So long as the Jedi make no distinction between the light and darkness, it is not enough to trust and believe that the Force will guide you in your decisions and actions.

Thank you for listening to me, Luke. I hope that the light is with you always, and that this message finds you well.

PART SIX

THE CHOSEN ONE

RECORDED 40 A.B.Y. · AUTHOR: TIONNE SOLUSAR

Because some Jedi have been able to use the Force to anticipate possible future events, it is not surprising that Jedi records relate various accounts of prophecies. The Great Holocron contains many references to the prophecy of the Chosen One:

> A Jedi will come
> To destroy the Sith
> And bring balance to the Force.

Records are unclear about this prophecy's exact origin, or whether the above words were the actual prophecy or a concise interpretation. Several accounts indicate that the prophecy was the subject of debate as far back as twelve hundred years ago, but it may in fact be much older. However, records do establish that approximately two hundred years before the Battle of Yavin, Jedi Masters became aware of an abrupt change in the shape of the Force, and many believed that a looming sense of dread pointed to the growing power of the dark side; some Jedi suggested that the Sith had returned, while others—maintaining that the Sith were extinct—dismissed this notion. But as time passed without any indication of Sith activity, the Jedi Master Yoda proposed that the gathering darkness was a sign of the coming fulfillment of the prophecy of the Chosen One. According to Master Yoda via the Great Holocron:

> Fully defeated by just anyone, the dark side cannot be, but only by the Chosen One. And who might be this Jedi? Know I

do not, but not yet born is he or she. This much, sense I can. A vessel of pure Force the Chosen One will be, more powerful than any Jedi in history.

Records reveal only occasional references on the subject of the Chosen One until 32 B.B.Y. It was in that year that the Jedi Master Qui-Gon Jinn told the Jedi Council on Coruscant that he believed he had found the Chosen One in the form of Anakin Skywalker. Evidently, this belief was prompted by Qui-Gon Jinn's discovery of Anakin's midi-chlorian count, which was by all accounts higher than any Jedi on record.

Was Anakin Skywalker the Chosen One? Contemporary Jedi have noted that Anakin and his alter ego, Darth Vader, were responsible for countless deaths, yet he ultimately returned to the light and defeated Emperor Palpatine at the Battle of Endor; furthermore, Anakin's own death, it seemed, brought an end to the Sith Order *at the time*. Palpatine's subsequent resurrection attests to the fact that Anakin did not completely destroy the Sith, leaving some to suggest that he failed to fulfill the prophecy, and wonder whether the prophecy has yet to be fulfilled. Some Jedi scholars have even suggested the possibility that an unknown Sith Lord conceived the prophecy as part of the Sith Order's long-term plan to conquer the galaxy, but this remains purely speculative.

Now, at a time when the Sith have once again revealed their existence, it may be overly generous

◀ SHMI SKYWALKER WATCHES THE JEDI MASTER QUI-GON JINN TAKE A BLOOD SAMPLE FROM ANAKIN SKYWALKER ON TATOOINE. *(Edwards)*

to say that Anakin Skywalker fulfilled the prophecy *from a certain point of view.* Still, all Jedi should be aware of his accomplishments and failings; his biography is not only a caution to the dark side but also a reminder that Sith Lords generally do not begin their lives as evil beings.

Because many official records of the Jedi were expunged, altered, or lost after Emperor Palpatine seized control of the Republic, there are relatively few records of Anakin Skywalker. If Anakin or Vader himself ever left a complete record, it has yet to be found. Anakin's actual birthplace remains unknown, but various sources confirm that he was born into slavery, probably in the Outer Rim Territories. It should be noted that slavery was illegal throughout the Republic at the time of his birth, but that Republic laws were seldom enforced in the Outer Rim.

It is believed that Anakin was about three years old when he and his mother, Shmi Skywalker, arrived on Tatooine, and that they were the property of Gardulla the Hutt. Not long after their arrival, they were acquired by a Toydarian junk dealer named Watto, who evidently obtained them by gambling with Gardulla. Implanted explosive transmitters discouraged the Skywalkers from escaping their masters.

Eight years after the Battle of Yavin, Leia Organa Solo obtained a datapad that had previously belonged to Anakin's mother, Shmi Skywalker. According to messages on the datapad, Anakin was nearly ten years old and had spent most of his childhood as a slave when Qui-Gon Jinn found him on Tatooine. Just five years ago, the astromech droid R2-D2 yielded recordings that shed light on the circumstances of Anakin's conversion to Darth Vader. More recently, the Great Holocron has provided even more accounts of Anakin's life, allowing us to assemble the most detailed biography to date.

TATOOINE CHILDHOOD

Recorded in 8 A.B.Y.
Author: Leia Organa Solo

My mission to Tatooine hardly went as expected. Han, Chewbacca, C-3PO, and I went in search of the Alderaanian moss-painting Killik Twilight, *which Lando Calrissian informed us had turned up on Tatooine and was scheduled to be auctioned at Mawbo's Performance Hall in Mos Espa. When Alderaan was destroyed,* Killik Twilight *was returning from a museum loan on Coruscant, and that was the last anyone knew of it for years. We'd hoped to bid on it without attracting attention to ourselves, but . . . I don't believe it's wise to go into details at this time, but I will say that our primary interest in acquiring the painting was cultural preservation.*

What I didn't expect was that the mission would evolve into a series of discoveries about my biological father, Anakin Skywalker. I might have anticipated at least some of what I learned if I hadn't so deliberately avoided any interest in his life. At some point, Luke had told me that he'd learned from the HoloNet that Anakin had grown up on Tatooine, but I know for a fact he never told me that Anakin had lived in Mos Espa, something I wish I'd known beforehand.

Sorry, I'm being unfair. Every time Luke mentioned anything about our father, I just shut him out. I didn't want to know. I didn't need to be reminded that I was related to Darth Vader. Whenever I thought of him, I still saw him overseeing my torture on the Death Star, or remember him standing behind me as Alderaan exploded, or ordering Han frozen in carbonite. Not exactly fond memories.

Anyway, after we arrived at the auction in Mos Espa, I was surprised to find myself distracted from our mission by an old holocube that was up for bid. The holocube showed an image of a blue-eyed young boy standing in front of a Podracer cockpit. His eyes reminded me of Luke's, and made me remember a strange dream I'd had earlier on the Millennium Falcon, just before we'd arrived on Tatooine. The dream had been...unnerving as well as strange, a vision of Tatooine's twin suns and a dark nebula transforming into Vader's helmet, then shifting into Luke's face. Even though I've come to understand that many of the diplomatic "gifts" I once attributed to intuition were really the glimmerings of Force sensitivity, I initially dismissed the dream. I shouldn't have, for I now realize it foretold that I would find on Tatooine a path to the Skywalkers' past.

Han tried to buy the holocube for me, but I made it more than clear that I wanted nothing to do with the thing. It wound up being bought by a Gotal for thirteen hundred credits. I eventually learned that the holocube had been put up for auction by Kitster Banai, a childhood friend of Anakin. I met Kitster as well as Wald, who'd also known Anakin as a boy, and I encountered others who'd known Anakin's mother. I even met an old Podracer pilot who once competed against Anakin, and who swore up and down that Anakin was one of the only pilots who never cheated. I found myself flummoxed to hear so many people speak of my father with such fondness and admiration, but then they had only known him as Anakin, and none of them ever saw him again after he left Tatooine. Wald absolutely refused to believe that his friend had become Darth Vader.

Years ago, Luke sold the place where

he was raised by Owen and Beru Lars to Siyla Darklighter and her husband, Jula. Last month, their daughter Anya found a datapad on the property. They knew it was old and didn't belong to them, so they set it aside, planning to forward it to Luke, but gave it to me instead. This datapad turned out to be a journal made by Anakin's mother, Shmi Skywalker. My grandmother. Her journal covers a ten-year period, and almost all of her entries are addressed to Anakin. Obviously, she had hoped to share it with him someday.

And so on Tatooine I learned that Anakin and Shmi, as well as Kitster and Wald, had been slaves. At age nine, Anakin met a Jedi named Qui-Gon Jinn, then won his freedom—along with a sum of credits—in a Podrace called the Boonta Eve Classic. I don't yet know Qui-Gon Jinn's exact role in the situation, but the following excerpt from Shmi Skywalker's journal seems to offer some explanation:

I can't tell you how I struggled with the decision to let you race for Qui-Gon that day. When you noticed his lightsaber, you were so convinced he had come to free the slaves...it crushed me to hear him tell you the truth. But as Qui-Gon himself said, you give without thinking of yourself. How could I say no when you hatched your plan to win the parts they needed to repair their ship?

A slave boy helping a Jedi. To me, it seemed matters should have been the other way around. I would have said no, and I know you would have forgiven me. But you wouldn't have forgotten, either. For the rest of your life, you would have remembered the Boonta Eve and how your mother wouldn't let you help a Jedi. And that wouldn't have been fair to you. I couldn't deny you the chance to be the hero you dreamed of.

Anakin was unable to buy his mother's freedom, something that must have pained him more than anyone imagined. He left Tatooine with Qui-Gon Jinn, who had promised to bring him to the Jedi Temple on Coruscant. Eventually, Shmi learned from a messenger, a female Falleen who might have been a Jedi, that Qui-Gon Jinn was slain at the Battle of Naboo, but was consoled by the knowledge that Anakin had been accepted for Jedi training. The Falleen also brought a gift from Qui-Gon Jinn, a valuable Tobal lens that Shmi eventually used to gain her freedom from Watto. Shmi wound up marrying a moisture farmer named Cliegg Lars, whose son Owen would later raise Luke.

Before he left Tatooine, Anakin gave some credits to Kitster, who used them to buy a flimsiplast copy of Par Ontham's Guide to Etiquette; a purchase he believes ultimately helped him secure his own freedom. Anakin also left behind a design for a swoop, which his mother gave to Kitster and Wald. Wald eventually used the plans to build a swoop that he flew in a race to win his freedom. Clearly, young Anakin Skywalker was an inspirational person to those who knew him on Tatooine, and a very different individual from Darth Vader.

ADDENDUM BY
TIONNE SOLUSAR

Leia Organa Solo's record resumes with her account of Anakin's return to Tatooine, ten years after the Battle of Naboo.

Although there are records of various Falleen Jedi, I have been unable to identify the messenger who delivered the Tobal lens to Shmi Skywalker.

It can now be revealed that the painting Killik Twilight contained a hidden code key for Shadowcast, a secret communications network that transmitted Rebel messages encrypted within Imperial propaganda programming via the HoloNet. Leia Organa Solo's allusion to "cultural preservation" referred to her desire to preserve the painting as well as maintain security for the Rebel agents whose lives and operations depended on the secrecy of Shadowcast.

PODRACER CHAMPION

11 A.B.Y.

Author: Teemto Pagalies

Hi. I'm Teemto Pagalies. From Tatooine. I hope this message reaches, um, Leia Organa Solo. Maybe you remember me? We met here, on Tatooine, about three years ago. I work for a lady named Ulda. At the Mos Espa Arena. Only I didn't know who you were at the time.

After you found out I was a Podracer, you asked me some funny questions about Anakin Skywalker, like if he ever cheated at Podracing. I thought that was a laugh. Since then, I learned some stuff from guys I know. Maybe you also remember Ody, Wald, and Kitster?

Anyway, I wasn't nosing around. It's just that some people talk. And sometimes I listen. Like Ody telling me that you wanted to buy that swoop to go looking for Kitster. Then a few days after you talked with me, I run into Wald. He was fuming. Said he met a lady who claimed that Anakin Skywalker grew up to be Darth Vader, and that he told her it was a lie. I had to agree with him, it sounded crazy. But I asked him what the lady looked like. He gave a good description.

And then a few weeks after that, I hear Ulda talking to some moisture farmers, and the name Skywalker comes up. I figured out they're talking about Anakin's mother, and about a diary that wound up going to Anakin's daughter. And I figured they're talking about you.

So a couple of years go by. But then just a few weeks back, we got the news about a new Jedi academy starting up. There was a vid about it that showed you and your brother. I recognized you straight off.

Then last week, Kitster comes out here to get yelled at by Ulda about something. They used to be married, you know. Anyway, when they're done, I go right up to Kitster— because I'd figured he was somehow connected to whatever you were doing on Tatooine—and I ask him, "Is it true that Anakin Skywalker became Darth Vader?"

Kitster glared at me a millisecond, then shrugged and said, "What do you think?"

I can still see pretty well with the one eye I've got left. Well enough to know when someone's trying to dodge me.

Well, I remembered our little conversation from three years ago. I told you I had a vid of the Boonta Eve Classic that your father won. I made a copy of it for you, and I'm transmitting it along with this message. Because for some reason, I want you to see what I saw that day. I want you to see that the kid never cheated. Not once, even when he could've. Anakin Skywalker was great. A Podracer champion, through and through. I don't know if that's important to you, but it is to me.

I don't know what else to say. All this talking has made my throat dry. I guess that's it.

Bye.

ARRIVAL AT THE JEDI TEMPLE

Recorded 32 B.B.Y.
Author: Jedi Master Ki-Adi-Mundi

Meditation is difficult.

Several months ago, I pursued the criminal Ephant Mon to Tatooine. At the time, I did not know of Anakin Skywalker's existence, let alone that Tatooine was his homeworld. The galaxy seemed less complicated then, when I believed the Sith were extinct. But upon meeting Skywalker, who is absolutely teeming with midichlorians and may very well be the Chosen One, I could not help questioning my own perceptive abilities.

Time and again, the Force has guided my heart and my weapon. I trust my most powerful ally, but cannot dismiss a sense of personal failure. I was on Tatooine before Qui-Gon Jinn discovered the boy. Although I sensed a disturbance in the Force there, how could I have not sensed the presence of one so strong with the Force? It is not that my own powers are more considerable than Qui-Gon's were, but that Skywalker is a beacon of power.

It is little consolation that every member of the Jedi Council was surprised by recent events: the discovery of Skywalker, the death of Qui-Gon Jinn, and the return of the Sith. Despite our initial refusal to allow Skywalker to be trained to become a Jedi, none of us anticipated the circumstances that would prompt us to revise our decision. This troubles us all.

Now evidence has surfaced that Sharad Hett may be alive, and once again I am traveling to that haven of mirages and lies called Tatooine. Before I left Coruscant, the Dark Woman herself told me she has had dreams of great dangers that await me at my destination. She has never given me any reason to dismiss the value of her dreams.

Tatooine cannot be a coincidence. I do not believe in coincidences.

"Events are moving too fast." Those were my own words, addressed to Qui-Gon on the occasion of the Council's decision to reject his request to train young Skywalker. So much has happened since then. I find it troubling that I am unable—even during meditation—to entirely suspend those words from my mind.

What disturbs me most of all is Anakin Skywalker himself. It is not in my nature to make assumptions about anyone based on appearance, and yet I find it almost alarming that the boy looks so entirely un-remarkable. If I didn't know better, I would have dismissed him as a harmless raga-muffin. His responses to our tests showed he was incredibly adept at using the Force to anticipate the immediate future, but could he really have been conceived by the midi-chlorians, as Qui-Gon suggested? And if he is the Chosen One, destined to bring balance to the Force, why do I sense some danger about this boy, as if he is a threat? I wish I knew.

Like Anakin, I was well past infancy when I began my training at the Jedi Temple. There was much concern about whether I was too old to learn the ways of the Force, that my Cerean childhood might cloud my judgments, but . . . I am not certain of how to express myself. My mind tells me I should feel empathy for Anakin, but my instinct tells me something else. Jedi are trained not to feel fear, but I believe that this may be the discomfort

I sense from Anakin. No, I'm not afraid of him. He is, after all, merely a boy. But as a father myself, I can positively attest that children can grow in unexpected ways, and this may be what I fear: not who Anakin Skywalker is, but what he might become.

With respect to Qui-Gon's memory, I will make every effort to treat Anakin as I would any Padawan, but I intend to be much more mindful of him than others. And given that the Sith have resumed their dark enterprise, I shall take some consolation in the knowledge that Anakin was not discovered by them instead.

ADDENDUM BY
TIONNE SOLUSAR

The preceding recording was made by Ki-Adi-Mundi during a voyage on a Republic Cruiser to the planet Tatooine, shortly after his first meeting with Anakin, and was found in a datapad among a collection of personal artifacts donated to the new Jedi library by Ki-Adi-Mundi's descendants on Cerea. According to the Great Holocron, Ki-Adi-Mundi was four years old when the Jedi known as the Dark Woman discovered him and brought him to the Jedi Temple on Coruscant. As previously noted, Ki-Adi-Mundi did find the renegade Jedi Knight Sharad Hett, whose son A'Sharad Hett became Ki-Adi-Mundi's Padawan apprentice.

JEDI TRAINING

Recorded 29 B.B.Y.
Author: Obi-Wan Kenobi

It has been three years since Anakin Skywalker became my Padawan learner. His powers continue to grow, and all of his instructors at the Jedi Temple acknowledge that his abilities exceed those not only of other students his age but of many instructors as well.

However, every Jedi Master has also noted that Anakin continues to exhibit behavior and emotions that are characteristic of Force-users who did not begin Jedi training at infancy. As might be expected of anyone who has been liberated from slavery, he can be outspoken regarding social injustices. I have assured him that all Jedi must develop a sense of patience, something he has difficulty maintaining. Of greater concern are his impulsiveness, competitiveness, and occasional arrogance. I admit there have been several times that I have been at a loss for words for his actions. I must remind myself of various instances when I confounded or disappointed my own Master, and that I, too, was once impatient to become a Jedi.

As my Padawan, Anakin has become a strong part of my life, yet he remains something of a mystery to me. Recently, I found him gazing up at the night sky. Although Coruscant's atmosphere is too polluted for stargazing, I suspected he was looking in the direction of the Tatooine system. I know that from an orbital skyhook, Tatooine's twin suns would appear to the naked eye as a dim, single star, and had found Anakin searching for that point of light on previous occasions. Feeling sympathetic, I asked him if he was thinking of his mother. He kept his eyes skyward as he answered, "No, I was thinking of yours."

His tone was not unkind or antagonistic, but I did sense a certain tension in his words. I asked why he was thinking of my mother, and he said, fixing me with an expression that indicated his answer was obvious, "Because someone should."

I didn't know what to say to that. Anakin knows that a Jedi must relinquish familial attachments, but...I suddenly found myself more concerned for his future than ever before. He misses his mother—I know this as well as anything. Although he left Tatooine willingly, he left a part of himself there. I can only offer him guidance, but if he is the Chosen One, it seems inevitable that he must free himself from that bond.

FIRST MISSION

Recorded 28 B.B.Y.
Author: Siri Tachi

Before I submit my report of my activities over the past year, I have reason to make a statement about Obi-Wan Kenobi and his Padawan, Anakin Skywalker.

As you know, because only members of the Jedi Council were aware of my assignment, Obi-Wan and Anakin were under the impression that I had betrayed our Order, and did not know of my mission to infiltrate the criminal syndicate operated by the pirate Krayn. It has come to my attention that some members of the Council have expressed dismay over the fact that Anakin unintentionally revealed me as a

Jedi operative to Krayn, and that the Council has also pondered whether Anakin acted honorably when he killed Krayn.

Furthermore, I am aware that the Galactic Senate, in response to Republic media reports regarding Anakin's actions at Nar Shaddaa, is considering the formation of an independent committee to investigate the legal and ethical ramifications of allowing Padawans to participate in "dangerous missions." I know it is not my place to criticize the Senate, but I will allow that I would sooner have any Padawan at my side in battle than I would any Senator.

Although it was through Anakin's actions that my identity was revealed to Krayn, it would be a grave injustice if any review board held Anakin accountable. Obi-Wan and Anakin had no way of knowing that our paths would cross, and had every reason to believe I had abandoned the Jedi Order. With all due respect, I remind the Council that Obi-Wan and Anakin did not happen upon me by accident. After all, it was the Council that sanctioned their mission to escort the Colicoids across treacherous territories.

Did Anakin act with impatience during his first mission as a Jedi? Yes. But those of you who know me well will recall that I was never good at patience exercises at the Temple, either. After Anakin realized I had not betrayed the Order, he proved to be most resourceful. More than anyone, he is responsible for liberating the slaves on Nar Shaddaa.

Was Anakin motivated by revenge to kill Krayn? Only Anakin can answer that question truthfully. But as a witness to their duel, and also as a Jedi, I can attest to the fact that had I been in Anakin's position, Krayn would have died by my lightsaber. In that capacity, I believe that Krayn's death was decided not by Anakin, but by the will of the Force.

ADDENDUM BY
TIONNE SOLUSAR

A contemporary of Obi-Wan Kenobi, Siri Tachi apprenticed to Jedi Council member Adi Gallia before she became a Jedi Knight. Drawn from the Great Holocron, the preceding excerpt of her report to the Council does not shed any additional light on Anakin Skywalker's role in the liberation of slaves on Nar Shaddaa or the death of the pirate and slaver named Krayn. Efforts have not revealed additional records of Anakin's activity on Nar Shaddaa in 28 B.B.Y., but there is confirmation that Krayn was accountable for at least five raids on Tatooine. One such raid occurred while Anakin was still living on that world, but no other data is currently available. Siri Tachi served in the Clone Wars, and died during a mission with Obi-Wan on the planet Azure in 20 B.B.Y.

RETURN TO TATOOINE

Recorded in 8 A.B.Y.
Author: Leia Organa Solo

From those who knew my father on Tatooine, I have learned that Anakin returned to the desert planet at least once after he became a Jedi. As best as I can figure, this happened just before the Battle of Geonosis, which kicked off the Clone Wars. About one month before Anakin's return, Shmi Skywalker made the following entry in her journal:

Today there are more Tuskens out on the plain. We can't see them, but the lowing of their banthas carries for kilometers. Owen and Cliegg keep saying we'll be all right as long as we don't go out at night. I'd feel better if they didn't make such a point of keeping their blasters within reach, even inside. But there isn't much food out here for banthas; the Tuskens will have to move on soon. And Cliegg is going to the Dorr Farm tomorrow, to start organizing local farmers. We'll be fine, Anakin, I'm sure.

This was the final entry in Shmi's journal. Luke's Aunt Beru had a younger sister, Dama Whitesun Brunk, who remained on Tatooine and is now an innkeeper in Anchorhead. It was Dama who told me that Shmi was taken by Sand People. She'd been gone for weeks by the time Anakin arrived at the Lars family's moisture farm.

I don't know how Anakin learned about his mother's situation, or even if other Jedi knew that he had traveled to Tatooine. According to Kitster Banai, it was Anakin's former master Watto who told him where to find Shmi. And according to Dama, Beru— who was Owen Lars's girlfriend at the time—

was out at the Lars homestead with Owen and his father, Cliegg, when Anakin arrived.

Anakin left the moisture farm by himself to search for his mother. Evidently, he tracked her to a Tusken camp, and he soon returned with her body. Beru told Dama that Shmi was dead when Anakin brought her back to the moisture farm. If Beru knew whether Shmi had still been alive when Anakin found her, she never told Dama.

Anakin buried his mother at the moisture farm. There used to be a headstone, but it seems Owen removed it. Beru told Dama that Owen said he didn't see a need for anyone to know where Shmi was buried.

I learned more about Shmi's death later, when Han and I arrived at the remains of an old Tusken camp. We had been searching for Kitster when a Jawa named Herat had directed us to the site, which was in an oasis deep in Tusken territory. According to Herat, it was a "ghost village" where an

entire tribe of Tuskens had been hacked to pieces by an angry ghost. The camp's ruins had become a sacred place to the nomadic Tuskens, who would present gifts and make sacrifices when they visited.

There were about thirty bantha wool huts still standing. I hadn't given much thought to Herat's description of the area, but it really was . . . well, it was haunted. I don't know how else to put it. When I first set eyes on the huts, I felt the area was alive with some kind of phantom pain.

There was one hut that stood apart from the others, still supported by an exterior framework of bantha bones. Its builders had taken care to sink its fabric walls deep into the sand, and a simple drawbar made of bantha bone locked its door from the outside. I realized it had been a holding cell. And I knew that this had been the place where the Tuskens had taken Shmi and . . . and they'd tortured her. This was the place where Anakin, three decades earlier, had found his mother. The place where he first surrendered to his anger.

For his mother's life, Anakin had taken the lives of dozens of Tuskens. Even the children. And in doing so, he not only avenged his mother but created a legacy of death for the area as well. In the three decades since Anakin slaughtered his mother's abductors, the Tuskens have transformed the site into their own. I found a pile of at least a hundred skulls, most of them human.

If the Tuskens still fear the "ghost" of Anakin Skywalker, I can't imagine why they continue to sacrifice captives. Why do Sand People do anything? No one knows. That's what makes them Sand People.

Still, what Anakin did was wrong. He was a Jedi. All I could think of was that he should have known better.

And perhaps he did know better. Kitster

Banai told me that after he'd heard that Anakin had visited Watto's junk shop in search of Shmi, he'd gone to the Lars farm, hoping to see Anakin. He arrived shortly after Shmi had been buried, but Anakin had already left on a starship. Beru told Kitster that when they buried Shmi, Anakin spoke to her grave, saying he had not been strong enough to save her. And then Anakin promised that he wouldn't fail again.

Kitster figured out on his own that Anakin had slain the Tuskens at the oasis. He didn't condone Anakin's actions, but when he thought about what Beru had told him, he thought that Anakin may have realized what a terrible mistake he had made, and knew that he'd failed as a Jedi. Kitster said that the Anakin Skywalker he knew would have been sorry for what he had done.

I'd like to believe that's true.

FORBIDDEN LOVE

As previously noted, Jedi of the Old Republic were generally forbidden to engage in romantic relationships. Although they did not dismiss love, they were cautious of emotional attachments, and knew that various possessive aspects of love could lead to the dark side of the Force.

In 21 B.B.Y., during the Clone Wars, Cularin Central Broadcasting reporter Yara Grugara interviewed Jedi Master Lanius Qel-Bertuk, then headmaster at the Jedi academy on Almas. Lanius told the following story, which illustrates how most Jedi of the Old Republic regarded emotional attachments:

There was a story I heard once, about a man who wanted to find the Force.

He believed he could reach a place on a faraway planet, or maybe a moon, where he would find a swirling white cloud made of pure Force energy. He traveled the galaxy from one side to the other in search of this swirling white cloud. He left his life behind, he left his family behind, and he left his children behind. All of his friends, all of his valuables, everything that had ever meant anything to him. He traveled by freighter, doing manual labor as he hopped from one planet to the next. He would get off, ask questions, describe the cloud, and then find a new freighter. He never held on to the disappointment of his failures, but they became many. I couldn't even guess how many planets he visited, how many languages he must have spoken, how many times he must have pushed himself to go on and try just one more world, because there he might find the Force.

I don't know if the cloud exists. But I know that he never found it, and that he died old and disappointed.

Because for all his leave-takings, for all the things he removed from his life, he retained one attachment, one thing that he valued above all others. Ironically, his attachment was to the Force itself, and for it, he gave up what could have been a productive life to chase a dream across a galaxy.

Friendship in the Jedi Order is one aspect of our philosophy. We are all part of the Force. As Master Yoda says, it surrounds us and penetrates us. All of us. The friendships that we have should be the same. So, no: friendship is not forbidden. It is part of who and what we are. We work together. At times, we may fight together. Sometimes we even die together. But we do not die to save another Jedi. We die—if

we must—knowing that all life is sacrosanct. We are all, every one of us, vital to the will of the Force.

We now know that Anakin Skywalker and Senator Padmé Amidala of Naboo married in secret in the year 22 B.B.Y., just after the Battle of Geonosis. It was only after the astromech droid R2-D2 divulged recordings of Anakin and Amidala that contemporary scholars became aware of their relationship. It is almost a certainty that Anakin told no one of his marriage, and subsequent interviews with Amidala's relatives have determined that family members were also oblivious.

After Leia Organa Solo discovered the identity of her mother, she realized that Pooja Naberrie—a former representative of Naboo and a friend she had known since her service in the Imperial Senate—was not only Padmé Amidala's niece but also her own first cousin. In 35 A.B.Y., Pooja Naberrie recalled meeting Anakin when she was a child, just prior to the Battle of Geonosis:

I was just a little girl, only four years old, when I first saw Anakin. Oh, my. I thought he was the most handsome man I'd ever seen, and so tall! My memory of him is entirely from a child's perspective, and I still envision him as a giant.

I was at my grandparents' home with my sister Ryoo, who's two years older, when he came to Naboo. He came walking up the street with Aunt Padmé, and they brought an R2 unit. Ryoo and I always got so excited when Padmé would visit, because we sometimes didn't see her for months at a time. And if you're four and six years old, months can seem like years! Anyway, if I remember right, I think Ryoo and I must have thought that Anakin had brought the droid to us as a present, because we just started dancing around it, right there in the street outside the house. We were so silly.

I'd overheard someone say that Anakin was Padmé's bodyguard, and I don't think I thought there was anything strange about that. Padmé was often accompanied by a security officer named . . . Oh, my, what was his name? Ty? No, Captain Typho! Anyway, I just imagined that Anakin was Padmé's boyfriend. I thought they both looked so beautiful together.

Well, Ryoo and I were just heartbroken when we learned that they weren't staying at the house. They left just a few hours later for the Lake Country. I recall our mother saying something about Padmé needing to get away from the city and rest for a few days. We cried because we wanted the droid to stay and play with us!

A few days later, I remember there was some concern in our house about no one knowing where Padmé was. She and Anakin had been staying at a retreat in the Lake Country, but then they'd left without telling anyone where they were going. My mother was a bit frantic until a few days later, when she received word that Padmé was alive and well.

It wasn't long after that that Padmé returned to Naboo with Anakin, and that was the second time I met him. I remember that encounter more clearly because of the way I reacted when I saw that his right hand had been replaced with a prosthetic. The fingertips were made of a gold-colored metal, and I thought it looked cold. And there were exposed wires. I guess it may have been just a temporary prosthetic. When my family and I greeted him and Padmé, I couldn't stop myself from staring at his new hand. And then I looked up into his eyes.

He looked . . . well, I thought he looked angry, and I just started crying. Maybe he was angry, but in hindsight, I'm certain it had

nothing to with me. My mother apologized for my behavior, but Anakin said there was no reason for anyone to be sorry. He knelt down beside me, held out his left hand to me, and asked me if I'd put my hand in his. I did. He smiled and gave my fingers a gentle squeeze, then said, "That's for good luck, so we'll all hang on to our fingers from now on." I'm sure he just wanted to make me feel better, and he did. But I still felt so awful for him for losing a hand.

And then, three years later, Padmé was dead. It was awful. She was so young. And no one in our family seemed to know how she had died, or at least no one told us. My sister and I did learn that there had been assassination attempts, and that was why Anakin had been acting as her bodyguard.

At her funeral, I didn't just weep for her. I thought Anakin was dead, too. We'd heard that the Jedi had attempted to overthrow the Republic, and that most of the Jedi had been killed. To Ryoo and me, Anakin was our hero. We couldn't imagine him doing anything wrong. I had all sorts of fantasies about how he might have been killed or injured while trying to save Padmé, or that he'd gone into hiding because he refused to participate in the so-called Jedi takeover. Silly dreams.

But all that was . . . How long ago? About fifty-five years, I think. And now, my dear friend Leia Organa Solo tells me about her discovery that Padmé was her mother, and of what became of Anakin. My head is still reeling. I've known Leia ever since we both served in the Imperial Senate, and to think that neither of us ever had the slightest inkling that we were first cousins.

If Leia hadn't told me herself, I don't think I ever would have believed that Anakin Skywalker became Darth Vader. It's just so . . . so entirely inconceivable

EMPEROR PALPATINE SUPERVISES DARTH VADER'S ▶
CYBERNETIC RECONSTRUCTION. (Edwards)

that that lovely young man could have become Vader. And yet that's exactly what happened, isn't it? To think I held his hand. His good hand. Oh, my.

Soon after Pooja Naberrie learned that Padmé Amidala and Anakin Skywalker were the parents of Leia Organa Solo and Luke Skywalker, she discovered the only known record of her aunt's wedding. The record was in a databook that had once belonged to a man who was an old friend to the Naberrie family. For ethical reasons, Pooja Naberrie refused to divulge the man's identity or provide a copy of the record, but she allowed that he was authorized to perform marriages and that the wedding took place at a villa in the Naboo Lake Country at a time that coincides with Anakin's first visit to Naboo following the Battle of Geonosis.

DARTH VADER

The actions of Darth Vader have been described throughout this record by various sources, and there is little more that can be added here that hasn't already been said. For all our efforts to understand how and why Anakin Skywalker became Darth Vader, we can only speculate whether Anakin might have turned to the dark side without Palpatine's influence. Given that he did not entirely destroy the Sith, and that his training of Lumiya led to the death of Mara Jade, it is difficult for most contemporary Jedi to attach any significance to the idea that he may have been the Chosen One of prophecy. Although Darth Vader may endure as an inspiration to those who seek darkness, he also serves as a caution to Jedi who aspire to keep to the light.

DARTH VADER WITH IMPERIAL INTELLIGENCE ▲
AGENT SHIRA BRIE. (*Trevas*)

Page numbers in *italics* refer to illustrations.

INDEX

THE SITH LORD DARTH SIDIOUS BESTOWS ▶
HIS NEW APPRENTICE, ANAKIN SKYWALKER,
WITH THE NAME DARTH VADER. (*Trevas*)

RAKATA AND THE STAR FORGE. ▶
(Trevas)

Q

R

S

ABOUT THE AUTHOR

Photo: Jill Palumbo

RYDER WINDHAM is a former editor of *Star Wars* comics and the author of more than fifty *Star Wars* books, including the *New York Times* bestsellers *Star Wars: The Ultimate Visual Guide* and *Revenge of the Sith Scrapbook*. He is also an instructor and the certificate program advisor for Comic and Sequential Art at Rhode Island School of Design Continuing Education. He lives with his family in Providence, Rhode Island.

ABOUT THE ILLUSTRATORS

Photo: Yuen Hom

CHRIS TREVAS first saw *Star Wars* at the impressionable age of three and has been fascinated with that far away galaxy ever since. He attended the College for Creative Studies in Detroit before beginning his official *Star Wars* career in 1995. Over the years he has created *Star Wars* artwork for several licensees including Wizards of the Coast, DK Publishing, Golden Books, Scholastic, and Topps among others. He is also a writer and illustrator for *Star Wars Insider* magazine. Chris previously illustrated *The New Essential Guide to Alien Species*.

www.christrevas.com

Photo: Melissa Edwards

TOMMY LEE EDWARDS is one of the most prolific *Star Wars* artists in recent years, having illustrated numerous RPG book covers, children's books, magazines, prints, essential guide books, and merchandising art for the franchise. After studying film and illustration at California's Art Center College of Design in the early 1990s, he moved to central North Carolina. Beyond the occasional business trip back to L.A. or to a film location, he enjoys keeping close to his wife, two kids, and dog by working in the studio behind his house. Various non–*Star Wars* projects in his portfolio include promotional and merchandising art for the films *Harry Potter, Batman Begins,* and *Superman Returns*. He's also storyboarded for the film *Sinbad* for DreamWorks, designed games like Command & Conquer for Electronic Arts, and created scores of comics for Marvel, DC, Dark Horse, and many more. TLE is currently hard at work on Marvel's 1985 series.

www.TommyLeeEdwards.com

EMPEROR FEL AND THE ▶
IMPERIAL KNIGHTS. *(Edwards)*

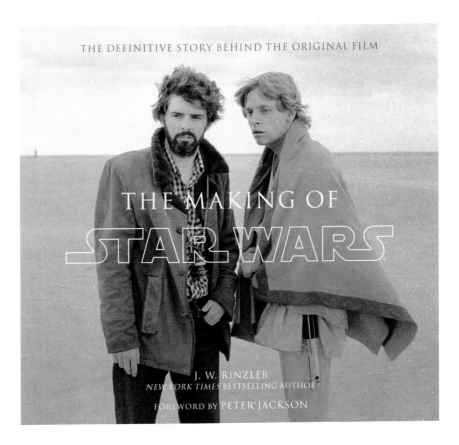

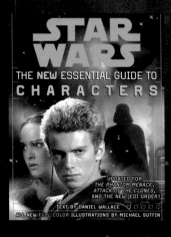
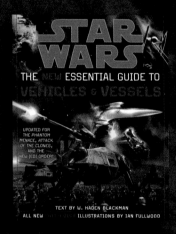
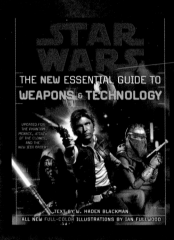

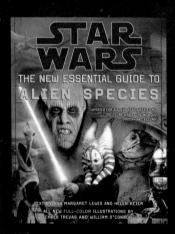
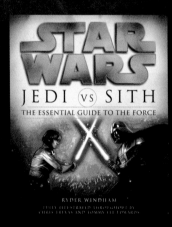